Philip Massinger, John Monck Mason

The Dramatick Works of Philip Massinger

Philip Massinger, John Monck Mason

The Dramatick Works of Philip Massinger

ISBN/EAN: 9783743407947

Manufactured in Europe, USA, Canada, Australia, Japa

Cover: Foto ©Thomas Meinert / pixelio.de

Manufactured and distributed by brebook publishing software (www.brebook.com)

Philip Massinger, John Monck Mason

The Dramatick Works of Philip Massinger

THE

DRAMATICK WORKS

OF

PHILIP MASSINGER.

IN FOUR VOLUMES.

VOL II.

THE

DRAMATICK WORKS

OF

PHILIP MASSINGER

COMPLETE,

IN FOUR VOLUMES.

REVISED AND CORRECTED,

WITH NOTES CRITICAL AND EXPLANATORY,

BY JOHN MONCK MASON, Esq.

TO WHICH ARE ADDED,

REMARKS AND OBSERVATIONS OF VARIOUS AUTHORS

CRITICAL REFLECTIONS ON THE OLD ENGLISH
DRAMATICK WRITERS;

AND

A SHORT ESSAY ON THE LIFE AND WRITINGS OF
MASSINGER, INSCRIBED TO DR. S. JOHNSON.

VOLUME THE SECOND.

LONDON:

Printed for T. DAVIES, in RUSSEL-STREET; T. PAYNE and
SON, at the MEWS-GATE; L. DAVIS, in HOLBOURN;
J. NICHOLS, RED-LION PASSAGE; T. EVANS,
in the STRAND; W. DAVIS, in PICCADILLY;
and H. PAYNE, in PALL-MALL.

MDCCLXXIX.

THE

RENEGADO.

A

TRAGI-COMEDY.

VOL. II.   A

TO THE

RIGHT HONOURABLE

GEORGE HARDING,

Baron *Barkley*, of *Barkley Caſtle*, and Knight
of the Honourable Order of the BATH.

My good Lord,

*T*O *be honoured for old Nobility, or hereditary Titles, is
not alone proper to yourſelf, but to ſome few of your
Rank, who may challenge the like Privilege with you : But
in our Age to vouchſafe (as you have often done) a ready Hand
to raiſe the dejeEted Spirits of the contemned Sons of the Mu-
ſes ; ſuch as would not ſuffer the glorious Fire of Poeſy to be
wholly extinguiſhed, is ſo remarkable and peculiar to your
Lordſhip, that with a full Vote and Suffrage, it is acknowledged that the Patronage and ProteEtion of the dramatic
Poem, is yours, and almoſt without a Rival. I deſpair not
therefore, but that my Ambition to preſent my Service in this
Kind, may in your Clemency meet with a gentle Interpretation.
Confirm it, my good Lord, in your gracious Acceptance of this
Trifle ; in which, if I were not confident there are ſome Pieces
worthy the Peruſal, it ſhould have been taught an humbler
Flight ; and the Writer (your Countryman) never yet made
happy in your Notice and Favour, had not made this an Advocate to plead for his Admiſſion among ſuch as are wholly and
ſincerely devoted to your Service. I may live to tender my
humble Thankfulneſs in ſome higher Strain ; and, till then,
comfort myſelf with Hope, that you deſcend from your Height,
to receive*

Your Honour's commanded Servant,

PHILIP MASSINGER.

A 2

Dramatis Personæ.	Original Actors.
Asambeg, Viceroy of *Tunis*.	JOHN BLANYE.
Mustapha, Basha of *Aleppo*.	JOHN SUMNER.
Vitelli, a Gentleman of *Venice*, disguis'd.	MICHAEL BOWIER.
Francisco, a Jesuit.	WILLIAM REIGNALDS.
Antonio Grimaldi, the Renegado.	WILLIAM ALLEN.
Carazie, an Eunuch.	WILLIAM ROBINS.
Gazet, Servant to *Vitelli*.	EDWARD SHAKERLEY.
Aga.	
Capiaga.	
Master.	
Boatswain.	
Sailors.	
Jailor.	
Three *Turks*.	
Donusa, Niece to *Amurath*.	EDWARD ROGERS.
Paulina, Sister to *Vitelli*.	THEO. BOURNE.
Manto, Servant to *Donusa*.	

The Scene, Tunis.

THE

RENEGADO.

ACT I. SCENE I.

Enter Vitelli *and* Gazet.

Vitelli.

YOU'VE hir'd a Shop, then?
    Gaz. Yes, Sir; and our Wares
('Tho' brittle as a Maidenhead at sixteen)
Are safe unladen; not a Cryftal crack'd,
Or China Difh needs ford'ring; our choice Pictures,
As they came from the Workman, without Blemifh;
And I have ftudied Speeches for each Piece;
And in a thrifty Tone, to fell 'em off,
Will fwear by *Mahomet* and *Termagant,* [1]

---

[1] *Will fwear by Mahomet and Termagant.*

Dr. *Percy,* in his Remarks on the ancient Ballad of *King Eftmere,* fays, that *Termagant* is the Name given by the Authors of the old Romances to the God of the *Saracens:* And as he was generally reprefented as a very furious Being, the Word *Termagant* was applied to any Perfon of a turbulent outrageous Difpofition, though at prefent it is appropriated to the female Sex: Dr. *Grey,* in his Annotations on *Hudibras,* is of the fame Opinion with Refpect to the original Signification of this Word, and in Confirmation of it, he cites a Paffage from *Chaucer,* and the following Lines from *Fairfax's* Tranflation of *Taffo's Jerufalem,* which are in the 84th Stanza of the firft Canto,

    The leffer Part in Chrift believed wele,
    In *Termagant* the more, and in *Mahowne.*

This Tranflation, however, is not warranted by the Original, for in that *Mahowne* only is mentioned.

That this is Miſtreſs to the great Duke of *Florence*,
That Niece to old King *Pepin*, and a third
An *Auſtrian* Princeſs by her *Roman* Noſe,
Howe'er my Conſcience tells me they are Figures
Of Bawds and common Courteſans in *Venice*.

Vitel. You make no Scruple of an Oath, then?

Gaz. Fye, Sir!
'Tis out of my Indentures; I'm bound there
To ſwear for my Maſter's Profit, as ſecurely
As your Intelligencer muſt for his Prince,
That ſends him forth an honourable. Spy
To ſerve his Purpoſes.   And, if it be lawful
In a Chriſtian Shopkeeper to cheat his Father,
I cannot find but, to abuſe a *Turk*
In the Sale of our Commodities, muſt be thought
A meritorious Work.

Vitel. I wonder, Sirrah,
What's your Religion?

Gaz. Troth, to anſwer truly,
I would not be of one that ſhould command me
To feed upon *Poor John*, when I ſee Pheaſants
And Partridges on the Table: Nor do I like
The other that allows us to eat Fleſh
In Lent, tho' it be rotten, rather than be
Thought ſuperſtitious, as your zealous *Cobler*
And learned *Botcher* preach at *Amſterdam* ²
Over a Hotchpotch.   I'd not be confin'd
In my Belief; when all your Sects and Sectaries

La debil Parte, et la Minore in Chriſto,
La grande et forte in *Macometto* crede.

Termagant is ſuppoſed to be derived, either from the *Latin ter-
magnus*, or from the *Saxon tyr Magon*, both of which ſignify emi-
nently great.   M. M.

☞ ² ————— *As your zealous Cobler*
And learned Botcher preach at Amſterdam.

Much about this Time the *Low Countries* were infeſted with a ſuperſtitious Crew of Puritans and Fanaticks, and the Perſons here allu-
ded to were perhaps the moſt noted: A Cobler and a Taylor,

Are grown of one Opinion, if I like it,
I will profeſs myſelf,—in the mean Time,
Live I in *England*, *Spain*, *France*, *Rome*, *Geneva*,
I'm of that Country's Faith.

Vitel. And what in *Tunis ?*
Will you turn *Turk* here ?

Gaz. No : So I ſhould loſe
A Collop of that Part my *Doll* enjoin'd me
To bring Home as ſhe left it : 'Tis her Venture,
Nor dare I barter that Commodity
Without her ſpecial Warrant.

Vitel. You're a Knave, Sir ;
Leaving your Roguery, think upon my Buſineſs :
It is no Time to fool now——
Remember where you are too : Tho' this Mart-time
We are allowed free Trading, and with Safety,
Temper your Tongue, and meddle not with the *Turks*,
Their Manners nor Religion.

Gaz. Take you Heed, Sir,
What Colours you wear. Not two Hours ſince, there
landed
An *Engliſh Pirate*'s Whore with a green Apron,
And, as ſhe walk'd the Streets, one of their Mufti's
(We call them Prieſts at *Venice*) with a Razor
Cuts it off, Petticoat, Smock and all, and leaves her
As naked as my Nail ; the young Fry wond'ring
What ſtrange Beaſt it ſhould be. I 'ſcap'd a Scouring,
My Miſtreſs' Buſk Point of that forbidden Colour
Then ty'd my Codpiece, had it been diſcover'd,
I had been capon'd.

Vitel. And had been well ſerv'd.
Haſte to the Shop, and ſet my Wares in Order,
I will not long be abſent.

Gaz. Tho' I ſtrive, Sir,
To put off Melancholy, to which you are ever
Too much inclin'd, it ſhall not hinder me
With my beſt Care to ſerve you.

[*Exit* Gaze

A 4

Enter Francisco.

Vitel. I believe thee.
O welcome, Sir! Stay of my Steps in this Life
And Guide to all my bleſſed Hopes hereafter!
What Comfort, Sir? Have your Endeavours proſ-
 per'd?
Have we tir'd Fortune's Malice with our Sufferings?
Is ſhe at length, after ſo many Frowns,
Pleas'd to vouchſafe one cheerful Look upon us?
 Fran. You give too much to Fortune and your Paſ-
  ſions,
O'er which a wiſe Man, if religious, triumphs.
That Name Fools worſhip, and thoſe Tyrants, which
We arm againſt our better Part, our Reaſon,
May add, but never take from our Afflictions.
 Vitel. Sir, as I am a ſinful Man, I cannot
But like one ſuffer.
 Fran. I exact not from you
A Fortitude inſenſible of Calamity,
To which the Saints themſelves have bow'd, and ſhew
They're made of Fleſh and Blood: All that I challenge
Is manly Patience. Will you, that were train'd up
In a religious School, where divine Maxims,
Scorning Compariſon with moral Precepts,
Were daily taught you, bear your Conſtancy's Trial,
Not like *Vitelli*, but a Village Nurſe,
With Curſes in your Mouth? Tears in your Eyes?
How poorly it ſhows in you.
 Vitel. I am ſchool'd, Sir,
And will hereafter to my utmoſt Strength
Study to be myſelf.
 Fran. So ſhall you find me
Moſt ready to aſſiſt you: Neither have I
Slept in your great Occaſions ſince I left you:
I have been at the Viceroy's Court, and preſs'd
As far as they allow a Chriſtian Entrance.
And ſomething I have learn'd that may concern
The Purpoſe of this Journey,

Vitel. Dear Sir, what is it?

Fran. By the Command of *Afambeg,* the Viceroy,
The City fwells with barbarous Pomp and Pride
For the Entertainment of ftout *Muftapha,*
The Bafha of *Aleppo,* who in Perfon
Comes to receive the Niece of *Amurath,*
The fair *Donufa,* for his Bride.

Vitel. I find not
How this may profit us.

Fran. Pray you give me Leave,
Among the reft that wait upon the Viceroy,
(Such as have under him Command in *Tunis)*
Who, as you've often heard, are all faife Pirates,
I faw the Shame of *Venice* and the Scorn
Of all good Men : The perjur'd *Renegado,*
Antonio Grimaldi.

Vitel. Ha! his Name
Is Poifon to me.

Fran. Yet again?

Vitel. I've done, Sir!

Fran. This debauch'd Villain, whom we ever thought
(After his impious Scorn done in St. *Mark's*
To me as I ftood at the holy Altar)
The Thief that ravifh'd your fair Sifter from you,
The virtuous *Paulina,* not long fince
(As I am truly given to underftand)
Sold to the Viceroy a fair Chriftian Virgin,
On whom, maugre his fierce and cruel Nature
Afambeg dotes extremely.

Vitel, 'Tis my Sifter :
It muft be fhe ; my better Angel tells me
'Tis poor *Paulina,* Farewel all Difguifes !
I'll fhow in my revenge that I am Noble.

Fran. You are not mad?

Vitel. No, Sir; my virtuous Anger
Makes ev'ry Vein an Artery ; I feel in me
The Strength of twenty Men ; and, being arm'd
With my good Caufe to wreak wrong'd Innocence,
I dare alone run to the Viceroy's Court

And with this Poniard, before his Face,
Dig out *Grimaldi*'s Heart.

　Fran. Is this religious?

　Vitel. Would you have me tame now? Can I know
　　　my Sister
Mew'd up in his Seraglio, and in Danger
Not alone to lose her Honour, but her Soul?
The Hell-bred Villain by too, that has sold both
To black Destruction, and not haste to send him
To the Devil his Tutor? To be patient now,
Were, in another Name, to play the Pander
To th' Viceroy's loose Embraces, and cry Aim
While he by Force or Flattery compels her
To yield her fair Name up to his foul Lust,
And after turn *Apostate* to the Faith
That she was bred in.

　Fran. Do but give me Hearing,
And you shall soon grant how ridiculous
This childish Fury is. A wise Man never
Attempts Impossibilities: 'Tis as easy
For any single Arm to quell an Army
As to effect your Wishes. We come hither
To learn *Paulina*'s Fate and to redeem her:
Leave your Revenge to Heaven. I oft have told you
Of a Relick that I gave her, which has Power
(If we may credit holy Men's Traditions)
To keep the Owner free from Violence:
This on her Breast she wears, and does preserve
The Virtue of it by her daily Prayers.
So, if she fall not by her own Consent,
(Which it were Sin to think) I fear no Force.
Be, therefore, patient; keep this borrow'd Shape,
Till Time and Opportunity present us
With some fit Means to see her; which perform'd,
I'll join with you in any desperate Course
For her Delivery.

　Vitel. You have charm'd me, Sir!
And I obey in all Things: Pray you, pardon
The Weakness of my Passion.

Fran. And excufe it.
Be cheerful, Man; for know that good Intents
Are, in the End, crown'd with as fair Events.

[*Exeunt.*

SCENE II.

A Room.

Enter Donufa, Manto, *and* Carazie.

Don. Have you feen the Chriftian Captive,
The great Bafhaw is fo enamour'd of?
Manto. Yes, an't pleafe your Excellency,
I took a full View of her, when fhe was
Prefented to him.
Don. Is fhe fuch a Wonder,
As 'tis reported?
Manto. She was drown'd in Tears then,
Which took much from her Beauty; yet, in fpite
Of Sorrow, fhe appear'd the Miftrefs of
Moft rare Perfections; and, tho' of low Stature,
Her well-proportion'd Limbs invite Affection:
And, when fhe fpeaks, each Syllable is Mufick
That does enchant the Hearers.—But your Highnefs,
That are not to be parallell'd, I never yet
Beheld her Equal.
Don. Come, you flatter me;
But I forgive it. We, that are born great,
Seldom diftafte our Servants, tho' they give us
More than we can pretend to. I have heard
That Chriftian Ladies live with much more Freedom
Than fuch as are born here. Our jealous *Turks*
Never permit their fair Wives to be feen
But at the public Bagnios or the Mofques;
And even then veil'd and guarded. Thou, *Carazie,*
Wert born in *England*; what's the Cuftom there
Among your Women? Come, be free and merry:

I'm no fevere Miftrefs; nor haft thou met with
A heavy Bondage.

 Car. Heavy ? I was made lighter
By two Stone Weight at leaft, to be fit to ferve you.
But to your Queftion, Madam ; Women in *England*,
For the moft Part, live like Queens. Your Country
    Ladies
Have Liberty to hawk, to hunt, to feaft ;
To give free Entertainment to all Comers,
To talk, to kifs : There's no fuch Thing known there
As an *Italian* Girdle. Your City Dame,
Without Leave, wears the Breeches, has her Hufband
At as much Command as her 'Prentice ; and, if Need be,
Can make him Cuckold by her Father's Copy.

 Don. But your Court-Lady ?

 Car. She, I affure you, Madam,
Knows nothing but her Will ; muft be allow'd
Her Footmen, her Coach, her Ufhers, her Pages,
Her Doctor, Chaplains ; and, as I have heard,
They're grown of late fo learn'd, that they maintain
A ftrange Pofition, which their Lords with all
Their Wit cannot confute.

 Don. What's that, I prithee ?

 Car. Marry, that it is not only fit but lawful
Your Madam there, her much Reft and high Feeding
Duly confider'd, fhould, to eafe her Hufband,
Be allow'd a private Friend. They have drawn a Bill
To this good Purpofe ; and, the next Affembly,
Doubt not to pafs it.

 Don. We enjoy no more
That are of the *Ottoman* Race, tho' our Religion
Allows all Pleafure. I am dull :—Some Mufick.
Take my Chapins off.[3] So, a lufty Strain—[*A Galliard.*
Who knocks there ?

 ☞ 3 *Take my Chapins off.*

 Chapin (Spanifh) a high Cork-heel'd Shoe, or rather a Kind of
Slipper.

Manto. 'Tis the Basha of *Aleppo,*
Who humbly makes Request he may present
His Service to you.

Don. Reach a Chair.—We must
Receive him like ourself, and not depart with
One Piece of Ceremony, State and Greatnefs,
That may beget Refpect and Reverence
In one that's born our Vaffal. Now admit him.

Enter Muftapha; *puts off his yellow Pantoufles.* 4

Mufta. The Place is facred, and I am to enter
The Room where fhe abides with fuch Devotion
As Pilgrims pay at *Meccha,* when they vifit
The Tomb of our great Prophet.

Don. Rife, the Sign
That we vouchfafe your Prefence.

[*The Eunuch takes up the Pantoufles.*

Mufta. May thofe Powers,
That rais'd the *Ottoman* Empire, and ftill guard it,
Reward your Highnefs for this gracious Favour
You throw upon your Servant. It hath pleas'd
The moft invincible, mightieft *Amurath,*
(To fpeak his other Titles would take from him
That in himfelf does comprehend all Greatnefs,)
To make me the unworthy Inftrument
Of his Command. Receive, divineft Lady,

[*Delivers a Letter.*

This Letter, fign'd by his victorious Hand,
And made authentick by th' imperial Seal.
There when you find me mention'd, far be it from you
To think it my Ambition to prefume
At fuch a Happinefs, which his pow'rful Will
From his great Mind's Magnificence, not my Merit,
Hath fhower'd upon me. But, if your Confent
Join with his good Opinion and Allowance
To perfect what his Favours have begun,

☞ 4 Pantoufles (*French*) Slippers; it is a Cuftom with the *Turks*
to be bare-footed whenever they appear before any of the royal Blood.

I fhall in my Obfequioufnefs and Duty
Endeavour to prevent all juft Complaints,
Which Want of Will to ferve you may call on me.

Don. His facred Majefty writes here that your Valour
Againft the *Perfian* hath fo won upon him,
That there's no Grace or Honour in his Gift
Of which he can imagine you unworthy ;
And, what's the greateft you can hope or aim at,
It is his Pleafure you fhould be receiv'd
Into his Royal Family—Provided,
(For fo far I am unconfin'd) that I
Affect and like your Perfon. I expect not
The Ceremony which he ufes in
Beftowing of his Daughters and his Nieces.
As that he fhould prefent you for my Slave,
To love you if you pleas'd me; or deliver
A Poniard on my leaft Diflike to kill you.
Such Tyranny and Pride agree not with
My fofter Difpofition. Let it fuffice
For my firft Anfwer, that thus far I grace you.
[*Gives him her Hand to kifs.*

Hereafter, fome Time fpent to make Enquiry
Of the good Parts and Faculties of your Mind,
You fhall hear further from me.

Mufta. Tho' all Torments
Really fuffer'd, or in Hell imagin'd
By curious Fiction, in one Hour's Delay
Are wholly comprehended : I confefs
That I ftand bound in Duty, not to check at
Whatever you command, or pleafe to impofe
For Trial of my Patience.

Don. Let us find
Some other Subject; too much of one Theme cloys me;
Is't a full Mart?

Mufta. A Confluence of all Nations
Are met together : There's Variety too
Of all that Merchants traffick for.

Don. I know not.—
I feel a Virgin's Longing to defcend
So far from my own Greatnefs, as to be,

Tho' not a Buyer, yet a Looker on
Their ftrange Commodities.

Mufta. If without a Train
You dare be feen abroad, I'll difmifs mine.
And wait upon you as a common Man,
And fatisfy your Wifhes.

Don. I embrace it.
Provide my Veil; and at the Poftern Gate
Convey us out unfeen. I trouble you.

Mufta. It is my Happinefs you deign to command me.
[*Exeunt.*

SCENE III.

A Shop difcovered, Gazet *in it.*

Francifco *and* Vitelli *walking by.*

Gaz. What do you lack? Your choice *China* Difhes,
your pure *Venetian* Cryftal of all Sorts, of all neat and
new Fafhions, from the Mirror of the Madam, to the
private Utenfil of the Chamber-maid; and curious Pictures of the rareft Beauties of *Europe:* What do you
lack, Gentlemen?

Fran. Take Heed, I fay; howe'er it may appear
Impertinent, I muft exprefs my Love,
My Advice and Counfel. You are young
And may be tempted; and thefe *Turkifh* Dames,
(Like *Englifh* Maftiffs, that increafe their Fiercenefs
By being chain'd up) from the Reftraint of Freedom,
If Luft once fire their Blood from a fair Object,
Will run a Courfe the Fiends themfelves would fhake at,
To enjoy their wanton Ends.

Vitel. Sir, you miftake me:
I am too full of Woe to entertain
One Thought of Pleafure, tho' all *Europe*'s Queens
Kneel'd at my Feet and courted me: Much lefs
To mix with fuch, whofe Difference of Faith
Muft, of Neceffity, (or I muft grant

Myfelf neglectful of all you have taught me)
Strangle fuch bafe Defires.

Fran. Be conftant in
That Refolution, I'll abroad again
And learn, as far as it is poffible,
What may concern *Paulina.* Some two Hours
Shall bring me back.

Vitel. All Bleffings wait upon you ! [*Exit* Francifco.
Gaz. Cold Doings, Sir ! a Mart do you call this ?
'Slight !
A Pudding-wife, or a Witch with a Thrum Cap
That fells Ale under-ground to fuch as come
To know their Fortunes in a dead Vacation,
Have, ten to one, more Stirring.

Vitel. We muft be patient.

Gaz. Your Seller by Retail ought to be angry
But when he's fingering Money.

Enter Grimaldi, *Mafter, Boatfwain, Sailors, and* Turks.

Vitel. Here are Company ;
Defend me, my good Angel, I behold
A Bafilifk !

Gaz. What do you lack ? What do you lack ? Pure
China Difhes, clear Cryftal Glaffes, a dumb Miftrefs
to make Love to ? What do you lack, Gentlemen ?

Grim. Thy Mother for a Bawd ; or, if thou haft
A handfome one, thy Sifter for a Whore ;
Without thefe, do not tell me of your Trafh,
Or I fhall fpoil your Market.

Vitel. —Old *Grimaldi !*

Grim. 'Zounds, wherefore do we put to Sea, or ftand
The raging Winds aloft, or pifs upon
The foamy Waves, when they rage moft? Deride
The Thunder of the Enemy's Shot, board boldly
A Merchant's Ship for Prize, tho' we behold
The defperate Gunner ready to give Fire
And blow the Deck up ? Wherefore fhake we off
Thofe fcrupulous Rags of Charity and Confcience,
Invented only to keep Churchmen warm,

Or feed the hungry Mouths of famifh'd Beggars;
But, when we touch the Shore, to wallow in
All fenfual Pleafures.

Mafter. Ay, but, noble Captain,
To fpare a little for an After-clap
Were not Improvidence.

Grim. Hang Confideration:
When this is fpent, is not our Ship the fame?
Our Courage too the fame to fetch in more?
The Earth, where it is fertileft, returns not
More than three Harvefts, while the glorious Sun
Pofts thro' the Zodiack and makes up the Year:
But the Sea, which is our Mother, (that embraceth
Both the rich *Indies* in her out-ftretch'd Arms)
Yields every Day a Crop if we dare reap it.
No, no, my Mates! let Tradefmen think of Thrift,
And Ufurers hoard up; let our Expence
Be as our Comings in are, without Bounds;
We are the *Neptunes* of the Ocean,
And fuch as traffick fhall pay Sacrifice
Of their beft Lading.   I'll have this Canvafs
Your Boy wears lin'd with Tiffue, and the Cates
You tafte, ferv'd up in Gold; tho' we caroufe
The Tears of Orphans in our *Greekifh* Wines,
The Sighs of undone Widows paying for
The Mufick bought to cheer us; ravifh'd Virgins
To Slav'ry fold for Coin to feed our Riots.
We will have no Compunction.

Gaz. Do you hear, Sir?
We have paid for our Ground.

Grim. Hum!

Gaz. And hum too,
For all your big Words, get you farther off,
And hinder not the Profpect of our Shop,
Or————

Grim. What will you do?

Gaz. Nothing, Sir,—but pray
Your Worfhip to give me Handfel.

–VOL. II.   B

Grim. By the Ears;
Thus, Sir; by the Ears.

Master. Hold, hold!——

Vitel. You'll still be prating?

Grim. Come, let's be drunk: Then each Man to
his Whore.

—'Slight, how you look! you had best go find a Corner
To pray in and repent. Do, do, and cry.
It will shew fine in Pirates.   [*Exit* Grimaldi.

Master. We must follow;
Or he will spend our Shares.

Boatsw. I fought for mine.

Master. Nor am I so precise but I can drab too:
We will not sit out for our Parts.

Boatsw. Agreed.
           [*Exeunt Master, Boatswain, and Sailors.*

Gaz. The Devil gnaw off his Fingers! If he were
In *London* among the Clubs, up went his Heels
For striking of a 'Prentice. What do you lack?
What do you lack, Gentlemen?

1 *Turk.* I wonder how the Viceroy can endure
The Insolence of this Fellow.

2 *Turk.* He receives Profit
From the Prizes he brings in; and that excuses
Whatever he commits.—Ha! what are these?

Enter Mustapha, *and* Donusa *veil'd.*

1 *Turk.* They seem of Rank and Quality; observe 'em.

Gaz. What do you lack? See what you please to
buy; Wares of all Sorts, most honourable Madona.

Vitel. Peace, Sirrah! Make no Noise: These are
not People
To be jested with

Don. Is this the Christians' Custom
In the vending their Commodities?

Musta. Yes, best Madam!
But you may please to keep your Way, here's nothing
But Toys and Trifles, not worth your observing.

Don. Yes, for Variety's Sake. Pray you shew us
    Friends

The chiefeft of your Wares.

Vitel. Your Ladyfhip's Servant;
And, if in Worth or Title you are more,
My Ignorance plead my Pardon.

Don. He fpeaks well.

Vitel. Take down the Looking-Glafs.——Here is a
    Mirrour

Steel'd fo exactly, neither taking from,
Nor flattering the Object, it returns
To the Beholder, that *Narciffus* might
(And never grow enamour'd of himfelf)
View his fair Feature in't.

Don. Poetical too!

Vitel. Here *China* Difhes to ferve in a Banquet,
Tho' the voluptuous *Perfian* fat a Gueft.
Here Cryftal Glaffes, fuch as *Ganymede*
Did fill with Nectar to the Thunderer,
When he drank to *Alcides*, and receiv'd him
In the Fellowfhip of the Gods, true to the Owners:
Corinthian Plate ftudded with Diamonds
Conceal oft deadly Poifon; this pure Metal
So innocent is and faithful to the Miftrefs
Or Mafter that poffeffes it, that rather
Than hold one Drop that's venomous, of itfelf
It flies in Pieces and deludes the Traitor.

Don. How movingly could this Fellow treat upon
A worthy Subject that finds fuch Difcourfe
To grace a Trifle!

Vitel. Here's a Picture, Madam;
The Mafter-piece of *Michael Angelo*,
Our great *Italian* Workman——Here's another,
So perfect in all Parts, that, had *Pygmalion*
Seen this, his Prayers had been made to *Venus*
T' have given it Life, and his carv'd Iv'ry Image
By Poets ne'er remember'd. They are, indeed,
The rareft Beauties of the Chriftian World,
And no where to be equall'd.

Don. You are partial
In the Cause of those you favour, I believe;
I instantly could shew you one, to theirs
Not much inferior.

Vitel. With your Pardon, Madam,
I am incredulous.

Don. Can you match me this?   [*Unveils herself.*

Vitel. What Wonder look I on! I'll search above,
And suddenly attend you.   [*Exit* Vitelli.

Don. Are you amaz'd?
I'll bring you to yourself.   [*Breaks the Glasses.*

Musta. Ha! what's the Matter!

Gaz. My Master's Ware?—We are undone!—O
strange!
A Lady to turn Roarer, and break Glasses!
'Tis Time to shut up Shop then.

Musta. You seem mov'd.
If any Language of these Christian Dogs
Have call'd your Anger on, in a Frown shew it,
And they are dead already.

Don. The Offence
Looks not so far. The foolish paltry Fellow
Shew'd me some Trifles, and demanded of me,
For what I valu'd at so many Aspers,
A thousand Ducats. I confess he mov'd me,
Yet I should wrong myself, should such a Beggar
Receive least Loss from me.

Musta. Is it no more?

Don. No, I assure you. Bid him bring his Bill
To-morrow to the Palace and enquire
For one *Donusa:* That Word gives him Passage
Thro' all the Guard; say there he shall receive
Full Satisfaction. Now when you please——

Musta. I wait you.
        [*Exeunt* Mustapha, Donusa, *and two* Turks.

1 *Turk.* We must not know them.—Let's shift off,
        and vanish.

Gaz. The Swine's-pox overtake you: There's a Curse
For a *Turk* that eats no Hog's Flesh.

Vitel. Is fhe gone?

Gaz. Yes: You may fee her Handy-work.

Vitel. No Matter:
Said fhe aught elfe?

Gaz. That you fhould wait upon her,
And there receive Court Payment; and to pafs
The Guards, fhe bids you only fay, you come
To one *Donufa.*

Vitel. How! remove the Wares.
Do it without Reply, The Sultan's Niece!
I have heard among the *Turks* for any Lady
To fhew her Face bare, argues Love or fpeaks
Her deadly Hatred. What fhould I fear? My Fortune
Is funk fo low there cannot fall upon me
Aught worth my fhunning.—I will run the Hazard.—
She may be a Means to free diftrefs'd *Paulina.*—
Or, if offended, at the worft, to die
Is a full Period to Calamity.   [*Exeunt.*

End of the Firft *Act.*

ACT II.   SCENE I.

A Room.

Enter Carazie *and* Manto.

Carazie.

IN the Name of Wonder, *Manto*, what hath my
        Lady
Done with herfelf fince yefterday?

Manto. I know not.
Malicious Men report we are all guided
In our Affections by a wand'ring Planet:
But fuch a fudden Change in fuch a Perfon,

May ſtand for an Example to confirm
Their falſe Aſſertion.

Car. She's now pettiſh, froward:
Muſick, Diſcourſe, Obſervance tedious to her.

Manto. She ſlept not the laſt Night; and yet
    prevented
The riſing Sun, in being up before him.
Call'd for a coſtly Bath, then will'd the Rooms
Should be perfum'd; ranſack'd her Cabinets
For her choiceſt, richeſt Jewels, and appears now
Like *Cynthia* in full Glory, waited on
By the faireſt of the Stars.

Car. Can you gueſs the Reaſon,
Why the *Aga* of the *Janizaries*, and he
That guards the Entrance of the inmoſt Port,
Were call'd before her?

Manto. They are both her Creatures,
And by her Grace preferr'd. But I am ignorant
To what Purpoſe they were ſent for.

Enter Donuſa.

Car. Here ſhe comes,
Full of ſad Thoughts: We muſt ſtand farther off.—
What a Frown was that!

Manto. Forbear.

Car. I pity her.

Don. What Magick hath transform'd me from my-
    ſelf?
Where is my Virgin Pride? How have I loſt
My boaſted Freedom? What new Fire burns up
My ſcorched Entrails? What unknown Deſires
Invade, and take Poſſeſſion of my Soul,
All virtuous Objects vaniſh'd? Have I ſtood
The Shock of fierce Temptations, ſtopp'd mine Ears
Againſt all *Syren* Notes Luſt ever ſung,
To draw my Bark of Chaſtity (that with Wonder
Hath kept a conſtant and an honour'd Courſe)
Into the Gulf of a deſerv'd ill Fame?
Now fall unpitied? And, in a Moment
With mine own Hands dig up a Grave to bury

The monumental Heap of all my Years,
Employ'd in noble Actions? O my Fate!
—But there is no refifting. I obey thee,.
Imperious God of Love, and willingly
Put mine own Fetters on to grace thy Triumph:
'Twere therefore more than Cruelty in thee
To ufe me like a Tyrant. What poor Means
Muft I make ufe of now? And flatter fuch,
To whom, till I betray'd my Liberty,
One gracious Look of mine would have erected
An Altar to my Service? How now, *Manto!*
My ever careful Woman; and *Carazie,*
Thou haft been faithful too.

Car. I dare not call
My Life mine own, fince it is yours; but gladly
Will part with it whene'er you fhall command me,
And think I fall a Martyr, fo my Death
May give Life to your Pleafures.

Manto. But vouchfafe
To let me underftand what you defire
Should be effected, I will undertake it
And curfe myfelf for Cowardice if I paus'd
To afk a Reafon Why.

Don. I'm comforted
In the Tender of your Service, but fhall be
Confirm'd in my full Joys in the Performance.
Yet, truft me, I will not impofe upon you
But what you ftand engag'd for, to a Miftrefs;
Such as I have been to you. All I afk
Is Faith and Secrecy.

Car. Say but you doubt me,
And, to fecure you, I'll cut out my Tongue,
I am lib'd in the Breech already.

Manto. Do not hinder
Yourfelf by thefe Delays.

Don. Thus then I whifper
My own Shame to you. O that I fhould blufh
To fpeak what I fo much defire to do!
And further— [*Whifpers, and ufes vehement Actions.*

B 4

Manto. Is this all?

Don. Think it not bafe;
Altho' I know the Office undergoes
A coarfe Conftruction.

Car. Coarfe? 'Tis but procuring;
A Smock Employment which has made more Knights,
In a Country I could name, than twenty Years
Of Service in the Field.

Don. You have my Ends.

Manto. Which fay you have arriv'd at, be not wanting
To yourfelf and fear not us.

Car. I know my Burthen:
I'll bear it with Delight.

Manto. Talk not, but do. [*Exeunt* Carazie *and* Manto.

Don. O Love! what poor Shifts thou doft force us to?
[*Exit* Donufa.

SCENE II.

Enter Aga, Capiaga, *and* Janizaries.

Aga. She was ever our good Miftrefs and our Maker,
And fhould we check at a little Hazard for her,
We were unthankful.

Cap. I dare pawn my Head,
'Tis fome difguifed Minion of the Court
Sent from great *Amurath*, to learn from her
The Viceroy's Actions.

Aga. That concerns not us;
His Fall may be our Rife: Whate'er he be,
He paffes thro' my Guards.

Cap. And mine—provided
He give the Word.

Enter Vitelli.

Vitel. To faint now, being thus far,
Would argue me of Cowardice.

Aga. Stand—the Word—

Or, being a Chriftian, to prefs thus far
Forfeits thy Life.

Vitel. Donu*fa.*

Aga. Pafs in Peace.   [*Exeunt* Aga *and* Janizaries.

Vitel. What a Privilege her Name bears!
'Tis wondrous ftrange!
If the great Officer,
The Guardian of the inner Port, deny not.—

Cap. Thy Warrant.—Speak,
Or thou art dead.

Vitel. Donu*fa.*

Cap. That protects thee; without Fear enter.
So—Difcharge the Watch. [*Exeunt* Vitelli *and* Capiaga.

S C E N E III.

Enter Carazie *and* Manto.

Car. Tho' he hath paft the *Aga* and chief Porter,
This cannot be the Man.

Manto. By her Defcription, I am fure it is.

Car. O Women, Women!
What are you? A great Lady dote upon
A Haberdafher of fmall Wares!

Manto. Pifh! thou haft none.

Car. No; if I had I might have ferv'd the Turn:
This 'tis to want Munition, when a Man
Should make a Breach and enter.

Enter Vitelli.

Manto. Sir! you're welcome:
Think what 'tis to be happy, and poffefs it.

Car. Perfume the Rooms there and make Way.
Let Mufick's choice Notes entertain the Man,
The Princefs now purpofes to honour.

Vitel. I am ravifh'd.   [*Exeunt.*

SCENE IV.

A Room of State.

A Table set forth, Jewels and Bags upon it : Loud Musick.

Enter Donusa, *takes a Chair ; to her* Carazie, Vitelli, *and* Manto.

Don. Sing o'er the Ditty that I last compos'd
Upon my Love-fick Paffion : Suit your Voice
To the Musick that's plac'd yonder, we shall hear you
With more Delight and Pleasure.
   Car. I obey you.   [*Song.*
   Vitel. Is not this *Tempe,* or the bleffed Shades,
Where innocent Spirits refide ? Or do I dream,
And this a heavenly Vifion ? Howfoever,
It is a Sight too glorious to behold
For fuch a Wretch as I am.   [*Stands amaz'd.*
   Car. He is daunted.
   Manto. Speak to him, Madam ! cheer him up, or
        you
Deftroy what you have built.
   Car. Would I were furnifh'd
With his Artillery, and if I ftood
Gaping as he does, hang me.
   Vitel. That I might 'ever dream thus.   [*Kneels.*
   Don. Banifh Amazement :
You wake ; your Debtor tells you fo, your Debtor :
And to affure you that I am Subftance,
And no aërial Figure, thus I raife you.
Why do you fhake ? My foft Touch brings no Ague ;
No biting Froft is in this Palm ; nor are
My Looks like to the *Gorgon*'s Head that turns
Men into Statues : Rather they have Power
(Or I have been abus'd) where they beftow
Their Influence (let me prove it Truth in you)
To give to dead Men Motion.

Vitel. Can this be?
May I believe my Senses? Dare I think
I have a Memory? Or that you are
That excellent Creature that of late disdain'd not
To look on my poor Trifles.

Don. I am She.

Vitel. The Owner of that blessed Name, *Donusa*,
Which, like a potent Charm, altho' pronounc'd
By my prophane, but much unworthier Tongue,
Hath brought me safe to this forbidden Place
Where Christian ne'er yet trod?

Don. I am the same.

Vitel. And to what End, great Lady, pardon me
That I presume to ask, did your Command
Command me hither? Or what am I to whom
You should vouchsafe your Favours? nay, your Anger?
If any wild or uncollected Speech
Offensively deliver'd, or my Doubt
Of your unknown Perfections, have displeas'd you,
You wrong your Indignation to pronounce
Yourself my Sentence: To have seen you only,
And to have touch'd that Fortune-making Hand,
Will with Delight weigh down all Tortures that
A flinty Hangman's Rage could execute,
Or rigid Tyranny command with Pleasure.

Don. How the Abundance of Good, flowing to thee,
Is wrong'd in this Simplicity? And these Bounties,
Which all our Eastern Kings have kneel'd in vain for,
Do by thy Ignorance, or wilful Fear,
Meet with a false Construction. Christian! know
(For till thou art mine by a nearer Name,
That Title, tho' abhorr'd here, takes not from
Thy Entertainment) that 'tis not the Fashion
Among the greatest and the fairest Dames,
This *Turkish* Empire gladly owns and bows to,
To punish where there's no Offence; or nourish
Displeasures against those, without whose Mercy
They part with all Felicity. Prithee, be wise,
And gently understand me; do not force her,
That ne'er knew aught but to command, nor e'er read
The Elements of Affection but from such

As gladly fu'd to her, in the Infancy
Of her new-born Defires, to be at once
Importunate and immodeft.

 Vitel. Did I know,
Great Lady, your Commands; or, to what Purpofe
This perfonated Paffion tends, (fince 'twere
A Crime in me deferving Death, to think
It is your own) I fhould, to make you Sport,
Take any Shape you pleafe t' impofe upon me;
And with Joy ftrive to ferve you.

 Don. Sport! Thou art cruel,
If that thou canft interpret my Defcent
From my high Birth and Greatnefs, but to be
A Part in which I truly act myfelf.
And I muft hold thee for a dull Spectator
If it ftir not Affection and invite
Compaffion for my Sufferings. Be thou taught
By my Example, to make Satisfaction
For Wrongs unjuftly offer'd. Willingly
I do confefs my Fault; I injur'd thee
In fome poor petty Trifles; thus I pay for
The Trefpafs I did to thee. Here—receive
Thefe Bags ftuff'd full of our imperial Coin;
Or, if this Payment be too light, take here
Thefe Gems for which the flavifh *Indian* dives
To th' Bottom of the Main: Or, if thou fcorn
Thefe as bafe Drofs (which take but common Minds)
But fancy any Honour in my Gift
(Which is unbounded as the *Sultan*'s Power)
And be poffeft of't.

 Vitel. I am overwhelm'd
With the Weight of Happinefs you throw upon me:
Nor can it fall in my Imagination
What Wrong I e'er have done you; and much lefs
How like a royal Merchant to return
Your great Magnificence.

 Don. They are Degrees,
Not Ends, of my intended Favours to thee,
Thefe Seeds of Bounty I yet fcatter on
A Glebe I have not try'd:—But, be thou thankful,
The Harveft is to come.

Vitel. What can be added
To that which I already have receiv'd,
I cannot comprehend.

Don. The Tender of
Myfelf.—Why doft thou ftart ! and in that Gift
Full Reftitution of that Virgin Freedom
Which thou haft robb'd me of. Yet, I profefs,
I fo far prize the lovely Thief that ftole it,
That, were it poffible thou couldft reftore
What thou unwittingly haft ravifh'd from me,
I fhould refufe the Prefent.

Vitel. How I fhake
In my conftant Refolution ! and my Flefh,
Rebellious to my better Part, now tells me,
(As if it were a ftrong Defence of Frailty,)
A Hermit in a Defert, trench'd with Prayers,
Could not refift this Battery.

Don. Thou an *Italian ?*
Nay more, I know't, a natural *Venetian,*[5])
Such as are Courtiers born to pleafe fair Ladies,
Yet come thus flowly on ?

Vitel. Excufe me, Madam,
What Imputation foe'er the World
Is pleas'd to lay upon us ; in myfelf
I am fo innocent, that I know not what 'tis
That I fhould offer.

Don. By Inftinct I'll teach thee,
And with fuch Eafe as Love makes me to afk it.
When a young Lady wrings you by the Hand—thus ;
Or with an amorous Touch preffes your Foot
Looks Babies in your Eyes, plays with your Locks,
Do not you find, without a Tutor's Help,
What 'tis fhe looks for.

Vitel. I am grown already
Skillful i' th' Myftery.

Don. Or, if thus fhe kifs you,
Then taftes your Lips again.——

5 A Native of *Venice.* The Venetians are celebrated for licentious Love and Gallantry above all other Italians : Baretti in his Reply to Sharp's Letters from Italy, feems to confirm this Opinion. *D.*

Vitel. That latter Blow
Has beat all chaste Thoughts from me.

   Don. Say, she points to
Some private Room the Sun Beams never enters,
Provoking Dishes passing by to heighten
Declined Appetite, active Musick ushering
Your fainting Steps, the Waiters too as born dumb,
Nor daring to look on you. [*Exit, inviting him to follow.*

   Vitel. Tho' the Devil
Stood by and roar'd, I follow : Now I find
That Virtue's but a Word, and no sure Guard,
If set upon by Beauty and Reward.   [*Exit.*

SCENE V.

Enter Aga, Capiaga, Grimaldi, *Mafter, Boatfwain,* &c.

   Aga. The Devil's in him, I think.
   Grim. Let him be damn'd too.
I'll look on him, tho' he star'd as wild as Hell ;
Nay, I'll go nearer to tell him to his Teeth,
If he mends not suddenly and proves more thankful,
We do him too much Service. Wer't not for Shame
       now,
I could turn honest, and forswear my Trade,
Which, next to being truss'd up at the Main-yard
By some low Country Butter-box, I hate
As deadly as I do Fasting or long Grace
When Meat cools on the Table.
   Cap. But take Heed,
You know his violent Nature.
   Grim. Let his Whores
And Catamites know't ; I understand myself,
And how unmanly 'tis to sit at home,
And rail at us that run abroad all Hazards,
If ev'ry Week we bring not Home new Pillage,
For the fatting his Seraglio.

      Enter Asambeg, Muftapha, *and* Aga.

   Aga. Here he comes.
   Cap. How terrible he looks !

Grim. To such as fear him :
The Viceroy *Asambeg !* were he the Sultan's felf,—
He'll let us know a Reason for his Fury,
Or we muft take Leave, without his Allowance,
To be merry with our Ignorance.

Afam. Mahomet's Hell
Light on you all—you crouch and cringe now. Where
Was the Terror of my juft Frowns when you fuffered
Thofe Thieves of *Malta,* almoft in our Harbour,
To board a Ship and bear her fafely off
While you ftood idle Lookers-on ?

Aga. The Odds
I' th'. Men and Shipping, and the Suddennefs
Of their Departure, yielding us no Leifure
To fend forth others to relieve our own,
Deterr'd us, mighty Sir.

Afam. Deterr'd you, Cowards ?
How durft you only entertain the Knowledge
Of what Fear was, but in the not Performance
Of our Command ? In me great *Amurath* fpake ;
My Voice did echo to your Ears his Thunder,
And will'd you, like fo many Sea-born Tritons,
Arm'd only with the Trumpets of your Courage,
To fwim up to her, and, like *Remoras*
Hanging upon her Keel, to ftay her Flight
Till Refcue, fent from us, had fetch'd you off.
You think you're fafe now ; who durft but difpute it,
Or make it queftionable, if this Moment
I charg'd you from yon hanging Cliff, ‘ that glaffes
His rugged Forehead in the neighbouring Lake,
To throw yourfelves down Headlong ? Or like Faggots
To fill the Ditches of defended Forts,
While on your Backs we march'd up to the Breach ?

Grim. That would not I.
Afam. Ha ?

6 *Southern* in his *Oroonoko* feems to have borrowed this beautiful
Image from *Maffinger.*

————O for a *Whirlwind's Wing*
To hurry us to yonder Clift that frowns
Upon the Flood.   Oroon. Act 5th. *D.*

Grim. Yet I dare as much
As any of the Sultan's boldeſt Sons,
(Whoſe Heaven and Hell hang on his Frown or
    Smile,)
His warlike Janizaries.

Aſam. Add one Syllable more;
Thou doſt pronounce upon thyſelf a Sentence
That, Earthquake-like, will ſwallow thee.

Grim. Let it open;
I'll ſtand the Hazard: Thoſe condemned Thieves
Your Fellow-pirates, Sir! the bold *Malteſe;*
Whom with your Looks you think to quell, at *Rhodes*
Laugh'd at great *Solyman*'s Anger: And, if Treaſon
Had not delivered them into his Power,
He had grown old in Glory as in Years,
At that ſo fatal Siege; or ris'n with Shame,
His Hopes and Threats deluded.

Aſam. Our great Prophet!
How have I loſt my Anger and my Power?

Grim. Find it, and uſe it on thy Flatterers,
And not upon thy Friends that dare ſpeak Truth.
Theſe Knights of *Malta,* but a Handful to
Your Armies that drank Rivers up, have ſtood
Your Fury at the Height, and with their Croſſes
Struck pale your horned Moons; theſe Men of *Malta,*
Since I took pay from you, I've met and fought with;
Upon Advantage too; yet, to ſpeak Truth,
By th' Soul of Honour, I have ever found them
As provident to direct, and bold to do,
As any train'd up in your Diſcipline,
Raviſh'd from other Nations.

Muſta. I perceive
The Lightning in his fiery Looks, the Cloud
Is broke already.

Grim. Think not, therefore, Sir,
That you alone are Giants; and ſuch Pigmies
You war upon.

Aſam. Villain, I'll make thee know
Thou haſt blaſphem'd the *Ottoman* Power, and ſafer
At Noon-day might have given Fire to St. *Mark*'s,

Your proud *Venetian* Temple.—Seize upon him;—
I am not so near reconcil'd to him,
To bid him die! That were a Benefit
The Dog's unworthy of, to our Use confiscate
All that he stands possess'd of: Let him taste
The Misery of Want, and his vain Riots,
Like to so many walking Ghosts, affright him
Where'er he sets his desperate Foot. Who is't
That does command you?

 Grim. Is this the Reward
For all my Service, and the Rape I made
On fair *Paulina?*

 Asam. Drag him hence,—he dies,
That dallies but a Minute.

 Boatsw. What's become
Of our Shares now, Master?
     [*Grimaldi dragg'd off, his Head covered.*

 Mast. Would he had been born dumb:
Patience, the Beggar's Cure, is all that's left us.
     [*Exeunt Master and Boatswain.*

 Musta. 'Twas but Intemperance of Speech, excuse
  him——
Let me prevail so far. Fame gives him out
For a deserving Fellow.

 Asam. At *Aleppo,*
I durst not press you so far: Give me Leave
To use my own Will and Command in *Tunis,*
And, if you please, my Privacy.

 Musta. I will see you,
When this high Wind's blown o'er. [*Exit* Mustapha.

 Asam. So shall you find me
Ready to do you Service. Rage, now leave me;
Stern Looks, and all the ceremonious Forms
Attending on dread Majesty, fly from
Transformed *Asambeg.* Why should I hug
     [*Plucks out a gilt Key.*
So near my Heart, what leads me to my Prison?
Where she, that is inthrall'd, commands her Keeper,
And robs me of the Fierceness I was born with.

Stout Men quake at my Frowns; and, in Return,
I tremble at her Softneſs. Baſe *Grimaldi*
But only nam'd *Paulina*, and the Charm
Had almoſt choak'd my Fury, ere I could
Pronounce his Sentence. Would! when firſt I ſaw her,
Mine Eyes had met with Lightning, and, in Place
Of hearing her inchanting Tongue, the Shrieks
Of Mandrakes had made Muſick to my Slumbers:
For now I only walk a loving Dream,
And, but to my Diſhonour, never wake;
And yet am blind, but when I ſee the Object,
And madly doat on it. Appear, bright Spark

       [*Opens a Door,* Paulina *diſcovered, comes forth.*

Of all Perfection! any Simile
Borrow'd from Diamonds or the faireſt Stars,
To help me to expreſs how dear I prize
Thy unmatch'd Graces, will riſe up, and chide me
For poor Detraction.

    Pau. I deſpiſe thy Flatteries:
Thus ſpit at 'em, and ſcorn 'em; and, being arm'd
In the Aſſurance of my innocent Virtue,
I ſtamp upon all Doubts, all Fears, all Tortures
Thy barbarous Cruelty, or, what's worſe, thy Dotage,
(The worthy Parent of thy Jealouſy)
Can ſhow'r upon me.

    Aſam. If theſe bitter Taunts
Raviſh me from myſelf, and make me think
My greedy Ears receive angelical Sounds;
How would this Tongue, tun'd to a loving Note,
Invade, and take Poſſeſſion of my Soul,
Which then I durſt not call mine own!

    Pau. Thou art falſe;
Falſer than thy Religion. Do but think me
Something above a Beaſt, nay more, a Monſter,
Would fright the Sun to look on, and then tell me,
If this baſe Uſage can invite Affection.
If to be mew'd up, and excluded from
Human Society; the Uſe of Pleaſures;
The neceſſary, not ſuperfluous, Duties

Of Servants to discharge those Offices,
I blush to name.

Asam. Of Servants ? Can you think
That I, that dare not trust the Eye of Heaven
To look upon your Beauties ; that deny
Myself the Happiness to touch your Pureness,
Will e'er consent an Eunuch, or bought Handmaid,
Shall once approach you ?—There is something in you
That can work Miracles, or I am cozen'd ;
Dispose and alter Sexes, to my Wrong,
In Spite of Nature : I will be your Nurse,
Your Woman, your Physician, and your Fool ;
Till, with your free Consent, which I have vow'd
Never to force, you grace me with a Name
That shall supply all these.

Pau. What is't ?

Asam. Your Husband.

Pau. My Hangman, when thou pleasest.

Asam. Thus I guard me
Against your further Angers.—

Pau. Which shall reach thee,
Tho' I were in the Center.

      [Puts to the Door, and locks it.

Asam. Such a Spirit,
In such a small Proportion I ne'er read of ;
Which Time must alter :—Ravish her I dare not ;
The Magick that she wears about her Neck,
I think, defends her, this Devotion paid
To this sweet Saint, Mistress of my sour Pain,
'Tis fit I take mine own rough Shape again.

        [Exit Asambeg.

SCENE VI.

Enter Francisco *and* Gazet.

Fran. I think he's lost.

Gaz. 'Tis ten to one of that ;
I ne'er knew Citizen turn Courtier yet,

But he loft his Credit, tho' he fav'd himfelf.
Why, look you, Sir! there are fo many Lobbies,
Out-offices, and Difputations⁷ here
Behind thefe *Turkifb* Hangings, that a Chriftian
Hardly gets off but circumcifed.

Enter Vitelli, Carazie *and* Manto.

Fran. I'm troubl'd,
Troubled exceedingly.—Ha! what are thefe?
 Gaz. One by his rich Suit fhould be fome *French*
   Ambaffador:
For his Train, I think they are *Turks.*
 Fran. Peace!—be not feen.
 Cara. You are now paft all the Guards, and undifco-
   ver'd
You may return.
 Vitel. There's for your Pains:—Forget not
My humbleft Service to the beft of Ladies.
 Manto. Deferve her Favour, Sir! in making Hafte
For a fecond Entertainment.
       [*Exeunt* Carazi *and* Manto.
 Vitel. Do not doubt me;
I fhall not live till then.
 Gaz. The Train is vanifh'd:
They've done him fome good Office, he's fo free
And liberal of his Gold. Ha! do I dream?
Or is this mine own natural Mafter?
 Fran. 'Tis he;
But ftrangely metamorphos'd. You have made, Sir,
A profperous Voyage; Heaven grant it be honeft!
I fhall rejoice then, too.
 Gaz. You make him blufh,
To talk of Honefty: You were but now
In the giving Vein, and may think of *Gazet,*
Your Worfhip's 'Prentice.

    ⁷ *Difputations.*
 This Word feems to convey here no Meaning: It is very probable
that the Author wrote Difpartations, a Word fignifying feparate
Apartments. *D.*

Vitel. There's Gold : Be thou free too,
And Mafter of my Shop, and all the Wares
We brought from *Venice.*

   Gaz. Rivo then.

   Vitel. Dear Sir !
This Place affords not Privacy for Difcourfe ;
But I can tell you Wonders : My rich Habit
Deferves leaft Admiration ; there's nothing,
That can fall in the Compafs of your Wifhes,
Tho' it were to redeem a thoufand Slaves
From the *Turkifh* Gallies, or at Home to erect
Some pious Work, to fhame all Hofpitals,
But I am Mafter of the Means.

   Fran. 'Tis ftrange.

   Vitel. As I walk, I'll tell you more.

   Gaz. Pray you, a Word, Sir !
And then I will put on. I have one Boon more—

   Vitel. What is't ? Speak freely.

   Gaz. Thus then : As I am Mafter
Of your Shop and Wares, pray you, help me to fome
         Trucking,
With your laft She-cuftomer ; tho' fhe crack'd my beft
         Piece,
I will endure it with Patience.

   Vitel. Leave your prating.

   Gaz. I may : You have been doing ; we will do too.

   Fran. I am amaz'd, yet will not blame nor chide you,
Till you inform me further : Yet muft fay,
They fteer not the right Courfe, nor traffick well,
That feek a Paffage to reach Heaven, thro' Hell.

                      [*Exeunt.*

End of the Second Act.

ACT III.   SCENE I.

Enter Donusa *and* Manto.

Donusa.

WHEN, said he, he would come again ?
        Manto. He swore,
Short Minutes should be tedious Ages to him,
Until the Tender of his second Service,
So much he seem'd transported with the first.
    Don. I'm sure I was.   I charge thee, *Manto*, tell me,
By all my Favours and my Bounties, truly,
Whether thou art a Virgin ; or, like me,
Hast forfeited that Name,
    Manto. A Virgin, Madam ?
At my Years, being a Waiting-woman, and in Court
        too ?
That were miraculous.   I so long since lost
That barren Burthen, I almost forget
That ever I was one. [8]
    Don. And could thy Friends
Read in thy Face, thy Maidenhead gone, that thou
Hadst parted with it ?
    Manto. No, indeed : I past
For current many Years after ; till, by Fortune,
Long and continued Practice in the Sport
Blew up my Deck : A Husband then was found out
By my indulgent Father, and to the World
All was made whole again.   What need you fear, then,
That at your Pleasure may repair your Honour ?
Durst any envious or malicious Tongue
Presume to taint it ?
    Don. How now ?

---

[8] *I almost forget*
    That ever I was one.
    This is little more than a Translation from *Petronius Arbiter.*
Quartilla, at Fourteen Years of Age, cannot recollect the Time
when she was a Virgin. *D.*

Enter Carazie.

Car. Madam, the Bafha
Humbly defires Accefs.

Don. If it had been
My neat *Italian,* thou hadft met my Wifhes.
—Tell him we would be private.

Car. So I did ;
But he is much importunate.

Manto. Beft difpatch him :
His ling'ring here elfe, will deter the other
From making his Approach.

Don. His Entertainment
Shall not invite a fecond Vifit.—Go,
Say we are pleas'd.

Enter Muftapha.

Mufta. All Happinefs.

Don. Be fudden.
'Twas faucy Rudenefs in you, Sir, to prefs
On my Retirements ; but ridiculous Folly
To wafte the Time that might be better fpent
In complimental Wifhes.

Car. There's a Cooling
For his hot Encounter.

Don. Come you here to ftare ?
If you have loft your Tongue and Ufe of Speech,
Refign your Government : There's a Mute's Place void
In my Uncle's Court, I hear, and you may work me
To write for your Preferment.

Mufta. This is ftrange !
I know not, Madam, what Neglect of mine
Has call'd this Scorn upon me.

Don. To the Purpofe——
My Will's a Reafon, and we ftand not bound
To yield Account to you.

Mufta. Not of your Angers,
But with erected Ears, I fhould hear from you

The Story of your good Opinion of me
Confirm'd by Love and Favours.

   Don. How deferv'd?
I have confidered you from Head to Foot,
And can find nothing in that Wainfcot Face,
That can teach me to dote; nor am I taken
With your grim Afpect, or tadpole-like Complexion.'
Thofe Scars you glory in I fear to look on;
And had much rather hear a merry Tale,
Than all your Battles won with Blood and Sweat,
Tho' you belch forth the Stink too in the Service,
And fwear by your Muftachios all is true.
You're yet too rough for me: Purge and take Phyfick,
Purchafe Perfumers; get me fome *French* Taylor
To new-create you; the firft Shape you were made with
Is quite worn out: Let your Barber wafh your Face too,
You look yet like a Bugbear to fright Children;
Till when I take my Leave—Wait me, *Carazie.*

                 [*Exeunt* Donufa *and* Carazie.

   Mufta. Stay you, my Lady's Cabinet-key!
   Manto. How's this, Sir?
   Mufta. Stay, and ftand quietly, or you fhall fall elfe;
Not to firk your Belly up, Flounder-like, but never
To rife again.   Offer but to unlock
Thefe Doors that ftop your fugitive Tongue (obferve me)
And, by my Fury, I'll fix there this Bolt

                 [*Draws ais Scymitar.*

To bar thy Speech for ever,—So.—Be fafe now,
And but refolve me (not of what I doubt,
But bring Affurance to a Thing believ'd)
Thou mak'ft thyfelf a Fortune; not depending
On the uncertain Favours of a Miftrefs,
But art thyfelf one.   I'll not fo far queftion
My Judgment and Obfervance, as to afk
Why I am flighted and contemn'd; but in
Whofe Favour it is done.   I, (that have read
The copious Volumes of all Women's Falfehood,
Commented on by the Heart-breaking Groans
Of abus'd Lovers; all the Doubts wafh'd off
With fruitlefs Tears the Spider's Cobweb Veil

Of Arguments, alleg'd in their Defence,
Blown off with Sighs of defperate Men, and they
Appearing in their full Deformity)
Know that fome other hath difplanted me,
With her Difhonour. Has fhe giv'n it up?
Confirm it in two Syllables.

Manto. She has.

Mufta. I cherifh thy Confeffion thus, and thus,

                      [Gives her Jewels.

Be mine.—Again I court thee thus, and thus:
Now prove but conftant to my Ends.

Manto. By all——

Mufta. Enough; I dare not doubt thee. O Land-
    Crocodiles,
Made of *Ægyptian* Slime, accurfed Women!
But 'tis no Time to rail: Come, my beft *Manto.*

                      [Exeunt.

SCENE II.

Enter Vitelli *and* Francifco.

Vitel. Sir, as you are my Confeffor, you ftand bound
Not to reveal whatever I difcover
In that religious Way: Nor dare I doubt you.
Let it fuffice you've made me fee my Follies,
And wrought, perhaps, Compunction; for I would not
Appear an Hypocrite: But, when you impofe
A Penance on me beyond Flefh and Blood
To undergo, you muft inftruct me how
To put off the Condition of a Man;
Or, if not pardon, at the leaft, excufe
My Difobedience. Yet, defpair not, Sir;
For, tho' I take mine own Way, I fhall do
Something that may hereafter; to my Glory,
Speak me your Scholar.

Fran. I enjoin you not
To go, but fend.

Vitel. That were a petty Trial;
Not worth one, fo long taught and exercis'd

Under so grave a Master.   Reverend *Francisco!*
My Friend, my Father ! in that Word, my All !
Rest confident you shall hear something of me
That will redeem me in your good Opinion,
Or judge me lost for ever.   Send *Gazet*
(She shall give Order that he may have Entrance)
To acquaint you with my Fortunes.   [*Exit* Vitelli.
     Fran. Go, and prosper.
Holy Saints guide and strengthen thee ! Howsoever,
As thy Endeavours are, so may they find
Gracious Acceptance.

                 Enter Gazet *and* Grimaldi, *in Rags.*

     Gaz. Now, you do not roar, Sir ;
You speak not Tempests, nor take Ear-rent from
A poor Shopkeeper.   Do you remember that, Sir ?
I wear your Marks here still.
     Fran. Can this be possible ?
All Wonders are not ceas'd then.
     Grim. Do, abuse me,
Spit on me, spurn me, pull me by the Nose !
Thrust out these fiery Eyes, that yesterday
Would have look'd thee dead.
     Gaz. O save me, Sir !
     Grim. Fear nothing !
I'm tame and quiet ; there's no Wrong can force me
To remember what I was.   I have forgot
I e'er had ireful Fierceness, a steel'd Heart,
Insensible of Compassion to others :
Nor is it fit that I should think myself
Worth mine own Pity.—Oh !
     Fran. Grows this Dejection
From his Disgrace, do you say ?
     Gaz. Why he's cashier'd, Sir !
His Ships, his Goods, his Livery-punks confiscate :
And there is such a Punishment laid upon him,
The miserable Rogue must steal no more,
Nor drink, nor drab.
     Fran. Does that torment him.

Gaz. O, Sir !
Should the State take Order to bar Men of Acres
From thefe two laudable Recreations,
Drinking and Whoring, how fhould Panders purchafe,
Or thrifty Whores build Hofpitals ? 'Slid ! if I,
That, fince I am made free, may write myfelf
A City Gallant, fhould forfeit two fuch Charters,
I fhould be fton'd to Death, and ne'er be pitied
By th' Liveries of thofe Companies.

Fran. You'll be whipp'd, Sir !
If you bridle not your Tongue. Hafte to the Palace,
Your Mafter looks for you.

Gaz. My quondam Mafter,
Rich Sons forget they ever had poor Fathers ;
In Servants 'tis more pardonable.—As a Companion,
Or fo, I may confent : But, is there Hope, Sir !
He has got me a good Chapwoman ? Pray you, write
A Word or two in my Behalf.

Fran. Out, Rafcal !

Gaz. I feel fome Infurrections.

Fran. Hence !

Gaz. I vanifh.   [*Exit* Gazet.

Grim. Why fhould I ftudy a Defence or Comfort,
In whom black Guilt and Mifery, if balanc'd,
I know not which would turn the Scale ? Look up-
            ward
I dare not ; for, fhould it but be believ'd
That I (dy'd deep in Hell's moft horrid Colours)
Should dare to hope for Mercy, it would leave
No Check or Feeling in Men innocent
To catch at Sins, the Devil ne'er taught Mankind yet.
No ! I muft downward, downward ; tho' Repentance [9]
Could borrow all the glorious Wings of Grace,

☞ 9 *No, I muft downward, downward; tho'. Repentance Could borrow all the glorious Wings, &c.*

The Beauty of this Paffage is inimitable, and truly original : *Shakefpeare* has, indeed, many that are fimilar to it ; but none that can be brought in Competition.

My mountainous Weight of Sins would crack their
     Pinions,
And sink them to Hell with me.

Fran. Dreadful! hear me,
Thou miserable Man!

Grim. Good Sir! deny not
But that there is no Punishment beyond
Damnation.

Enter Master and Boatswain.

Master. Yonder he is: I pity him.

Boatsw. Take Comfort, Captain: We live still to
    serve you.

Grim. Serve me? I am a Devil already.—Leave me!"
Stand farther off! you're blasted, else. I've heard
Schoolmen affirm, Man's Body is compos'd
Of the four Elements; and, as in League together
They nourish Life, so each of them affords
Liberty to the Soul, when it grows weary
Of this fleshy Prison.—Which shall I make Choice of?
The Fire? No; I shall feel that hereafter.
The Earth will not receive me.—Should some Whirl-
    wind
Snatch me into the Air, and I hang there,
Perpetual Plagues would dwell upon the Earth,
And those superior Bodies, that pour down
Their cheerful Influence, deny to pass it
Thro' those vast Regions I have infected.
The Sea; I," that is Justice, there I plow'd up

---

10 ————————*Leave me!*
    Stand farther off! you're blasted else.

Whenever the Mind is harrassed by the Stings of Conscience, or
the Horrors of Guilt, the Senses are liable to infinite Delusions, and
startle at hideous imaginary Monsters. The Poet, who can touch
such Incidents with happy Dexterity, and paint such Images of Con-
sternation, will infallibly work upon the Minds of others.
                   The Rev. Mr. SMITH.

11 In all the ancient Poets, *I* is used for *Ay.* M. M.

Mifchief as deep as Hell: There, I'll hide
This curfed Lump of Clay: May it turn Rocks,
Where Plummet's Weight could never reach the
    Sands!
And grind the Ribs of all fuch Barks as prefs
The Ocean's Breaft in my unlawful Courfe.
I hafte then to thee: Let thy rav'nous Womb,
Whom all Things elfe deny, be now my Tomb!" [12]
                     [*Exit* Grimaldi.

   Mafter. Follow him, and reftrain him.
   Fran. Let this ftand
For an Example to you. I'll provide
A Lodging for him, and apply fuch Cures
To his wounded Confcience as Heaven hath lent me.
He's now my fecond Care; and my Profeffion
Binds me to teach the Defperate to repent,
As far as to confirm the Innocent.   [*Exeunt.*

SCENE III.

Enter Afambeg, Muftapha, Aga *and* Capiaga.

   Afam. Your Pleafure?
   Mufta. 'Twill exact your private Ear;
And, when you have receiv'd it, you will think
Too many know it.   [*Exeunt* Aga *and* Capiaga.
   Afam. Leave the Room; but be
Within our Call.——Now, Sir, what burning Secrets
    bring you
(With which it feems you are turn'd Cinders)
To quench in my Advice or Power?
   Mufta. The Fire
Will rather reach you.——
   Afam. Me?

---

  12 *Whom all Things elfe deny, be now my Tomb!*

    This is a Latinifm unufual in our Language; the pronoun *whom*
refers to *me* underftood, and comprized in the Pronoun poffeffive
my. M. M.

Mufta. And confume both;
For 'tis impoffible to be put out,
But with the Blood of thofe that kindle it:
And yet one Vial of it is fo precious,
In being borrow'd from the *Ottoman* Spring,
That better 'tis, I think, both we fhould perifh
Than prove the defp'rate Means that muft reftrain it
From fpreading farther.

Afam. To the Point and quickly:
Thefe winding Circumftances in Relations
Seldom environ Truth.

Mufta. Truth, *Afambeg?*

Afam. Truth, *Muftapha.* I faid it, and add more:
You touch upon a String that to my Ear
Does found *Donufa.*

Mufta. You then underftand
Who 'tis I aim at.

Afam. Take Heed, *Muftapha;*
Remember what fhe is, and whofe we are.
'Tis her Neglect, perhaps, that you complain of;
And, fhould you practife to revenge her Scorn,
With any Plot to taint her in her Honour.—

Mufta. Hear me.

Afam. I will be heard firft; there's no Tongue
A Subject owes, that fhall out-thunder mine.

Mufta. Well, take your Way.

Afam. I then again repeat it,
If *Muftapha* dares with malicious Breath
(On jealous Suppofitions) prefume
To blaft the Bloffom of *Donufa*'s Fame,
Becaufe he is deny'd a Happinefs
Which Men of equal, nay, of more Defert,
Have fu'd in vain for—

Mufta. More?

Afam. More. 'Twas I fpake it,
The Bafha of *Natolia* and myfelf
Were Rivals for her; either of us brought
More Victories, more Trophies to plead for us
To our great Mafter, than you dare lay claim to;
Yet ftill, by his Allowance, fhe was left

To her Election : Each of us ow'd Nature
As much for outward Form and inward Worth,
To make Way for us to her Grace and Favour,
As you brought with you.   We were heard, repuls'd ;
Yet thought it no Dishonour to sit down
With the Disgrace ; if not to force Affection
May merit such a Name.

 Musta. Have you done yet ?

 Asam. Be therefore more than sure the Ground on
  which
You raise your Accusation, may admit
No undermining of Defence in her :
For if with pregnant and apparent Proofs,
Such as may force a Judge, more than inclin'd,
Or partial in her Cause, to swear her guilty ;
You win not me to set off your Belief :
Neither our ancient Friendship, nor the Rites
Of sacred Hospitality (to which
I would not offer Violence) shall protect you.
—Now when you please.

 Musta. I will not dwell upon
Much Circumstance ; yet cannot but profess,
With the Assurance of a Loyalty
Equal to yours, the Reverence I owe
The Sultan, and all such his Blood makes sacred :
That there is not a Vein of mine, which yet is
Unemptied in his Service, but this Moment
Should freely open, so it might wash off
The Stains of her Dishonour.   Could you think ?
Or, tho' you saw it, credit your own Eyes ?
That she, the Wonder and Amazement of
Her Sex, the Pride and Glory of the Empire,
That hath disdain'd you, slighted me, and boasted
A frozen Coldness, which no Appetite
Or Height of Blood could thaw, should now so far
Be hurry'd with the Violence of her Lust,
As, in it burying her high Birth and Fame,
Basely descend to fill a Christian's Arms ?
And to him yield her Virgin Honour up ?
Nay, sue to him to take't !

Afam. A Christian?

Mufta. Temper

Your Admiration :—And what Christian think you?
No Prince difguis'd; no Man of Mark nor Honour;
No daring Undertaker in our Service,
But one, whofe Lips her Foot fhould fcorn to touch,
A poor Mechanick Pedlar.

Afam. He?

Mufta. Nay, more;

Whom do you think fhe made her Scout, nay Bawd,
To find him out, but me? What Place makes Choice of
To wallow in her foul and loathfome Pleafures,
But in the Palace? Who the Inftruments
Of clofe Conveyance, but the Captain of
Your Guard, the *Aga*, and, that Man of Truft,
The Warden of the inmoft Port?—I'll prove this;
And, tho' I fail to fhew her in the Act,
Glu'd like a neighing Gennet to her Stallion,
Your Incredulity fhall be convinc'd
With Proofs I blufh to think on.

Afam. Never yet

This Flefh felt fuch a Fever.—By the Life
And Fortune of great *Amurath*, fhould our Prophet
(Whofe Name I bow to) in a Vifion fpeak this,
'Twould make me doubtful of my Faith.—Lead on;
And, when my Eyes and Ears are, like yours, guilty,
My Rage fhall then appear; for I will do
Something;—but what, I am not yet determin'd.

[*Exeunt.*

SCENE IV.

Enter Carazie, Manto, *and* Gazet.

Car. They're private to their Wifhes.

Manto. Doubt it not!

Gaz. A pretty Structure this! a Court do you call it?
Vaulted and arch'd: O! here has been old jumbling
Behind this Arras.

Car. Pry'thee let's have fome Sport
With this frefh Codfhead.

Manto. I am out of Tune,
But do as you pleafe. My Confcience!—Tufh! the
    Hope
Of Liberty does throw that Burthen off;
I muft go watch, and make Difcovery.   [*Exit.*

Car. He's mufing,
And will talk to himfelf; he cannot hold;
The poor Fool's ravifh'd.

Gaz. I am in my Mafter's Clothes;
They fit me to a Hair too; let but any
Indifferent Gamefter meafure us Inch by Inch,
Or weigh us by the Standard, I may pafs:
I have been prov'd, and prov'd again, true Metal.

Car. How he furvey's himfelf.

Gaz. I've heard, that fome
Have fool'd themfelves at Court into good Fortunes,
That never hop'd to thrive by Wit i' th' City,
Or Honefty i' th' Country.   If I do not
Make the beft laugh at me, I'll weep for myfelf:
If they give me Hearing.—'Tis refolv'd—I'll try
What may be done. By your Favour, Sir! I pray
    you,
Were you born a Courtier?

Car. No, Sir; why do you afk?

Gaz. Becaufe I thought that none could be preferr'd
But fuch as were begot there.

Car. O, Sir! many;
And, howfoe'er you are a Citizen born,
Yet if your Mother were a handfome Woman,
And ever long'd to fee a Mafk at Court,
It is an even Lay, but that you had
A Courtier to your Father; and I think fo,
You bear yourfelf fo fprightly.

Gaz. It may be;
But pray you, Sir! had I fuch an Itch upon me
To change my Copy, is there Hope a Place
May be had here for Money?

Car. Not without it;
That I dare warrant you.

Gaz. I have a pretty Stock,
And would not have my good Parts undiscover'd,
What Places of Credit are there?

Car. There's your *Beglerbeg.* [13]

Gaz. By no Means that; it comes too near the Beggar;
And most prove so that come there.

Car. Or your *Sangiack.* [14]

Gaz. Saucy Jack? Fie! none of that.

Car. Your *Chiaus.* [15]

Gaz. Nor that.

Car. Chief Gardener!

Gaz. Out upon't!
'Twill put me in Mind my Mother was an Herb-woman.
What is your Place, I pray you?

Car. Sir! an Eunuch.

Gaz. An Eunuch? Very fine! I Faith! an Eunuch!
And what are your Employments? Neat and easy.

Car. In the Day I wait on my Lady when she eats,
Carry her Pantoufles, bear up her Train;
Sing her asleep at Night, and, when she pleases,
I am her Bedfellow.

Gaz. How? Her Bedfellow?
And lie with her?

Car. Yes, and lie with her.

☞ 13 *There's your* Beglerberg.

(i. e. Lord of Lords*)* a chief Governor of a *Turkish* Province.

☞ 14 Or your *Sangiack.*

A *Turkish* Governor of a City or Province.

☞ 15 Your *Chiaus.*

An Officer in the *Turkish* Court, who performs the Duty of an Usher, and also an Ambassador to foreign Princes and States.

Gaz. O rare!
I'll be an Eunuch, tho' I fell my Shop for't,
And all my Wares.
   Car. It is but parting with
A precious Stone or two. I know the Price on't.
   Gaz. I'll part with all my Stones; and, when I am
An Eunuch, I'll fo tofs and towfe the Ladies;
Pray you help me to a Chapman.
   Car. The Court-Surgeon
Shall do you that Favour.
   Gaz. I am made! an Eunuch!

Enter Manto.

Manto. *Carazie,* quit the Room.
   Car. Come, Sir! we'll treat of
Your Bufinefs further.
   Gaz. Excellent! an Eunuch?   [*Exeunt.*

SCENE V.

Enter Donufa *and* Vitelli.

Vitel. Leave me, or I am loft again: No Prayers,
No Penitence can redeem me.
   Don. Am I grown
Old or deform'd fince yefterday?
   Vitel. You are ftill,
Altho' the fating of your Luft hath fullied
Th' immaculate Whitenefs of your Virgin Beauties,
Too fair for me to look on: And, tho' Purenefs,
The Sword with which you ever fought and conquer'd,
Is ravifh'd from you by unchafte Defires,
You are too ftrong for Flefh and Blood to treat with,
Tho' Iron Grates were interpos'd between us,
To warrant me from Treafon.
   Don. Whom do you fear?

Vitel. That human Frailty I took from my Mother,
That, as my Youth increas'd, grew ftronger on me;
That ftill purfues me, and, tho' once recover'd,
In Scorn of Reafon, and, what's more, Religion,
Again feeks to betray me.

　Don. If you mean, Sir,
To my Embraces, you turn Rebel to
The Laws of Nature, the great Queen and Mother
Of all Productions, and deny Allegiance,
Where you ftand bound to pay it.

　Vitel. I will ftop
Mine Ears againft thefe Charms, which, if *Ulyffes*
Could live again, and hear this fecond *Syren*,
Tho' bound with Cables to his Maft, his Ship too
Faften'd with all her Anchors, this Inchantment
Would force him, in Defpite of all Refiftance,
To leap into the Sea and follow her;
Altho' Deftruction with outftretched Arms,
Stood ready to receive him.

　Don. Gentle Sir;
Tho' you deny to hear me, yet vouchfafe
To look upon me. Tho' I ufe no language,
The Grief for this unkind Repulfe, will print
Such a dumb Eloquence upon my Face,
As will not only plead but prevail for me.

　Vitel. I am a Coward: I will fee and hear you;
The Trial, elfe, is nothing, nor the Conqueft,
My Temperance fhall crown me with hereafter,
Worthy to be remember'd. Up, my Virtue!
And holy Thoughts and Refolutions arm me
Against this fierce Temptation! give me Voice
Tun'd to a zealous Anger, to exprefs
At what an Over-value I have purchas'd
The wanton Treafure of your Virgin Bounties,
That in their falfe Fruition heap upon me
Defpair and Horror—That I could with that Eafe
Redeem my forfeit Innocence, or caft up
The Poifon I receiv'd into my Entrails,
From the alluring Cup of your Enticements,
As now I do deliver back the Price　*[Returns the Cafket.*

And Salary of your Luſt ! or thus unclothe me
Of Sin's gay Trappings, (the proud Livery
                              [*Throws off his Cloak and Doublet.*
Of wicked Pleaſure) which but worn and heated
With the Fire of Entertainment and Conſent,
Like to *Alcides'* fatal Shirt, tears off
Our Fleſh and Reputation both together,
Leaving our ulcerous Follies bare and open
To all malicious Cenſure.

   Don. You muſt grant,
If you hold that a Loſs to you, mine equals,
If not tranſcends it. If you then firſt taſted
That Poiſon, as you call it, I brought with me
A Palate unacquainted with the Reliſh
Of thoſe Delights, which moſt (as I have heard)
Greedily ſwallow; and then the Offence
(If my Opinion may be believ'd)
Is not ſo great; howe'er, the Wrong no more
Than if *Hippolitus* and the Virgin Huntreſs,
Should meet and kiſs together.

   Vitel. What Defences
Can Luſt raiſe to maintain a Precipice
                              [*Aſambeg and* Muſtapha *above.*
To the Abyſs of Looſeneſs ? But affords not
The leaſt Stair, or the faſt'ning of one Foot,
To re-aſcend that glorious Height we fell from.

   Muſta. By *Mahomet* ſhe courts him !

   Aſam. Nay, kneels to him :
Obſerve the ſcornful Villain turns away too,
As glorying in his Conqueſt.

   Don. Are you Marble ?   [*Kneels.*
If Chriſtians have Mothers, ſure they ſhare in
The Tygreſs Fierceneſs ; for, if you were Owner
Of human Pity, you could not endure
A Princeſs to kneel to you, or look on
Theſe falling Tears which hardeſt Rocks would ſoften,
And yet remain unmov'd. Did you but give me
A Taſte of Happineſs in your Embraces,
That the Remembrance of the Sweetneſs of it

Might leave perpetual Bitterneſs behind it?
Or ſhew'd me what it was to be a Wife,
To live a Widow ever?

Enter Capiaga *and* Aga *with others.*

Aſam. She has confeſt it;——
Seize on him, Villains! O the Furies!
　Don. How?—　　[Aſambeg *and* Muſtapha *deſcend.*
Are we betray'd?
　Vitel. The better; I expected
A *Turkiſh* Faith.
　Don. Who am I, that you dare this?
'Tis I that do command you to forbear
A Touch of Violence.
　Aga. We already, Madam,
Have ſatisfied your Pleaſure further than
We know to anſwer it.
　Cap. Would we were well off;
We ſtand too far engag'd I fear.
　Don. For us?
We'll bring you ſafe off. Who dares contradict
What is our Pleaſure?

Enter Aſambeg *and* Muſtapha.

Aſam. Spurn the Dog to Priſon!
I'll anſwer you anon.
　Vitel. What Puniſhment
So e'er I undergo, I'm ſtill a Chriſtian
　　　　　　　　　　[*Exit* Vitelli *guarded.*
　Don. What bold Preſumption's this? Under what
　　　Law
Am I to fall, that ſet my Foot upon
Your Statutes and Decrees?
　Muſta. The Crime committed
Our *Alcoran* calls Death.
　Don. Tuſh! who is here,'
That is not *Amurath*'s Slave, and ſo unfit
To ſit a Judge upon his Blood?

Afam. You've loft
And fham'd the Privilege of it; robb'd me too
Of my Soul, my Underftanding, to behold
Your bafe, unworthy Fall from your high Virtue.

   Don. I do appeal to *Amurath.*

   Afam. We'll offer
No Violence to your Perfon, till we know
His facred Pleafure; till when, under Guard
You fhall continue here.

   Don. Shall?

   Afam. I have faid it.

   Don. We fhall remember this.

   Afam. It ill becomes
Such, as are guilty, to deliver Threats
Againft the Innocent.   [*The Guard leads off* Donufa.
I could tear this Flefh now,
But 'tis in vain; nor muft I talk, but do:
Provide a well-mann'd Galley for *Conftantinople:*
Such fad News never came to our great Mafter.
As he directs, we muft proceed, and know
No Will but his, to whom what's ours we owe.
                             [*Exeunt.*

End of the Third Act.

ACT IV.   SCENE I.

Enter Mafter and Boatfwain.

Mafter.

H E does begin to eat?
   Boatf. A little, Mafter:
But our beft Hope for his Recovery is, that
His Raving leaves him; and thofe dreadful Words,

Damnation and Defpair, with which he ever
Ended all his Difcourfes, are forgotten.

Mafter. This Stranger is a moft religious Man fure,
And I am doubtful, whether his Charity
In the relieving of our Wants, or Care
To cure the wounded Confcience of *Grimaldi*,
Deferves more Admiration.

Boatf. Can you guefs
What the Reafon fhould be, that we never mention
The Church, or the high Altar, but his Melancholy
Grows, and increafes on him?

Mafter. I have heard him
(When he gloried to profefs himfelf an Atheift)
Talk often, and with much Delight and Boafting,
Of a rude Prank he did ere he turn'd Pirate,
The Memory of which, as it appears,
Lies heavy on him.

Boatf. 'Pray you, let me underftand it.

Mafter. Upon a folemn Day, when the whole City
Join'd in Devotion, and with barefoot Steps
Pafs'd to S. *Mark*'s, the Duke and the whole Signiory,
Helping to perfect the religious Pomp
With which they were received; when all Men elfe
Were full of Tears, and groan'd beneath the Weight
Of paft Offences (of whofe heavy Burden
They came to be abfolv'd and freed,) our Captain,
Whether in Scorn of thofe fo pious Rites
He had no Feeling of, or elfe drawn to it
Out of a wanton, irreligious Madnefs,
(I know not which) ran to the holy Man,
As he was doing of the Work of Grace,
And, fnatching from his Hands the fanctify'd Means,
Dafh'd it upon the Pavement.

Boatf. How efcap'd he?
It being a Deed deferving Death with Torture.

Mafter. The general Amazement of the People
Gave him Leave to quit the Temple, and a Gondola,
(Prepar'd, it feems, before) brought him aboard,
Since which he ne'er faw *Venice.* the Remembrance
Of this, it feems, torments him; aggravated

With a ftrong Belief he cannot receive Pardon
For this foul Fact, but from his Hands, 'gainft whom
It was committed.

Boatf. And what Courfe intends
His heavenly Phyfician, reverend *Francifco*,
To beat down this Opinion?

Mafter. He promis'd
To ufe fome holy and religious Fineffe,
To this good End; and, in the mean Time, charg'd me
To keep him dark, and to admit no Vifitants;
But on no Terms to crofs him.—Here he comes.

Enter Grimaldi, *with a Book.*

Grim. For Theft, he that reftores treble the Value, [16]
Makes Satisfaction; and, for want of Means,
To do fo, as a Slave, muft ferve it out
Till he hath made full Payment.—There's Hope left
 here;
Oh! with what Willingnefs would I give up
My Liberty to thofe that I have pillag'd;
And wifh the Numbers of my Years, tho' wafted
In the moft fordid Slavery, might equal
The Rapines I have made; till with one Voice,
My patient Sufferings might exact from my
Moft cruel Creditors, a full Remiffion,
An Eye's Lofs with an Eye, Limb's with a Limb; [17]
A fad Account!—yet, to find Peace within here,
Tho' all fuch as I have maim'd and difmember'd

16 *For Theft, he that reftores treble the Value, makes Satisfaction,* &c.

This, and the following Part of this Speech alludes to the Law of *Mofes:* As in *Exodus* we read, "If a Man fhall fteal an Ox or a "Sheep, and kill it, or fell it, he fhall reftore five Oxen for an "Ox; and four Sheep for a Sheep.—If he have nothing, then he "fhall be fold for his Theft." Chap. 22. Ver. 1, 3.

17 *An Eye's Lofs with an Eye, Limb's with a Limb.*

Thefe are common Expreffions both in the Old and in the New Teftament.

In drunken Quarrels, or o'ercome with Rage,
When they were giv'n up to my Power, ſtood here now,
And cry'd for Reſtitution to appeaſe 'em,
I'd do a bloody Juſtice on myſelf;
Pull out theſe Eyes, that guided me to raviſh
Their Sight from others; lop theſe Legs, that bore me
To barbarous Violence;. with this Hand cut off
This Inſtrument of wrong, till nought were left me
But this poor bleeding limbleſs Trunk, which gladly
I would divide among them.——Ha! what think I

Enter Franciſco *in a Cope like a Biſhop.*

Of petty Forfeitures! in this reverend Habit,
(All that I am turn'd into Eyes) I look on
A Deed of mine ſo fiend-like, that Repentance,
Tho' with my Tears I taught the Sea new Tides,
Can never waſh off: All my Thefts, my Rapes
Are venial Treſpaſſes, compar'd to what
I offer'd to that Shape; and in a Place too,
Where I ſtood bound to kneel to't.   [*Kneels.*
    Fran. 'Tis forgiven;
I with his Tongue (whom in theſe ſacred Veſtments
With impure Hands thou didſt offend) pronounce it;
I bring Peace to thee; ſee that thou deſerve it
In thy fair Life hereafter.
    Grim. Can it be?
Dare I believe this Viſion? Or hope
A Pardon e'er may find me?
    Fran. Purchaſe it
By zealous Undertakings, and no more
'Twill be remembered.
    Grim. What celeſtial Balm
I feel now pour'd into my wounded Conſcience!
What Penance is there I'll not undergo;
Tho' ne'er ſo ſharp and rugged, with more Pleaſure
Than Fleſh and Blood e'er taſted! ſhew me true Sorrow,
Arm'd with an Iron Whip, and I will meet
The Stripes ſhe brings along with her, as if
They were the gentle Touches of a Hand

That comes to cure me. Can good Deeds redeem me?
I will rife up a Wonder to the World,
When I have giv'n ftrong Proofs how I am alter'd,
i that have fold fuch as profefs'd the Faith
That I was born in to Captivity,
Will make their Number equal, that I fhall
Deliver from the Oar ; and win as many
By the Clearnefs of my Actions, to look on
Their Mifbelief, and loath it. I will be
A Convoy for all Merchants ; and thought worthy
To be reported to the World hereafter
The Child of your Devotion, nurs'd up,
And made ftrong by your Charity, to break thro'
All Dangers Hell can bring forth to oppofe me :
Nor am I, tho' my Fortunes were thought defperate,
Now you have reconcil'd me to myfelf,
So void of worldly Means, but, in Defpight
Of the proud Viceroy's Wrongs, I can do fomething
To prove that I have Power when you pleafe try me,
And I will perfect what you fhall injoin me
Or fall a joyful Martyr.

   Fran. You will reap
The Comfort of it ; live yet undifcover'd,
And with your holy Meditations ftrengthen
Your Chriftian Refolution ; ere long,
You fhall hear further from me.

                     [*Exit* Francifco.

   Grim. I'll attend
All your Commands with Patience ;—come, my Mates!
I hitherto have liv'd an ill Example ;
And as your Captain led you on to Mifchief ;
But now will truly labour, that good Men
May fay hereafter of me, to my Glory,
Let but my Power and Means hand with my Will,
" His good Endeavours did weigh down his Ill."

          [*Exeunt* Grimaldi, *Mafter and Boatfwain.*

Enter Francifco.

Fran. This Penitence is not counterfeit; howfoever
Good Actions are in themfelves rewarded;
My Travail's to meet with a double Crown;
If that *Vitelli* come off fafe, and prove
Himfelf the Mafter of his wild Affections.——

Enter Gazet.

Oh! I fhall have Intelligence; how now, *Gazet!*
Why thefe fad Looks and Tears?
   Gaz. Tears, Sir? I have loft
My worthy Mafter.   Your rich Heir feems to mourn
         for
A miferable Father, your young Widow
Following a Bed-rid Hufband to his Grave,
Would have her Neighbours think fhe cries and roars,
That fhe muft part with fuch a Goodman Do-nothing;
When 'tis, becaufe he ftays fo long above Ground
And hinders a rich Suitor:—All's come out, Sir!
We are fmok'd for being Cunny-catchers; My Mafter
Is put in Prifon; his She-cuftomer
Is under Guard too.—Thefe are Things to weep for;
But mine own Lofs confider'd, and what a Fortune
I have had, as they fay, fnatch'd out of my Chops,
Would make a Man run mad.
   Fran. I fcarce have Leifure,
I am fo wholly taken up with Sorrow
For my lov'd Pupil, to enquire thy Fate;
Yet I will hear it.
   Gaz. Why, Sir! I had bought a Place,
A Place of Credit too, and I had gone thro' with it;
I fhould have been made an Eunuch.—There was Ho-
         nour
For a late poor 'Prentice! when upon the fudden
There was fuch a Hurly-burly in the Court,
That I was glad to run away, and carry
The Price of my Office with me.

Fran. Is that all?
You've made a faving Voyage.   We muft think now,
Tho' not to free, to comfort fad *Vitelli* ;
My griev'd Soul fuffers for him.

Gaz. I am fad too ;
But, had I been an Eunuch——

Fran. Think not on it.   [*Exeunt.*

SCENE II.

Enter Afambeg, *unlocks the Door, and leads forth* Paulina.

Afam. Be your own Guard : Obfequioufnefs and Service
Shall win you to be mine.   Of all Reftraint
For ever take your Leave : No Threats fhall awe you ;
No jealous Doubts of mine Difturb your Freedom :
No fee'd Spies wait upon your Steps.   Your Virtue
And due Confideration in yourfelf,
Of what is noble, are the faithful Helps
I leave you as Supporters to defend you
From falling bafely.

Paul. This is wondrous ftrange !
Whence flows this Alteration ?

Afam. From true Judgment,
And ftrong Affurance : Neither Grates of Iron,
Hemm'd in with Walls of Brafs, ftrict Guards, high
          Birth,
The Forfeiture of Honour, nor the Fear
Of Infamy or Punifhment, can ftay
A Woman flav'd to Appetite from being
Falfe and unworthy.

Paul. You are grown fatirical
Againft our Sex.   Why, Sir, I durft produce
Myfelf in our Defence, and from you challenge
A Teftimony that's not to be denied ;
All fall not under this unequal Cenfure.
I, that have ftood your Flatteries, your Threats,

Borne up againſt your fierce Temptations; ſcorn'd
The cruel Means you practis'd to ſupplant me,
Having no Arms to help me to hold out,
But Love of Piety and conſtant Goodneſs;
If you are unconfirm'd, dare again boldly
Enter into the Liſts and combat with
All Oppoſites Man's Malice can bring forth
To ſhake me in my Chaſtity, built upon
The Rock of my Religion.

   Aſam. I do wiſh
I could believe you; but, when I ſhall ſhew you
A moſt incredible Example of
Your Frailty in a Princeſs, ſu'd and ſought to
By Men of Worth, of Rank, of Eminence; courted
By Happineſs itſelf, and her cold Temper
Approv'd by many Years; yet ſhe to fall,
Fall from herſelf, her Glories, nay her Safety,
Into a Gulf of Shame and black Deſpair;
I think you'll doubt yourſelf, or, in beholding
Her Puniſhment, for ever be deterr'd
From yielding baſely.

   Paul. I would ſee this Wonder;
'Tis Sir, my firſt Petition.

   Aſam. And thus granted;——
Above, you ſhall obſerve all.   [*Paulina ſteps aſide.*

Enter Muſtapha.

   Muſta. Sir, I ſought you,
And muſt relate a Wonder.   Since I ſtudied
And knew what Man was, I was never Witneſs
Of ſuch invincible Fortitude as this Chriſtian
Shews in his Sufferings: All the Torments that
We could preſent him with, to fright his Conſtancy,
Confirm'd, not ſhook it; and thoſe heavy Chains
That eat into his Fleſh, appear'd to him
Like Bracelets made of ſome lov'd Miſtreſs' Hairs,
We kiſs in the Remembrance of her Favours.
I'm ſtrangely taken with it, and have loſt
Much of my Fury.

Asam. Had he suffer'd poorly,
It had call'd on my Contempt; but manly Patience,
And all-commanding Virtue, wins upon
An Enemy. I shall think upon him. Ha!

Enter Aga, *with a Black Box.*

So soon return'd? This Speed pleads in Excuse
Of your late Fault, which I no more remember.
What's the Grand Signior's Pleasure?
  Aga. 'Tis inclos'd here.
The Box too that contains it may inform you
How he stands affected: I am trusted with
Nothing but this.—On Forfeit of your Head,
She must have a speedy Trial.
  Asam. Bring her in
In Black, as to her Funeral: 'Tis the Colour
Her Fault wills her to wear; and which, in Justice,
I dare not pity. Sit, and take your Place:
However in her Life she has degenerated,
May she die nobly and in that confirm
Her Greatness and high Blood.

Solemn Musick. A Guard. The Aga and Capiaga, leading
in Donusa *in Black; her Train borne up by* Carazie *and*
Manto.

  Musta. I now could melt;——
But soft Compassion leave me.
  Manto. I am affrighted
With this dismal Preparation. Should the enjoying
Of loose Desires find ever such Conclusions
All Women would be Vestals.   [*Aside.*
  Don. That you clothe me
In this sad Livery of Death, assures me
Your Sentence is gone out before, and I
Too late am call'd for, in my guilty Cause
To use Qualification or Excuse——
Yet must I not part so with mine own Strength,
But borrow from my Modesty Boldness, to enquire

By whofe Authority you fit
My Judges, and whofe Warrant digs my Grave
In the Frowns you dart againft my Life?

Afam. See here!
This fatal Sign and Warrant! This, brought to
A General fighting at the Head of his
Victorious Troops, ravifhes from his Hand
His e'en then conqu'ring Sword: This fhewn unto
The Sultan's Brothers, or his Sons, delivers
His deadly Anger; and, all Hopes laid by,
Commands them to prepare themfelves for Heaven;
Which would ftand with the Quiet of your Soul,
To think upon and imitate.

Don. Give me Leave
A little to complain: Firft, of the hard
Condition of my Fortune, which may move you,
Tho' not to rife up Interceffors for me,
Yet, in Remembrance of my former Life,
(This being the firft Spot tainting mine Honour)
To be the Means to bring me to his Prefence;
And then I doubt not, but I could alledge
Such Reafons in mine own Defence, or plead
So humbly (my Tears helping) that it fhould
Awake his fleeping Pity.

Afam. 'Tis in vain!
If you have aught to fay, you fhall have Hearing,
And in me think him prefent.

Don. I would thus then
Firft kneel, and kifs his Feet; and after, tell him
How long I'd been his Darling; what Delight
My infant Years afforded him; how dear
He priz'd his Sifter in both Bloods, my Mother;
That fhe, like him, had Frailty, that to me
Defcends as an Inheritance; then conjure him
By her bleft Afhes, and his Father's Soul;
The Sword that rides upon his Thigh; his right Hand
Holding the Scepter and the *Ottoman* Fortune;
To have Compaffion on me.

Afam. But fuppofe

(As I am fure) he would be deaf, what then
Could you infer?

Don. I, then, would thus rife up;
And to his Teeth tell him he was a Tyrant,
A moft voluptuous and infatiable Epicure
In his own Pleafures; which he hugs fo dearly,
As proper and peculiar to himfelf,
That he denies a moderate lawful Ufe
Of all Delight to others. And to thee,
Unequal Judge, I fpeak as much, and charge thee
But with impartial Eyes to look into
Thyfelf, and then confider with what Juftice
Thou canft pronounce my Sentence. Unkind Nature!
To make weak Women Servants; proud Men, Mafters.
Indulgent *Mahomet!* Do thy bloody Laws
Call my Embraces with a Chriftian, Death?
Having my Heat and *May* of Youth, to plead
In my Excufe? and yet want Power to punifh
Thefe that with Scorn break thro' thy Cobweb-edicts,
And laugh at thy Decrees? To tame their Lufts
There's no religious Bit. [13] Let her be fair,
And pleafing to the Eye, tho' *Perfian, Moor,*
Idolatrefs, *Turk* or *Chriftian,* you are privileg'd,
And freely may enjoy her. At this Inftant,
I know, unjuft Man! thou haft in thy Power
A lovely Chriftian Virgin; thy Offence
Equal, if not tranfcending mine: Why, then,
We being both guilty, doft thou not defcend
From that ufurp'd Tribunal, and with me
Walk Hand in Hand to Death?

Afam. She raves! and we
Lofe Time to hear her:—Read the Law.

Don. Do! do!——
I ftand refolv'd to fuffer.

[13] I read in this Line *Bar,* inftead of *Bit,* as the latter is not
Senfe. *M. M.*

Bit or *Curb,* by which Horfes are tamed, is the Author's Allufion,
and certainly very good Senfe. *D.*

Aga. If any Virgin, of what Degree or Quality foever, born a natural *Turk*, ſhall be convicted of corporal Looſeneſs, and Incontinence with any Chriſtian, ſhe is, by the Decree of our great Prophet *Mahomet*, to loſe her Head.

Aſam. Mark that! then tax our Juſtice.

Aga. Ever provided, That if ſhe, the ſaid Offender, by any Reaſons, Arguments, or Perſuaſion, can win and prevail with the ſaid Chriſtian, offending with her, to alter his Religion and marry her, that then the Winning of a Soul to the *Mahometan* Sect ſhall acquit her from all Shame Diſgrace and Puniſhment whatſoever.

Don. I lay hold on that Clauſe, and challenge fromyou
The Privilege of the Law.

Muſta. What will you do?

Don. Grant me Acceſs and Means, I'll undertake
To turn this *Chriſtian Turk*, and marry him:
This Trial you cannot deny.

Muſta. O baſe!
Can Fear to die make you deſcend ſo low
From your high Birth, and brand the *Ottoman* Line
With ſuch a Mark of Infamy?

Aſam. This is worſe
Than the parting with your Honour.—Better ſuffer
Ten thouſand Deaths, and without Hope to have
A Place in our great Prophet's Paradiſe,
Than have an Act to After-times remember'd
So foul as this is.

Muſta. Chear your Spirits, Madam!
To die is nothing; 'tis but parting with
A Mountain of Vexations.

Aſam. Think of your Honour:
In dying nobly, you make Satisfaction
For your Offence; and you ſhall live a Story
Of bold heroick Courage.

Don. You ſhall not fool me
Out of my Life: I claim the Law, and ſue for
A ſpeedy Trial; if I fail, you may
Determine of me as you pleaſe.

Afam. Bafe Woman!

—But ufe thy Ways, and fee thou profper in 'em :
For, if thou fall again into my Power,
Thou fhalt in vain, after a thoufand Tortures,
Cry out for Death, that Death which now thou fly'ft
    from.
Unloofe the Prifoner's Chains.—Go! lead her on
To try the Magick of her Tongue——I follow :—
I'm on the Rack.——Defcend, my beft *Paulina.*
                       [*Exeunt.*

SCENE III.

Enter Francifco *and Jailor.*

Fran. I come not empty-handed ;—I will purchafe
Your Favour at what Rate you pleafe.—There's Gold.

Jailor. 'Tis the beft Oratory. I will hazard
A Check for your Content.—Below there !

Vitel. Welcome !——   [Vitelli *under the Stage.*
Art thou the happy Meffenger that brings me
News of my Death ?

    Jailor. Your Hand !   [Vitelli *pluck'd up.*
    Fran. Now, if you pleafe,
A little Privacy.

    Jailor. You have bought it, Sir ;
Enjoy it freely.   [*Exit Jailor.*
    Fran. O, my deareft Pupil !
Witnefs thefe Tears of Joy : I never faw you,
'Till now, look lovely ; nor durft I ever glory
In the Mind of any Man I had built up
With the Hands of virtuous and religious Precepts,
'Till this glad Minute. Now you have made good
My Expectation of you. By my Order !
All *Roman Cæfars*, that led Kings in Chains,
Faft bound to their triumphant Chariots, if
Compar'd with that true Glory and full Luftre
You now appear in ; all their boafted Honours,

Purchas'd with Blood and Wrong, would lose their
      Names
And be no more remember'd.

   Vitel. This Applause,
Confirm'd in your Allowance, joys me more
Than if a thousand full-cramm'd Theatres
Should clap their eager Hands, to witness that
The Scene I act did please, and they admire it.
But these are, Father, but Beginnings, not
The Ends of my high Aims.   I grant t' have master'd
The rebel Appetite of Flesh and Blood
Was far above my Strength; and still owe for it
To that great Power that lent it.   But, when I
Shall make't apparent the grim Looks of Death
Affright me not; and that I can put off
The fond Desire of Life (that, like a Garment,
Covers and cloathes our Frailty) hast'ning to
My Martyrdom, as to a heavenly Banquet,
To which I was a choice invited Guest.
Then you may boldly say you did not plough,
Or trust the barren and ungrateful Sands
With the fruitful Grain of your religious Counsels.

   Fran. You do instruct your Teacher.   Let the Sun
Of your clear Life (that lends to good Men Light)
But set as gloriously as it did rise,
Tho' sometimes clouded, you may write *nil ultra*
To human Wishes.

   Vitel. I have almost gain'd
The End o' th' Race, and will not faint or tire now.

Enter Aga and Jailor.

   Aga. Sir, by your Leave (nay stare not) I bring
     Comfort;
The Viceroy, taken with the constant Bearing
Of your Afflictions; and presuming too
You will not change your Temper, does command
Your Irons should be ta'en off.   Now arm yourself

With your old Refolution : Suddenly

                           [The Chains taken off.

You fhall be vifited.   You muft leave the Room too ;
And do it without Reply.

    Fran. There's no contending :
Be ftill thyfelf, my Son ;   *[Exit* Francifco.
    Vitel. 'Tis not in Man

    Enter Donufa, Afambeg, Muftapha *and* Paulina.

To change or alter me.

    Paul. Whom do I look on ?——
My Brother ?—'Tis he !—But no more my Tongue !
Thou wilt betray all.   *[Afide.*

    Afam. Let us hear this Temptrefs :
The Fellow looks as he would ftop his Ears
Againft her powerful Spells.

    Paul. He is undone elfe.
    Vitel. I'll ftand th' Encounter—Charge me home.
    Don. I come, Sir !   *[Bows herfelf.*

A Beggar to you, and doubt not to find
A good Man's Charity, which if you deny,
You're cruel to yourfelf; a Crime a wife Man
(And fuch I hold you) would not willingly
Be guilty of ; nor let it find lefs Welcome,
Tho' I (a Creature you contemn) now fhew you
The Way to certain Happinefs; nor think it
Imaginary or fantaftical,
And fo not worth th' acquiring, in refpect
The Paffage to it is not rough nor thorny !
No fteep Hills in the Way which you muft climb up ;
No Monfters to be conquer'd ; no Inchantments
To be diffolv'd by Counter-charms, before
You take Poffeffion of it.

    Vitel. What ftrong Poifon
Is wrapp'd up in thefe fugar'd Pills ?

    Don. My Suit is,
That you would quit your Shoulders of a Burthen,
Under whofe ponderous Weight you wilfully

Have too long groan'd, to caft thofe Fetters off,
With which, with your own Hands, you chain your
        Freedom :
Forfake a fevere, nay, imperious Miftrefs,
Whofe Service does exact perpetual Cares,
Watchings and Troubles ; and give Entertainment
To one that courts you, whofe leaft Favours are
Variety, and Choice of all Delights
Mankind is capable of.

   Vitel. You fpeak in Riddles.
What Burthen, or what Miftrefs ? or what Fetters
Are thofe you point at ?

   Don. Thofe which your Religion,
The Miftrefs you too long have ferv'd, compels
To bear with Slave-like Patience.

   Vitel. Ha !

   Paul. How bravely
The virtuous Anger fhows !   [*Afide.*

   Don. Be wife, and weigh
The profperous Succefs of Things ; if Bleffings
Are Donatives from Heaven (which, you muft grant,
Were Blafphemy to queftion) and that
They are call'd down and pour'd on fuch as are
Moft gracious with the great Difpofer of 'em,
Look on our flourifhing Empire, if the Splendor,
The Majefty, the Glory of it dim not
Your feeble Sight, and then turn back, and fee
The narrow Bounds of yours ; yet that poor Remnant
Rent in as many Factions and Opinions
As you have petty Kingdoms ; and then, if
You are not obftinate againft Truth and Reafon,
You muft confefs the Deity you worfhip
Wants Care or Power to help you.

   Paul. Hold out now,
And then thou art victorious.

   Afam. How he eyes her !

   Mufta. As if he would look thro' her.

   Afam. His Eyes flame too,
As threat'ning Violence.

Vitel. But that I know
The Devil, thy Tutor, fills each Part about thee,
And that I cannot play the Exorcift
To difpoffefs thee, unlefs I fhould tear
Thy Body Limb by Limb, and throw it to
The Furies that expect it, I would now
Pluck out that wicked Tongue, that hath blafphem'd
The great Omnipotency, at whofe Nod
The Fabrick of the World fhakes. Dare you bring
Your juggling Prophet in Comparifon with
That moft infcrutable and infinite Effence
That made this All, and comprehends his Work?
The Place is too prophane to mention him
Whofe only Name is facred. O *Donufa!*
How much in my Compaffion I fuffer,
That thou, on whom this moft excelling Form,
And Faculties of Difcourfe, beyond a Woman,
Were by his liberal Gift conferr'd, fhouldft ftill
Remain in Ignorance of him that gave it!
I will not foul my Mouth to fpeak the Sorceries
Of your Seducer, his bafe Birth, his Whoredoms,
His ftrange Impoftures; nor deliver how
He taught a Pigeon to feed in his Ear;
Then made his credulous Followers believe
It was an Angel that inftructed him
In the framing of his *Alcoran.* Pray you, mark me.——
  Afam. Thefe Words are Death, were he in nought
     elfe guilty.
  Vitel. Your Intent to win me
To be of your Belief, proceeded from
Your Fear to die. Can there be Strength in that
Religion, that fuffers us to tremble
At that which every Day, nay Hour, we hafte to?
  Don. This is unanfwerable, and there's fomething
     tells me
I err in my Opinion.
  Vitel. Cherifh it!
It is a heavenly Prompter; entertain
This holy Motion, and wear on your Forehead

E 4

The facred Badge he arms his Servants with,
You fhall, like me, with Scorn look down upon
All Engines Tyranny can advance to batter
Your conftant Refolution : Then you fhall
Look truly fair, when your Mind's Purenefs anfwers
Your outward Beauties.

Don. I came here to take you,
But I perceive a yielding in myfelf
To be your Prifoner.

Vitel. 'Tis an Overthrow,
That will outfhine all Victories· O *Donufa !*
Die in my Faith like me; and 'tis a Marriage
At which celeftial Angels fhall be Waiters,
And fuch as have been fainted welcome us.
—Are you confirm'd ?

Don. I would be ; but the Means
That may affure me ?

Vitel. Heaven is merciful,
And will not fuffer you to want a Man.
To do that facred Office, build upon it.

Don. Then thus I fpit at *Mahomet.*

Afam. Stop her Mouth :
In Death to turn Apoftate ! I'll not hear
One Syllable from any ;—wretched Creature :
With the next rifing Sun prepare to die.
Yet Chriftian, in Reward of thy brave Courage,
Be thy Faith right or wrong, receive this Favour.
In Perfon I'll attend thee to thy Death ;
And boldly challenge all that I can give,
But what's not in my Grant, which is to live. [*Exeunt.*

End of the Fourth Act.

ACT V. SCENE I.

Enter Vitelli *and* Francisco.

Francisco.

YOU'RE wond'rous brave and jocund.
  Vitel. Welcome, Father!
Should I spare Cost, or not wear cheerful Looks
Upon my Wedding Day, it were ominous,
And shew'd I did repent; which I dare not,
It being a Marriage, howsoever sad
In the first Ceremonies that confirm it,
That will for ever arm me against Fears,
Repentance, Doubts, or Jealousies, and bring
Perpetual Comforts, Peace of Mind, and Quiet
To the glad Couple.
  Fran. I well understand you;
And my full Joy to see you so resolv'd
Weak Words cannot express. What is the Hour
Design'd for this Solemnity?
  Vitel. The sixth;
Something before the setting of the Sun,
We take our last Leave of his fading Light,
And with our Soul's Eyes seek for Beams eternal.
Yet there's one Scruple with which I am much
Perplex'd and troubl'd, which I know you can.
Resolve me of.
  Fran. What is't?
  Vitel. This, Sir; my Bride,
Whom I first courted, and then won (not with
Loose Lays, poor Flatteries, apish Compliments,
But sacred and religious Zeal) yet wants
The holy Badge that should proclaim her fit
For these celestial Nuptials: Willing she is,
I know, to wear it as the choicest Jewel.

On her fair Forehead ; but to you, that well
Could do that Work of Grace, I know the Viceroy
Will never grant Accefs. Now, in a Cafe -
Of this Neceffity, I would gladly learn,
Whether in me a Layman, without Orders,
It may not be religious and lawful,
As we go to our Deaths to do that Office ?

    Fran. A Queftion in itfelf with much Eafe anfwer'd ;
Midwives upon Neceffity perform it ;
And Knights that in the holy Land fought for
The Freedom of *Jerufalem,* when full·
Of Sweat and Enemy's Blood, have made their Helmets
The Fount, out of which with their holy Hands
They drew that heavenly Liquor : 'Twas approved then
By the holy Church, nor muft I think it now
In you a Work lefs pious.

    Vitel. You confirm me ;
I will find a Way to do it. In the mean Time
Your holy Vows affift me.

    Fran. They fhall ever
Be prefent with you.

    Vitel. You fhall fee me act
This laft Scene to the Life.

    Fran. And tho' now fall,
Rife a blefs'd Martyr.

    Vitel. That's my End, my All.   [*Exeunt.*

S C E N E II.

Enter Grimaldi, *Mafter, Boatfwain and Sailors.*

    Boatf. Sir, if you flip this Opportunity,
Never expect the like.

    Mafter. With as much Eafe now
We may fteal the Ship out of the Harbour, Captain,
As ever Gallants in a wanton Bravery
Have fet upon a drunken Conftable,
And bore him from a fleepy rug-gown'd Watch :
Be therefore wife.

Grim. I muſt be honeſt too,
And you ſhall wear that Shape : You ſhall obſerve me,
If that you purpoſe to continue mine.
Think you Ingratitude can be the Parent
To our unfeign'd Repentance ? Do I owe
A Peace within here, Kingdoms could not purchaſe,
To my religious Creditor, to leave him
Open to Danger, the great Benefit
Never rememb'red ? No ; tho' in her Bottom
We could ſtow up the Tribute of the *Turk ;*
Nay, grant the Paſſage ſafe too ; I will never
Conſent to weigh an Anchor up, till he,
That only muſt, commands it.
    Boatſ. This Religion
Will keep us Slaves and Beggars.
    Maſter. The Fiend prompts me
To change my Copy : Plague on't, we are Seamen :
What have we to do with't, but for a Snatch or ſo,
At the End of a long Lent ?

Enter Franciſco.

    Boatſ. Mum, See, who is here !
    Grim. My Father !
    Fran. My good Convert ! I am full
Of ſerious Buſineſs which denies me Leave
To hold long Conference with you : Only thus much
Briefly receive ;—a Day or two at the moſt,
Shall make me fit to take my Leave of *Tunis,*
Or give me loſt for ever.
    Grim. Days nor Years,
Provided that my Stay may do you Service,
But to me ſhall be Minutes.
    Fran. I much thank you :
In this ſmall Scroll you may in private read
What my Intents are ; and as they grow ripe
I will inſtruct you further : In the mean Time
Borrow your late diſtracted Looks and Geſture ;

The more dejected you appear the lefs
The Viceroy muft fufpect you.

 Grim. I am nothing,
But what you pleafe to have me be.

 Fran. Farewell, Sir!——
Be cheerful, Mafter! fomething we will do
That fhall reward itfelf in the Performance;
And that's true Prize indeed.

 Mafter. I am obedient.

   [*Exeunt* Grimaldi, *Mafter and Boatfwain.*

 Boatf. And I:—There's no contending.
 Fran. Peace to you all.
Profper, thou great Exiftence! my Endeavours,
As they religioufly are undertaken,
And diftant equally from fervile Gain,

   Enter Paulina, Carazie *and* Manto.

Or glorious Oftentation.—I am heard
In this bleft Opportunity, which in vain
I long have waited for.—I muft fhow myfelf!
O, fhe has found me! now if fhe prove right
All Hope will not forfake us.

 Paul. Farther off!
And in that Diftance know your Duties too!
You were beftow'd on me as Slaves to ferve me,
And not as Spies to pry into my Actions;
And after to betray me. You fhall find
If any Look of mine be unobferv'd,
I am not ignorant of a Miftrefs' Power,
And from whom I receive it.

 Car. Note this *Manto,*
The Pride and Scorn with which fhe entertains us!
Now we are made her's by the Viceroy's Gift.
Our fweet condition'd Princefs, fair *Donufa,*
(Reft in her Death wait on her!) never us'd us
With fuch Contempt. I would he had fent me
To the Gallies, or the Gallows, when he gave me
To this proud little Devil.   [*Afide.*

Manto. I expect
All tyrannous Ufage, but I muft be patient;
And, though ten Times a Day, fhe tears thefe Locks,
Or makes this Face her Footftool, 'tis but Juftice.
[*Afide.*

Paul. 'Tis a true Story of my Fortunes, Father!
My Chaftity preferv'd by Miracle,
Or your Devotions for me; and, believe it,
What outward Pride fo e'er I counterfeit,
Or State to thefe appointed to attend me,
I am not in my Difpofition alter'd,
But ftill your humble Daughter, and fhare with you,
In my poor Brother's Sufferings.—All Hell's Tor-
    ments
Revenge it on accurs'd *Grimaldi*'s Soul,
That in his Rape of me, gave a Beginning
To all the Miferies that fince have follow'd.

Fran. Be charitable, and forgive him, gentle Daugh-
    ter!
He's a chang'd Man, and may redeem his Fault
In his fair Life hereafter. You muft bear too
Your forc'd Captivity (for 'tis no better,
Tho' you wear golden Fetters) and of him,
Whom Death affrights not, learn to hold out nobly.

Paul. You are ftill the fame good Counfellor.

Fran. And who knows,
(Since what above is purpos'd, is infcrutable)
But that the Viceroy's extreme Dotage on you
May be the Parent of a happier Birth
Than yet our Hopes dare fafhion. Longer Conference
May prove unfafe for you and me, however,
Perhaps for Trial, he allows you Freedom.
[*Delivers a Paper.*

From this learn therefore what you muft attempt,
Tho' with the Hazard of yourfelf,—Heaven guard
    you,
And give *Vitelli* Patience: then I doubt not

But he will have a glorious Day, since some
Hold truly, such as suffer, overcome. [19]   [*Exeunt.*]

SCENE III.

Enter Asambeg, Mustapha, Aga *and* Capiaga.

Asam. What we commanded, see perform'd; and fail
  not
In all Things to be punctual.

Aga. We shall, Sir!   [*Exeunt* Aga *and* Capiaga.

Musta. 'Tis strange, that you should use such Circumstance
To a Delinquent of so mean Condition!

Asam. Had he appear'd in a more sordid Shape
Than disguis'd Greatness ever deign'd to mask in,
The gallant bearing of his present Fortune
Aloud proclaims him noble.

Musta. If you doubt him
To be a Man built up for great Employments,
And, as a cunning Spy, sent to explore
The Cities Strength, or Weakness, you by Torture
May force him to discover it.

Asam. That were base;
Nor dare I do such Injury to Virtue
And bold assured Courage; neither can I
Be won to think, but if I should attempt it,
I shoot against the Moon. He that hath stood
The roughest Battery, that Captivity
Could ever bring to shake a constant Temper;
Despis'd the Fawnings of a future Greatness,
By Beauty in her full Perfection tender'd;
That hears of Death as of a quiet Slumber,
And, from the Surplusage of his own Firmness,
Can spare enough of Fortitude, to assure
A feeble Woman; will now, *Mustapha*, never
Be alter'd in his Soul for any Torments

---

[19] That is, do overcome.

We can afflict his Body with ?

Mufta, Do your Pleafure !
I only offer'd you a Friend's Advice,
But without Gall or Envy to the Man
That is to fuffer.—But what do you determine
Of poor *Grimaldi ?* The Difgrace call'd on him,
I hear, has run him mad.

Afam. There weigh the Difference
In the true Temper of their Minds. The one,
A Pirate fold to Mifchiefs, Rapes, and all
That make a Slave relentlefs and obdurate ;
Yet, of himfelf wanting the inward Strengths
That fhould defend him, finks beneath Compaffion
Or Pity of a Man; whereas this Merchant,
Acquainted only with a civil Life,
Arm'd in himfelf, intrench'd and fortify'd
With his own Virtue, valuing Life and Death
At the fame Price, poorly does not invite
A Favour, but commands us do him right ;
Which unto him, and her (we both once honour'd)
As a juft Debt I gladly pay 'em—they enter ;
Now fit equal Hearers.   [*A dreadful Mufick at one Door.*

The Aga, *Janizaries,* Vitelli, Francifco, *and* Gazet : *at
the other* Donufa, Paulina, Carazie *and* Manto.

Mufta. I fhall hear
And fee, Sir ! without Paffion ; my Wrongs arm me.
Vitel. A joyful Preparation ! to whofe Bounty
Owe we our Thanks for gracing thus our Hymen ?
The Notes, tho' dreadful to the Ear, found here
As our *Epithalamium* were fung
By a Cœleftial Choir, and a full Chorus
Affur'd us future Happinefs. Thefe that lead me
Gaze not with wanton Eyes upon my Bride,
Nor for their Service are repaid by me
With Jealoufies or Fears; nor do they envy
My Paffage to thofe Pleafures from which Death
Cannot deter me. Great Sir, pardon me !
Imagination of the Joys I haften to

Made me forget my Duty; but the Form
And Ceremony paſt, I will attend you,
And with our conſtant Reſolution feaſt you,
Not with coarſe Cates, forgot as ſoon as taſted,
But ſuch as ſhall, while you have Memory,
Be pleaſing to the Palate.

 Fran. Be not loſt
In what you purpoſe.   [*Exit* Franciſco.

 Gaz. Call you this a Marriage?
It differs little from Hanging; I cry at it.

 Vitel. See, where my Bride appears! in what full
     Luſtre!

As if the Virgins that bear up her Train,
Had long contended to receive an Honour
Above their Births in doing her this Service.
Nor comes ſhe fearful to meet thoſe Delights,
Which, once paſt o'er, immortal Pleaſures follow.
I need not, therefore, comfort or encourage
Her forward Steps; and I ſhould offer Wrong
To her Mind's Fortitude, ſhould I but aſk
How ſhe can brook the rough high-going Sea,
Over whoſe foamy Back, our Ship, well rigg'd
With Hope and ſtrong Aſſurance, muſt tranſport us.
Nor will I tell her, when we reach the Haven
(Which Tempeſts ſhall not hinder) what loud Welcome
Shall entertain us; nor commend the Place,
To tell whoſe leaſt Perfection would ſtrike dumb
The Eloquence of all boaſted in Story,
Tho' join'd together.

 Don. 'Tis enough, my deareſt:
I dare not doubt you; as your humble Shadow,
Lead where you pleaſe, I follow.

 Vitel. One Suit, Sir!
And willingly I ceaſe to be a Beggar;
And that you may with more Security hear it,
Know, 'tis not Life I'll aſk, nor to defer
Our Deaths but a few Minutes.

 Aſam. Speak; 'tis granted.

 Vitel. We being now to take our lateſt Leave,
And grown of one Belief, I do deſire

I may have your Allowance to perform it,
But in the Fashion which we Christians use,
Upon the like Occasions.

Asam. 'Tis allow'd of.

Vitel. My Service: Haste, *Gazet*, to the next Spring,
And bring me of it.

Gazet. Would I could as well
Fetch you a Pardon; I would not run but fly,
And be here in a Moment.

Musta. What's the Mystery of this? Discover it.

Vitel. Great Sir! I'll tell you.
Each Country hath its own peculiar Rites:
Some, when they are to die, drink Store of Wine,
Which pour'd in liberally does oft beget
A bastard Valour, with which arm'd they bear
The not-to-be declined Charge of Death
With less Fear and Astonishment: Others take
Drugs to procure a heavy Sleep, that so
They may insensibly receive the Means
That casts them in an everlasting Slumber;
Others—O welcome!

Enter Gazet *with Water.*

Asam. Now the Use of yours?

Vitel. The Clearness of this is a perfect Sign
Of Innocence; and as this washes off
Stains and Pollutions from the Things we wear,
Thrown thus upon the Forehead, it hath Power
To purge those Spots that cleave unto the Mind,
                                   [*Throws it on her Face.*
If thankfully receiv'd.

Asam. 'Tis a strange custom!

Vitel. How do you entertain it, my *Donusa!*
Feel you no Alteration? No new Motives?
No unexpected Aids that may confirm you
In that to which you were inclin'd before?

Don. I am another Woman,—till this Minute
I never liv'd, nor durst think how to die.

How long have I been blind! yet on the sudden,
By this blest Means I feel the Films of Error
Ta'en from my Soul's Eyes. O divine Physician!
That hast bestow'd a Sight on me, which Death,
Tho' ready to embrace me in his Arms,
Cannot take from me. Let me kiss the Hand
That did this Miracle, and seal my Thanks
Upon those Lips from whence these sweet Words va-
            nish'd,
That freed me from the cruellest of Prisons,
Blind Ignorance and Misbelief: false Prophet!
Impostor *Mahomet!*

   Asam. I'll hear no more;
You do abuse my Favours, sever 'em:
Wretch, if thou hadst another Life to lose,
This Blasphemy deserv'd it,—instantly
Carry them to their Deaths.

   Vitel. We part now, blest one!
To meet hereafter in a Kingdom, where
Hell's Malice shall not reach us.

   Paul. Ha! ha! ha!

   Asam. What means my Mistress?

   Paul. Who can hold her Spleen,
When such ridiculous Follies are presented;
The Scene too made Religion? O, my Lord,
How from one Cause two contrary Effects
Spring up upon the sudden.

   Asam. This is strange!

   Paul. That which hath fool'd her in her Death, wins
      me,
That hitherto have barr'd myself from Pleasure,
To live in all Delight.

   Asam. There's Musick in this.

   Paul. I now will run as fiercely to your Arms
As ever longing Woman did, borne high
On the swift Wings of Appetite.

   Vitel. O Devil!

   Paul. Nay more; for there shall be no odds betwixt
      us,
I will turn *Turk.*

Gazet. Moſt of your Tribe do ſo,
When they begin in Whore.   [*Aſide.*
   Aſam. You are ſerious, Lady?
   Paul. Serious :—But ſatisfy me in a Suit
That to the World may witneſs that I have
Some Power upon you, and to-morrow challenge
Whatever's in my Gift; for I will be
At your Diſpoſal.
   Gazet. That's ever the Subſcription
To a damn'd Whore's falſe Epiſtle.   [*Aſide.*
   Aſam. Aſk this Hand,
Or, if thou wilt, the Heads of theſe.   I am rapt
Beyond myſelf with Joy.—Speak, ſpeak, what is it?
   Paul. But twelve ſhort Hours Reprieve for this baſe
            Couple,
   Aſam. The Reaſon, ſince you hate them?
   Paul. That I may
Have Time to triumph o'er this wretched Woman :
I'll be myſelf her Guardian; I will feaſt,
Adorned in her Choice and richeſt Jewels :
Commit him to what Guards you pleaſe.   Grant this,
I am no more mine own but yours,
   Aſam. Enjoy it.
Repine at it who dares.   Bear him ſafe off
To the Black Tower, but give him all Things uſeful ;
The contrary was not in your Requeſt.
   Paul. I do contemn him.
   Don. Peace in Death deny'd me?
   Paul. Thou ſhalt not go in Liberty to thy Grave,
For one Night a Sultana is my Slave.
   Muſta. A terrible little Tyranneſs.
   Aſam. No more ;
Her Will ſhall be a Law.   'Till now ne'er happy.
                                     [*Exeunt.*

SCENE IV.

Enter Francisco, Grimaldi, *Master,* Boatswain, *and Sailors.*

Grim. Sir ! all Things are in Readiness; the *Turks*
That seiz'd upon my Ship stow'd under Hatches;
My Men resolv'd and cheerful.   Use but Means
To get out of the Ports, we will be ready
To bring you aboard, and then (Heaven be but pleas'd)
This for the Viceroy's Fleet.
 Fran. Discharge your Parts,
In mine I'll not be wanting : Fear not, Master !
Something will come along to fraught your Bark,
That you will have just Cause to say you never
Made such a Voyage.
 Master. We will stand the Hazard.
 Fran. What's the best Hour ?
 Boats. After the second Watch.
 Fran. Enough ;—each t'his Charge.
 Grim. We will be careful.   [*Exeunt.*

SCENE V.

Enter Paulina, Donusa, Carazie, *and* Manto.

Paul. Sit, Madam ! it is fit that I attend you;
And pardon, I beseech you, my rude Language,
To which the sooner you will be invited,
When you shall understand, no Way was left me
To free you from a present Execution,
But by my personating that which never
My Nature was acquainted with.
 Don. I believe you.
 Paul. You will, when you shall understand I may
Receive the Honour to be known unto you
By a nearer Name.—And, not to rack you further,

The Man you pleafe to favour is my Brother;
No Merchant, Madam, but a Gentleman
Of the beft Rank in *Venice*.

Don. I rejoice in't;
But what's this to his Freedom? For myfelf,
Were he well off, I were fecure.

Paul. I have
A prefent Means, not plotted by myfelf,
But a religious Man, my Confeffor,
That may preferve all, if we had a Servant
Whofe Faith we might rely on.

Don. She, that's now
Your Slave, was once mine; had I twenty Lives,
I durft commit them to her Truft.

Manto. Oh! Madam!
I have been falfe,—forgive me.—I'll redeem it
By any Thing, however defperate,
You pleafe t'impofe upon me.

Paul. 'Troth thefe Tears—
I think, cannot be counterfeit,—I believe her,
And if you pleafe will try her.

Don. At your Peril;
There is no further Danger can look towards me.

Paul. This only then—canft thou ufe Means to carry
This bak'd Meat to *Vitelli*?

Manto. With much Eafe;
I am familiar with the Guard; befide,
It being known 'twas I that did betray him,
My Entrance hardly will of them be queftion'd.

Paul. About it then.—Say, it was fent to him
From his *Donufa*: Bid him fearch the midft of't,
He there fhall find a Cordial.

Manto. What I do
Shall fpeak my Care and Faith.   [*Exit* Manto.

Don. Good Fortune with thee!
Paul. You cannot eat.
Don. The Time we thus abufe
We might employ much better.

Paul. I am glad
To hear this from you.   As for you *Carazie!*
If our Intents do profper, make Choice, whether
You'll fteal away with your two Miftreffes,
Or take your Fortune.
    Car. I'll be gelded twice firft;
Hang him that ftays behind.
    Paul. I wait you Madam.
Were but my Brother off, by the Command
Of the doting Viceroy there's no Guard dare ftay me;
And I will fafely bring you to the Place
Where we muft expect him.
 — *Don.* Heaven be gracious to us.

                                  [*Exeunt.*

S C E N E VI.

Enter Vitelli, Aga, *and a Guard.*

Vitel. *Paulina* to fall off thus! 'tis to me
More terrible than Death; and, like an Earthquake
Totters this walking Building (fuch I am)
And in my fudden Ruin would prevent,
By choaking up at once my vital Spirits
This pompous Preparation for my Death.
But I am loft; that good Man, good *Francifco,*
Deliver'd me a Paper, which till now
I wanted Leifure to perufe.   [*Reads the Paper.*
    Aga. This Chriftian
Fears not, it feems, the near approaching Sun
Whofe fecond Rife he never muft falute.

Enter Manto *with the bak'd Meat.*

    1 *Guard.* Who's that?
    2 *Guard.* Stand!
    Aga. Manto?
    Manto. Here's the Viceroy's Ring
Gives Warrant to my Entrance.   Yet you may

Partake of any Thing I fhall deliver;
'Tis but a Prefent to a dying Man
Sent from the Princefs that muft fuffer with him.

   Aga. Ufe your own Freedom.

   Manto. I would not difturb
This his laft Contemplation.

   Vitel. O, 'tis well! *
He has reftor'd all, and I at Peace again
With my *Paulina.*

   Manto. Sir! the fad *Donufa*
Grieved for your Suff'rings, more than for her own,
Knowing the long and tedious Pilgrimage
You are to take, prefents you with this Cordial,
Which privately fhe wifhes you fhould tafte of,
And fearch the middle Part, where you fhall find
Something that hath the Operation to
Make Death look lovely.

   Vitelli. I will not difpute
What fhe commands, but ferve it.   [*Exit* Vitelli.

   Aga. Pr'ythee, *Manto!*
How hath the unfortunate Princefs fpent this Night
Under her proud new Miftrefs?

   Manto. With fuch Patience
As it o'ercomes the other's Infolence;
Nay triumphs o'er her Pride. My much Hafte now
Commands me hence; but, the fad Tragedy, paft,
I'll give you Satisfaction to the full
Of all hath pafs'd, and a true Character,
Of the proud Chriftian's Nature.   [*Exit* Manto.

   Aga. Break the Watch up.—
What fhould we fear i' th' midft of our own Strengths?
'Tis but the Bafhaw's Jealoufy. Farewell, Soldiers.
                       · [*Exeunt.*

---

   * This is fpoken after *Vitelli* has read the Paper from *Francifco.* D.

SCENE VII.

Enter Vitelli, *with the bak'd Meats above.*

Vitel. There's fomething more in this than means to
    cloy
A hungry Appetite,—which I muft difcover.
She will'd me fearch the midft.—Thus, thus I pierce it:
—Ha! what is this? A Scroll bound up in Packthread?
What may the myftery be?   [*He reads the Scroll.*

  " Son, let down this Packthread at the Weft Win-
" dow of the Caftle. By it you fhall draw up a Ladder
" of Ropes, by which you may defcend; your deareft
" *Donufa*, with the reft of your Friends, below attend
" you. Heaven profper you!"

                          Francifco.

O beft of Men! he that gives up himfelf
To a true religious Friend, leans not upon
A falfe deceiving Reed, but boldly builds
Upon a Rock; which now with Joy I find
In reverend *Francifco*, whofe good Vows,
Labours and Watchings in my hoped-for Freedom,
Appear a pious Miracle.—I come,
I come, good Man, with Confidence; though the De-
    fcent
Were fteep as Hell, I know I cannot flide
Being call'd down by fuch a faithful Guide.
                       [*Exit* Vitelli.

SCENE *the laft.*

Afambeg, Muftapha, *and Janizaries.*

Afam. Excufe me *Muftapha*, tho' this Night to me
Appear as tedious as that treble one
Was to the World, when *Jove* on fair *Alcmena*

Begot *Alcides*. Were you to encounter
Thofe ravifhing Pleafures, which the flow-pac'd Hours
(To me they are fuch) bar me from, you would
With your continu'd Wifhes ftrive to imp.
New Feathers to the broken Wings of Time,
And chide the amorous Sun, for too long Dalliance
In *Thetis'* wat'ry Bofom.

   Mufta. You are too violent
In your Defires, of which you are yet uncertain;
Having no more Affurance to enjoy 'em
Than a weak Woman's Promife, on which wife Men
Faintly rely.

   Afam. Tufh! fhe is made of Truth;
And what fhe fays fhe will do, holds as firm
As Laws in Brafs that know no Change: What's this?
Some new Prize brought in, fure.—Why are thy Looks
                             [*A Piece fhot off.*
So ghaftly.—Villain, fpeak!

Enter Aga.

   Aga. Great Sir! hear me,
Then after kill me.—We are all betray'd,
The falfe *Grimaldi* funk in your Difgrace,
With his Confederates, have feiz'd his Ship,
And thofe that guarded it ftow'd under Hatches:
With him the condemn'd Princefs, and the Merchant,
That with a Ladder made of Ropes defcended
From the black Tower in which he was inclos'd
And your fair Miftrefs.—

   Afam. Ha!
   Aga. With all their Train,
And choiceft Jewels, are gone fafe aboard,
Their Sails fpread forth, and with a Fore-gale [20]
Leaving our Coaft, in Scorn of all Purfuit
As a Farewell they fhew'd a Broadfide to us.

    20 —————— *With a right Fore-gale.*

  The Infertion of the Word right is neceffary both for the Senfe
and the Metre. *M. M.*

Afam. No more.——

Mufta. Now note your Confidence!

Afam. No more.——

O my Credulity! I am too full
Of Grief and Rage to fpeak.—Dull heavy Fool!
Worthy of all the Tortures that the Frown
Of thy incenfed Mafter can throw on thee
Without one Man's Compaffion. I will hide
This Head among the Defarts, or fome Cave
Fill'd with my Shame and me; where I alone
May die without a Partner in my Moan.

[*Exeunt.*

F I N I S:

THE

BONDMAN.

AN

ANCIENT STORY.

Dramatis Perſonæ.

TIMOLEON, the General of *Corinth*.
ARCHIDAMUS, the Prætor of *Syracuſa*.
DIPHILUS, a Senator of *Syracuſa*.
CLEON, a fat impotent Lord.
PISANDER (diſguis'd) a Gentleman of *Thebes*.
POLIPHRON (diſguis'd) Friend to PISANDER.
LEOSTHENES, a Gentleman of *Syracuſa*, enamour'd of
      CLEORA.
ASOTUS, a fooliſh Lover, and the Son of CLEON.
TIMAGORAS, the Son of ARCHIDAMUS.
CLEORA, Daughter of ARCHIDAMUS.
CORISCA, a proud wanton Lady, Wife to CLEON.
OLYMPIA, a rich Widow.
STATILIA, Siſter to PISANDER, Slave to CLEORA.
ZANTHIA, Slave to CORISCA.
GRACCULO, ⎫
CIMBRIO,   ⎬ Bondmen.
A Jailor.

THE

BONDMAN.*

ACT I. SCENE I.

Enter Timagoras *and* Leofthenes.

Timagoras.

WHY fhould you droop, *Leofthenes*, or defpair
My Sifter's Favour? What before you pur-
chas'd
By Courtfhip, and fair Language, in thefe Wars
(For, from her Soul, you know, fhe loves a Soldier)
You may deferve by Action.

   Leoft. Good *Timagoras*,
When I have faid my Friend, think all is fpoken
That may affure me yours; and pray you, believe
The dreadful Voice of War, that fhakes the City,
The thund'ring Threats of *Carthage*, nor their Army,

☞ * The Tale of this Play is one of the fimpleft and beft of any
among the Works of the old *Englifh* Writers.——It confifts of but
one regular Vein, and has all its Parts, Paufes, and Incidents marked
in fo judicious a Manner, that nothing is either improbable, incon-
fiftent, or unentertaining.—'Tis indeed clogg'd with fome ridiculous
comick Characters; but then they have no Share in the Bufinefs of
the Play, and may be rejected at Pleafure.—Some State Affairs too
are introduced, which, though they don't immediately relate to the
Plot, yet are fo affiftant to the Incidents of it, as not to be fpared on
any Account. Befide which, they are in themfelves entertaining,
and ferve to introduce his principal Woman in a Manner wholly
grand, novel, and furprifing. The Tale itfelf is calculated to fhew
the ill Effects of Jealoufy in Love, and the Force of Addrefs and
Management.

Rais'd to make good thofe Threats, affright not me,
If fair *Cleora* were confirm'd his Prize,
That has the ftrongeft Arm and fharpeft Sword,
I'd court *Bellona* in her horrid Trim,
As if fhe were a Miftrefs, and blefs Fortune
That offers my young Valour to the Proof,
How much I dare do for your Sifter's Love.
But, when that I confider how averfe
Your noble Father, great *Archidamus*,
Is, and hath ever been, to my Defires,
Reafon may Warrant me to doubt and fear,
What Seeds 'foever I fow in thefe Wars
Of noble Courage, his determinate Will
May blaft, and give my Harveft to another
That ne'er toil'd for it.

 Timag. Prithee, do not nourifh
Thefe jealous Thoughts; I'm thine, and, pardon me,
Tho' I repeat it, my *Leofthenes*,
That, for thy Sake, when the bold *Theban* fu'd
Far-fam'd *Pifander* for my Sifter's Love,
Sent him difgrac'd and difcontented Home;
I wrought my Father then; and I, that ftopp'd not
In the Career of my Affection to thee,
When that renowned Worthy, brought with him [1]
High Birth, Wealth, Courage, as fee'd Advocates
To mediate for him, never will confent,
A Fool, that only has the Shape of Man,
Afotus, tho' he be rich *Cleon*'s Heir,
Shall bear her from thee.

 Leoft. In that Truft I live.

 Timag. Which never fhall deceive you.

Enter Pifander.

Pifan. Sir, the General
Timoleon, by his Trumpets hath giv'n Warning
For a Remove.

---

 [1] *When that renowned Worthy, that brought with him*
Leaving out the Word *that*, which deftroys both Senfe and Metre. *M. M.*

Timag. 'Tis well; provide my Horſe.

Piſan. I ſhall, Sir. [*Exit* Piſander.

Leoſt. This Slave has a ſtrange Aſpect!

Timag. Fit for his Fortune; 'tis a ſtrong-limb'd
       Knave;

My Father bought him for my Siſter's Litter.

O Pride of Women! Coaches are too common,

They ſurfeit in the Happineſs of Peace,

And Ladies think they keep not State enough,

If, for their Pomp and Eaſe, they are not borne

In Triumph on Men's Shoulders.

Leoſt. Who commands

The *Carthaginian* Fleet?

Timag. Giſco's their Admiral,

And, 'tis our Happineſs, a raw young Fellow,

One never train'd in Arms, but rather faſhion'd

To tilt with Ladies Lips, than crack a Lance,

Raviſh a Feather from a Miſtreſs' Fan,

And wear it as a Favour. A Steel Helmet,

Made horrid with a glorious Plume, will crack

His Woman's Neck.

Leoſt. No more of him.—The Motives

That *Corinth* gives us Aid?

Timag. The common Danger:

For *Sicily* being on Fire, ſhe is not ſafe;

It being apparent that ambitious *Carthage,*

(That to enlarge her Empire ſtrives to faſten

An unjuſt Gripe on us, that live free Lords

Of *Syracuſa* will not end, till *Greece*

Acknowledge her their Sovereign.

Leoſt. I'm ſatisfy'd.

What think you of our General?

Timag. He is a Man

Of ſtrange [a] and reſerv'd Parts; but a great Soldier.'

              [*A Trumpet ſounds.*

His Trumpets call us; I'll forbear his Character:

---

[a] *Strange* ſignifies here *diſtant.*

To-morrow, in the Senate-houſe, at large
He will expreſs himſelf.

Leoſt. I'll follow you.   [*Exeunt.*

SCENE II.

Enter Cleon, Coriſca, *and* Gracculo.

Coriſ. Nay, good Chuck.——

Cleon. I've ſaid it : Stay at home ;
I cannot brook your Gadding, you're a fair one,
Beauty invites Temptation, and ſhort Heels
Are ſoon tripp'd up.

Coriſ. Deny me ? By my Honour
You take no Pity on me. I ſhall ſwoon
As ſoon as you are abſent ;—aſk my Man elſe ;
You know he dares not tell a Lie.

Grac. Indeed,
You are no ſooner out of Sight, but ſhe
Does feel ſtrange Qualms ; then ſends for her young
        Doctor,
Who miniſters Phyſick to her on her Back,
Her Ladyſhip lying as ſhe were entranc'd.
(I've peep'd in at the Key-hole, and obſerv'd them)
And ſure his Potions never fail to work,
For ſhe's ſo pleaſant in the taking them,
She tickles again.

Coriſ. And all's to make you merry
When you come Home.

Cleon. You flatter me ; I'm old,
And Wiſdom cries, beware.

Coriſ. Old ! Duck ? To me
You are a young *Adonis.*

Grac. Well ſaid, *Venus !*
I am ſure ſhe *Vulcans* him.   [*Aſide.*

Coriſ. I will not change thee
For twenty boiſt'rous young Things without Beards.
Theſe Briſtles give the gentleſt Titillations,
And ſuch a ſweet Dew flows on them, it cures

My Lips without Pomatum :—Here's a round Belly,
'Tis a down Pillow to my Back. I fleep
So quietly by it ; and this tunable Nofe
(Faith when you hear it not) affords fuch Mufick,
That I curfe all Night-fidlers.

   Grac. This is grofs ;
Not finds fhe flouts him ?   [*Afide.*

   Corif. As I live, I am jealous.

   Cleon. Jealous of me, Wife ?

   Corif. Yes ; and I have a Reafon,
Knowing how lufty and active a Man you are.

   Cleon. Hum ! Hum !   [*Struts.*

   Grac. This is no cunning Quean ! 'flight, fhe will
      make him
To think, that, like the Stag, he has caft his Horns,
And is grown young again.   [*Afide.*

   Corif. You have forgot
What you did in your Sleep, and when you wak'd
Call'd for a Caudle.

   Grac. It was in his Sleep ;
For, waking, I durft truft my Mother with him. [*Afide.*

   Corif. I long to fee the Man of War ; *Cleora,*
Archidamus's Daughter, goes, and rich *Olympia* ;
I will not mifs the Show.

   Cleon. There's no contending :
—For this Time I am pleas'd ; but I'll no more on't.
                  [*Exeunt.*

SCENE III.

The Senate Houfe.

Enter Archidamus, Cleon, Diphilus, Olympia, Corif-
    ca, Cleora, *and* Zanthia.

   Archid. So carelefs we have been, my noble Lords,
In the difpofing of our own Affairs,
And ignorant in the Art of Government,
           G 2

That now we need a stranger to instruct us.
Yet we are happy that our Neighbour *Corinth*
(Pitying the unjust Gripe *Carthage* would lay
On *Syracusa*) hath vouchsaf'd to lend us
Her Man of Men, *Timoleon*, to defend
Our Country and our Liberties.

   Diph. 'Tis a Favour
We are unworthy of, and we may blush
Necessity compells us to receive it.

   Archid. O Shame! that we, that are a populous Na-
       tion,
Engag'd to lib'ral Nature, for all Blessings
An Island can bring forth; we that have Limbs,
And able Bodies, Shipping, Arms and Treasure,
The Sinews of the War, now we are call'd
To stand upon our Guard, cannot produce
One fit to be our General.

   Cleon. I'm old and fat;
I could say something else.

   Archid. We must obey
The Time and our Occasions; ruinous Buildings,
Whose Bases and Foundations are infirm,
Must use Supporters: We are circled round
With Danger; o'er our Heads with Sail-stretch'd
       Wings
Destruction hovers, and a Cloud of Mischief
Ready to break upon us; no Hope left us
That may divert it, but our sleeping Virtue
Rous'd up by brave *Timoleon*.

   Cleon. When arrives he?

   Diph. He is expected every Hour.

   Archid. The Braveries
Of *Syracusa*, among whom my Son
Timagoras, *Leosthenes* and *Asotus*,
(Your hopeful Heir Lord *Cleon*) two Days since
Rode forth to meet him, and attend him to
The City; every Minute we expect
To be bless'd with his Presence.

   Cleon. What Shout's this?   [*Shout at a Distance.*

Diph. 'Tis feconded with loud Mufick.

                 [*Trumpets flourifh within.*

Archid. Which confirms
His wifh'd-for Entrance. Let us entertain him
With all Refpeſt, Solemnity, and Pomp
A Man may merit, that comes to redeem us
From Slavery and Oppreffion.

    Cleon. I'll lock up
My Doors and guard my Gold; thefe Lads of *Corinth*
Have nimble Fingers, and I fear them more,
Being within our Walls, than thofe of *Carthage*;
They are far off.

    Archid. And, Ladies, be it your Care
To welcome him and his Followers with all Duty:
For reft refolv'd, their Hands and Swords muft keep
      you
In that full Height of Happinefs you live:
A dreadful Change elfe follows.

                [*Exeunt* Arch. Cleon. *and* Diph.

    Olymp. We are inftruſted.

    Corif. I'll kifs him for the Honour of my Country,
With any She in *Corinth.*

    Olymp. Were he a Courtier,
I've Sweetmeat in my Clofet fhall content him,
Be his Palate ne'er fo curious.

    Corif. And if Need be,
I have a Couch and a Banqueting-houfe in my Orchard,
Where many a Man of Honour has not fcorn'd
To fpend an Afternoon.

    Olymp. Thefe Men of War,
As I have heard, know not to court a Lady.
They cannot praife our Dreffings, kifs our Hands,
Ufher us to our Litters, tell Love-ftories,
Commend our Feet and Legs, and fo fearch upwards;
A fweet becoming Boldnefs! They are rough,
Boift'rous and faucy, and at the firft Sight
Ruffle and touze us, and, as they find their Stomachs,
Fall roundly to it.

Corif. 'Troth, I like 'em the better :
I can't endure to have a perfum'd Sir
Stand cringing in the Hams, licking his Lips
Like a Spaniel over a Furmety-pot, and yet
Has not the Boldnefs to come on, or offer
What they know we expect.

Olymp. We may commend
A Gentleman's Modefty, Manners, and fine Language,
His Singing, Dancing, riding of great Horfes,
The Wearing of his Clothes, his fair Complexion ;
Take Prefents from him, and extol his Bounty :
Yet, though he obferve, and wafte his 'State upon us,
³ If he be ftaunch, and bid not for the Stock
That we were born to traffick with ;—the Truth is,
We care not for his Company.

Corif. Mufing, *Cleora ?*
Olymp. She's ftudying how to entertain thefe Stran-
gers,
And to ingrofs them to herfelf.

Cleora. No, furely ;
I will not cheapen any of their Wares,
'Till you have made your Market ; you will buy,
I know, at any Rate.

Corif. She has given it you.
Olymp. No more ; they come.
The firft Kifs for this Jewel.   [*Flourifh of Trumpets.*

Enter Timagoras, Leofthenes, Afotus, Timoleon *in*
black, led in by Archidamus, Diphilus, *and* Cleon ;
followed by Pifander, Gracculo, Cimbrio, *and other*
Slaves.

Archid. It is your Seat.
Which with a general Suffrage,

---

3 *If he be ftaunch,* &c.

I don't think that *ftaunch* can be Senfe in this Paffage ; we fhould
probably read *ftarch'd,* that is *precife, formal.* M. M.

As to the fupreme Magiftrate, *Sicily* tenders,
And prays *Timoleon* to accept.

Timol. Such Honours
To one ambitious of Rules or Titles, *
Whofe Heaven on Earth is plac'd in his Command,
And abfolute Power o'er others, would with Joy,
And Veins fwoln high with Pride be entertain'd.
They take not me; for I have ever lov'd
An equal Freedom, and proclaim all fuch
As would ufurp another's Liberties,
Rebels to Nature, to whofe bounteous Bleffings
All Men lay Claim as true legitimate Sons.
But fuch as have made forfeit of themfelves
By vicious Courfes, and their Birthright loft,
'Tis not Injuftice they are mark'd for Slaves
To ferve the virtuous. For myfelf, I know
Honours and great Employments are great Burthens,
And muft require an *Atlas* to fupport them.
He that would govern others, firft fhould be
The Mafter of himfelf, richly indu'd
With Depth of Underftanding, Height of Courage,
And thofe remarkable Graces which I dare not
Afcribe unto myfelf.

Archid. Sir, empty Men
Are Trumpets of their own Deferts; but you,
That are not in Opinion, but in Proof,
Really good, and full of glorious Parts,
Leave the Report of what you are to Fame;

☞ 4 ——— *Such Honours*
To one ambitious of Rule, &c.

Maffinger has here finely drawn the Character of *Timoleon*, and
been very true to Hiftory; I fhall take the Liberty to tranfcribe fuch
Parts as may be not only entertaining, but likewife throw a Luftre
on feveral Parts of the Play before us: *Timoleon* was defcended from
one of the nobleft Families in *Corinth*, loved his Country paffionately,
and difcovered upon all Occafions a fingular Humanity of Temper,
except againft Tyrants and bad Men. He was an excellent Captain;
and as in his Youth he had all the Maturity of Age, in Age he had
all the Fire and Courage of the moft ardent Youth.

Which, from the ready Tongues of all good Men,
Aloud proclaims you.

Diph. Besides, you stand bound,
Having so large a Field to exercise
Your active Virtues offer'd you, to impart
Your Strength to such as need it.

Timol. 'Tis confessed :
And, since you'll have it so, such as I am,
For you, and for the Liberty of *Greece*,
I am most ready to lay down my Life :
But yet consider, Men of *Syracusa*,
Before that you deliver up the Power
(Which yet is yours) to me, to whom 'tis giv'n ;
To an impartial Man, with whom nor Threats
Nor Prayers shall e'er prevail ; for I must steer
An even Course.

Archid. Which is desir'd of all.

Timol. *Timophanes*, my Brother, for whose Death [5]
I'm tainted in the World, and foully tainted ;
In whose Remembrance I have ever worn,
In Peace and War, this Livery of Sorrow,
Can witness for me, how much I detest
Tyrannous Usurpation ; with Grief
I must remember it : For, when no Persuasion
Could win him to desist from his bad Practice,
To change the Aristocracy of *Corinth*

---

5 Timophanes, *my Brother, for whose Death*
I'm tainted in the World, &c.

Timoleon had an elder Brother, called *Timophanes*, whom he tenderly loved, as he had demonstrated in a Battle, in which he covered him with his Body, and saved his Life at the great Danger of his own ; but his Country was still dearer to him. That Brother having made himself Tyrant of it, so black a Crime gave him the sharpest Affliction. He made Use of all possible Means to bring him back to his Duty : Kindness, Friendship, Affection, Remonstrances, and even Menaces. But, finding all his Endeavours ineffectual, and that nothing could prevail upon an Heart abandoned to Ambition, he caused his Brother to be assassinated in his Presence by two of his Friends and Intimates, and thought, that upon such an Occasion, the Laws of Nature ought to give Place to those of his Country.

Into an abfolute Monarchy, I chofe rather
To prove a pious and obedient Son
To my Country, my beft Mother, than to lend
Affiftance to *Timophanes*, tho' my Brother,
That, like a Tyrant, ftrove to fet his Foot
Upon the City's Freedom.

Timag. Twas a Deed
Deferving rather Trophies than Reproof.

Leoft. And will be ftill remembered to your Honour,
If you forfake us not.

Diph. If you free *Sicily*
From barbarous *Carthage's* Yoke, it will be faid
In him you flew a Tyrant.

Archid. But, giving Way
To her Invafion, not vouchfafing us
(That fly to your Protection) Aid and Comfort,
'Twill be believ'd, that for your private Ends
You kill'd a Brother.

Timol. As I then proceed,
To all Pofterity may that Act be crown'd
With a deferv'd Applaufe, or branded with
The Mark of Infamy—Stay yet; ere I take
This Seat of Juftice, or engage myfelf
To fight for you abroad, or to reform
Your State at home, fwear all upon my Sword,
And call the Gods of *Sicily* to witnefs
The Oath you take; that whatfoe'er I fhall
Propound for Safety of your Commonwealth,
Not circumfcrib'd or bound in, fhall by you
Be willingly obey'd.

Archid. Diphilus, Cleon. So may we profper,
As we obey in all Things!

Timog. Leofthenes, Afotus. And obferve
All your Commands as Oracles!

Timol. Do not repent it.   [*Takes the State.*

Olymp. He afk'd not our Confent.

Coril. He's a Clown, I warrant him.

Olymp. I offer'd myfelf twice, and yet the Churl
Would not falute me.

Corif. Let him kifs his Drum!
I'll fave my Lips, I reft on it.
 Olymp. He thinks Women
No Part of the Republick.
 Corif. He fhall find
We are a Commonwealth.
 Cleora. The lefs your Honour.
 Timol. Firft then, a Word or two, but without Bit-
  ternefs,
(And yet miftake me not, I am no Flatterer)
Concerning your ill Government of the State.
In which the greateft, nobleft, and moft rich,
Stand, in the firft File, guilty.
 Cleon. Ha! how's this?
 Timol. You have not, as good Patriots fhould do,
  ftudied
The public Good, but your particular Ends;
Factious among yourfelves, preferring fuch
To Offices and Honours, as ne'er read
The Elements of faving Policy;
But deeply fkill'd in all the Principles
That ufher to Deftruction.
 Leoft. Sharp.
 Timag. The better.
 Timol. Your Senate-houfe, which us'd not to admit
A Man, however popular, to ftand
At the Helm of Government, whofe Youth was not
Made glorious by Action; whofe Experience
Crown'd with grey Hairs, gave Warrant to his Counfels,
Heard and receiv'd with Reverence; is now fill'd
With green Heads that determine of the State
Over their Cups, or when their fated Lufts
Afford them Leifure; or fupply'd by thofe
Who, rifing from bafe Arts and fordid Thrift,
Are eminent for Wealth, not for their Wifdom:
Which is the Reafon that to hold a Place
In Council, which was once efteem'd an Honour,
And a Reward for Virtue, hath quite loft
Luftre and Reputation, and is made
A mercenary Purchafe.

Timag. He fpeaks home.

Leoſt. And to the Purpofe.

Timol. From whence it proceeds
That the Treafure of the City is ingrofs'd
By a few private Men, the publick Coffers
Hollow with Want; and they, that will not fpare
One Talent for the common Good, to feed
The Pride and Bravery of their Wives, confume
In Plate, in Jewels, and fuperfluous Slaves,
What would maintain an Army.

Coriſ. Have at us!

Olymp. We thought we were forgot.

Cleora. But it appears
You will be treated of.

Timol. Yet in this Plenty,
And Fat of Peace, your young Men ne'er were train'd
In martial Difcipline, and your Ships unrigg'd
Rot in the Harbour: No Defence prepar'd,
But thought unufeful; as if that the Gods,
Indulgent to your Sloth, had granted you
A Perpetuity of Pride and Pleafure,
Nor Change fear'd or expected. Now you find
That *Carthage*, looking on your ftupid Sleeps,
And dull Security, was invited to
Invade your Territories.

Archid. You've made us fee, Sir,
To our Shame, the Country's Sicknefs: Now from you,
As from a careful and a wife Phyfician,
We do expect the Cure.

Timol. Old fefter'd Sores
Muft be lanc'd to the quick and cauteriz'd:
Which, borne with Patience, after I'll apply
Soft Unguents: For the Maintenance of the War,
It is decreed all Monies in the Hands
Of private Men, fhall inftantly be brought
To th' publick Treafury.

Timag. This bites fore.

Cleon. The Cure
Is worfe than the Difeafe; I'll never yield to't:
What could the Enemy, tho' victorious,

Inflict more on us? All that my Youth hath toil'd for,
Purchas'd with Industry, and preserv'd with Care,
Forc'd from me in a Moment.

   Diph. This rough Course
Will never be allow'd of.

   Timol. O blind Men!
If you refuse the first Means that is offer'd
To give you Health, no Hope's left to recover
Your desp'rate Sickness. Do you prize your Muck
Above your Liberties: And rather choose
To be made Bondmen, than to part with that
To which already you are Slaves? Or can it
Be probable in your flattering Apprehensions,
You can capitulate with the Conqueror,
And keep that yours which they come to possess,
And, while you kneel in vain, will ravish from you?
—But take your own Ways; brood upon your Gold,
Sacrifice to your Idol, and preserve
The Prey intire, and merit the Report
Of careful Stewards: Yield a just Account
To your proud Masters, who with Whips of Iron
Will force you to give up what you conceal,
Or tear it from your Throats; adorn your Walls
With *Persian* Hangings wrought of Gold and Pearl;
Cover the Floors on which they are to tread,
With costly *Median* Silks; perfume the Rooms
With Cassia and Amber, where they are
To feast and revel; while, like servile Grooms
You wait upon their Trenchers; feed their Eyes
With massy Plate, until your cupboards crack
With the Weight that they sustain; set forth your
        Wives
And Daughters in as vary'd Shapes
As there are Nations, to provoke their Lusts,
And let them be embrac'd before your Eyes,
The Object may content you; and, to perfect
Their Entertainment, offer up your Sons,
And able Men for Slaves; while you, that are
Unfit for Labour, are spurn'd out to starve,
Unpity'd, in some Desert, no Friend by,

Whofe Sorrow may fpare one compaffionate Tear
In the Remembrance of what once you were.

Leoft. The Blood turns.

Timag. Obferve how old *Cleon* fhakes,
As if in Picture he had fhown him what
He was to fuffer.

Corif. I am fick ; the Man
Speaks Poignards and Difeafes.

Olymp. Oh ! my Doctor !
I never fhall recover.

Cleora. If a Virgin,
Whofe Speech was ever yet ufher'd with Fear;
One knowing Modefty and humble Silence
To be the choiceft Ornaments of our Sex,
I'th' Prefence of fo many Reverend Men,
Struck dumb with Terror and Aftonifhment,
Prefume to clothe her Thought in vocal Sounds, !
Let her find Pardon.   Firft, to you, great Sir !
A bafhful Maid's Thanks, and her zealous Prayers
Wing'd with pure Innocence bearing them to Heaven,
For all Profperity that the Gods can give
To one whofe Piety muft exact their Care ;
Thus low I offer.

Timol. 'Tis a happy Omen.
Rife, bleft one, and fpeak boldly : On my Virtue
I am thy Warrant, from fo clear a Spring.
Sweet Rivers ever flow.

Cleora. Then thus to you,
My noble Father, and thefe Lords, to whom
I next owe Duty ; no Refpect forgotten
To you, my Brother, and thefe bold young Men
(Such I would have them) that are, or fhould be,
The City's Sword and Target of Defence ;
To all of you I fpeak ; and, if a Blufh
Steal on my Cheeks, it is fhown to reprove
Your Palenefs (willingly I would not fay
Your Cowardice or Fear :) Think you all Treafure
Hid in the Bowels of the Earth, or fhipwreck'd
In *Neptune*'s watry Kingdom, can hold Weight,
When Liberty and Honour fill one Scale,

Triumphant Juſtice ſitting on the Beam?
Or dare you but imagine that your Gold is
Too dear a Salary for ſuch as hazard
Their Blood and Lives in your Defence? For me,
An ignorant Girl, bear Witneſs, Heaven! ſo far
I prize a Soldier, that, to give him Pay,
With ſuch Devotion as our *Flamens* offer
Their Sacrifices at the holy Altar,
I do lay down theſe Jewels, will make ſale
Of my ſuperfluous Wardrobe; to ſupply
The meaneſt of their Wants.

   Timol. Brave maſculine Spirit!

   Diph. We are ſhown, to our Shame, what we in Honour
Should have taught others.

   Archid. Such a fair Example
Muſt needs be follow'd.

   Timag. Ever my dear Siſter;
But now our Family's Glory.

   Leoſt. Were ſhe deform'd,
The Virtues of her Mind would force a Stoick
To ſue to be her Servant.

   Cleon. I muſt yield;
And, tho' my Heart-blood part with it, I will
Deliver in my Wealth.

   Aſot. I would ſay ſomething;
But, the Truth is, I know not what.

   Timol. We have Money;
And Men muſt now be thought on.

   Archid. We can preſs
Of Labourers in the Country (Men inur'd
To Cold and Heat) ten Thouſand.

   Diph. Or, if Need be,
Inrol of Slaves, luſty and able Varlets,
And fit for Service.

   Cleon. They ſhall go for me;
I will not pay and fight too.

   Cleora. How! your Slaves?
O Stain of Honour!—Once more, Sir, your Pardon;
And to their Shames let me deliver what
I know in Juſtice you may ſpeak.

Timol. Moſt gladly :
I could not wiſh my Thoughts a better Organ
Than your Tongue to expreſs them.
　　Cleora. Are you Men ?
(For Age may qualify, tho' not excuſe,
The Backwardneſs of theſe) able young Men ?
Yet, now your Country's Liberty's at Stake,
Honour and glorious Triumph made a Garland
For ſuch as dare deſerve them ; a rich Feaſt
Prepar'd by Victory, of immortal Viands,
Not for baſe Men, but ſuch as with their Swords
Dare force Admittance, and will be her Gueſts ;
And can you coldly ſuffer ſuch Rewards
To be propos'd to Labourers and Slaves ?
While you, that are born Noble (to whom theſe
Valu'd at their beſt Rate, are next to Horſes,
Or other Beaſts of Carriage) cry, Ay me [6] !
Like idle Lookers on, till their proud Worth
Make them become your Maſters ?

⠀⠀[6] ⸻⸻⸻⸻⸻⸻*Cry, Ay me!*
　⠀*Like idle Lookers-on,* &c.

This is wrong: Inſtead of *Cry, Ay me!* we ſhould read, *Cry Aim.*
—To *cry aim,* is a Phraſe which frequently occurs in the old Dramatick Writers, and ſeems to imply, to *encourage,* or to *direct.*

　⠀⸻⸻⸻⸻⸻Muſt I *cry aim*
⠀To this unheard-of Inſolence ?
　　　　⠀⠀*Beaum.* and *Fletch.* Vol. IX. p. 419.

⠀Glut yourſelf with him,
⠀I will *cry aim.*
　　⠀*Maſſinger's Guardian,* Vol. III. Scene VIII.

　⠀⸻⸻⸻⸻⸻To be patient now,
⠀Were, in another Time, to play the Pander
⠀To the Viceroy's baſe Embraces, and *cry aim,*
⠀While he, &c.
　　　⠀*Maſſinger's Renegado,* Act I. Scene I.

⠀The Phraſe, perhaps, may owe its Origin to Archery, which was
much practiſed in thoſe Days, both as an Amuſement and a military
Exerciſe, or perhaps to the Paſtime of playing at Bowls ; the Perſon who points out to the Bowler the Ground he ought to take,
might poſſibly, at that Time, be ſaid to *cry aim* to him. But theſe
are merely Conjectures, unſupported by any Authority.

Timol. By my Hopes,
There's Fire and Spirit enough in this to make
Therſites valiant.

Cleora. No; far, far be it from you!
Let thoſe of meaner Quality contend,
Who can endure moſt Labour; plow the Earth,
And think they are rewarded when their Sweat
Brings home a fruitful Harveſt to their Lords;
Let them prove good Artificers and ſerve you
For Uſe and Ornament; but not preſume
To touch at what is noble: if you think them
Unworthy to taſte of thoſe Cates you feed on,
Or wear ſuch coſtly Garments, will you grant them
The Privilege and Prerogative of great Minds,
Which you were born to? Honour won in War;
And to be ſtil'd Preſervers of their Country,
Are Titles fit for free and generous Spirits,
And not for Bondmen. Had I been born a Man,
And ſuch ne'er dying Glories made the Prize
To bold heroic Courage, by *Diana,*
I would not to my Brother, nay, my Father,
Be brib'd to part with the Piece of Honour
I ſhould gain in this Action.

Timol. She's inſpir'd,
Or in her ſpeaks the Genius of your Country,
To fire your Blood in her Defence: I am rapp'd
With the Imagination.—Noble Maid,
Timoleon is your Soldier, and will ſweat
Drops of his beſt Blood, but he will bring home
Triumphant Conqueſt to you. Let me wear
Your Colours, Lady; and, tho' youthful Heats
That look no farther than your outward Form,
Are long ſince buried in me, while I live,
I am a conſtant Lover of your Mind,
That does tranſcend all Precedents.

Cleora. 'Tis an Honour,　　　　　　[*Gives her a Scarf.*
And ſo I do receive it.

---

7 It is *Cleora* that gives her a Scarf to *Timoleon,* not he that gives
her one: *In* the Days of Chivalry the higheſt Favour a Knight could

Corif. Plague upon it !
She has got the ftart of us : I could ev'n burft
With Envy at her Fortune,
   Olymp. A raw, young Thing !
We've too much Tongue fometimes, our Hufband**s**
     fay ;
And fhe outftrip us !
   Leoft. I am for the Journey.
   Timag. May all Difeafes Sloth and Letchery bring,
Fall upon him that ftays at home.
   Archid. Tho' old,
I will be there in Perfon.
   Diph. So will I.
Methinks I am not what I was : Her Words
Have made me younger by a Score of Years,
Than I was when I came hither.
   Cleon. I am ftill
Old *Cleon,* fat and unweildy ; I fhall never
Make a good Soldier, and therefore defire
To be excus'd at home.
   Afot. 'Tis my Suit too :
I am a Griftle, and thefe Spider Fingers
Will never hold a Sword.—Let us alone
To rule the Slaves at Home, I can fo yerk 'em ;
But in my Confcience I fhall never prove
Good Juftice in the War.
   Timol. Have your Defires ;
You would be Burthens to us, no Way Aids.
Lead, Faireft, to the Temple ; firft we'll pay
A Sacrifice to the Gods for good Succefs :
For all great Actions the wifh'd Courfe do run,
That are, with their Allowance, well begun.
               [*Exeunt all but the Slaves.*

receive from his Miftrefs, was a Scarf, which he wore over his Armour ; and it is this Favour *Timoleon* requefts from *Cleora,* when he defires to wear her *Colours* in the Speech preceding. *M. M.*

Pisan. Stay, *Cimbrio* and *Gracculo:*

Cimb. The Business?

Pisan. Meet me to-morrow Night near to the Grove,
Neighbouring the east Part of the City.

Grac. Well.

Pisan. And bring the rest of our Condition with you:
I've something to impart may break our Fetters,
If you dare second me.

Cimb. We'll not fail.

Grac. A Cart-rope
Shall not bind me at home.

Pisan. Think on't and prosper.

[*Exeunt.*

End of the First Act.

ACT II.   SCENE I,

Enter Archidamus, Timagoras, Leosthenes, *with Gorgets, and* Pisander.

Archidamus.

SO, so, 'tis well: How do I look?

Pisan. Most sprightfully.

Archid. I shrink not in the Shoulders; tho' I'm old
I'm tough; Steel to the Back: I have not wasted
My Stock of Strength in Feather Beds.—Here's an
Arm too;
There's Stuff in't, and I hope will use a Sword
As well as as any beardless Boy of you all.

Timag. I'm glad to see you, Sir, so well prepar'd
To endure the Travail of the War.

Archid. Go to, Sirrah!
I shall endure, when some of you keep your Cabins,
For all your flaunting Feathers.—Nay, *Leosthenes*,
You're welcome too, all Friends and Fellows now.

Leost. Your Servant, Sir.

Archid. Pish! leave these Compliments,
They stink in a Soldier's Mouth; I could be merry,
(For, now my Gown's off, farewel Gravity,)
And must be bold to put a Question to you,
Without Offence, I hope.

Leost. Sir, what you please.

Archid. And you will answer truly?

Timag. On our Words, Sir.

Archid. Go to, then! I presume you will confess
That you are two notorious Whoremasters.
Nay, spare your Blushing, I've been wild myself;
A Smack or so for Physick does no Harm;
Nay, it is Physick, if us'd moderately:
But to lie at Rack and Manger——

Leost. Say we grant this,
(For if we should deny't you'll not believe us)
What will you infer upon it?

Archid. What you'll groan for,
I fear, when you come to the Test. Old Stories tell us,
There's a Month call'd *October*; which brings in
Cold Weather; there are Trenches too, 'tis rumour'd,
In which to stand all Night to th' Knees in Water,
In Gallants breeds the Tooth-ach; there's a Sport too,
Nam'd, *lying perdue*, do you mark me? 'tis a Game
Which you must learn to play at, now in these Seasons)
And choice Variety of Exercises,
(Nay I come to you) and fasts not for Devotion;
Your rambling Hunt-smock feels strange Alterations,
And in a frosty Morning looks as if
He could with Ease creep in a Pottle-pot,
Instead of his Mistress' Placket.—Then he curses
The Time he spent in Midnight Visitations,
And finds what he superfluously parted with,
To be reported good and well breath'd,

H 2

But if retriev'd into his Back again,
Would keep him warmer than a Scarlet Waistcoat.

Enter Diphilus *and* Cleora.

Or an Armour lin'd with Furr. O welcome, welcome!
You've cut off my Discourse, but I will perfect
My Lecture in the Camp.

Diph. Come, we are stay'd for;
The General's afire for a Remove,
And longs to be in Action.

Archid. 'Tis my Wish too.
We must part.—Nay, no Tears, my best *Cleora*;
I shall melt too, and that were ominous.
Millions of Blessings on thee! All that's mine
I give up to thy Charge; and, Sirrah, look
You with that Care and Rev'rence observe her
As you would pay to me.—A Kiss, farewell! Girl!

Diph. Peace wait upon you, fair One!
                    [*Exit* Archid. Diph. *and* Pisander.

Timag. 'Twere Impertinence
To wish you to be careful of your Honour,
That ever keep in Pay a Guard about you
Of faithful Virtues.—Farewell: Friend, I leave you
To wipe our Kisses off; I know that Lovers
Part with more Circumstance and Ceremony;
Which I give Way to.   [*Exit* Timag.

Leost. 'Tis a noble Favour,
For which I ever owe you.—We're alone:
But how I should begin, or in what Language
Speak the unwilling Word of parting from you,
I'm yet to learn.

Cleora. And still continue ignorant;
For I must be most cruel to myself,
If I should teach you.

Leost. Yet it must be spoken,
Or you will chide my Slackness: You have fir'd me
With the Heat of noble Action to deserve you;
And the least Spark of Honour that took Life
From your sweet Breath, still fann'd by it and cherish'd,

Muſt mount up in a glorious Flame, or I
Am much unworthy.

Cleora. May it yet burn here,
And, as a Sea-mark, ſerve to guide true Lovers
(Toſs'd on the Ocean of luxurious Wiſhes)
Safe from the Rocks of Luſt, into the Harbour
Of pure Affection riſing up an Example
Which After-times ſhall witneſs to our Glory,
Firſt took from us Beginning!

Leoſt. 'Tis a Happineſs
My Duty to my Country, and mine Honour
Cannot conſent to; beſides, add to theſe,
It was your Pleaſure, fortify'd by Perſuaſion
And Strength of Reaſon, for the general Good,
That I ſhould go.

Cleora. Alas! I then was witty
To plead againſt myſelf; and mine Eye, fix'd
Upon the Hill of Honour, ne'er deſcended
To look into the Vale of certain Dangers,
Thro' which you were to cut your Paſſage to it.

Leoſt. I'll ſtay at home, then.

Cleora. No, that muſt not be;
For ſo, to ſerve my own Ends, and to gain
A petty Wreath myſelf, I rob you of
A certain Triumph, which muſt fall upon you;
Or Virtue's turn'd a Hand-maid to blind Fortune:
How is my Soul divided! to confirm you
In the Opinion of the World moſt worthy
To be belov'd (with me you're at the Height,
And can advance no farther) I muſt ſend you
To court the Goddeſs of ſtern War, who, if
She ſee you with my Eyes, will ne'er return you,
But grow enamour'd of you.

Leoſt. Sweet, take Comfort!
And what I offer you you muſt vouchſafe me
Or I am wretched: All the Dangers that
I can encounter in the War are Trifles;
My Enemies abroad to be contemn'd;

H 3

The dreadful Foes, that have the Pow'r to hurt me,
I leave at home with you.

 Cleora. With me?

 Leoſt. Nay, in you,
In every Part about you, they are arm'd
To fight againſt me.

 Cleora. Where?

 Leoſt. There's no Perfection
That you are Miſtreſs of, but muſters up
A Legion againſt me, and all ſworn
To my Deſtruction.

 Cleora. This is ſtrange!

 Leoſt. But true, Sweet:
Exceſs of Love can work ſuch Miracles.
Upon this Ivory Forehead are intrench'd
Ten thouſand Rivals, and theſe Suns command
Supplies from all the World, on Pain to forfeit
Their comfortable Beams; theſe Ruby Lips,
A rich Exchequer to aſſure their Pay;
This Hand, *Sibylla's* golden Bough to guard them
Thro' Hell and Horror to the *Elyſian* Springs;
Which who'll not venture for? and, ſhould I name
Such as the Virtues of your Mind invite,
Their Numbers would be infinite.

 Cleora. Can you think
I may be tempted?

 Leoſt. You were never prov'd.
For me, I have convers'd with you no farther
Than would become a Brother.   I ne'er tun'd
Looſe Notes to your chaſte Ears; or brought rich Pre-
   ſents
For my Artillery, to batter down
The Fortreſs of your Honour; nor endeavour'd
To make your Blood run high at ſolemn Feaſts
With Viands that provoke (the ſpeeding Philtres):
I work'd no Bawds to tempt you; never practis'd
The cunning and corrupting Arts they ſtudy,
That wander in the wild Maze of Deſire;
Honeſt Simplicity and Truth were all
The Agents I employ'd; and when I came

To fee you, it was with that Reverence
As I beheld the Altars of the Gods;
And Love, that came along with me, was taught
To leave his Arrows, and his Torch behind,
Quench'd in my Fear to give Offence.

Cleora. And 'twas
That Modefty that took me and preferves me,
Like a frefh Rofe, in mine own natural Sweetnefs;
Which, fully'd with the Touch of impure Hands,
Lofes both Scent and Beauty.

Leoft. But, *Cleora,*
When I am abfent, as I muft go from you,
(Such is the Cruelty of my Fate) and leave you,
Unguarded, to the violent Affaults
Of loofe Temptations; when the Memory
Of my fo many Years of Love and Service,
Is loft in other Objeets; you are courted
By fuch as keep a Catalogue of their Conquefts
Won upon credulous Virgins; when nor Father
Is here to awe you, Brother to advife you,
Nor your poor Servant by, to keep fuch off,
By Luft inftructed how to undermine
And blow your Chaftity up; when your weak Senfes,
At once affaulted, fhall confpire againft you,
And play the Traitors to your Soul, your Virtue;
How can you ftand? 'Faith, tho' you fall, and I
The Judge, before whom you then ftood accus'd,
I fhould acquit you.

Cleora. Will you then confirm
That Love and Jealoufy, tho' of different Natures,
Muft of Neceffity be Twins; the Younger
Created only to defeat the Elder,
And fpoil him of his Birthright? 'tis not well.
But being to part, I will not chide, I will not;
Nor with one Syllable or Tear, exprefs
How deeply I am wounded with the Arrows
Of your Diftruft: But when that you fhall hear
At your Return how I have borne myfelf,
And what an auftere Penance I take on me,

To satisfy your Doubts : When like a Vestal
I shew you, to your Shame, the Fire still burning,
Committed to my Charge by true Affection,
The People joining with you in the Wonder :
When, by the glorious Splendor of my Suff'rings,
The prying Eyes of Jealousy are struck blind,
The Monster too that feeds on, Fears, ev'n starv'd
For Want of seeming Matter to accuse me,
Expect, *Leosthenes*, a sharp Reproof
From my just Anger.

   Leost. What will you do ?
   Cleora. Obey me,
Or from this Minute you're a Stranger to me ;
And do't without Reply.—All-seeing Sun,
Thou Witness of my Innocence, thus I close
Mine Eyes against thy comfortable Light,
'Till the Return of this distrustful Man.

                   [He binds her Eyes.

Now bind them sure ;---nay, do't : If uncompell'd
I loose this Knot, until the Hands that made it
Be pleas'd t' untie it, may consuming Plagues
Fall heavy on me ! Pray you, guide me to your Lips,
This Kiss, when you come back, shall be a Virgin
To bid you welcome.---Nay, I have not done yet :
I will continue dumb ; and, you once gone,
No Accent shall come from me : Now to my Chamber ;
My Tomb, if you miscarry : There I'll spend
My Hours in silent Mourning, and thus much
Shall be reported of me to my Glory,
And you confess it, whether I live or die,
My Chastity triumphs o'er your Jealousy.   *[Exeunt.*

SCENE II.

Asotus driving in Gracculo.

   Asot. You Slave ! you Dog ! down, Cur.
   Gra.. Hold, good young Master,
 For Pity's Sake !

Afot. Now am I in my Kingdom.
Who fays I am not valiant ?—I begin
To frown again : Quake, Villain.

Grac. So I do, Sir;
Your Looks are Agues to me.

Afot. Are they fo, Sir ?
'Slight, if I had them at this Bay, that flout me,
And fay I look like a Sheep and an Afs, I'd make 'em
Feel, that I am a Lion.

Grac. Do not roar, Sir,
As you're a valiant Beaft—But do you know
Why you ufe me thus ?

Afot. I'll beat thee a little more,
Then ftudy for a Reafon.———O ! I have it :
One brake a Jeft on me, and then I fwore,
Becaufe I durft not ftrike him, when I came home
That I would break thy Head.

Grac. Pox on his Mirth;
I'm fure I mourn for't.   [*Afide.*

Afot. Remember too, I charge you,
To teach my Horfe good Manners ; for this Morning
As I rode to take the Air, th' untutor'd Jade
Threw me, and kick'd me.

Grac. I thank him for't.   [*Afide.*

Afot. What's that ?

Grac. I fay, Sir, I'll teach him to hold his Heels,
If you will hold your Fingers.

Afot. I'll think upon't

Grac I am bruis'd to Jelly.—Better be a Dog,
Than Slave to a Fool or Coward.   [*Afide.*

Afot. Here's my Mother.

Enter Corifca *and* Zanthia.

She is chaftifing too—How brave we live,
That have our Slaves to beat, to keep us in Breath
When we want exercife !

Corif. Carelefs Harlotary,   [*Striking her.*
Look to't; if a Curl fall, or Wind or Sun

Take my complexion off, I will not leave
One Hair upon thine Head.

Grac. Here's a fecond Show
Of the Family of Pride.

Corif. Fie on thefe Wars!
I'm ftarv'd for want of Action, not a Gamefter left
To keep a Woman play : If this World laft
A little longer with us, Ladies muft Study
Some new-found Myftery to cool one another,
We fhall burn to Cinders elfe. I have heard there have
  been
Such Arts in a long Vacation; would they were
Reveal'd to me! They've made my Doctor too
Phyfician to the Army, he was us'd
To ferve the Turn at a Pinch; but I am now
Quite unprovided.

Afot. My Mother-in-Law is fure
At her Devotion.   [*Afide,*

Corif. There are none but our Slaves left;
Nor are they to be trufted.—Some great Women,
Which I could name, in a Dearth of Vifitants,
Rather than be idle, have been glad to play
At fmall Game; but I am fo fqueafy-ftomach'd,
And from my Youth have been fo us'd to Dainties,
I cannot tafte fuch grofs Meat. Some that are hungry
Draw on their Shoemakers, and take a Fall
From fuch as mend Mats in their Galleries;
Or when a Taylor fettles a Petticoat on,
Take Meafure of his Bodkin.—Fie upon't,
'Tis bafe; for my Part, I could rather lie with
A Gallant's Breeches, and conceive upon 'em
Than ftoop fo low.

Afot. Fair Madam, and my Mother——

Corif. Leave the laft out, it fmells rank of the Coun-
  try,
And fhews coarfe Breeding; your true Courtier knows
  not
His Niece, or Sifter from another Woman,
If fhe be apt and cunning.—I could tempt now
This Fool: but he will be fo long a working:

Then he's my Husband's Son.—The fitter to
Supply his Wants, I have the Way already.
I'll try if it will take——When were you with
Your Miſtreſs, fair *Cleora* ?

Aſot. Two days ſithence,
But ſhe's ſo coy, forſooth, that ere I can
Speak a penn'd Speech I've bought and ſtudy'd for her,
Her woman calls her away.

Coriſ. Here's a dull Thing !
But better taught, I hope.—Send off your Man.

Aſot. Sirrah, be gone.

Grac. This is the firſt good Turn
She ever did me.   [*Aſide.*]   [*Exit* Gracculo.

Corriſ. We'll have a ſcene of Mirth ;
I muſt not have you ſham'd for want of Practice.
I ſtand here for *Cleora* ; and, do you hear, Minion ?
(That you may tell her what her Woman ſhould do)
Repeat the Leſſon over that I taught you
When my young Lord came to viſit me ; if you miſs
In a Syllable or Poſture——

Zant. I am perfect.

Aſot. Would I were ſo : I fear I ſhall be out.

Coriſ. If you are, I'll help you in.—Thus I walk
     muſing :
You are to enter, and, as you paſs by,
Salute my Woman :—Be but bold enough,
You'll ſpeed, I warrant you : Begin.

Aſot. Have at it——
'Save thee, Sweet heart.—A Kiſs.

Zant. Venus forbid, Sir,
I ſhould preſume to taſte your Honour's Lips
Before my Lady.

Coriſ. This is well on both Parts.

Aſot. How does thy Lady ?

Zant. Happy in your Lordſhip,
As often as ſhe thinks on you.

Coriſ. Very good
This Wench will learn in Time.

Aſot. Does ſhe think of me ?

Zant. O, Sir! and speaks the best of you; admires
Your Wit, your Cloaths, Discourse; and swears, but
   that
You are not forward enough for a Lord, you were
The most compleat and absolute Man,---I'll shew
Your Lordship a Secret.

 Asot. Not of thine own?

 Zant. O! no, Sir;
'Tis of my Lady:—But, upon your Honour,
You must conceal it.

 Asot. By all Means,

 Zant. Sometimes
I lie with my Lady, as the last Night I did;
She could not say her Pray'rs for thinking of you:
Nay, she talk'd of you in her Sleep, and sigh'd out
O sweet *Asotus!* sure thou art so backward
That I must ravish thee; and in that Fervour
She took me in her Arms, threw me upon her,
Kiss'd me, and hugg'd, and then wak'd, and wept
——Because 'twas but a Dream.

 Coris. This will bring him on,
Or he's a Block.—A good Girl!

 Asot. I am mad,
'Till I am at it.

 Zant. Be not put off, Sir,
With, *Away, I dare not*; *Fie, you are immodest*;
My Brother's up; *my Father will hear.*—Shoot home,
   Sir,
You cannot miss the Mark.

 Asot. There's for thy Counsel. [*Gives her Money,*
This is the fairest Interlude; if it prove earnest,
I shall wish I were a Player.

 Coris. Now my Turn comes.——
I am exceeding sick, pray you send my Page
For young *Asotus*; I cannot live without him;
Pray him to visit me; yet, when he's present,
I must be strange to him.

 Asot. Not so; you're caught:
Lo, whom you wish, behold *Asotus* here!

Corif. You wait well, Minion; shortly I shall not
    speak
My Thoughts in my private Chamber, but they must
Lie open to Discovery.
   Asot. 'Slid, she's angry.
   Zant. No, no, Sir, she but seems so.—To her again.
   Asot. Lady, I would descend to kiss your Hand,
But that 'tis glov'd, and Civit makes me sick;
And to presume to taste your Lips not safe,
Your Woman by.
   Corif. I hope she's no Observer
Of whom I grace.   [*Zant. looks on a Book.*
   Asot. She's at her Book, O rare!   [*Kisses her.*
   Corif. A Kiss for Entertainment is sufficient:
Too much of one Dish cloys me.
   Asot. I would serve in
The second Course; but still I fear your Woman.
   Corif. You're very cautious.   [*Zant. seems to sleep.*
   Asot. 'Slight she's asleep!
'Tis Pity these Instructions are not printed;
They would sell well to Chambermaids.—'Tis no Time
    now
To play with my good Fortune, and your Favour;
Yet to be taken, as they say—a Scout,
To give the Signal when the Enemy comes,
              [*Exit* Zanthia.
Were now worth Gold.---She's gone to watch.——
A Waiter so train'd up were worth a Million
To a wanton City-Madam.
   Corif. You're grown conceited.
   Asot. You teach me.—Lady, now—your Cabinet
   Corif. You speak as it were yours.
   Asot. When we are there,
I'll shew you my best Evidence.
   Corif. Hold! you forget;
I only play *Cleora*'s Part.
   Asot. No Matter;
Now we've begun, let's end the Act.
   Corif. Forbear, Sir!
Your Father's Wife?

Afot. Why, being Heir, I am bound,
Since he can make no Satisfaction to you,
To fee his Debts paid.

Enter Zanthia *running.*

Zant. Madam, my Lord.——
Corif. Fall off;
I muſt trifle with the Time too! Hell confound it!
Afot. Plague on his toothleſs Chaps! he cannot do't
Himſelf, yet hinders ſuch as have good Stomachs.

Enter Cleon.

Cleon. Where are you, Wife? I fain would go
        Abroad;
But cannot find my Slaves that bear my Litter.
I'm tir'd :—Your Shoulder, Son ;—nay, Sweet, thy
        Hand too;
A Turn or two in the Garden, and then to Supper,
And ſo to Bed.
Afot. Never to riſe, I hope, more.
                                        [*Exeunt.*

SCENE III.

Piſander and Poliphron *bringing forth a Table.*

Piſan. 'Twill take, I warrant thee.
Polip. You may do your Pleaſure :
But, in my Judgment, better to make Uſe of
The preſent Opportunity.
Piſan. No more.
Polip. I'm ſilenc'd
Piſan. More Wine; pry'thee drink hard, Friend,
And when we're hot, whatever I propound,

Enter Cimbrio, Gracculo, *and other Slaves.*

Second with Vehemency.—Men of your Words, all
    welcome!
Slaves ufe no Ceremony; fit down, here's a Health.
  Polip. Let it run round, fill every man his Glafs.
  Grac. We look for no Waiters; this is Wine.
  Pifan. The better,
Strong, lufty Wine: Drink deep, this Juice will
    make us
As free as our Lords,   [*Drinks.*
  Grac. But, if they find we tafte it,
We are all damn'd to the Quarry during Life,
Without Hope of Redemption.
  Pifan. Pifh! for that
We'll talk anon: Another Rouze, we lofe Time;
                       [*Drinks.*
When our low Blood's wound up a little higher,
I'll offer my Defign;—nay, we are cold yet
Thefe Glaffes contain nothing;—do me right
               [*Takes the Bottle.*
As e'er you hope for Liberty. 'Tis done bravely;
How do you feel yourfelves now?
  Cimb. I begin
To have ftrange Conumdrums in my Head.
  Grac. And I
To loath bafe Water: I would be hang'd in Peace
    now,
For one Month of fuch Holidays.
  Pifan. An Age, Boys;
And yet defy the Whip, if you are Men,
Or dare believe you've Souls.
  Cimb. We are no Brokers:
  Grac. Nor Whores, whofe Marks are out of their
    Mouths:
They hardly can get Salt enough to keep 'em
From ftinking above Ground.
  Pifan. Our Lords are no Gods?
  Grac. They are Devils to us, I am fure.

Pisan. But subject to
Cold, Hunger, and Diseases.

Grac. In Abundance :
Your Lord that feels no Ach in his Chine at Twenty,
Forfeits his Privilege ; how should their Chirurgeons
        build else,
Or ride on their Foot-cloaths ?

Pisan. Equal Nature fashion'd us
All in one Mold : The Bear serves not the Bear,
Nor the Wolf the Wolf ; 'twas odds of Strength in
        Tyrants,
That pluck'd the first Link from the Golden Chain
With which that Thing of Things[8] bound in the
        World.
Why then, since we are taught, by their Examples,
To love our Liberty, if not command,
Should the Strong serve the Weak, the fair deform'd
        ones ?
Or such as know the Cause of Things, pay Tribute
To ignorant Fools ? All's but the outward Gloss
And politic Form that does distinguish us.
Cymbrio, thou art a strong Man ; if, in Place
Of carrying Burthens, thou hadst been train'd up
In martial Discipline, thou might'st have prov'd
A General, fit to lead and fight for *Sicily*,
As fortunate as *Timoleon*.

Cymbrio. A little fighting
Will serve a General's Turn.

Pisan. Thou, *Gracculo*,
Hast Fluency of Language, quick Conceit ;
And I think, cover'd with a Senator's Robe,
Formally set on the Bench, thou wouldst appear
As brave a Senator——

Grac. Would I had Lands,
Or Money to buy a Place ; and if I did not
Sleep on the Bench with the drowsiest of 'em,

---

8 *Thing of Things* is so harsh an Expression, and so little in *Massinger's* stile, that probably we should read *King of Kings*. I will
not however alter the Text : If *Thing of Things* be the right Reading, it is probably intended as a literal Translation of *Ens Entium*.
M. M.

Play with my Chain,
Look on my Watch when my Guts chim'd Twelve,
    and wear
A State Beard, with my Barber's Help; rank with 'em
In their moſt choice peculiar Gifts; degrade me
And put me to drink Water again, which (now
I've taſted Wine) were Poiſon.

   Piſan. 'Tis ſpoke nobly,
And like a Gown-man:—None of theſe, I think too,
But would prove good Burghers.

   Grac. Hum! the Fools are modeſt:
I know their Inſides.—Here's an ill-fac'd Fellow
(But that will not be ſeen in a dark Shop,)
If he did not in a Month learn to out-ſwear,
In the ſelling of his Wares, the cunningeſt Tradeſman
In *Syracuſa,* I've no Skill.—Here's another,
Obſerve but what a couſ'ning Look he has,
(Hold up thy Head Man) if for drawing Gallants
Into Mortgages for Commodities, cheating Heirs
With your new counterfeit Gold Thread, and gumm'd
    Velvets,
He does not tranſcend all that went before him,
Call in his Patent. Paſs the reſt; they'll all make
Sufficient *Beccos,* and with their Brow-antlers,
Bear up the Cap of Maintenance.

   Piſan. Is't not Pity, then,
Men of ſuch eminent Virtues ſhould be Slaves?

   Cimb. Our Fortune!

   Piſan. 'Tis your Folly: Daring Men
Command, and make their Fates.——Say, at this
    Inſtant,
I mark'd you out a Way to Liberty;
Poſſeſs'd you of thoſe Bleſſings our proud Lords
So long have ſurfeited in; and, what is ſweeteſt,
Arm you with Pow'r, by ſtrong Hand to avenge
Your Stripes, your unregarded Toil, the Pride,
The Inſolence of ſuch as tread upon
Your patient Sufferings; fill your famiſh'd Mouths,
With the Fat and Plenty of the Land; redeem you

From the dark Vale of Servitude, and seat you
Upon a Hill of Happiness : What would you do
To purchase this and more ?

Grac. Do any Thing :
To burn a Church or two, and dance by the Light on't
Were but a May-game.

Poliph. I have a Father living ;
But, if the cutting of his Throat could work this,
He should excuse me.

Cimb. I would cut mine own,
Rather than miss it, so I might but have
A Taste on't ere I die.

Pisan. Be resolute Men,
You shall run no such Hazard ; nor groan under
The Burthen of such crying Sins.

Cimb. The Means ?

Grac. I feel a Woman's Longing.

Polip. Don't torment us
With Expectation.

Pisan. Thus then : Our proud Masters,
And all the able Freemen of the City
Are gone unto the Wars—

Poliph. Observe but that.

Pisan. Old Men, and such as can make no Resistance,
Are only left at Home.

Grac. And the proud young Fool
My Master—If this take, I'll hamper him.

Pisan. Their Arsenal, their Treasure's in our Power,
If we have Hearts to seize 'em. If our Lords fall
In the present Action, the whole Country's ours.
Say they return victorious, we have Means
To keep the Town against them ; at the worst
To make our own Conditions. Now, if you dare
Fall on their Daughters and their Wives, break up
Their Iron Chests, banquet on their rich Beds,
And carve yourselves of all Delights and Pleasures
You have been barr'd from, with one Voice cry with
     me,
Liberty, Liberty !

All. Liberty, Liberty !

Pifan. Go then, and take Poffeffion : Ufe all Free-
    dom ;
But fhed no Blood.—So, this is well begun ;
But not to be commended till't be done.

           [*Exeunt all, crying Liberty.*

End of the Second Act.

ACT III.   SCENE I.

Pifander, *and* Timandra.

Pifander.

WHY, think you that I plot againft myfelf?
    Fear nothing; you are fafe : Thefe thick-
      fkin'd Slaves,
I ufe as Inftruments to ferve my Ends,
Pierce not my deep Defigns ; nor fhall they dare
To lift an Arm againft you.
    Timand. With your Will :
But turbulent Spirits, rais'd beyond themfelves
With Eafe are not fo foon laid : They oft prove
Dangerous to him that call'd them up.
    Pifan. 'Tis true,
In what is rafhly undertook. Long fince
I have confider'd ferioufly their Natures,
Proceeded with mature Advice, and know
I hold their Will and Faculties in more Awe
Than I can do my own. Now, for their Licence,
And Riot in the City, I can make
A juft Defence and Ufe : It may appear too
A politic Prevention of fuch Ills
As might with greater Violence and Danger
Hereafter be attempted ; tho' fome fmart for't

I 2

It matters not:—However, I'm refolv'd;
And fleep you with Security. Holds *Cleora*
Conftant to her rafh Vow?

   Timand. Beyond Belief;
To me that fee her hourly, it feems a Fable.
By Signs I guefs at her Commands, and ferve 'em
With Silence; fuch her Pleafure is made known
By holding her fair Hand thus. She eats little,
Sleeps lefs, as I imagine: Once a Day
I lead her to this Gallery, where fhe walks
Some half a dozen Turns, and, having offer'd
To her abfent Saint a Sacrifice of Sighs,
She points back to her Prifon.

   Pifan. Guide her hither,
And make her underftand the Slaves Revolt;
And with your utmoft Eloquence enlarge
Their Infolence and Rapes done in the City.
Forget not too I am their Chief, and tell her
You ftrongly think my extreme Dotage on her,
As I am *Marullo*, caus'd this fudden Uproar
To make Way to enjoy her.

   Timand. Punctually
I will difcharge my Part.   [*Exit* Timandra.

Enter Poliphron.

   Poliph. O, Sir, I fought you:
You've mifs'd the Sport. Hell, I think's broke loofe,
There's fuch Variety of all Diforders,
As Leaping, Shouting, Drinking, Dancing, Whoring,
Among the Slaves; anfwer'd with Crying, Howling,
By the Citizens and their Wives; fuch a Confufion,
(In a Word, not to tire you) as I think
The like was never read of.

   Pifan. I fhare in
The Pleafure though I'm abfent. This is fome
Revenge for my Difgrace.

   Poliph. But, Sir, I fear,
If your Authority reftrain them not,
They'll fire the City, or kill one another,

They are fo apt to Outrage ; neither know I
Whether you wifh it, and came therefore to
Acquaint you with fo much.

Pifan. I will among 'em ;
But muft not long be abfent.

Poliph. At your Pleafure. [*Exeunt.*

SCENE II.

Cleora, Timandra, *a Chair, a Shout within.*

Timand. They're at our Gates, my Heart ! affrights
   and Horrors
Increafe each Minute : No Way left to fave us,
No flattering Hope to comfort us, or Means
By Miracle to redeem us from bafe Luft
And lawlefs Rapine ? Are there Gods, yet fuffer
Such innocent Sweetnefs to be made the Spoil
Of brutifh Appetite ? Or, fince they decree
To ruin Nature's Mafter piece (of which
They have not left one Pattern) muft they choofe,
To fet their Tyranny off, Slaves to pollute
The Spring of Chaftity, and poifon it
With their moft loth'd Embraces ? And of thofe
He that fhould offer up his Life to guard it ?
Marullo, curs'd *Marullo,* your own Bondman,
Purchas'd to ferve you, and fed by your Favours.
          [Cleora *ftarts.*

Nay, ftart not : It is he ; he, the grand Captain
Of thefe libidinous Beafts, that have not left
One cruel Act undone that barbarous Conqueft
Yet ever practis'd in a captive City.
He, doting on your Beauty, and to have Fellows
In his foul Sin, hath rais'd thefe mutinous Slaves,
Who have begun the Game by violent Rapes,
Upon the Wives and Daughters of their Lords :
And he, to quench the Fire of his bafe Luft,

By Force comes to enjoy you :—Do not wring
         [Cleora *wrings her Hands.*
Your innocent Hands, 'tis bootlefs ; ufe the Means
That may preferve you. 'Tis no Crime to break
A Vow when you are forc'd to it ; fhew your Face,
And with the Majefty of commanding Beauty
Strike dead his loofe Affections : If that fail,
Give Liberty to your Tongue, and ufe Entreaties ;
There cannot be a Breaft of Flefh and Blood,
Or Heart fo made of Flint, but muft receive
Impreffion from your Words ; or Eyes fo ftern,
But from the clear Reflection of your Tears,
Muft melt and bear them Company ; will you not
Do thefe good Offices to yourfelf ? Poor I then
Can only weep your Fortune :—Here he comes.

Enter Pifander *fpeaking at the Door.*

  Pifand. He that advances
A Foot beyond this, comes upon my Sword.
You have had your Ways, difturb not mine.
  Timand. Speak gently,
Her Fears may kill her elfe.
  Pifand. Now Love infpire me !
Still fhall this Canopy of envious Night
Obfcure my Suns of Comfort ? And thofe Dainties
Of pureft white and Red, which I take in at
My greedy Eyes, deny'd my famifh'd Senfes ?
The Organs of your Hearing are yet open ;
And you infringe no Vow, tho' you vouchfafe
To give them Warrant to convey unto
Your underftanding Parts, the Story of
A tortur'd and defpairing Lover, whom
Not Fortune but Affection marks your Slave :
         [Cleora *fhakes.*
Shake not, beft Lady ! for believ't, you are
As far from Danger as I am from Force :
All Violence I'll offer, tends no farther
Than to relate my Sufferings, which I dare not

Prefume to do, till by fome gracious Sign
You fhew you're pleas'd to hear me.

Timand. If you are,
Hold forth your Right-hand.

     [*Cleora holds forth her right Hand.*

 Pifan. So, 'tis done; and I
With my glad Lips feal humbly on your Foot,
My Soul's Thanks for the Favour: I forbear
To tell you who I am, what Wealth, what Honours
I made Exchange of to become your Servant:
And, tho' I knew worthy *Leofthenes*
(For fure he muft be worthy, for whofe Love
You have endur'd fo much) to be my Rival;
When Rage and Jealoufy counfel'd me to kill him,
(Which then I could have done with much more Eafe,
Than now, in Fear to grieve you, I dare fpeak it)
Love, feconded with Duty boldly told me
The Man I hated, fair *Cleora* favour'd:
And that was his Protection.   [*Cleora bows.*

 Timand. See, fhe bows
Her Head in Sign of Thankfulnefs.

 Pifan. He remov'd,
By th' Occafion of the War (my Fires increafing
By being clos'd and ftopp'd up) frantic Affection
Prompted me to do fomething in his Abfence
That might deliver you into my Power,
Which you fee is effected; and even now,
When my rebellious Paffions chide my Dulnefs,
And tell me how much I abufe my Fortunes;
Now 'tis in my Power to bear you hence,

       [*Cleora ftarts,*

Or take my Wifhes here, (nay, fear not, Madam,
True Love's a Servant, brutifh Luft a Tyrant,
I dare not touch thofe Viands that ne'er tafte well,
But when they're freely offer'd; Only thus much,
Be pleas'd I may fpeak in my own dear Caufe;
And think it worthy your Confideration
I have lov'd truly, (cannot fay deferv'd;
Since Duty muft not take the Name of Merit)

That I so far prize your Content, before
All Blessings that my Hope can fashion to me,
That willingly I entertain Despair,
And for your Sake embrace it.   For I know,
This Opportunity lost by no Endeavour
The like can be recover'd.   To conclude,
Forget not that I lose myself to save you.
For what can I expect but Death and Torture,
The War being ended ? And what is a Task
Would trouble *Hercules* to undertake,
I do deny you to myself, to give you
A pure unspotted Present to my Rival.
I've said : If it dictate not, best of Virgins,
Reward my Temperance with some lawful Favour,
Tho' you contemn my Person.

> [*Cleora kneels, then pulls off her Glove, and offers
> her Hand to* Pisander.

Timand. See, she kneels,
And seems to call upon the Gods to pay
The Debt she owes your Virtue : To perform which,
As a sure Pledge of Friendship, she vouchsafes you
Her Right-hand.

Pisan. I am paid for all my Sufferings.
Now, when you please, pass to your private Chamber,
My Love and Duty, faithful Guards, shall keep you

> [*Makes a low Courtesy as she goes off.*

From all Disturbance ; and when you are sated
With thinking of *Leosthenes*, as a Fee
Due to my Service, spare one Sigh for me.   [*Exeunt.*

SCENE III.

Enter Gracculo, *leading* Asotus *in an Ape's Habit, with a
Chain about his Neck.* Zanthia *in* Corisca's *Clothes, she
bearing up her Train.*

Grac. Come on, Sir.
Asot. Oh !

Grac. Do you grumble? You were ever
A brainlefs Afs; but, if this hold, I'll teach you
To come aloft, and do Tricks like an **Ape.**
Your Morning's Leffon! if you mifs—

Afot. O no, Sir!   [*Afotus makes Mouths.*

Grac. What for the *Carthaginians*?—A good Beaft.
What for ourfelf, your Lord?—Exceeding well.
                                                  [*Dances.*

There's your Reward. Not kifs your Paw? So, fo, fo.

Zant. Was ever Lady, the firft Day of her Honour,
So waited on by a wrinkled Crone? She looks now,
Without her Painting, Curling and Perfumes,
Lik the laft Day of *January*; and ftinks worfe
Than a hot Brach in the Dog-days. Farther off!
So—ftand there like an Image;—if you ftir,
'Till with a quarter of a Look I call you,
You know what follows.

Corif. O, what am I fallen to!
But 'tis a Punifhment for my Luft and Pride,
Juftly return'd upon me.

Grac. How doft thou like
Thy Ladyfhip, *Zanthia?*

Zant. Very well; and bear it
With as much State as your Lordfhip.

Grac. Give me thy Hand:
Let us like conqu'ring *Romans* walk in Triumph,
Our Captives following: Then mount our Tribunals,
And make the Slaves our Footftools.

Zant. Fine, by *Jove!*
Are your Hands clean, Minion?

Corif. Yes, forfooth.

Zant. Fall off then—
So, now come on; and, having made your three Duties,
—Down, I fay, (are you ftiff in the Hams?) now kneel,
And tie our Shoe. Now kifs it, and be happy.

Grac. This is State, indeed.

Zant. It is fuch as fhe taught me;
A tickling Itch of Greatnefs, your proud Ladies
Expect from their poor Waiters: We have chang'd
        Parts;

She does what she forc'd me to do in her Reign,
And I must practise it in mine.

Grac. 'Tis Justice;
O! here come more.

Enter Cimbrio, Cleon, Poliphron *and* Olympia.

Cimb. Discover to a Drachma,
Or I will famish thee.

Cleon. O! I'm pin'd already.

Cimb. Hunger shall force thee to cut off the Brawns
From thy Arms and Thighs, then broil them on the Coals
For Carbonades.

Poliph. Spare the old Jade, he's founder'd.

Grac. Cut his Throat then,
And hang him out for a Scarecrow.

Poliph. You have all your Wishes
In your Revenge, and I have mine. You see
I use no Tyranny: When I was her Slave
She kept me as a Sinner to lie at her Back
In frosty Nights, and fed me with high Dainties
Which still she had in her Belly again ere Morning;
And in Requital of those Courtesies,
Having made one another free, we are married,
And, if you wish us Joy, join with us in
A Dance at our Wedding.

Grac. Agreed; for I have thought of
A most triumphant one, which shall express
We are our Lords, and these our Slaves.

Poliph. But we shall want
A Woman.

Grac. No, here's *Jane of Apes* shall serve;——
Carry your Body swimming: Where's the Musick?

Poliph. I have plac'd it in yon Window.

                     [*The Dance at the End.*

Grac. Begin then sprightly.

Enter Pisander *unseen.*

Poliph. Well done on all Sides. I have prepar'd a Banquet;
Let's drink and cool us.

Grac. A good Motion.

Cimb. Wait here :——

You have been tired with Feafting, learn to faft now.

Grac, I'll have an Apple for *Jack,* and may be fome Scraps
May fall to your Share.

[*Exeunt* Gracculo, Zanthia, Cimbrio, Poliphron, *and* Olympia.

Corif. Whom can we accufe
But ourfelves for what we fuffer ? Thou art juft,
Thou all-creating Power! and Mifery
Inftructs me now, (that Yefterday acknowledg'd
No Deity beyond my Luft and Pride)
There is a Heaven above us, that looks down
With Eyes of Juftice, upon fuch as number
Thofe Bleffings freely given, in the Accompt
Of their poor Merits ; Elfe it could not be,
Now, miferable I, to pleafe whofe Palate
The Elements were ranfack'd, yet complain'd
Of Nature, as not liberal enough
In her Provifion of Rarities
To footh my Tafte and pamper my proud Flefh,
Should wifh in vain for Bread.

Cleon. Yes, I do wifh too
For what I fed my Dogs with.

Corif. I, that forgot
I was made of Flefh and Blood, and thought the Silks
Spun by the diligent Worm, out of their Entrails,
Too coarfe to clothe me, and the fofteft Down
Too hard to fleep on ; that difdain'd to look
On Virtue being in Rags : that ftopp'd my Nofe
At thofe that did not ufe adulterate Arts
To better Nature ; that from thofe that ferv'd me
Expected Adoration, am made juftly
The Scorn of my own Bondwoman.

Afot. I am punifh'd,
For feeking to cuckold mine own natural Father.
Had I been gelded then, or us'd myfelf
Like a Man, I had not been transform'd and forc'd
To play an o'ergrown Ape,

Cleon. I know I cannot
Laſt long, that's all my Comfort : Come, I forgive both;
It is in vain to be angry ; let us, therefore,
Lament together like Friends.

Piſan. What a true Mirrour
Were this ſad Spectacle for ſecure **Greatneſs** !
Here they, that never ſee themſelves, but in
The Glaſs of ſervile Flattery, might behold
The weak Foundation upon which they build
That truſt in human Frailty.   Happy are thoſe,
That knowing in their Births, they are ſubject to
Uncertain Change, are ſtill prepar'd, and arm'd
For either Fortune ! a rare Principle,
And with much Labour, learn'd in Wiſdom's School !
For, as theſe Bondmen by their Actions ſhew
That their Proſperity, like too large a Sail
For their ſmall Bark of Judgment, ſinks them with
A fore-right Gale of Liberty, ere they reach
The Port they long to touch at : So theſe Wretches,
Swoln with the falſe Opinion of their Worth,
And proud of Bleſſings left them, not acquir'd ;
That did believe they could with Giant Arms
Fathom the Earth, and were above their Fates,
Thoſe borrow'd Helps that did ſupport them vaniſh'd,
Fall of themſelves, and by unmanly ſuff'ring,
Betray their proper Weakneſs, and make known
Their boaſted Greatneſs was lent, not their own,

Cleon. O for ſome Meat : They ſit long.

Coriſ. We forgot,
When we drew out intemperate Feaſts till Midnight :
Their Hunger was not thought on, nor their Watchings;
Nor did we hold ourſelves ſerv'd to the Height,
But when we did exact and force their Duties
Beyond their Strength and Power.

Aſot. We pay for't now :
I now could be content to have my Head
Broke with a Rib of Beef, or for a Coffin,
Be bury'd in the Dripping-pan.

Enter Poliphron, Cimbrio, Gracculo, Zanthia, *and*
    Olympia, *drunk and quarrelling*.

Cimb. Do not hold me :
Not kifs the Bride ?
 Poliph. No, Sir.
Cimb. She's common Good,
And fo we'll ufe her.
 Grac. We'll have nothing private.
Olymp. Hold :—
Zant. Here, *Marullo.*—
Olymp. He's your Chief.
Cimb. We are Equals,
I will know no Obedience.
 Grac. Nor Superior.—
Nay, if you are Lion-drunk, I will make one ;
For lightly ever he that parts the Fray,
Goes away with the Blows.
 Pifan. Art thou mad too ?
No more, as you refpeft me.
 Poliph. I obey, Sir,
 Pifan. Quarrel among yourfelves ?
Cimb. Yes, in our Wine, Sir,
And for our Wenches.
 Grac. How could we be Lords elfe ?
 Pifan. Take Heed ; I've News will cool this Heat,
    and make you
Remember what you were.
 Cimb. How !
 Pifan. Send off thefe,
And then I'll tell you.   [Zanthia *beating* Corifca.
 Olymp. This is Tyranny,
Now fhe offends not.
 Zant. 'Tis for Exercife,
And to help Digeftion : What is fhe good for elfe ?
To me it was her Language.
 Pifan. Lead her off ;
And take Heed, Madam Minx, the Wheel may turn.
Go to your Meat, and Reft ; and from this Hour

Remember, He that is a Lord to Day,
May be a Slave To-morrow.

   Cleon. Good Morality!

   [*Exeunt* Cleon, Asotus, Zanthia, Olympia *and* Corisca.

   Cimb. But what would you impart?

   Pisan. What must invite you
To stand upon your Guard and leave your Feasting;
Or but imagine what it is to be
Most miserable, and rest assur'd you are so.
Our Masters are victorious,

   All. How!

   Pisan. Within
A Day's March of the City, flesh'd with Spoil,
And proud of Conquest; the *Armado* sunk;
The *Carthaginian* Admiral, Hand to Hand,
Slain by *Leosthenes.*

   Cimb. I feel the Whip
Upon my Back already.

   Grac. Every Man
Seek a convenient Tree and hang himself.

   Poliph. Better die once, than live an Age to suffer
New Tortures every Hour.

   Cimb. Say, we submit,
And yield us to their Mercy.

   Pisan. Can you flatter
Yourselves with such false Hopes? Or dare you think
That your imperious Lords, that never fail'd
To punish with Severity petty Slips
In your Neglect of Labour, may be won
To pardon those licentious Outrages,
Which noble Enemies forbear to practise
Upon the conquer'd? What have you omitted,
That may call on their just Revenge with Horror
And studied Cruelty? We have gone too far
To think now of retiring; in our Courage,
And During[9], lies our Safety; if you are not
Slaves in your abject Minds, as in your Fortunes,
Since to die is the worst, better expose

   9 *During*, unless *during* shall mean *enduring*. M. M.

Our naked Breaſts to their keen Swords, and ſell
Our Lives with the moſt Advantage, than to truſt
In a foreſtall'd Remiſſion, or yield up
Our Bodies to the Furnace of their Fury,
Thrice heated with Revenge.

 Grac. You led us on.

 Cimb. And 'tis but Juſtice you ſhould bring us off.

 Grac. And we expect it.

 Piſan. Hear then, and obey me;
And I will either ſave you or fall with you.
Man the Walls ſtrongly, and make good the Ports;
Boldly deny their Entrance, and rip up
Your Grievances, and what compell'd you to
This deſperate Courſe: If they diſdain to hear
Of Compoſition, we have in our Powers
Their aged Fathers, Children, and their Wives,
Who, to preſerve themſelves, muſt willingly
Make Interceſſion for us. 'Tis not Time now
To talk, but do. A glorious End, or Freedom
Is now propos'd us; ſtand reſolv'd for either,
And, like good Fellows, live or die together.

          [*Exeunt.*

SCENE IV.

Enter Leoſthenes *and* Timagoras.

 Timag. I am ſo far from Envy, I am proud
You have outſtripp'd me in the Race of Honour.
Oh! 'twas a glorious Day, and bravely won!
Your bold Performance gave ſuch Luſtre to
Timoleon's wiſe Directions, as the Army
Reſts doubtful, to whom they ſtand moſt engag'd
For their ſo great Succeſs.

 Leoſt. The Gods firſt honour'd,
The Glory be the General's; 'tis far from me
To be his Rival.

 Timag. You abuſe your Fortune,
To entertain her Choice and gracious Favours

With a contracted Brow; plum'd Victory
Is truly painted with a cheerful Look,
Equally distant from proud Insolence,
And base Dejection.

 Leost. O *Timagoras!*
You only are acquainted with the Cause,
That loads my sad Heart with a Hill of Lead;
Whose pond'rous Weight, neither my new-got Honour,
Assisted by the general Applause
The Soldiers crown it with, nor all War's Glories
Can lessen or remove: And, would you please,
With fit Consideration, to remember,
How much I wrong'd *Cleora*'s Innocence
With my rash Doubts; and what a grievous Penance
She did impose upon her tender Sweetness,
To pluck away the Vulture Jealousy
That fed upon my Liver, you cannot blame me,
But call it a fit Justice on myself,
Though I resolve to be a Stranger to
The Thought of Mirth or Pleasure.

 Timag. You have redeem'd
The Forfeit of your Fault with such a Ransom
Of honourable Action, as my Sister
Must of Necessity confess her Sufferings
Weigh'd down by your fair Merits; and, when she
   views you,
Like a triumphant Conqueror, carried thro'
The Streets of *Syracusa*, the glad People
Pressing to meet you, and the Senators
Contending who shall heap most Honours on you;
The Oxen crown'd with Garlands led before you
Appointed for the Sacrifice; and the Altars
Smoking with thankful Incense to the Gods:
The Soldiers chaunting loud Hymns to your Praise;
The Windows fill'd with Matrons and with Virgins,
Throwing upon your Head, as you pass by,
The choicest Flowers, and silently invoking
The Queen of Love, with their particular Vows,
To be thought worthy of you; can *Cleora*,

(Tho', in the Glafs of Self-love, fhe behold
Her beft Deferts) but with all Joy acknowledge,
What fhe endur'd was but a noble Trial
You made of her Affection? And her Anger,
Rifing from your too am'rous Fears, foon drench'd
In *Lethe*, and forgotten.

    Leoft. If thofe Glories
You fo fet forth were mine they might plead for me:
But I can lay no Claim to the leaft Honour
Which you with foul Injuftice ravifh from her.
Her Beauty in me wrought a Miracle,
Taught me to aim at Things beyond my Power,
Which her Perfections purchas'd, and gave to me
From her free Bounties; fhe infpir'd me with
That Valour which I dare not call mine own;
And, from the fair Reflexion of her Mind,
My Soul receiv'd the fparkling Beams of Courage.
She, from the Magazine of her proper Goodnefs
Stock'd me with virtuous Purpofes; fent me forth
To trade for Honour: and, fhe being the Owner
Of the Bark of my Adventures, I muft yield her
A juft Account of all, as 'fits a Factor:
And, howfoever others think me happy,
And cry aloud I've made a profp'rous Voyage,
One Frown of her Diflike at my Return,
(Which, as a Punifhment for my Fault, I look for)
Strikes dead all Comfort.

    Timag. Tufh! thefe Fears are needlefs,
She cannot, muft not, fhall not be fo cruel.
A free Confeffion of a Fault wins Pardon,
But, being feconded by Defert commands it.
The General is your own, and fure my Father
Repents his Harfhnefs: For myfelf, I am
Ever your Creature;—one Day fhall be happy
In your Triumph and your Marriage.

    Leoft. May it prove fo,
With her Confent and Pardon.

Timag. Ever touching
On that harſh String ? She is your own, and you
Without Diſturbance ſeize on what's your Due.

[*Exeunt.*

End of the Third Act.

ACT IV. SCENE I.

Enter Piſander *and* Timandra.

Piſander.

SHE has her Health, then ?
 Timand. Yes, Sir, and as often
As I ſpeak of you lends attentive Ear
To all that I deliver ; nor ſeems tir'd,
Tho' I dwell long on the Relation of
Your Suff'rings for her, heaping Praiſe on Praiſe
On your unequal'd Temperance and Command
You hold o'er your Affections.
 Piſan. To my Wiſh :
Have you acquainted her with the Defeat
Of the *Carthaginians,* and with what Honours
Leoſtheues comes crown'd home with ?
 Timand. With all Care.
 Piſan. And how does ſhe receive it ?
 Timand. As I gueſs,
With a ſeeming kind of Joy ; but yet appears not
Tranſported, or proud of his happy Fortune.
But when I tell her of the certain Ruin
You muſt encounter with at their Arrival
In *Syracuſa,* and that Death with Torments
Muſt fall upon you, which you yet repent not,
Eſteeming it a glorious Martyrdom,
And a Reward of pure unſpotted Love,

Preferv'd in the white Robe of Innocence,
Tho' she were in your Pow'r; and, still spurr'd on
By insolent Lust, you rather chose to suffer
The Fruit untasted, for whose glad Possession
You have call'd on the Fury of your Lord,
Than that she should be griev'd or tainted in
Her Reputation.

Pisan. Doth it work Compunction?
Pities she my Misfortune?

Timand. She exprefs'd
All Signs of Sorrow, which her Vow obferv'd,
Could witnefs a griev'd Heart.   At the first Hearing
She fell upon her Face, rent her fair Hair,
Her Hands held up to Heav'n, and vented Sighs
In which she silently seem'd to complain
Of Heav'n's Injustice.

Pisan. 'Tis enough.   Wait carefully,
And, upon all watch'd Occasions, continue
Speech and Difcourfe of me : 'Tis Time must work her.

Timand. I'll not be wanting ; but still strive to serve
     you.   [*Exit* Timand.

Enter Poliphron.

Pisan. Now, *Poliphron,* the News?
Poliph. The conquering Army
Is within Ken.

Pisan. How brook the Slaves the Object?
Poliph. Cheerfully yet; they do refuse no Labour,
And feem to fcoff at Danger : 'Tis your Prefence
That must confirm them; with a full Confent
You're chofen to relate the Tyranny
Of our proud Masters; and what you fubfcribe to,
They gladly will allow of, or hold out
To the last Man.

Pisan. I'll instantly among them :
If we prove conftant to ourfelves, good Fortune
Will not, I hope, forfake us.

Poliph. 'Tis our best Refuge.   [*Exeunt.*

SCENE II.

Enter Timoleon, Archidamus, Diphilus, Leofthenes,
Timagoras, *and others.*

Timol. Thus far we are return'd victorious; crown'd
With Wreaths triumphant, (Famine, Blood and
   Dearth,
Banifh'd your peaceful Confines) and bring home
Security and Peace. 'Tis therefore fit,
That fuch as boldly ftood the Shock of War,
And With the dear Expence of Sweat and Blood
Have purchas'd Honour, fhould with Pleafure reap
The Harveft of their Toil; and we ftand bound
Out of the firft File of the beft Defervers,
(Tho' all muft be confider'd to their Merits)
To think of you, *Leofthenes,* that ftand,
And worthily, moft dear in our Efteem,
For your heroic Valour.
 Archid. When I look on
(The Labour of fo many Men and Ages)
This well-built City, not long fince defign'd
To Spoil and Rapine, by the Favour of
The Gods, and you their Minifters, preferv'd,
I cannot, in my Height of Joy, but offer
Thefe Tears for a glad Sacrifice.
 Diph. Sleep the Citizens?
Or are they overwhelm'd with the Excefs
Of Comfort that flows to them?
 Leoft. We receive
A filent Entertainment.
 Timag. I long fince
Expected that the Virgins and the Matrons,
The old Men ftriving with their Age, the Priefts,
Carrying the Images of their Gods before 'em,
Should have met us with Proceffion.—Ha! the Gates
Are fhut againft us!

Archid. And upon the Walls
Arm'd Men feem to defy us!

Enter above Pifander, Poliphron, Cimbrio, Gracculo, *&c.*

Diph. I fhould know
Thefe Faces.—They are our Slaves.
Timag. The Myftery, Rafcals!
Open the Ports, and play not with an Anger
That will confume you.
Timol. This is above Wonder!
Archid. Our Bondmen ftand againft us?
Grac. Some fuch Things
We were in Man's Remembrance.—The Slaves are
  turn'd
Lords of the Town, or fo.—Nay, be not angry:
Perhaps, on good Terms, giving Security
You will be quiet Men, we may allow you
Some Lodgings in our Garrets or Out-houfes:
Your great Looks cannot carry it.
Cimb. The Truth is,
We've been bold with your Wives, toy'd with your
  Daughters——
Leoft. O my prophetic Soul!
Grac. Rifled your Chefts,
Been bufy with your Wardrobes.
Timag. Can we endure this?
Leoft. O! my *Cleora!*
Grac. A Caudle for the Gentleman,
He'll die o' th' Pip elfe.
Timag. Scorn'd too? Are you turn'd Stone?
Hold Parley with our Bondmen? Force our Entrance,
Then, Villains, expect——
Timol. Hold! you wear Men's Shapes,
And if, like Men, you've Reafon, fhew a Caufe
That leads you to this defperate Courfe, which muft
  end
In your Deftruction.

Grac. That, as pleafe the Fates;
But we vouchfafe.—Speak, Captain.

Timag. Hell and Furies!

Archid. Bay'd by our own Curs?

Cimb. Take heed you be not worry'd.

Poliph. We are fharp fet.

Cimb. And fudden.

Pifand. Briefly thus then,
Since I muft fpeak for all.—Your Tyranny
Drew us from our Obedience. Happy thofe Times
When Lords were ftyl'd Fathers of Families,
And not imperious Mafters! when they number'd
Their Servants almoft equal with their Sons,
Or one Degree beneath them; when their Labours
Were cherifh'd and rewarded, and a Period
Set to their Sufferings; when they did not prefs
Their Duties or their Wills beyond the Power
And Strength of their Performance; all Things
            order'd
With fuch Decorum as [10] wife Law-makers,
From each well-govern'd private Houfe deriv'd
The perfect Model of a Common-wealth.
Humanity then lodg'd i' th' Hearts of Men,
And thankful Mafters carefully provided
For Creatures wanting Reafon.   The noble Horfe,
That in his fiery Youth from his wide Noftrils
Neigh'd Courage to his Rider, and broke thro'
Groves of oppofed Pikes, bearing his Lord
Safe to triumphant Victory, old or wounded,
Was fet at Liberty and freed from Service.
The *Athenian* Mules, that from the Quarry drew
Marble, hew'd for the Temples of the Gods,
The great Work ended, were difmifs'd, and fed
At the publick Coft; nay, faithful Dogs have found
Their Sepulchres; but Man to Man more cruel,
Appoints no End to th' Sufferings of his Slave;
Since Pride ftepp'd in and Riot, and o'erturn'd
This goodly Frame of Concord, teaching Mafters

---

[10] *As*, in this Paffage, has the Force of *that*. M. M.

To glory in the Abuſe of ſuch as are
Brought under their Command ; who, grown unuſeful,
Are leſs eſteem'd than Beaſts.—This you have practis'd
Practis'd on us with Rigour ; this hath forc'd us
To ſhake our heavy Yokes off ; and, if Redreſs
Of theſe juſt Grievances be not granted us,
We'll right ourſelves, and by ſtrong Hand defend
What we are now poſſeſs'd of.

 Grac. And not leave
One Houſe unfir'd.

 Cimb. Or Throat uncut of thoſe
We have in our Power.

 Poliph. Nor will we fall alone ;
You ſhall buy us dearly.

 Timag. O the Gods !
Unheard of Inſolence !

 Timol. What are your Demands ?

 Piſan. A general Pardon firſt for all Offences
Committed in your Abſence : Liberty
To all ſuch as deſire to make Return
Into their Countries ; and to thoſe that ſtay
A Competence of Land freely allotted
To each Man's proper Uſe ; no Lord acknowledged.
Laſtly, with your Conſent, to chooſe them Wives
Out of your Families.

 Timag. Let the City ſink firſt.

 Leoſt. And Ruin ſeize on all, ere we ſubſcribe
To ſuch Conditions.

 Archid. Carthage, tho' victorious,
Could not have forc'd more from us.

 Leoſt. Scale the Wall !
Capitulate after.

 Timol. He that wins the Top firſt,
Shall wear a Mural Wreath.   [*Exeunt.*

 Piſan. Each to his Place.   [*Flouriſh and Arms.*
Or Death or Victory.—Charge them home, and fear
  not.

K 4

Enter Timoleon, Archidamus, *and Senators.*

Timol. We wrong ourfelves, and we are juftly pu-
    nifh'd,
To deal with Bondmen as if we encounter'd
An equal Enemy.
    Archid. They fight like Devils ;
And run upon our Swords, as if their Breafts
Were Proof beyond their Armour.

Enter Leofthenes *and* Timagoras.

Timag. Make a firm Stand.——
The Slaves not fatisfy'd they've beat us off,
Prepare to fally forth.
    Timol. They are wild Beafts,
And to be tam'd by Policy.——Each Man take
A tough Whip in his Hand, fuch as you us'd
To punifh them with as Mafters : In your Looks
Carry Severity and Awe ; 'twill frighten them
More than your Weapons : Salvage Lions fly from
The Sight of Fire ; and thefe that have forgot
That Duty you ne'er taught them with your Swords,
When, unexpected, they behold thofe Terrors
Advanc'd aloft that they were made to fhake at,
'Twill force them to remember what they are
And ftoop to due Obedience.

Enter Cimbrio, Gracculo, *and other Slaves.*

Archid. Here they come.
    Cimb. Leave not a Man alive : A Wound is but a
        Flea-biting,
To what we fuffer'd being Slaves.
    Grac. O, my Heart !
Cimbrio, what do we fee ? The Whip ! our Mafters ![11]

☞ 11 ————*The Whip ! our Mafters !*
    This reducing the Slaves by the Sight of rhe Whip, is taken
from the Story of the *Scythian* Slaves.

Timag. Dare you rebél, Slaves? ⸻

[*Senators fhake their Whips, and they throw
away their Weapons, and run off.*

Cimb. Mercy! Mercy! where ⸻
Shall we hide us from their Fury?

Grac. Fly! they follow.
Oh! we fhall be tormented.

Timol. Enter with them,
But yet forbear to kill 'em. Still remember
They are Part of your Wealth; and being difarm'd,
There is no Danger.

Archid. Let us firft deliver
Such as they have in Fetters, and at Leifure
Determine of their Punifhment.

Leoft. Friend, to you
I leave the Difpofition of what's mine:
I cannot think I am fafe without your Sifter.
She's only worth my Thought: and, 'till I fee
What fhe has fuffer'd I am on the Rack
And Furies my Tormentors.   [*Exeunt.*

SCENE III.

Enter Pifander *and* Timandra.

Pifan. I know I am purfu'd; nor would I fly,
Altho' the Ports were open, and a Convoy
Ready to bring me off.—The Bafenefs of
Thefe Villains from the Pride of all my Hopes,
Have thrown me to the bottomlefs Abyfs
Of Horror and Defpair. Had they ftood firm,
I could have bought *Cleora*'s free Confent
With the Safety of her Father's Life and Brother's;
And forc'd *Leofthenes* to quit his Claim,
And kneel a Suitor to me.

Timand. You muft not think
What might have been, but what muft now be practis'd,
And fuddenly refolve.

Pifand. All my poor Fortunes
Are at the Stake, and I muſt run the Hazard.
Unſeen, convey me to *Cleora's* Chamber;
For, in her Sight, if it were poſſible,
I would be apprehended.—Do not enquire
The Reaſon why but help me.

    Timand. Make Haſte.—One knocks.

                  [*Exit* Piſander.

Enter Leoſthenes.

Jove turn all to the beſt,—You are welcome, Sir.

    Leoſt. Thou giv'ſt it in a heavy Tone.

    Timand. Alas! Sir,
We have ſo long fed on the Bread of Sorrow,
Drinking the bitter Water of Afflictions,
Made loathſome too by our continued Fears,
Comfort's a Stranger to us.

    Leoſt. Fears? Your Suff'rings,
For which I am ſo overgone with Grief,
I dare not aſk without compaſſionate Tears
The Villain's Name that robb'd thee of thy Honour,
For being train'd up in Chaſtity's cold School,
And taught by ſuch a Miſtreſs as *Cleora,*
'Twere impious in me to think *Timandra*
Fell with her own Conſent.

    Timand. How mean you? Fell, Sir?
I underſtand you not.

    Leoſt. I would thou did'ſt not,
Or that I could not read upon thy Face,
In bluſhing Characters, the Story of
Libidinous Rape.—Confeſs it, for you ſtand not
Accountable for a Sin, againſt whoſe Strength
Your o'ermatch'd Innocence could make no Reſiſtance,
Under which Odds I know *Cleora* fell too,
Heav'ns Help in vain invok'd!—the amazed Sun
Hiding his Face behind a Maſk of Clouds,
Not daring to look on it.—In her Sufferings
All Sorrow's comprehended.—What *Timandra,*

Or the City has endur'd, her Lofs confider'd,
Deferves not to be nam'd.

Timand. Pray you, do not bring Sir,
In the Chimeras of your jealous Fears,
New Monfters to affright us.

Leoft. O *Timandra*,
That I had Faith enough but to believe thee!
I fhould receive it with a Joy beyond
Affurance of *Elyfian* Shades hereafter,
Or all the Bleffings in this Life a Mother
Could wifh her Children crown'd with,—But I muft not
Credit Impoffibilities ; yet I ftrive
To find out that whofe Knowledge is a Curfe,
And Ignorance a Bleffing.—Come, difcover
What Kind of Look he had that forc'd thy Lady,
(Thy Ravifher I will enquire at Leifure)
That when hereafter I behold a Stranger
But near him in Afpect, I may conclude
(Tho' Men and Angels fhould proclaim him honeft)
He is a hell-bred Villain.

Timand. You're unworthy
To know fhe is preferv'd, preferv'd untainted.
Sorrow (but ill beftow'd) hath only made
A Rape upon her Comforts in your Abfence.

[*Exit, and returns with* Cleora [12].
Come forth, dear Madam,

Leoft. Ha! [*Kneels.*

Timand. Nay, fhe deferves
The bending of your Heart, that to content you,
Has kept a Vow, the Breach of which a Veftal
(Tho' the infringing it had call'd upon her
A living Funeral) muft of Force have fhrunk at.
No Danger could compel her to difpenfe with
Her cruel Penance ; tho' hot Luft came arm'd
To feize upon her ; when one Look or Accent
Might have redeem'd her.

[12] A Gentleman, diftinguifhed not more for his Learning than his fine Genius, obferved that this Scene between *Leoftbenes* and *Cleora* was one of the beft that he ever read.

Leoſt. Might ? O do not ſhew me
A Beam of Comfort, and ſtraight take it from me.
—— The Means by which ſhe was freed ?—Speak, O
        ſpeak quickly !
Each Minute of Delay's an Age of Torment :
O ! ſpeak *imandra !*
    Timand. Free her from the Oath,
Herſelf can beſt deliver it.   [*Takes off the Scarf,*
    Leoſt. O bleſt Office !
Never did Galley-ſlave ſhake off his Chains,
Or look'd on his Redemption from the Oar,
With ſuch true Feeling of Delight as now
I find myſelf poſſeſs'd of.—Now I behold
True Light indeed : For, ſince theſe faireſt Stars
(Cover'd with Clouds of your determinate Will)
Deny'd their Influence to my Optick Senſe,
The Splendor of the Sun appear'd to me
But as ſome little Glimpſe of his bright Beams
Convey'd into a Dungeon, to remember
The dark Inhabitants there how much they wanted,
Open theſe long-ſhut Lips, and ſtrike mine Ears
With Muſick more harmonious than the Spheres
Yield in their heav'nly Motions : And, if ever
A true Submiſſion for a Crime acknowledg'd
May find a gracious Hearing, teach your Tongue
In the firſt ſweet articulate Sounds it utters,
To ſign my wiſh'd-for Pardon.
    Cleora. I forgive you.
    Leoſt. How greedily I receive this ! Stay, beſt Lady,
And let me by Degrees aſcend the Height
Of human Happineſs ! All at once deliver'd,
The Torrent of my Joys will overwhelm me ;——
So, now a little more ; and pray excuſe me,
If like a wanton Epicure I deſire
The pleaſant Taſte theſe Cates of Comfort yield me,
Should not too ſoon be ſwallow'd. Have you not
(By your unſpotted Truth I do conjure you
To anſwer truly) ſuffer'd in your Honour

(By Force, I mean, for in your Will I free you) ...
Since I left *Syracufa* ?

    Cleora. I reftore
.This Kifs, (fo help me Goodnefs!) which I borrow'd
When I laft faw you.

    Leoft. Miracle of Virtue!
One Paufe more, I befeech you :—I am like
A Man whofe vital Spirits confum'd and wafted
With a long and tedious Fever, unto whom
Too much of a ftrong Cordial at once taken,
Brings Death and not reftores him... Yet I cannot
Fix here; but muft enquire the Man to whom
I ftand indebted for a Benefit,
Which to requite at full, tho' in this Hand
I grafp'd all Scepters the World's Empire bows to,
Would leave me a poor Bankrupt.—Name him, Lady,
If of a mean Eftate, I'll gladly part with
My utmoft Fortunes to him—but if Noble,
In thankful Duty ftudy how to ferve him :
Or, if of higher Rank, erect him Altars,
And as a God adore him..

    Cleora. If that Goodnefs
And noble Temperance, the Queen of Virtues,
Bridling rebellious Paffions (to whofe Sway
Such as have conquer'd Nations have liv'd Slaves)
Did ever wing great Minds to fly to Heaven ;
He that preferv'd mine Honour, may hope boldly
To fill a Seat among the Gods and fhake off
Our frail Corruption.

    Leoft. Forward.

    Cleora. Or if ever
The Powers above did mafk in human Shapes,
To teach Mortality, not by cold Precepts
Forgot as foon as told, but by Examples
To imitate their Purenefs, and draw near
To their celeftial Natures—I believe
He's more than Man.

    Leoft. You do defcribe a Wonder.

Cleora. Which will increase, when you shall un
stand
He was a Lover.

Leost. Not yours, Lady?

Cleora. Yes;
Lov'd me, *Leosthenes*; nay more, so doted,
(If e'er Affections scorning gross Desires
May without Wrong be styl'd so) that he durst not
With an immodest Syllable or Look,
In Fear it might take from me, whom he made
The Object of his better Part, discover
I was the Saint he su'd too.

Leost. A rare Temper!

Cleora. I cannot speak it to the Worth : All Praise
I can bestow upon it, will appear
Envious Detraction. Not to rack you further,
Yet make the Miracle full ; tho', of all Men,
He hated you, *Leosthenes*, as his Rival ;
So high yet prized he my Content, that, knowing
You were a Man I favour'd, he disdain'd not
Against himself to serve you.

Leost. You conceal still
The Owner of these Excellencies.

Cleora. 'Tis *Marullo*,
My Father's Bondman.

Leost. Ha, ha, ha!

Cleora. Why do you laugh?

Leost. To hear the lab'ring Mountain of your Praise
Deliver'd of a Mouse.

Cleora. The Man deserves not
This Scorn I do assure you.

Leost. Do you call
What was his Duty Merit?

Cleora. Yes, and place it
As high in my Esteem, as all the Honours
Descended from your Ancestors, or the Glory,
Which you may call your own, got in this Action,
In which, I must confess, you have done nobly,
And I could add as I desir'd ;—but that
I fear 'twould make you proud.

Leoft. Why, Lady, can you
Be won to give Allowance that your Slave
Should dare to love you ?

Cleora. The immortal Gods [13]
Accept the meaneſt Altars that are rais'd
By pure Devotions ; and ſometimes prefer
An Ounce of Frankincenſe, Honey or Milk,
Before whole *Hecatombs* or *Sabæan* Gums
Offer'd in Oſtentation.—Are you ſick   [*Aſide.*
Of your old Diſeaſe ? I'll fit you.

Leoft. You ſeem mov'd.

Cleora. Zealous, I grant, in the Defence of Virtue.
Why, good *Leoſthenes,* tho' I endur'd
A Penance for your Sake above Example,
I have not ſo far ſold myſelf, I take it,
To be at your Devotion, but I may
Cheriſh Deſert in others where I find it.
How would you tyrannize, if you ſtood poſſeſs'd of
That which is only yours in Expectation,
That now preſcribe ſuch hard Conditions to me ?

Leoft. One Kiſs, and I am ſilenc'd.

Cleora. I vouchſafe it ;
Yet, I muſt tell you 'tis a Favour that
Marullo, when I was his, not mine own,
Durſt not preſume to aſk : No ; when the City
Bow'd humbly to licentious Rapes and Luſt ;
And when I was, of Men and Gods forſaken,
Deliver'd to his Power, he did not preſs me
To grace him with one Look or Syllable,
Or urg'd the Diſpenſation of an Oath
Made for your Satisfaction—The poor Wretch
Having related only his own Suff'rings,
And kiſs'd my Hand which I could not deny him,
Defending me from others, never ſince

☞ [13] *The immortal Gods
Accept the meaneſt Altars,* &c.

Milton's Invocation on the Opening of *Paradiſe Loſt* is not unlike this.

And chiefly thou, O Spirit, that doſt prefer
Before all Temples th' upright Heart and pure.

Solicited my Favours.

Leoſt. Pray you end ;
The Story does not pleaſe me.

Cleora. Well, take Heed
Of Doubts and Fears ;—for know, *Leoſthenes,*
A greater Injury cannot be offer'd
To innocent Chaſtity than unjuſt Suſpition.
I love *Marullo*'s fair Mind, not his Perſon ;
Let that ſecure you. And I here command you,
If I have any Power in you, to ſtand
Between him and all Puniſhment, and oppoſe
His Temperance to his Folly ; if you fail——
No more ; I will not threaten. [*Exit.*

Leoſt. What a Bridge
Of Glaſs I walk upon over a River
Of certain Ruin ! Mine own weighty Fears
Cracking what ſhould ſupport me :—And thoſe Helps,
Which Confidence yields to others, are from me
Raviſh'd by Doubts and wilful Jealouſy. [*Exit.*

SCENE IV.

Enter Timagoras, Cleon, Aſotus, Coriſca, *and* Olympia.

Cleon. But are you ſure we're ſafe ?

Timag. You need not fear :
They are all under Guard ; their Fangs par'd off :
The Wounds their Inſolence gave you to be cur'd
With the Balm of your Revenge.

Aſot. And ſhall I be
The Thing I was born my Lord ?

Timag. The ſame wiſe Thing——
'Slight, what a Beaſt they have made thee ! *Africk* never
Produc'd the like.

Aſot. I think ſo.—Nor the Land
Where Apes and Monkeys grow, like Crabs and Wal-
nuts
On the ſame Tree. Not all the Catalogue
Of Conjurers or wiſe Women, bound together

Could have so soon transform'd me, as my Rascal
Did with his Whip; Not in Outside only,
But in my own Belief, I thought myself
As perfect a Baboon——

Timag. An Ass thou wert ever.

Asot. And would have giv'n one Leg, with all my Heart,
For good Security to have been a Man
After three Lives, or one and twenty Years,
Tho' I had dy'd on Crutches.

Cleon. Never Varlets
So triumph'd o'er an old fat Man—I was famish'd.

Timag. Indeed you are fall'n away.

Asot. Three Years of Feeding
On Cullises and Jelly, tho' his Cooks
Lard all he eats with Marrow, or his Doctors
Pour in his Mouth Restoratives as he sleeps,
Will not recover him.

Timag. But your Ladyship looks
Sad on the Matter, as if you had miss'd
Your ten-crown Amber Posfets, good to smooth
The *Cutis* *, as you call it, and prepare you
Active, and high for an Afternoon's Encounter
With a rough Gamester on your Couch. Fie on't,
You are grown thrifty; smell like other Women,
The College of Physicians have not sat,
As they were us'd in Council, how to fill
The Crannies in your Cheeks, or raise a Rampire
With Mummy, Ceruses, or Infants' Fat
To keep off Age and Time.

Corif. Pray you, forbear;
I am an alter'd Woman.

Timag. So it seems ;—
A Part of your Honour's Ruff stands out of Rank too.

Corif. No Matter; I have other Thoughts.

Timag. O strange!
Not ten Days since it would have vex'd you more
Than th' Loss of your good Name; Pity, this Cure

Vol. II.   L

* That is, the Skin.

For your proud Itch came no fooner !—Marry, *Olympia*
Seems to bear up ftill.

 Olymp. I complain not, Sir !
I have borne my Fortune patiently.

 Timag. Thou wert ever
An excellent Bearer ; fo is all your Tribe,
If you may choofe your Carriage :—How now, Friend,
Looks our *Cleora* lovely ?

Enter Leofthenes, *and* Diphilus, *with a Guard.*

 Leoft. In my Thoughts, Sir.
 Timag. But why this Guard ?
 Diph. It is *Timoleon*'s Pleafure ;
The Slaves have been examin'd, and confefs
Their Riot took Beginning from your Houfe :
And the firft Mover of them to Rebellion,
Your Slave *Marullo.*

 Leoft. Ha ! I more than fear——
 Timag. They may fearch boldly.

Enter Timandra.

 Timand. You are unmanner'd Grooms
To pry into my Lady's private Lodgings ;
There's no *Marullos* there.

Enter Diphilus *with* Pifander.

 Timag. Now I fufpect too ;——
Where found you him ?

 Diph. Clofe hid in your Sifter's Chamber.
 Timag. Is that the Villain's Sanctuary ?
 Leoft. This confirms
All fhe deliver'd, falfe.

 Timag. But that I fcorn
To ruft my Sword in thy flavifh Blood,
Thou now wert dead.

 Pifan. He's more a Slave than Fortune

Or Mifery can make me, that infults
Upon unweapon'd Innocence.

Timag. Prate you, Dog?

Pifan. Curs fnap at Lions in the Toil, whofe Looks
Frighted them, being free.

Timag. As a wild Beaft,
Drive him before you.

Pifan. O divine *Cleora!*

Leoft. Dar'ft thou prefume to name her?

Pifan. Yes, and love her:
And may fay have deferv'd her.

Timag. Stop his Mouth:
Load him with Irons too.   [*Exit Guard with* Pifand.

Cleon. I am deadly fick
To look on him.

Afot. If he get loofe, I know it,
I caper like an Ape again—I feel
The Whip already.

Timand. This goes to my Lady.   [*Afide.*

Timag. Come, cheer you, Sir; we'll urge his Punifh-
    ment
To the full Satisfaction of your Anger.

Leoft. He is not worth my Thoughts.—No Corner
    left
In all the fpacious Rooms of my vex'd Heart,
But is fill'd with *Cleora:* And the Rape
She has done upon her Honour, with my Wrong,
The heavy Burthen of my Sorrow's Song.   [*Exeunt.*

End of the Fourth Act.

ACT V. SCENE I.

Enter Archidamus *and Cleora.*

Archidamus.

THOU art thine own Difpofer.—Were his Ho-
   nours
And Glories centupled, (as I muft confefs,
Leofthenes is moft worthy) yet I will not,
However I may counfel, force Affection.
 Cleora. It needs not, Sir; I prize him to his Worth,
Nay, love him truly; yet would not live flav'd
To his jealous Humours: Since, by the Hopes of Hea-
   ven,
As I am free from Violence, in a Thought
I am not guilty.
 Archid. 'Tis believ'd, *Cleora*;
And much the rather, (our great Gods be prais'd for't)
In that I find, beyond my Hopes, no Sign
Of Riot in my Houfe, but all Things order'd
As if I had been prefent.
 Cleora. May that move you
To pity poor *Marullo.*
 Archid. 'Tis my Purpofe
To do him all the Good I can, *Cleora:*
But this Offence being againft the State,
Muft have a publick Trial.—In the mean Time,
Be careful of yourfelf, and ftand engag'd
No further to *Leofthenes* than you may
Come off with Honour: For, being once his Wife,
You are no more your own, nor mine, but muft
Refolve to ferve and fuffer his Commands,
And not difpute 'em—ere it be too late,
Confider it duly. I muft to the Senate. [*Exit Archid.*

Cleora. I'm much diftracted; in *Leofthenes*
I can find nothing juftly to accufe,
But this Excefs of Love, which I have ftudied
To cure with more than common Means; yet ftill
It grows upon him. And, if I may call
His Sufferings Merit, I ftand bound to think on
Marullo's Dangers—tho' I fave his Life,
His love is unrewarded,—I confefs,
Both have deferv'd me; yet of Force I muft be
Unjuft to one—Such is my Deftiny.

Enter Timandra.

How now ? Whence flow thefe Tears ?
   Timand. I have met, Madam,
An Object of fuch Cruelty, as would force
A Savage to Compaffion.
   Cleora. Speak—What is it ?
   Timand. Men pity Beafts of Rapine, if o'ermatch'd,
Tho' baited for their Pleafure :—But thefe Monfters,
Upon a Man that can make no Refiftance,
Are fenfelefs in their Tyranny.—Let it be granted,
Marullo is a Slave; he's ftill a Man ;——
A Capital Offender ; yet in Juftice
Not to be tortur'd, till the Judge pronounce
His Punifhment.
   Cleora. Where is he ?
   Timand. Dragg'd to Prifon
With more than barb'rous Violence, fpurn'd and fpit on
By the infulting Officers; his Hands
Pinion'd behind his Back ; loaden with Fetters ;
Yet, with a Saint-like Patience, he ftill offers
His Face to their rude Buffets.
   Cleora. O my griev'd Soul !
By whofe Command ?
   Timand. It feems, my Lord your Brother,
For he's a Looker-on :—And it takes from
Honour'd *Leofthenes* to fuffer it,

For his Refpects to you, whofe Name in vain
The griev'd Wretch loudly calls on.

 Cleora. By *Diana*,
'Tis bafe in both, and to their Teeth I'll tell 'em
That I am wrong'd in't.   [*As going forth.*

 Timand. What will you do?

 Cleora. In Perfon
Vifit and comfort him.

 Timand. That will bring Fuel
To the jealous Fires which burn too hot already]
In Lord *Leofthenes.*

 Cleora. Let them confume him;——

I am Miftrefs of myfelf. Where Cruelty reigns,
There dwells nor Love nor Honour. [*Exit* Cleora.

 Timand. So, it works.
Tho' hitherto I've run a defp'rate Courfe
To ferve my Brother's Purpofes, now 'tis fit

   Enter Leofthenes *and* Timagoras.

I ftudy mine own Ends. They come.—Affift me
In thefe my Undertakings, Love's great Patron,
As my Intents are honeft.

 Leoft. 'Tis my Fault.
Diftruft of others fprings, *Timagoras*,
From Diffidence in ourfelves. But I will ftrive,
With the Affurance of my Worth and Merits,
To kill this Monfter Jealoufy.

 Timag. 'Tis a Gueft
In Wifdom, never to be entertain'd
On trivial Probabilities; but when
He does appear in pregnant Proofs, not fafhion'd
By idle Doubts and Fears, to be receiv'd,
They make their own Horns that are too fecure,
As well as fuch as give them Growth and Being
From meer Imagination. Though I prize
Cleora's Honour equal with mine own;
And know what large Additions of Power
This Match brings to our Family, I prefer
Our Friendfhip, and your Peace of Mind fo far

Above my own Refpeḋts or hers, that if
She hold not her true Value in the Teſt,
'Tis far from my Ambition for her Cure,
That you ſhould wound yourſelf.

   Timand. This argues for me.   [*Aſide.*

   Timag. Why ſhe ſhould be ſo paſſionate for a Bond-
      man,
Falls not in Compaſs of my Underſtanding,
But for ſome nearer Intereſt; or he raiſe
This Mutiny, if he lov'd her (as, you ſay,
She does confeſs he did) but to enjoy,
By fair or foul Play, what he ventur'd for,
To me's a Riddle.

   Leoſt. 'Pray you, no more; already
I have anſwer'd that objeḋtion in my ſtrong
Aſſurance of her Virtue.

   Timag. 'Tis unfit then,
That I ſhould preſs it farther.

   Timand. Now I muſt

              [Timandra *ſteps out diſtraḋtedly.*
Make in, or all is loſt.

   Timag. What would *Timandra ?*

   Leoſt. How wild ſhe looks !—How is it with thy
      Lady ?

   Timag. Colleḋt thyſelf and ſpeak.

   Timand. As you are noble,
Have Pity, or love Pity. Oh !——

   Leoſt. Take Breath.

   Timag. Out with it boldly.

   Timan. Oh ! the beſt of Ladies,
I fear, is gone for ever.

   Leoſt. Who, *Cleora ?*

   Timag. Deliver, how.—'Sdeath, be a Man, Sir! ſpeak.

   Timand. Take it then in as many Sighs as Words :
My Lady——

   Timag. What of her ?

   Timand. No ſooner heard
Marullo was impriſon'd, but ſhe fell
Into a deadly Swoon.

Timag. But she recover'd?
Say so, or he will sink too: Hold, Sir! fie,
This is unmanly.

Timand. Brought again to Life,
But with much Labour, she awhile stood silent,
Yet in that Interim vented Sighs, as if
They labour'd from the Prison of her Flesh,
To give her griev'd Soul Freedom. On the sudden
Transported on the Wings of Rage and Sorrow,
She flew out of the House, and, unattended,
Enter'd the common Prison.

Leost. This confirms
What but before I fear'd.

Timand. There you may find her;
And, if you love her as a Sister——

Timag. Damn her!

Timand. Or you respect her Safety, as a Lover
Procure *Marullo's* Liberty.

Timag. Impudence
Beyond Expression!

Leost. Shall I be a Bawd
To her Lust and my Dishonour?

Timand. She'll run mad, else,
Or do some violent Act upon herself.
My Lord, her Father, sensible of her Suff'rings,
Labours to gain his Freedom:

Leost. O, the Devil!
Has she bewitch'd him too?

Timag. I'll hear no more:
Come, Sir, we'll follow her; and if no Persuasion
Can make her take again her natural Form,
Which by Lust's powerful Spell she has cast off,
This Sword shall disenchant her.

Leost. O my Heart-Strings!

[*Exeunt* Leosthenes *and* Timagoras.

Timand. I knew 'twould take. Pardon me, fair
Cleora,
Though I appear a Traytress; which thou wilt do
In pity of my Woes, when I make known
My lawful Claim, and only seek mine own.   [*Exit.*

SCENE II.   *A Prison.*

Enter Cleora, *Jaylor, and* Pifander.

Cleora. There's for your Privacy.—Stay, unbind his
    Hands.
Jaylor. I dare not, Madam.
Cleora. I will buy thy Danger,
Take more Gold.—Do not trouble me with Thanks;
I do fuppofe it done.   [*Exit Jaylor.*
    Pifan. My better Angel
Affumes this Shape to comfort me, and wifely;
Since from the Choice of all celeftial Figures,
He could not take a vifible Form fo full
Of glorious Sweetnefs.   [*Kneels.*
    Cleora. Rife—I am Flefh and Blood,
And do partake thy Tortures.
    Pifan. Can it be?
That Charity fhould perfuade you to defcend
So far from your own Height as to vouchfafe
To look upon my Suff'rings? How I blefs
My Fetters now, and ftand engag'd to Fortune
For my Captivity—no, my Freedom rather!
For who dare think that Place a Prifon, which
You fanctify with your Prefence? Or believe,
Sorrow has Power to ufe her Sting on him,
That is in your Compaffion arm'd, and made
Impregnable? Tho' Tyranny raife at once
All Engines to affault him.
    Cleora. Indeed Virtue,
With which you have made evident Proofs that you
Are ftrongly fortified, can't fall, tho' fhaken
With the Shock of fierce Temptations; but ftill
      triumphs
In Spight of Oppofition. For myfelf,
I may endeavour to confirm your Goodnefs,
(A fure Retreat which never will deceive you)

And with unfeigned Tears exprefs my Sorrow
For what I cannot help——   [*Weeps.*

 Pifan. Do you weep for me!
O! fave that precious Balm for noble Ufes!
I am unworthy of the fmalleft Drop,
Which, in your Prodigality of Pity,
You throw away on me. Ten of thefe Pearls
Were a large Ranfom to redeem a Kingdom
From a confuming Plague, or ftop Heav'n's Vengeance,
Call'd down by crying Sins, tho' at that Inftant
In dreadful Flafhes falling on the Roofs
Of bold Blafphemers. I am juftly punifh'd
For my Intent of Violence to fuch Purenefs;
And all the Torments Flefh is fenfible of
A foft and gentle Penance.
 Cleora. Which is ended
In this your free Confeffion.

Enter Leofthenes and Timagoras unfeen.

 Leoft. What an Object
Have I encounter'd?
 Timag. I am blafted too!
Yet hear a little further.
 Pifan. Could I expire now,
Thefe white and innocent Hands clofing my Eyes thus,
'Twere not to die, but in a heav'nly Dream
To be tranfported, without the Help of *Charon,*
To the *Elyfian* Shades,—You make me bold;
And, but to wifh fuch Happinefs, I fear,
May give Offence——
 Cleora. No, for believ't *Marullo,*
You've won fo much upon me, that I know not
That Happinefs in my Gift but you may challenge.
 Leoft. Are you yet fatisfied?
 Cleora. Nor can you wifh
But what my Vows will fecond, tho' it were
Your Freedom firft, and then in me full Power
To make a fecond Tender of myfelf,
And you receive the Prefent. By this Kifs

(From me a Virgin Bounty) I will practife
All Arts for your Deliverance ; and that purchas'd
In what concerns your farther Aims, I fpeak it,
Do not defpair, but hope.

 Timag. To have the Hangman,
When he is married to the Crofs, in Scorn
To fay, Gods give you Joy.

 Leoft. But look on me,   [*To* Cleora.
And be not too indulgent to your Folly ;
And then (but that Grief ftops my Speech) imagine
What Language I fhould ufe.

 Cleora. Againft thyfelf.——
Thy Malice cannot reach me.

 Timag. How ?

 Cleora. No, Brother !
Tho' you join in the Dialogue t' accufe me,
What I have done, I'll juftify ; and thefe Favours,
Which you prefume will taint me in my Honour :
Tho' Jealoufy ufe all her Eyes to fpy out
One Stain in my Behaviour, or Envy
As many Tongues to wound it, fhall appear
My beft Perfections.   For, to the World,
I can in my Defence alledge fuch Reafons,
As my Accufers fhall ftand dumb to hear 'em ;
When in his Fetters this Man's Worth and Virtues,
But truly told, fhall fhame your boafted Glories,
Which Fortune claims a Share in.

 Timag. The bafe Villain
Shall never live to hear it.

    [*Offers to ftab* Pifander, Cleora *interpofes.*
 Cleora. Murther ! help !
Thro' me you fhall pafs to him.

  Enter Archidamus, Diphilus, *and Officers.*

 Archid. What's the Matter ?
On whom is your Sword drawn ? Are you a Judge ?
Or elfe ambitious of the Hangman's Office
Before it be defign'd you ? You are bold too !
Unhand my Daughter.

Leoſt. She's my Valour's Prize.

Archid. With her Conſent, not otherwiſe.   You may
     urge
Your Title in the Court; if it prove good,
Poſſeſs her freely : Guard him ſafely off too.

Timag. You'll hear me, Sir ?

Archid. If you have aught to ſay,
Deliver it in public ; all ſhall find
A juſt Judge of *Timoleon.*

Diphil. You muſt
Of Force now uſe your Patience.

          [*Exeunt* Archidamus, Diphilus, *and Guards.*

Timag. Vengeance rather !
Whirlwinds of Rage poſſeſs me ! you are wrong'd
Beyond a Stoick's Suff'rance ; yet you ſtand
As you were rooted.

Leoſt. I feel ſomething here,
That boldly tells me all the Love and Service
I pay *Cleora* is another's Due,
And therefore cannot proſper.

Timag. Melancholy !
Which now you muſt not yield to.

Leoſt. 'Tis apparent.
In Fact your Siſter's innocent, however
Chang'd by her violent Will.

Timag. If you believe ſo,
Follow the Chace ſtill ; and in open Court
Plead your own Intereſt : We ſhall find the Judge
Our Friend, I fear not.

Leoſt. Something I ſhall ſay,
But what——

Timag. Collect yourſelf as we walk thither.
                              [*Exeunt.*

SCENE III.[14]

The Court of Justice.

Enter Timoleon, Archidamus, Cleora, *and Officers.*

Timol. 'Tis wond'rous ftrange! nor can it fall within
The Reach of my Belief, a Slave fhould be
The Owner of a Temperance which this Age
Can hardly parallel in free-born Lords,
Or Kings proud of their Purple.

   Archid. 'Tis moft true;
And, tho' at firft it did appear a Fable,
All Circumftances meet to give it Credit;
Which works fo on me, that I am compell'd
To be a Suitor, not to be deny'd,
He may have equal Hearing.

   Cleora. Sir, you grac'd me
With the Title of your Miftrefs; but my Fortune
Is fo far diftant from Command, that I
Lay by the Power you gave me, and plead humbly
For the Preferver of my Fame and Honour.
And pray you, Sir, in Charity believe,
That, fince I had Ability of Speech,
My Tongue hath been fo much inur'd to Truth,
I know not how to lie.

   Timol. I'll rather doubt
The Oracles of the Gods, than queftion what
Your Innocence delivers; and, as far
As Juftice with mine Honour can give Way,
He fhall have Favour. Bring him in unbound:

                        [*Exeunt Officers.*
And 'tho' *Leofthenes* may challenge from me,
For his late worthy Service, Credit to
All Things he can alledge in his own Caufe,

☞ 14 This laft Scene is one of the beft concerted and the moft
furprifing Cataftrophe, that ever I met with in any Play whatever.

Marullo (ſo I think you call his Name)
Shall find I do reſerve one Ear for him

Enter Cleon, Aſotus, Diphilus, Olympia, *and* Coriſca.

To let in Mercy: Sit, and take your Places:
The Right of this fair Virgin firſt determin'd,
Your Bondmen ſhall be cenſur'd.

  Cleon. With all Rigour
We do expect.————
  Coriſ. Temper'd, I ſay, with Mercy.

Enter at one Door Leoſthenes *and* Timagoras; *at the
other, Officers with* Piſander *and* Timandra.

  Timol. Your Hand, *Leoſthenes:* I cannot doubt
You that have been victorious in the War,
Should in a Combat, fought with Words, come off
But with aſſured Triumph.

  Leoſt. My Deſerts, Sir,
(If without Arrogance I may ſtile them ſuch)
Arm me from Doubt and Fear.

  Timol. 'Tis nobly ſpoken!
Nor be thou daunted (howſoe'er thy Fortune
Has mark'd thee out a Slave) to ſpeak thy Merits;
For Virtue, tho' in Rags, may challenge more
Than Vice ſet off with all the Trim of Greatneſs,

  Piſan. I'd rather fall under ſo juſt a Judge,
Than be acquitted by a Man corrupt
And partial in his Cenſure.

  Archid. Note his Language!
It reliſhes of better Breeding than
His preſent State dares promiſe.

  Timol. I obſerve it.————
Place the fair Lady in the Midſt, that both,
Looking with covetous Eyes upon the Prize
They are to plead for, may, from the fair Object,
Teach *Hermes* Eloquence.

  Leoſt. Am I fall'n ſo low?
My Birth, my Honour, and, what's deareſt to me,

My Love, and Witnefs of my Love, my Service,
So undervalu'd that I muft contend
With one where my excefs of Glory muft
Make his O'erthrow a Conqueft? Shall my Fulnefs
Supply Defeéts in fuch a Thing, that never
Knew any Thing but Want and Emptinefs,
Give him a Name, and keep it fuch from this
Unequal Competition? If my Pride,
Or any bold Affurance of my Worth,
Has pluck'd this Mountain of Difgrace upon me,
I'm juftly punifh'd, and fubmit; but if
I have been modeft, and efteem'd myfelf
More injur'd in the Tribute of the Praife,
Which no Defert of mine priz'd by Self-Love
Ever exaéted; may this Caufe and Minute
For ever be forgotten. I dwell long
Upon mine Anger, and now turn to you,
Ungrateful Fair One; and, fince you are fuch,
'Tis lawful for me to proclaim myfelf,
And what I have deferv'd.

    Cleora. Negleét and Scorn
From me for this proud Vaunt.

    Leoft. You nourifh, Lady,
Your own Difhonour in this harfh Reply,
And almoft prove what fome hold of your Sex,
You're all made up of Paffion: For, if Reafon
Or Judgment could find Entertainment with you,
Or that you would diftinguifh of the Objeéts
You look on in a true Glafs; not feduc'd
By the falfe Light of your too violent Will,
I fhould not need to plead for that which you
With Joy fhould offer.—Is my high Birth a Blemifh?
Or does my Wealth, which all the vain Expence
Of Women cannot wafte, breed Loathing in you?
The Honours I can call mine own thought Scandals?
Am I deform'd, or for my Father's Sins
Muléted by Nature? If you interpret thefe
As Crimes, 'tis fit I fhould yield up myfelf
Moft miferably guilty: But, perhaps,
(Which yet I would not credit) you have feen

This Gallant pitch the Bar, or bear a Burthen
Would crack the Shoulders of a weaker Bondman;
Or any other boist'rous Exercise,
Assuring a strong Back to satisfy
Your loose Desires insatiate as the Grave.

 Cleora. You are foul-mouth'd.

 Archid. Ill-manner'd too.

 Leost. I speak
In the Way of Supposition, and intreat you,
With all the Fervour of a constant Lover,
That you would free yourself from these Aspersions,
Or any Imputation black tongu'd Slander
Could throw on your unspotted Virgin Whiteness;
To which there is no easier Way, than by
Vouchsafing him your Favour; him, to whom
Next to the General, and to the Gods,
The Country owes her Safety.

 Timag. Are you stupid?
'Slight, leap into his Arms, and there ask Pardon——
Oh! you expect your Slave's Reply; no Doubt
We shall have a fine Oration; I will teach
My Spaniel to howl in sweeter Language,
And keep a better Method.

 Archid. You forget
The Dignity of the Place.

 Diph. Silence!

 Timol. Speak boldly.

 Pisan. 'Tis your Authority gives me a Tongue,
I should be dumb else; and I am secure,
I cannot clothe my Thoughts, and just Defence
In such an abject Phrase, but 'twill appear
Equal, if not above, my low Condition,
I need no Bombast Language, stoln from such
As make Nobility from prodigious Terms
The Hearers understand not; I bring with me
No Wealth to boast of, neither can I number
Uncertain Fortune's Favours with my Merits;
I dare not force Affection, or presume
To censure her Discretion, that looks on me
As a weak Man, and not her Fancy's Idol.

How I have lov'd, and how much I have suffer'd,
And with what Pleasure undergone the Burthen
Of my ambitious Hopes (in aiming at
The glad Poffeffion of a Happinefs,
The Abftract of all Goodnefs in Mankind
Can at no Part deferve) with my Confeffion
Of mine own Wants, is all that can plead for me.
But if that pure Defire, not blended with
Foul Thoughts, that like a River keeps his Courfe,
Retaining ftill the Clearnefs of the Spring
From whence it took Beginning, may be thought
Worthy Acceptance; then I dare rife up,
And tell this gay Man to his Teeth, I never
Durft doubt her Conftancy, that like a Rock
Beats off Temptations, as that mocks the Fury
Of the proud Waves; nor from my jealous Fears
Queftion that Goodnefs, to which, as an Altar
Of all Perfection, he that truly loves,
Should rather bring a Sacrifice of Service,
Than raze it with the Engines of Sufpition;
Of which, when he can wafh an *Æthiope* white,
Leofthenes may hope to free himfelf;
But, till then, never.

   Timag. Bold, prefumptuous Villain!

   Pifan. I will go farther, and make good upon him
I'th' Pride of all his Honours, Birth and Fortunes,
He's more unworthy than myfelf.

   Leoft. Thou lyeft.

   Timag. Confute him with a Whip, and, the Doubt
       decided,
Punifh him with a Halter.

   Pifan. O the Gods!
My Ribs, tho' made of Brafs, cannot contain
My Heart, fwoln big with Rage—The Lye! A Whip!
                [*Plucks off his Difguife.*
Let Fury then difperfe thefe Clouds; in which
I long have mafk'd, difguis'd; that, when they know
Whom they have injur'd, they may faint with Horror

Of my Revenge, which, wretched Men! expect,
As sure as Fate, to suffer!

Leost. Ha! *Pisander?*

Timag. 'Tis the bold *Theban!*

Asot. There's no Hope for me then!
I thought I should have put in for a Share,
And borne *Cleora* from them both: But now
This Stranger looks so terrible, that I dare not
So much as look on her.

Pisan. Now, as myself,
Thy Equal at thy best, *Leosthenes.*——
For you, *Timagoras,* praise Heav'n you were born
Cleora's Brother, 'tis your safest Armour.——
But I lose Time.——The base Lie cast upon me,
I thus return. Thou art a perjur'd Man,
False and perfidious, and hast made a Tender
Of Love and Service to this Lady, when
Thy Soul (if thou hast any) can bear Witness,
That thou wert not thine own.——For Proof of this
Look better on this Virgin, and consider,
This *Persian* Shape laid by, and she appearing
In a *Greekish* Dress, such as when first you saw her,
If she resemble not *Pisander's* Sister,
One call'd *Statilia?*

Leost. 'This the same! my Guilt
So chokes my Spirits, I cannot deny
My Falsehood, nor excuse it.

Pisan. This is she,
To whom thou wert contracted: This the Lady,
That when thou wert my Prisoner fairly taken
In the *Spartan* War, that begg'd thy Liberty,
And with it gave herself to thee, ungrateful!

Timand. No more, Sir, I intreat you: I perceive
True Sorrow in his Looks, and a Consent
To make me Reparation in mine Honour;
And then I am most happy.

Pisan. The Wrong done her
Drew me from *Thebes* with a full Intent to kill thee:
But this fair Object met me in my Fury,

And quite difarm'd me.—Being deny'd to have her
By you, my Lord *Archidamus*, and not able
To live far from her, Love (the Miftrefs of
All quaint Devices,) prompted me to treat
With a Friend of mine, who as a Pirate fold me
For a Slave to you, my Lord, and gave my Sifter
As a Prefent to *Cleora*.

Timol. Strange *Meanders!*

Pifan. There how I bare myfelf needs no Relation,
But, if fo far defcending from the Height
Of my then flourifhing Fortunes, to the loweft
Condition of a Man, to have Means only
To feed my Eye with the Sight of what I honour'd;
The Dangers too I underwent; the Suff'ring;
The Clearnefs of my Intereft may deferve
A noble Recompence in your lawful Favour;
Now 'tis apparent that *Leofthenes*
Can claim no Intereft in you, you may pleafe
To think upon my Service.

Cleora. Sir, my Want
Of Power to fatisfy fo great a Debt,
Makes me accufe my Fortune; but if that
Out of the Bounty of your Mind, you think,
A free Surrender of myfelf full Payment,
I gladly tender it.

Archid. With my Confent too,
All Injuries forgotten.

Timag. I will ftudy
In my future Service to deferve your Favour
And good Opinion.

Leoft. Thus I gladly fee
This Advocate to plead for me.   [*Kiffing* Statilia.

Pifan. You will find me
An eafy Judge, when I have yielded Reafons
Of your Bondmen's falling off from their Obedience,
Then after, as you pleafe, determine of me.
I found their Natures apt to mutiny
From your too cruel Ufage; and made Trial
How far they might be wrought on; to inftruct you

To look with more Prevention, and Care
To what they may hereafter undertake
Upon the like Occasions—The Hurt's little
They have committed, nor was ever Cure
But with some Pain effected. I confess,
In Hope to force a Grant of fair *Cleora*
I urg'd them to defend the Town against you:
Nor had the Terror of your Whips, but that
I was preparing for Defence elsewhere,
So soon got Entrance;—In this I am guilty:
Now, as you please, your Censure.

    Timol. Bring them in;
And, tho' you've given me Power, I do intreat
Such as have undergone their Insolence,
It may not be offensive, tho' I study
Pity more than Revenge.

    Coris. 'Twill best become you.

    Cleon. I must consent.

    Asot. For me, I'll find a Time
To be reveng'd hereafter.

Enter Gracculo, Cimbrio, Poliphron, Zanthia, *and the
other Slaves with Halters about their Necks.*

    Grac. Give me Leave;
I'll speak for all.

    Timol. What canst thou say, to hinder
The Course of Justice?

    Grac. Nothing.—You may see
We are prepar'd for Hanging, and confess
We have deserv'd it. Our most humble Suit is,
We may not twice be executed.

    Timol. Twice? How mean'st thou?

    Grac. At the Gallows first, and after in a Ballad
Sung to some villainous Tune. There are Ten-groat
        Rhimers
About the Town grown fat on these Occasions.——
Let but a Chapel fall, or a Street be fir'd,
A foolish Lover hang himself for pure Love, |
Or any such like Accident, and before

They are cold in their Graves, fome damn'd Ditty's
    made
Which makes their Ghofts walk.—Let the State take
    Order
For the Redrefs of this Abufe, recording
'Twas done by my Advice, and for my Part,
I'll cut as clean a Caper from the Ladder
As ever merry *Greek* did.
    Timol. Yet I think
You would fhew more Activity to delight
Your Mafter for a Pardon.
    Grac. O! I would dance
As I were all Air and Fire.
    Timol. And ever be
Obedient and humble?
    Grac. As his Spaniel,
Tho' he kick'd me for Exercife ;—and the like
I promife for all the reft.
    Timol. Rife then, you have it.
    All Slaves. Timoleon! Timoleon!
    Timol. Ceafe thefe Clamours.——
And now, the War being ended to our Wifhes,
And fuch as want the Pilgrimage of Love,
Happy in full Fruition of their Hopes,
'Tis lawful, Thanks paid to the Powers divine,
To drown our Cares in honeft Mirth and Wine.
                     [*Exeunt.*

I don't recollect any Play whatfoever, that begins or ends in a
Manner fo pleafing, uncommon and ftriking, as this of *The Bondman.*
    The Introduction of *Cleora* in the firft Act, and the Difcovery of
Pifander in the laft, are moft happily conceived, and muft have an
admirable Effect in the Reprefentation. It was probably this Circumftance that determined *Betterton*, the famous Actor, to revive
this Comedy. I muft fuppofe that he fuppreffed fome of the moft
ludicrous Parts, and particularly the Scene between *Corifca, Afotus,*
and *Zanthia*, in the fecond Act, which deferves indeed a more harfh
Appellation: There is little elfe neceffary to adapt it to the Stage,
where it could not fail of a favourable Reception. *M. M.*

End of THE BONDMAN.

THE

FATAL DOWRY.

A

TRAGEDY.

Dramatis Personæ.

CHARALOIS,	FLORIMEL. ⎫
ROMONT,	BELLAPERT. ⎬
CHARMI.	AYMER.
NOVALL, Sen.	NOVALL, Jun.
LILADAM.	Advocates.
DU CROY.	Three Creditors.
ROCHFORT,	Officers,
BEAUMONT.	Priest.
PONTALIER,	Taylor.
MALOTIN,	Barber.
BEAUMELLE.	Perfumer.

The Scene, Dijon *in* Burgundy,

THE

FATAL DOWRY.*

ACT I. SCENE I.

Enter Charalois *with a Paper,* Romont *and* Charmi.

Charmi.

SIR, I may move the Court to ferve your Will;
But therein fhall both wrong you and myfelf.
Rom. Why think you fo, Sir?
Charmi. 'Caufe I am familiar
With what will be their Anfwer: They will fay,
'Tis againft Law, and argue me of Ignorance,
For off'ring them the Motion.
Rom. You know not, Sir,
How, in this Caufe, they may difpenfe with Law,
And therefore frame not you their Anfwer for them,
But do your Parts.
Charmi. I love the Caufe fo well,
That I could run the Hazard of a Check for't.
Rom. From whom?
Charmi. Some of the Bench that watch to give it,
More than to do the Office that they fit for:
But give me, Sir, my Fee.
Rom. Now you are noble.

---

* *Maffinger* was affifted in writing this Tragedy by Mr. *Nathaniel Field*, the Author of two Comedies befide; and, as a Poet, very much efteemed by the Cotemporaries of the Age in which he lived.

Charmi. I fhall deferve this better yet, in giving
My Lord fome Counfel (if he pleafe to hear it)
Than I fhall do with Pleading.

Rom. What may it be, Sir?

Charmi. That it would pleafe his Lordfhip, as the
   Prefidents
And Counfellors of Court come by, to ftand
Here and but fhew yourfelf, and to fome one
Or two make his Requeft: There is a Minute,
When a Man's Prefence fpeaks in his own Caufe,
More than the Tongues of twenty Advocates.

Rom. I have urg'd that.

Enter Rochfort *and* Du Croy.

Charmi. Their Lordfhips here are coming,
I muft go get me a Place.—You'll find me in Court,
And at your Service.   [*Exit* Charmi.

Rom. Now, put on your Spirits!

Du Croy. The Eafe that you prepare yourfelf, my
   Lord,
In giving up the Place you hold in Court,
Will prove, I fear, a Trouble in the State;
And that no flight one.

Roch. Pray you, Sir, no more.

Rom. Now, Sir, lofe not this offer'd Means: Their
   Looks
Fix'd on you with a pitying Earneftnefs,
Invite you to demand their Furtherance
To your good Purpofe.—This fuch a Dulnefs,
So foolifh and untimely, as——

Du Croy. You know him?

Roch. I do; and much lament the fudden Fall
Of his brave Houfe. It is young *Charalois;*
Son to the Marfhal, from whom he inherits
His Fame and Virtues only.

Rom. Ha! they name you.

Du Croy. His Father died in Prifon two Days fince.

Roch. Yes, to the Shame of this ungrateful State;
That fuch a Mafter in the Art of War,

So noble and fo highly meriting
From this forgetful Country, fhould, for Want
Of Means to.fatisfy his Creditors
The Sum he took up for the general Good,
Meet with an End fo infamous.

Rom. Dare you ever hope for like Opportunity?
Du Croy. My good Lord!
Roch. My Wifh bring Comfort to you,
Du Croy. The Time calls us.
Roch. Good morrow, Colonel!

                   [*Exeunt* Rochfort *and* Du Croy.

Rom. This obftinate Spleen,
You think becomes your Sorrow, and forts well
With your black Suits: But, grant me Wit or Judg-
      ment,
And, by the Freedom of an honeft Man,
And a true Friend to boot, I fwear, 'tis fhameful;
And therefore flatter not yourfelf with Hope,
Your fable Habit, with the Hat and Cloak,
No, tho' the Ribbons help, have Power to work 'em
To what you would: For thofe that had no Eyes
To fee the great Acts of your Father, will not,
From any Fafhion Sorrow can put on,
Be taught to know their Duties.

Char. If they will not,
They are too old to learn, and I too young
To give them Counfel; fince, if they partake
The Underftanding and the Hearts of Men,
They will prevent my Words and Tears: If not,
What can Perfuafion, tho' made eloquent
With Grief, work upon fuch as have chang'd Natures
With the moft favage Beaft? Bleft, bleft be ever
The Memory of that happy Age, when Juftice
Had no Guards to keep off wrong'd Innocence
From flying to her Succours, and, in that,
Affurance of Redrefs: Whereas now, *Romont,*
The Damn'd with more Eafe may afcend from Hell,
Than we arrive at her. One *Cerberus* there
Forbids the Paffage; in our Courts a thoufand,
As loud and fertile-headed; and the Client

That wants the Sops to fill their rav'nous Throats,
Muſt hope for no Acceſs.   Why ſhould I, then,
Attempt Impoſſibilities, you, Friend, being
Too well acquainted with my Dearth of Means
To make my Entrance that Way?

   Rom. Would I were not.
But, Sir! you have a Cauſe, a Cauſe ſo juſt,
Of ſuch Neceſſity, not to be deferr'd,
As would compel a Maid, whoſe Foot was never
Set o'er her Father's Threſhold, nor within
The Houſe where ſhe was born, ever ſpake Word
Which was not uſher'd with pure Virgin Bluſhes,
To drown the Tempeſt of a Pleader's Tongue,
And force Corruption to give back the Hire
It took againſt her:—Let Examples move you.
You ſee Men great in Birth, Eſteem and Fortune,
Rather than loſe a Scruple of their Right,
Fawn baſely upon ſuch, whoſe Gowns put off,
They would diſdain for Servants.

   Char. And to theſe can I become a Suitor?

   Rom. Without Loſs:
Would you conſider, that, to gain their Favours,
Our chaſteſt Dames put off their Modeſties,
Soldiers forget their Honours, Uſurers
Make Sacrifice of Gold, Poets of Wit,
And Men religious part with Fame and Goodneſs.
Be therefore won to uſe the Means that may
Advance your pious Ends.

   Char. You ſhall o'ercome.

   Rom. And you receive the Glory.   Pray you now
       practiſe.
'Tis well.

   Enter Old Novall, Liladam, *and three Creditors.*

   Char. Not look on me!

   Rom. You muſt have Patience——Offer it again.

   Char. And be again contemn'd!

   Nov. I know what's to be done.——

1 *Cred.* And, that your Lordfhip
Will pleafe to do your Knowledge, we offer firft
Our thankful Hearts here, as a bounteous Earneft
To what we will add.——

Nov. One Word more of this,
I am your Enemy. Am I a Man,
Your Bribes can work on ? Ha ?

· *Lilad.* Friends ! you miftake
The Way to win my Lord ;—he muft not hear this,
But I, as one in Favour, in his Sight,
May hearken to you for my Profit. Sir !
—I pray hear 'em.

Nov. 'Tis well.

Lilad. Obferve him now.

Nov. Your Caufe being good, and your Proceed-
           ings fo,
Without Corruption I am your Friend,
Speak your Defires.

2 *Cred.* Oh, they are charitable ;
The Marfhal ftood engag'd unto us three
Two hundred thoufand Crowns, which by his Death
We are defeated of. For which great Lofs
We aim at nothing but his rotten Flefh ;
Nor is that Cruelty.

1 *Cred.* I have a Son
That talks of nothing but of Guns and Armour,
And fwears he'll be a Soldier ; 'tis an Humour
I would divert him from; and I am told,
That if I minifter to him, in his Drink,
Powder made of this Bankrupt Marfhal's Bones,
Provided that the Carcafe rot above Ground,
'Twill cure his foolifh Frenzy.

Nov. You fhew in it
A Father's Care. I have a Son myfelf,
A fafhionable Gentleman, and a peaceful :
And, but I am affur'd he's not fo given,
He fhould take of it too.—Sir ! what are you ?

Char. A Gentleman.

Nov. So are many that rake Dunghills.
If you have any Suit, move it in Court:
I take no Papers in Corners.

    Rom. Yes, as the Matter may be carried; and
       whereby
To manage the Conveyance———Follow him.

    Lilad. You're rude: I say he shall not pass.

           [*Exeunt* Novall, Charalois, *and Advocates.*

    Rom. You say so? On what Assurance?
For the well cutting of his Lordship's Corns,
Picking his Toes, or any Office else
Nearer to Baseness?

    Lilad. Look upon me better;
Are these the Ensigns of so coarse a Fellow?
Be well advis'd.

    Rom. Out, Rogue! do not I know   [*Kicks him.*
These glorious Weeds spring from the sordid Dunghill
Of thy officious Baseness? Wert thou worthy
Of any Thing from me, but my Contempt,
I would do more than this,—more, you Court-Spider!

    Lilad. But that this Man is lawless; he should find
That I am valiant.

    1 *Cred.* If your Ears are fast,
'Tis nothing. What's a Blow or two? As much:

    2 *Cred.* These Chastisements as useful are as fre-
       quent
To such as would grow rich.

    Rom. Are they so, Rascals? I will befriend you
       then—   [*Kicks them.*

    1 *Cred.* Bear Witness, Sirs!

    Lilad. Truth, I have born my Part already, Friends!
In the Court you shall hear more.   [*Exit.*

    Rom. I know you for
The worst of Spirits, that strive to rob the Tombs
Of what is their Inheritance, the Dead:
For Usurers bred by a riotous Peace;
That hold the Charter of your Wealth and Freedom,
By being Knaves and Cuckolds, that never pray'd,
But when you fear the rich Heirs will grow wise,
To keep their Lands out of your Parchment Toils;

And then, the Devil your Father's call'd upon,
T' invent fome Ways of Luxury ne'er thought on.
Be gone, and quickly, or I'll leave no Room
Upon your Foreheads for your Horns to fprout on;
Without a Murmur, or I will undo you,
For I will beat you honeft.

   1 *Cred.* Thrift forbid!
We will bear this rather than hazard that.

[Exit Creditor.

Enter Charalois.

   Rom. I am fomewhat eas'd in this yet.—
   Char. Only Friend!
To what vain Purpofe do I make my Sorrow
Wait on the Triumph of their Cruelty?
Or teach their Pride from my Humility,
To think it has o'ercome? They are determin'd
What they will do; and it may well become me,
To rob them of the Glory they expect
From my fubmifs Intreaties.
   Rom. Think not fo, Sir!
The Difficulties that you encounter with,
Will crown the Undertaking——Heaven! you weep
And I could do fo to; but that I know,
There's more expected from the Son and Friend
Of him whofe fatal Lofs now fhakes our Natures,
Than Sighs or Tears, in which a Village Nurfe,
Or cunning Strumpet, when her Knave is hang'd,
May overcome us. We are Men, young Lord,
Let us not do like Women.—To the Court,
And there fpeak like your Birth: Wake fleeping Juftice,
Or dare the Axe. This is a Way will fort
With what you are: I call you not to that
I will fhrink from myfelf, I will deferve
Your Thanks, or fuffer with you—O how bravely
That fudden Fire of Anger fhews in you!
Give Fuel to it, fince you're on a Shelf,
Of extreme Danger, fuffer like yourfelf.   [*Exeunt.*

SCENE II.

Enter Rochfort, Novall *sen.* Charmi, Du Croy, *Advocates,* Beaumont, *Officers, and three Presidents.*

Du Croy. Your Lordship's seated. May this Meeting prove
Prosperous to us, and to the general Good of *Burgundy.*
Nov. sen. Speak to the Point!
Du Croy. Which is
With Honour to dispose the Place and Power
Of Premier President, which this reverend Man,
Grave *Rochfort,* (whom for Honour's Sake I name)
Is purpos'd to resign; a Place, my Lords,
In which he hath, with such Integrity,
Perform'd the first and best Parts of a Judge;
That, as his Life transcends all fair Examples
Of such as were before him in *Dijon,*
So it remains to those that shall succeed him,
A Precedent that they may imitate, but not equal.
Roch. I may not sit to hear this.
Du Croy. Let the Love
And Thankfulness we're bound to pay to Goodness,
In this o'ercome your Modesty.
Roch. My Thanks
For this great Favour shall prevent your Trouble.
The honourable Trust that was impos'd
Upon my Weakness, since you witness for me,
It was not ill discharg'd, I will not mention;
Nor now, if Age had not depriv'd me of
The little Strength I had to govern well
The Province that I undertook, forsake it.
Nov. sen. That we could lend you of our Years!
Du Croy. Or Strength!
Nov. sen. Or, as you are, persuade you to continue
The noble Exercise of your knowing Judgment!
Roch. That may not be; nor can your Lordship's
Goodness,
Since your Employments have conferr'd upon me

Sufficient Wealth, deny the Ufe of it ;
And, tho' old Age, when one Foot's in the Grave,
In many, when all Humours elfe are fpent
Feeds no Affection in them, but Defire
To add Height to the Mountain of their Riches :
In me it is not fo : I reft content
With th' Honours and Eftate I now poffefs.
And, that I may have Liberty to ufe,
What Heav'n, ftill bleffing my poor Induftry,
Hath made me Mafter of, I pray the Court
To eafe me of my Burthen ; that I may
Employ the fmall Remainder of my Life
In living well and learning how to die fo.

Enter Romont *and* Charalois.

Rom. See Sir our Advocate.
Du Croy. The Court intreats
Your Lordfhip will be pleas'd to name the Man,
Which you would have your Succeffor, and in me
All promife to confirm it.
Roch. I embrace it
As an Affurance of their Favour to me,
And name my Lord *Novall.*
Du Croy. The Court allows it.
Roch. But there are Suitors wait here, and their
      Caufes
May be of more Neceffity to be heard,
And therefore wifh that mine may be deferr'd,
And theirs have Hearing.
Du Croy. If your Lordfhip pleafe
To take the Place, we will proceed.
Charmi. The Caufe
We come to offer to your Lordfhip's Cenfure,
Is in itfelf fo noble, that it needs not
Or Rhetorick in me that plead, or Favour
From your grave Lordfhips, to determine of it ;
Since to the Praife of your impartial Juftice
(Which guilty, nay, condemn'd Men, dare not fcandal)

It will erect a Trophy of your Mercy
Which marry'd to that Justice——

Nov. sen. Speak to the Cause.

Charmi. I will, my Lord! to say; the late dead
    Marshal,
The Father of this young Lord here, my Client,
Hath done his Country great and faithful Service
Might tax me of Impertinence, to repeat
What your grave Lordships cannot but remember;
He, in his Life, became indebted to
These thrifty Men, (I will not wrong their Credits,
By giving them the Attributes they now merit)
And failing, by the Fortune of the Wars,
Of Means to free himself from his Engagements,
He was arrested, and for Want of Bail,
Imprison'd at their Suit: And not long after
With Loss of Liberty ended his Life.
And, tho' it be a Maxim in our Laws,
All Suits die with the Person, these Men's Malice
In Death find Matter for their Hate to work on,
Denying him the decent Rites of Burial,
Which the sworn Enemies of the Christian Faith
Grant freely to their Slaves: May it therefore please
Your Lordships so to fashion your Decree,
That, what their Cruelty doth forbid, your Pity
May give Allowance to.

Nov. sen. How long have you, Sir, practis'd in
    Court?

Charmi. Some twenty Years, my Lord.

Nov. sen. By your gross Ignorance, it should appear,
Not twenty Days.

Charmi. I hope I have giv'n no Cause in this, my
    Lord——

Nov. sen. How dare you move the Court
To the dispensing with an Act confirm'd
By Parliament, to the Terror of all Bankrupts?
Go home! and with more Care peruse the Statutes:
Or the next Motion, favouring of this Boldness,
May force you to leap (against your Will)
Over the Place you plead at.

Charmi. I forefaw this.

Rom. Why, does your Lordfhip think the moving of
A Caufe, more honeft than this Court had ever
The Honour to determine, can deferve
A Check like this?

Nov. fen. Strange Boldnefs!

Rom. 'Tis fit Freedom:
Or, do you conclude, an Advocate cannot hold
His Credit with the Judge, unlefs he ftudy
His Face more than the Caufe for which he pleads?

Charmi. Forbear!

Rom. Or cannot you, that have the Power
To qualify the Rigour of the Laws
When you are pleafed, take a little from
The Strictnefs of your four Decrees, enacted
In Favour of the greedy Creditors
Againft the o'erthrown Debtor?

Nov. fen. Sirrah! you that prate
Thus faucily, what are you?

Rom. Why, I'll tell you,
Thou Purple-colour'd Man! I'm one to whom
Thou ow'ft the Means thou haft of fitting there
A corrupt Elder.

Charmi. Forbear!

Rom. The Nofe thou wear'ft is my Gift, and thofe
Eyes,
That meet no object fo bafe as their Mafter,
Had been long fince torn from that guilty Head,
And thou thyfelf Slave to fome needy *Swifs*,
Had I not worn a Sword, and us'd it better
Than in thy Prayers thou ever didft thy Tongue.

Nov. fen. Shall fuch an Infolence pafs unpunifh'd?

Charmi. Hear me!

Rom. Yet I, that in my Service done my Country,
Difdain to be put in the Scale with thee,
Confefs myfelf unworthy to be valu'd
With the leaft Part, nay Hair of the dead Marfhal,
Of whofe fo many glorious Undertakings,
Make Choice of any one, and that the meaneft,

Perform'd againſt the ſubtle Fox of *France*
The politick *Lewis*, or the more deſperate *Swiſs*,
And 'twill outweigh all the good Purpoſe,
Tho' put in Act, that ever Gownman practis'd.

Nov. ſen. Away with him to Priſon!

Rom. If that Curſes,
Urg'd juſtly, and breath'd forth ſo, ever fell
On thoſe that did deſerve them; let not mine
Be ſpent in vain now, that thou from this Inſtant
May'ſt, in thy Fear that they will fall upon thee,
Be ſenſible of the Plagues they ſhall bring with them.
And for denying of a little Earth,
To cover what remains of our great Soldier,
May all your wives prove Whores, your Factors
              Thieves,
And, while you live, your riotous Heirs undo you.
And thou, the Patron of their Cruelty,
Of all thy Lordſhips live not to be Owner
Of ſo much Dung as will conceal a Dog,
Or, what is worſe, thyſelf in. And thy Years,
To th' End thou mayſt be wretched, I wiſh many;
And, as thou haſt deny'd the Dead a Grave,
May Miſery in thy Life make thee deſire one,
Which Men and all the Elements keep from thee:
I have begun well; imitate; exceed. [1]

Roch. Good Counſel, were it a praiſe-worthy Deed.

                    [*Exit Officers with* Romont.

Du Croy. Remember what we are.

Char. Thus low my Duty
Anſwers your Lordſhip's Counſel. I will uſe
In the few Words with which I am to trouble
Your Lordſhip's Ears the Temper that you wiſh me;
Not that I fear to ſpeak my Thoughts as loud,
And with a Liberty beyond *Romont*:
But that I know, for me, that am made up
Of all that's wretched, ſo to haſte my End,
Would ſeem to moſt rather a Willingneſs
To quit the Burthen of a hopeleſs Life,

---

[1] This Line is addreſſed to *Charalois.* M. M.

Than Scorn of Death or Duty to the Dead.
I, therefore, bring the Tribute of my Praife
To your Severity, and commend the Juftice
That will not, for the many Services
That any Man hath done the Commonwealth,
Wink at his leaft of Ills : What tho' my Father
Writ Man before he was fo, and confirm'd it,
By numb'ring that Day no Part of his Life,
In which he did not Service to his Country ;
Was he to be free therefore from the Laws,
And ceremonious Form in your Decrees?
Or elfe, becaufe he did as much as Man,
In thofe three memorable Overthrows,
At *Granfon, Morat, Nancy*, where his Mafter,
The warlike *Charalois* (with whofe Misfortunes
I bear his Name) loft Treafure, Men and Life,
To be excus'd from Payment of thofe Sums
Which (his own Patrimony fpent) his Zeal
To ferve his Country, forc'd him to take up ?

  Nov. fen. The Precedent were ill.

  Char. And yet, my Lord, thus much
I know you'll grant ; after thofe great Defeatures,
Which in their dreadful Ruins buried quick

Enter Officers.

Courage and Hope in all Men but himfelf,
He forc'd the proud Foe, in his Height of Conqueft,
To yield unto an honourable Peace,
And in it fav'd an hundred thoufand Lives
To end his own, that was fure Proof againft
The fcalding Summer's Heat, and Winter's Froft,
Ill Airs, the Cannon, and the Enemy's Sword,
In a moft loathfome Prifon.

  Du Croy. 'Twas his Fault
To be fo prodigal.

  Nov. fen. He had from the State
Sufficient Entertainment for the Army.

Char. Sufficient, my Lord? You fit at home,
And, tho' your Fees are boundlefs at the Bar,
Are thrifty in the Charges of the War,
But your Wills be obey'd.   To thefe I turn,
To thefe foft-hearted Men, that wifely know
They're only good Men that pay what they owe.

  2 Cred. And fo they are.

  1 Cred. 'Tis the City Doctrine;
We ftand bound to maintain it.

  Char. Be conftant in it;
And, fince you are as mercilefs in your Natures,
As bafe and mercenary in your Means
By which you get your Wealth, I will not urge
The Court to take away one Scruple from
The Right of their Laws, or one good Thought
In you to mend your Difpofition with.
I know there is no Mufic to your Ears
So pleafing as the Groans of Men in Prifon,
And that the Tears of Widows, and the Cries
Of famifh'd Orphans, are the Feafts that take you,
That to be in your Danger, with more Care
Should be avoided than infectious Air,
The loath'd Embraces of difeafed Women,
A Flatterer's Poifon, or the Lofs of Honour.
Yet, rather than my Father's reverend Duft
Shall want a Place in that fair Monument,
In which our noble Anceftors lie intomb'd,
Before the Court I offer up myfelf
A Prifoner for it: Load me with thofe Irons
That have worn out his Life; in my beft Strength
I'll run to the Encounter of cold Hunger,
And choofe my Dwelling where no Sun dares enter,
So he may be releas'd.

  1 Cred. What mean you, Sir?

  2 Advo. Only your Fee again: There's fo much faid
Already in this Caufe, and faid fo well,
That, fhould I only offer to fpeak in it,
I fhould not be heard, or laugh'd at for it,

1 *Cred.* 'Tis the firſt Money Advocate e'er gave
    back,
'Tho' he ſaid nothing.

Roch. Be advis'd, young Lord,
And well conſiderate ; you throw away
Your Liberty and Joys of Life together :
Your Bounty is employ'd upon a Subject
That is not ſenſible of it, with which wiſe Man
Never abus'd his Goodneſs ; the great Virtues
Of your dead Father vindicate themſelves
From theſe Mens Malice, and break ope the Priſon,
Tho' it contain his Body.

Nov. ſen. Let him alone :
If he love Cords, a God's Name, let him wear 'em,
Provided theſe conſent.

Char. I hope they are not
So ignorant in any Way of Profit,
As to neglect a Poſſibility
To get their own, by ſeeking it from that
Which can return them nothing but ill Fame,
And Curſes for their barbarous Cruelties.

3 *Cred.* What think you of the Offer ?

2 *Cred.* Very well.

1 *Cred.* Accept it by all Means : Let's ſhut him up,
He is well ſhap'd, and has a villainous Tongue,
And, ſhould he ſtudy that Way of Revenge,
As I dare almoſt ſwear he loves a Wench,
We have no Wives, nor ever ſhall get Daughters
That will hold out againſt him.

Du Croy. What's your Anſwer ?

2 *Cred.* Speak you for all.

1 *Cred.* Why, let our Executions
That lie upon the Father, be return'd
Upon the Son, and we releaſe the Body.

Nov. ſen. The Court muſt grant you that.

Char. I thank your Lordſhips,
They have in it confirm'd on me ſuch Glory,
As no Time can take from me : I am ready,
Come, lead me where you pleaſe : Captivity,

That comes with Honour, is true Liberty.

           [*Exit* Charalois, *Creditors and Officers.*

  Nov. sen. Strange Rashness.

  Roch. A brave Resolution rather,
Worthy a better Fortune; but, however,
It is not now to be disputed : therefore
To my own Cause. Already I have found
Your Lordships bountiful in your Favours to me;
And that should teach my Modesty to end here,
And press your Loves no farther.

  Du Croy. There is nothing
The Court can grant, but with Assurance you
May ask it, and obtain it.

  Roch. You encourage a bold Petitioner, and 'tis not
      fit
Your Favours should be lost. Besides 'thas been
A Custom many Years, at the surrend'ring
The Place I now give up, to grant the President
One Boon that parted with it. And, to confirm
Your Grace towards me, against all such as may
Detract my Actions and Life hereafter,
I now prefer it to you.

  Du Croy. Speak it freely,

  Roch. I then desire the Liberty of *Romont*,
And that my Lord *Novall*, whose private Wrong
Was equal to the Injury that was done
To the Dignity of the Court, will pardon it,
And now sign his Enlargement.

  Nov. sen. Pray you demand
The Moiety of my Estate, or any Thing
Within my Power but this.

  Roch. Am I deny'd then—my first and last Request?

  Du Croy. It must not be.

  2 *Pre.* I have a Voice to give in it,

  3 *Pre.* And I.
And, if Persuasion will not work him to it,
We will make known our Power.

  Nov. sen. You are too violent;
You shall have my Consent. But would you had
Made Trial of my Love in any thing

But this, you fhould have found then—But it fkills not,
You have what you defire.

 Roch. I thank your Lordfhips.

 Du Croy. The Court is up—Make Way.

     [*Exeunt all but* Rochfort *and* Beaumont.

 Roch. I follow you—*Beaumont !*

 Beaum. My Lord.

 Roch. You are a Scholar, *Beaumont !*
And can fearch deeper into th' Intents of Men,
Than thofe that are lefs knowing. How appear'd
The Piety and brave Behaviour of
Young *Charalois* to you ?

 Beaum. It is my Wonder,
Since I want Language to exprefs it fully ;
And fure the Colonel——

 Roch. Fie ! he was faulty.—What prefent Money
  have I ?

 Beaum. There is no Want
Of any Sum a private Man has Ufe for.

 Roch. 'Tis well :
I am ftrangely taken with this *Charalois* ;
Methinks, from his Example, the whole Age
Should learn to be good, and continue fo.
Virtue works ftrangely with us ; and his Goodnefs
Rifing above his Fortune, feems to me,
Prince-like, to will, not afk a Courtefy.   [*Exeunt.*

End of the Firft Act.

ACT II.   SCENE I.

Enter Pontalier, Malotin *and* Beaumont.

Malotin.

'TIS ſtrange.
   Beaum. Methinks ſo.
Pont. In a Man but young,
Yet old in Judgment; theorick and practick,
In all Humanity, and (to increaſe the Wonder)
Religious, yet a Soldier, that he ſhould
Yield his free-living Youth a Captive, for
The Freedom of his aged Father's Corps,
And rather chooſe to want Life's Neceſſaries,
Liberty, Hope of Fortune, than it ſhould
In Death be kept from Chriſtian Ceremony.
   Malot. Come, 'tis a golden Precedent in a Son
To let ſtrong Nature have the better Hand,
(In ſuch a Caſe) of all affected Reaſon.
What Years ſit on this *Charalois?*
   Beaum. Twenty-eight;
For ſince the Clock did ſtrike him ſeventeen old,
Under his Father's Wing this Son hath fought,
Serv'd and commanded, and ſo aptly both,
That ſometimes he appear'd his Father's Father,
And never leſs than his Son; the old Man's Virtues
So recent in him as the World may ſwear,
Nought but a fair Tree could ſuch fair Fruit bear.
   Pont. But wherefore lets he ſuch a barb'rous Law,
And Men more barbarous to execute it,
Prevail on his ſoft Diſpoſition,
That he had rather die alive for Debt
Of the old Man in Priſon, than they ſhould
Rob him of Sepulture, conſidering
Theſe Monies borrow'd bought the Lenders Peace,

And all their Means they enjoy, nor was diffus'd
In any impious or licentious Path?
Beaum. True! for my Part, were it my Father's
    Trunk,
The tyrannous Ram-heads, with their Horns fhould
    gore it,
Or caft it to their Curs than they lefs currifh,
Ere prey on me fo, with their Lion-law,
Being in my free Will (as in his) to fhun it.
    Pont. Alas! he knows himfelf in Poverty loft:
For in this partial avaricious Age
What Price bears Honour? Virtue? Long ago
It was but prais'd and freez'd, but now-a-days
'Tis colder far, and has nor Love nor Praife;
Very Praife now freezeth too: For Nature
Did make the Heathen far more Chriftian then,
Than Knowledge us (lefs heathenifh) Chriftian.
    Malo. This Morning is the Funeral.
    Pont. Certainly!
And from this Prifon 'twas the Son's Requeft,
That his dear Father might Interment have,
                   [*Recorders Mufick.*
See the young Son interr'd a lively Grave. [2]
    Beaum. They come—Obferve their Order.

Enter Funeral. The Body borne by four. Captains and
*   Soldiers, Mourners, 'Scutcheons, &c. in very good Order.*
*   Charalois and Romont meet it. Charalois fpeaks.*
*   Romont weeping. Solemn Mufick. Three Creditors.*

    Char. How like a filent Stream fhaded with Night,
And gliding foftly with our windy Sighs,

> 2 *That his dear Father fhould Interment have,*
>   *See the young Son interr'd a lively Grave.*

Thefe Lines, as they ftand, cannot be reconciled to Senfe. I
fhould therefore read the laft Line thus:

    See, the young Son enters alive the Grave.

(That is, the Prifon.)

Moves the whole Frame of this Solemnity!
Tears, Sighs and Blacks filling the Simile!
Whilst I, the only Murmur in this Grove
Of Death, thus hollowly break forth!—Vouchsafe
To stay awhile.—Rest, rest in Peace dear Earth!
Thou that brought'st Rest to their unthankful Lives,
Whose Cruelty deny'd thee Rest in Death!
Here stands thy poor Executor, thy Son,
That makes his Life Prisoner to bail thy Death:
Who gladlier puts on this Captivity,
Than Virgins, long in Love, their Wedding Weeds;
Of all that ever thou hast done Good to,
These only have good Memories; for they
Remember best forget not Gratitude.
I thank you for this last and friendly Love.
And tho' this Country, like a vip'rous Mother,
Not only hath eat up ungratefully
All Means of thee her Son, but last thyself,
Leaving thy Heir so bare and indigent,
He cannot raise thee a poor Monument,
Such as a Flatterer or an Usurer hath.
Thy Worth, in every honest Breast, builds one,
Making their friendly Hearts thy Funeral Stone.
    Pont. Sir!
   Char. Peace! O Peace! This Scene is wholly mine.
What! Weep ye, Soldiers?—Blanch not.—*Romont*
       weeps.
Ha! let me see! my Miracle is eas'd:
The Jailors and the Creditors do weep:
E'en they that make us weep do weep themselves.
Be these thy Body's Balm: These and thy Virtue
Keep thy Fame ever odoriferous,
Whilst the great, proud, rich, undeserving Man,
Alive stinks in his Vices, and, being vanish'd,
The golden Calf that was an Idol, deck'd
With Marble Pillars, Jet and Porphyry,
Shall quickly both in Bone and Name consume,
Tho' wrapt in Lead, Spice, Searcloth and Perfume.
   1 *Cred.* Sir!

Char. What!—Away, for Shame! you, prophane
    Rogues!
Muſt not be mingled with theſe holy Relicks:
This is a Sacrifice—Our Show'r ſhall crown
His Sepulchre with Olive, Myrrh and Bays,
The Plants of Peace, of Sorrow, Victory;
Your Tears would ſpring but Weeds.
    1 *Cred.* Would they ſo?
We'll keep them to ſtop Bottles then.
    Rom. No, keep 'em for your own Sins, you Rogues,
'Till you repent; you'll die elſe, and be damn'd.
    2 *Cred.* Damn'd, ha! ha! ha!
    Rom. Laugh ye?
    3 *Cred.* Yes, faith, Sir; we would be very glad
To pleaſe you either Way.
    1 *Cred.* Ye're ne'er content,
Crying nor laughing.
    Rom. Both with a Birth, ye rogues.
    2 *Cred.* Our Wives, Sir, taught us.
    Rom. Look, look, you Slaves! your thankleſs Cru-
    elty,
And ſavage Manners of unkind *Dijon,*
Exhauſt theſe Floods, and not his Father's Death.
    1 *Cred.* 'Slid, Sir! what would you, you're ſo cho-
    lerick?
    1 *Cred.* Moſt Soldiers are ſo, i'faith.—Let him alone.
They've little elſe to live on; we've not had
A Penny of him, have we?
    3 *Cred.* 'Slight, would you have our Hearts?
    1 *Cred.* We've nothing but his Body here in Du-
    rance
For all our Money.
    Prieſt. On.
    Char. One Moment more,
But to beſtow a few poor Legacies,
All I have left in my dead Father's Right,
And I have done. Captain, wear thou theſe Spurs,
That yet ne'er made his Horſe run from a Foe.
Lieutenant, thou this Scarf; and may it tie
Thy Valour and thy Honeſty together:

For fo it did in him. Enfign, this Cuirafs,
Your General's Necklace once. You gentle Bearers,
Divide this Purfe of Gold : This other ftrew
Among the Poor.—'Tis all I have. *Romont*,
Wear thou this Medal of himfelf, that like
A hearty Oak, grew'ft clofe to this tall Pine,
(E'en in the wildeft Wildernefs of War)
Whereon Foes broke their Swords, and tir'd themfelves;
Wounded and hack'd ye were but never fell'd.
For me, my Portion provide in Heaven :
My Root is earth'd, and I, a defolate Branch,
Left fcatter'd in the Highway of the World;
Trod under Foot, that might have been a Column
Mainly fupporting our demolifh'd Houfe,
This would I wear [3] as my Inheritance.
And what Hope can arife to me from it,
When I and it are here both Prifoners ?
Only may this, if ever we be free,
Keep or redeem me from all Infamy.

S O N G.

Fie ! ceafe to wonder !
Tho' you hear Orpheus, *with his Ivory Lute,*
Move Trees and Rocks,
Charm Bulls, Bears, and Men more favage, to be mute.
Weak foolifh Singer, here is one
Would have transform'd thyfelf to Stone.

1 *Cred.* No farther ! look to 'em at your own Peril.
2 *Cred.* No, as they pleafe :—Their Mafter's a good
    Man.
I would they were at the *Bermudas*.
    Jailor. You muft no farther.——
The Prifon limits you, and the Creditors
Exact the Strictnefs.
    Rom. Out, you wolfifh Mongrels !
Whofe Brains fhould be knock'd out, like Dogs in

---

3 Pointing to his Father's Sword. *M. M.*

July,
Left your Infection poifon a whole Town.
   Char. They grudge our Sorrow.—Your ill Wills,
      perforce,
Turn now to Charity: They would not have us
Walk too far mourning; Ufurers Relief
Grieves if the Debtors have too much of Grief.

                         [*Exeunt.*

SCENE II.

    Enter Beaumelle, Florimel *and* Bellapert.

   Beaumel. I pr'ythee tell me, *Florimel*, why do Women marry?
   Flor. Why truly, Madam, I think, to lie with their
Hufbands.
   Bellap. You are a Fool. She lies, Madam; Women
      marry Hufbands,
To lie with other Men.
   Flor. Faith, e'en fuch a Woman wilt thou make. By
this Light, Madam, this Wagtail will fpoil you, if you
take Delight in her Licence.
   Beaumel. 'Tis true, *Florimel*, and thou wilt make me
too good for a young Lady. What an Electuary found
my Father out for his Daughter, when he compounded
you two my Women? for thou, *Florimel*, art e'en a
Grain too heavy—fimply for a Waiting-gentlewoman.
   Flor. And thou, *Bellapert*, a Grain too light.
   Bellap. Well, go thy Ways, goodly Wifdom, whom
no-body regards. I wonder, whether be elder, thou
or thy Hood: You think, becaufe you ferve my Lady's
Mother, are thirty-two Years old, which is a pip [4] out,
you know.
   Flor. Well faid, Whirligig.
   Bellap. You are deceiv'd: I want a Peg i'th' Middle:
Out of thefe Prerogatives, you think to be Mother of

---

   4 A *Pip* means a Spot upon a Card; and this Paffage alludes to
to fome Kind of Play, where Thirty-one made the Game, and of
Courfe Thirty-two was a Pip too much.

the Maids here, and mortify 'em with Proverbs : Go,
go, govern the Sweet-meats, and weigh the Sugar, that
the Wenches steal none : Say your Prayers twice a
Day, and, as I take it, you have performed your Func-
tion.

Flor. I may be even with you.

Bellap. Hark ! the Court's broke up. Go, help my
old Lord out of his Caroch, and scratch his Head till
Dinner-time.

Flor. Well.   [*Exit.*

Bellap. Fie, Madam ! how you walk ! By my Maidenhead, you look seven Years older than you did this
Morning : Why there can be nothing under the Sun
valuable, to make you thus a Minute.

Boaumel. Ah my sweet *Bellapert !* thou Cabinet
To all my Counsels, thou dost know the Cause
That makes thy Lady wither thus in Youth.

Bellap. Uds-light, enjoy your Wishes : Whilst I live,
One Way or other you shall crown your Will.
Would you have him your Husband that you love,
And can it not be ? He is your Servant, tho',
And may perform the Office of a Husband.

Beaumel. But there is Honour Wench.

Bellap. Such a Disease
There is inded, for which ere I would die——

Beaumel. Pr'ythee, distinguish me a Maid and Wife.

Bellap. 'Faith, Madam, one may bear any Man's
                 Children,
T'other must bear no Man's.

Beaumel. What is a Husband ?

Bellap. Physic, that, tumbling in your Belly, will
make you sick i' th' Stomach. The only Distinction
betwixt a Husband and a Servant is, the first will lie
with you, when he pleases ; the last shall lie with you,
when you please. Pray tell me, Lady do you love, to
marry after ; or would you marry, to love after ?

Beaumel. I would meet Love and Marriage both at
once.

Bellap. Why then you are out of the Fashion, and
will be contemn'd : For, I'll assure you, there are few

Women in the World, but either they have married
firft and love after; or love firft and married after.
You muft do as you may, not as you would : Your
Father's Will is the Goal you muft fly to. *If a Hufband approach you, you would have farther off, is he
your Love the lefs near you ? A Hufband in thefe
Days is but a·Cloak to be oftener laid *upon* your Bed,
than *in* your Bed.

Beaumel. 'Hum !

Bellap. Sometimes you may wear him on your Shoulder; and now and then under your Arm; but feldom
or never let him cover you; for 'tis not the Fafhion.

Enter Novall *jun.* Pontalier, Malotin, Liladam, *and*
Aymer.

Nov. jun. Beft Day to Nature's Curiofity,
Star of *Dijon,* the Luftre of all *France !*
Perpetual Spring dwell on thy rofy Cheeks,
Whofe Breath is Perfume to our Continent,
See *Flora* turn'd in her Varieties.[6]

Bellap. Oh divine Lord !

Nov. jun. No Autumn nor no Age ever approach
This heavenly Piece, which Nature having wrought,
She loft her Needle, and did then defpair
Ever to work fo lively and fo fair.

Lilad. Uds-light, my Lord, one of the Purls of
your Band ·
Is, without all Difcipline, fall'n out of his Rank.

Nov. jun. How? I would not for a thoufand Crowns
fhe had feen't. Dear *Liladam,* reform it.

5 If a Hufband approach, you would have farther off, is he your
Love, the lefs near you ? This is the Manner in which thefe Lines
fhould be printed. *M. M.*

☞ 6 *See* Flora *turn'd in her Varieties.*

Thus it ftands in the old Copies; but certainly falfe : We ought
to read
See Flora trim'd *in her Varieties.*

Bellap. Oh Lord! *Per se*, Lord! Quinteffence of Honour! fhe walks not under a Weed that could deny thee any Thing.

Beaumel. Pr'ythee Peace, Wench! thou doft but blow the Fire that flames too much already.

[*Liladam and* Aymer *trim* Novall, *whilft* Bellapert *her Lady*.

Aymer. By Gad, my Lord, you have the divineft Taylor in *Chriftendom*; he hath made you look like an Angel in your Cloth of Tiffue Doublet.

Pont. This is a three-legg'd Lord: There's a frefh Affault. Oh! that Men fhould fpend Time thus!— See, fee how her Blood drives to her Heart, and ftrait vaults to her Cheeks again.

Malot. What are thefe?

Pont. One of 'em there, the lower, is a good, fool-ifh, knavifh, fociable Gallimaufry of a Man, and has much caught my Lord with Singing; he is Mafter of a Mufick Houfe. The other is his Dreffing Block, upon whom my Lord lays all his Cloaths and Fafhions, ere he vouchfafes 'em his own Perfon; you fhall fee him i' th' Morning in the Galley-foift,[7] at Noon in the Bul-lion, i' th' Evening in Querpo, and all Night in —.

Malat. A Bawdy-houfe.

Pont. If my Lord deny, they deny; if he affirm, they affirm: They fkip into my Lord's caft Skins fome twice a Year; and thus they live to eat, eat to live, and live to praife my Lord.

Malot. Good Sir, tell me one Thing.

Pont. What's that?

Malot. Dare thefe Men ever fight on any Caufe?

Pont. Oh, no, 'twould fpoil their Cloaths, and put their Bands out of Order.

---

7 The *Galley-foift* and the *Bullion* were probably Taverns diftin-guifhed by thofe Signs. *Bullion* is a Corruption of *Boulogne*, which from the Time that City was taken by *Henry* the Eighth became a popular Sign. *M. M.*

Galley-foift, I think, means a *Barge* or *fmall Veffel* in which it was cuftomary for young Perfons of both Sexes to divert themfelves on the *Thames*. *D.*

Nov. jun. Muſt you hear the News : Your Father
has reſign'd his Preſidentſhip to my Lord my Father.

Malot. And Lord *Charalois* undone for ever.

Pont. Troth, 'tis Pity, Sir !
A braver Hope of ſo aſſur'd a Father
Did never comfort *France.*

Lilad. A good dumb Mourner.

Aymer. A ſilent Black.

Nov. jun. Oh, fie upon him, how he wears his
    Cloaths !
As if he had come this *Chriſtmas* from *St. Omers,*
To ſee his Friends, and return'd after Twelf-tide.

Lilad. His Colonel looks finely like a Drover.—

Nov. jun. That had a Winter lain perdieu i' th' Rain.

Aymer. What he that wears a Clout about his Neck ?
His Cuffs in's Pocket, and his Heart in's Mouth ?

Nov. jun. Now, out upon him !

Beaumel. Servant, tie my Hand.
How your Lips bluſh, in Scorn that they ſhould pay
Tribute to Hands when Lips are in the Way !

Nov. jun. I thus recant; yet now your Hand looks
    white,
Becauſe your Lips robb'd it of ſuch a Right.
Monſieur Aymer, I prythee ſing the Song
Devoted to my Miſtreſs.   [*Muſick.*

S O N G.

A Dialogue between a Man and a Woman. [8]

Man.   *Set* Phœbus ! *ſet ; a fairer Sun doth riſe*
        From the bright Radiance of my Miſtreſs' Eyes
        Than ever thou begat'ſt : I dare not look ;
        Each Hair a Golden Line, each Word a Hook
        The more I ſtrive, the more ſtill I am took.

---

8 *Maſſinger's* poetical Talents ſeem to be confined to the Drama ;
the Odes and Songs introduced into his Plays are wretched Compo-
ſitions; in this reſpect he is much inferior to *Beaumont* and *Fletcher,*
who have given us in their Plays ſome pretty little Poems, eſpecially
the Invocation to Melancholy in the *Paſſionate Madman,* which (to
ſpeak in the faſhionable Jargon) is a delicious Morſel. *M. M.*

Wom. *Fair Servant! come; the Day these Eyes do lend*
         To warm thy Blood, thou dost so vainly spend,
         Come strangle Breath.

Man.   *What Note so sweet as this*
         That calls the Spirits to a further Bliss?

Wom.   *Yet this out-savours Wine, and this Perfume,*

Man.   *Let's die, I languish, I consume.*

After the Song, enter Rochfort *and* Beaumont.

Beaum. Romont will come, Sir, straight.

Roch. 'Tis well.

Beaumel. My Father.

Nov. jun. My honourable Lord.

Roch. My Lord *Novall!* this is a Virtue in you,
So early up and ready before Noon!
That are the Map of Dressing through all *France.*

Nov. jun. I rise to say my Prayers, Sir, here's my
         Saint.

Roch. 'Tis well and courtly;—you must give me
         Leave,
I have some private Conference with my Daughter,
Pray use my Garden, you shall dine with me.

Lilad. We'll wait on you.

Nov. jun. Good morn unto your Lordship,
Remember what you have vow'd—   [*To* Beaumelle.
                [*Exeunt all but* Rochfort *and* Beaumelle.

Beau. Perform I must.

Roch. Why how now, *Beaumelle,* thou look'st not
         well.
Th'art sad of late,—come cheer thee; I have found
A wholesome Remedy for these maiden Fits,
A goodly Oak whereon to twist my Vine,
Till her fair Branches grow up to the Stars.
Be near at Hand, Success crown my Intent,
My Business fills my little Time so full,
I cannot stand to talk: I know thy Duty
Is Handmaid to my Will, especially
When it presents nothing but good and fit.

Beaum. Sir, I am yours.—Oh! if my Tears prove true,
Fate hath wrong'd Love and will deftroy me too.
        [*Exit* Beaumelle.

Enter Romont *and Keeper.*

Rom. Sent you for me, Sir?
Roch. Yes.
Rom. Your Lordfhip's Pleafure?
Roch. Keeper, this Prifoner I will fee forth coming.
Upon my Word—Sit down, good Colonel.
        [*Exit Keeper.*

Why I did wifh you hither, noble Sir,
Is to advife you from this Iron Carriage,
Which, fo affected, *Romont,* you will wear
To pity, and to Counfel you fubmit
With Expedition to the great *Novall:*
Recant your ftern Contempt and flight Neglect
Of the whole Court and him, and opportunely,
Or you will undergo a heavy Cenfure
In public very fhortly.
 Rom. Reverend Sir,
I have obferv'd you, and do know you well;
And am now more afraid you know not me,
By wifhing my Submiffion to *Novall,*
Than I can be of all the bellowing Mouths
That wait upon him to pronounce the Cenfure,
Could it determine me to Torments and Shame.
Submit and crave Forgivenefs of a Beaft?
'Tis true, this Boil of State wears purple Tiffue,
Is high fed, proud:—So is his Lordfhip's Horfe,
And bears as rich Caparifons. I know
This Elephant carries on his Back not only
Tow'rs, Caftles, but the ponderous Republick,
And never ftoops for't, with his ftrong breath'd Trunk
Snuffs other's Titles, Lordfhips, Offices,
Wealth, Bribes, and Lives, under his ravenous Jaws:
What's this unto my Freedom? I dare die;

And therefore aſk this Camel, if theſe Bleſſings
(For ſo they would be underſtood by a man)
But mollify one Rudeneſs in his Nature,
Sweeten the eager Reliſh of the Law,
At whoſe great Helm he ſits.   Helps he the Poor
In a juſt Buſineſs ? Nay, does he not croſs
Every deſerved Soldier and Scholar,
As if, when Nature made him, ſhe had made
The general Antipathy of all Virtue ?
How ſavagely and blaſphemouſly he ſpake
Touching the General, the brave General dead!
I muſt weep when I think on't.
 Roch. Sir.
 Rom. My Lord, I am not ſtubborn; I can melt, you
  ſee,
And prize a Virtue better than my Life ;
For tho' I be not learn'd, I ever lov'd
That holy Mother9 of all Iſſues good,
Whoſe white Hand for a Scepter holds a File,
To poliſh rougheſt Cuſtoms, and in you
She has her Right ; See ! I am calm as Sleep,
But when I think of the groſs Injuries,
The godleſs Wrong done to my General dead,
I rave indeed, and could eat this *Novall* ;
A Soul-leſs Dromedary !
 Roch. Oh ! be temperate,
Sir, tho' I would perſuade, I'll not conſtrain ;
Each Man's Opinion freely is his own,
Concerning any Thing, or any Body,
Be it right or wrong, 'tis at the Judge's Peril.

Enter Beaumont.

 Beaum. Theſe Men, Sir ! wait without ; my Lord
  is come too.
 Roch. Pay 'em thoſe Sums upon the Table ; take
Their full Releaſes :—Stay—I want a witneſs :
Let me intreat you, Colonel, to walk in,

9 Meaning Virtue. *M. M.*

And ſtand but by to ſee this Money paid,
It does concern you and your Friend ; it was
The better Cauſe you were ſent for, tho' ſaid other-
    wiſe.
The Deed ſhall make this my Requeſt more plain.
   Rom. I ſhall obey your Pleaſure, Sir, tho' ignorant
To what it tends?   [*Exit* Romont *and Servant.*

Enter Charalois.

   Roch. Worthieſt Sir,
You are moſt welcome : Fie, no more of this :
You have out-wept a Woman, noble *Charalois!*
No Man but has or muſt bury a Father.
   Char. Grave Sir ! I buried Sorrow for his Death
In the Grave with him. I did never think
He was immortal—tho' I vow I grieve,
And ſee no Reaſon why the vicious,
Virtuous, valiant, and unworthy Men,
Should die alike.
   Roch. They do not.
   Char. In the Manner
Of dying Sir, they do not, but all die,
And therein differ not : But I have done.
I ſpy'd the lively Picture of my Father,
Paſſing your Gallery, and that caſt this Water
Into mine Eyes : See,—fooliſh that I am,
To let it do ſo.
   Roch. Sweet and gentle Nature !
How ſilken is this well ¹⁰ comparatively
To other Men ; I have a Suit to you Sir.
   Char. Take it ; 'tis granted.
   Roch. What?
   Char. Nothing, my Lord.

***

   10 *How ſilken is this well, &c.*

  I ſuſpect that there is ſome Conception in this Paſſage, but if *well*
be the right reading, it is a quaint Alluſion to the Tears of *Charalois,*
and muſt be conſidered as a Noun Subſtantive. *M. M.*

Roch. Nothing is quickly granted.

Char. Faith, my Lord!
That nothing granted is even all I have,
For all know I have nothing left to grant.

Roch. Sir, have you any Suit to me? I'll grant
You some Thing, any Thing.

Char. Nay, surely I that can
Give nothing, will but sue for that again.
No Man will grant me any Thing I sue for.
But begging nothing, every Man will give't.

Roch. Sir! the Love I bore your Father, and the Worth
I see in you, so much resembling his,
Made me thus send for you.   And tender here
                                         [*Draws a Curtain.*
Whatever you will take, Gold, Jewels, both,
All, to supply your Wants, and free yourself.
Where heavenly Virtue in high-blooded Veins
Is lodg'd, and can agree, Men should kneel down,
Adore and sacrifice all that they have;
And well they may, it is so seldom seen.
Put off your Wonder, and here freely take
Or send your Servants: Nor, Sir, shall you use
In aught of this a poor Man's Fee, or Bribe
Unjustly taken of the Rich, but what's
Directly gotten, and yet by the Law.

Char. How ill, Sir, it becomes those Hairs to mock!

Roch. Mock? Thunder strike me then.

Char. You do amaze me.
But you shall wonder too; I will not take
One single Piece of this great Heap.   Why should I
Borrow, that have not Means to pay; nay, am
A very Bankrupt, even in flatt'ring Hope
Of ever raising any.   All my begging
Is *Romont*'s Liberty.

Enter Romont, Beaumont, *and Creditors loaded with Money.*

Roch. Here is your Friend,
Enfranchised ere you spake.   I give him you:

And, *Charalois*, I give you to your Friend,
As free a Man as he : Your Father's Debts
Are taken off.

   Char. How ?

   Rom. Sir, it is moſt true.
I am the Witneſs.

   1 *Cred.* Yes, faith, we are paid.

   2 *Cred.* Heaven bleſs his Lordſhip—I did think him
      wiſer.

   3 *Cred.* He a Stateſman ?. He an Aſs—Pay other
      Men's Debts ?

   1 *Cred.* That he was never bound for.

   Rom. One more ſuch
Would ſave the reſt of Pleaders.

   Char. Honour'd *Rochfort.*
Lie ſtill my Tongue, and Bluſhes ſcald my Cheeks,
That offer Thanks in Words for ſuch great Deeds.

   Roch. Call in my Daughter :—Still I have a Suit to
      you.   [*Exit* Beaumont.
Would you requite me.

   Rom. With his Life, I aſſure you.

   Roch. Nay, would you make me now your Debtor,
      Sir !

Enter Beaumelle.

This is my only Child : What ſhe appears,
Your Lordſhip well may ſee : for Education, *Beaumelle*
Follows not any : For her Mind, I know it
To be far fairer than her Shape, and hope
It will continue ſo : If now her Birth
Be not too mean for *Charalois,* take her
This Virgin by the Hand, and call her Wife;
Indow'd with all my Fortunes : Bleſs me ſo,
Requite me thus, and make me happier,
In joining my poor empty Name to yours,
Than if my 'State were multiplied tenfold.

   Char. Is this the Payment, Sir, that you expect ?
Why, you precipitate me more in Debt,
That nothing but my Life can ever pay.

This Beauty being your Daughter (in which yours
I muſt conceive Neceſſity of her Virtue)
Without all Dowry is a Prince's Aim.
Then, as ſhe is, for poor and worthleſs me
How much too worthy!—Waken me, *Romont*,
That I may know I dream'd, and find this vaniſh'd.

  Rom. Sure I ſleep not.
  Roch. Your Sentence—Life or Death.
  Char. Fair *Beaumelle*, can you love me?
  Beaum. Yes, my Lord.

Enter Novall *jun.* Ponta, Malotin, Liladam, *and* Aymer.
All ſalute.

  Char. You need not queſtion me if I can you.
You are the faireſt Virgin in *Dijon*,
And *Rochfort* is your Father.
  Nov. jun. What's this Change?
  Roch. You met my Wiſhes, Gentlemen.
  Rom. What make
Theſe Dogs in Doublets here?
  Beaum. A Viſitation, Sir.
  Char. Then thus, fair *Beaumelle!* I write my Faith,
Thus ſeal it in the Sight of Heaven and Men.
Your Fingers tie my Heart-ſtrings with this Touch,
In true-love Knots, which nought but Death ſhall looſe.
And let theſe Tears (an Emblem of our Loves)
Like Cryſtal Rivers individually
Flow into one another; make one Source,
Which never Man diſtinguiſh, leſs divide!
Breath marry Breath; and Kiſſes mingle Souls;
Two Hearts and Bodies here incorporate:
And, tho' with little wooing I have won,
My future Life ſhall be a wooing Time,
And every Day new as the Bridal one.
Oh, Sir! I groan under your Courteſies,
More than my Father's Bones under his Wrongs,
You, *Curtius*-like, have thrown into the Gulf,
Of this his Country's foul Ingratitude,
Your Life and Fortunes, to redeem their Shames,

Roch. No more, my Glory! come, let's in, and
    haften
This Celebration.

Romont, Malotin, Pontalier *and* Beaumont.

All fair Blifs upon it.
        [*Exeunt* Rochfort, Charalois, Romont, Beau-
            mont *and* Malotin.
Nov. jun. Miftrefs!
Beaum. Oh Servant, Virtue ftrengthen me!
Thy Prefence blows round my Affection's Vane:
You will undo me if you fpeak again.
                                [*Exit* Beaumelle.
Lilad. Aym. Here will be Sport for you. This works.
                [*Exeunt* Liladam *and* Aymer.
Nov. jun. Peace! Peace!
Pont. One Word, my Lord *Novall!*
Nov. jun. What, thou would'ft Money—there.
Pont. No, I'll none, I'll not be bought a Slave,
A Pandar, or a Parafite, for all
Your Father's Worth; tho' you have fav'd my Life,
Refcu'd me often from my Wants, I muft not
Wink at your Follies that will ruin you.
You know my blunt Way, and my Love to Truth:
Forfake the Purfuit of this Lady's Honour,
Now you do fee her made another Man's,
And fuch a Man's fo good, fo popular;
Or you will pluck a thoufand Mifchiefs on you.
The Benefits you've done me are not loft,
Nor caft away, they are purs'd here in my Heart,
But let me pay you, Sir, a fairer Way
Than to defend your Vices, or to footh 'em.
    Nov. jun. Ha, ha, ha! what are my Courfes unto
        thee?
Good Coufin *Pontalier*, meddle with that
That fhall concern thyfelf.
                            [*Exit* Novall.

Pont. No more but Scorn?
Move on then, Stars! work your pernicious Will!
Only the wise rule, and prevent your Ill.   [*Exit.*

H A U T B O Y S.

*Here a Passage over the Stage, while the Act is playing for
the Marriage of* Charalois *with* Beaumelle, *&c.*

End of the Second Act.

A C T III.   S C E N E I.

Enter Novall *jun.* and Bellapert.

Novall *jun.*

FLY not to these Excuses: Thou hast been
     False in thy Promise—and, when I have said
Ungrateful, all is spoke.
  Bellap. Good my Lord! but hear me only.
  Nov. jun. To what Purpose, Trifler?
Can any Thing that thou canst say make void
The Marriage? Or those Pleasures but a Dream,
Which *Charalois* (oh *Venus!*) hath enjoy'd?
  Bellap. I yet could say that you receive Advantage
In what you think a Loss, would you vouchsafe me;
That you were never in the Way till now
With Safety to arrive at your Desires;
That Pleasure makes Love to you, unattended
By Danger or Repentance?
  Nov. jun. That I could
But apprehend one Reason how this might be,
Hope would not then forsake me.
  Bellap. The enjoying
Of what you most desire; I say th' enjoying

Shall, in the full Poſſeſſion of your Wiſhes,
Confirm that I am faithful.

Nov. jun. Give ſome Reliſh
How this may appear poſſible.

Bellap. I will.
Reliſh and taſte, and make the Banquet eaſy.
You ſay my Lady's married—I confeſs it :
That *Charalois* hath enjoyed her—'tis moſt true :
That with her he's already Maſter of
The beſt Part of my Lord's 'State. Still better :
But that the firſt or laſt ſhould be your Hindrance,
I utterly deny : For, but obſerve me,
While ſhe went for, and was, I ſwear, a Virgin,
What Courteſy could ſhe with her Honour give;
Or you receive with Safety—take me with you ;
When I ſay Courteſy, do not think I mean
A Kiſs ; the tying of her Shoe or Garter ;
An Hour of private Conference : Thoſe are Trifles.
In this Word Courteſy, we that are Gameſters point at
The Sport direct, where not alone the Lover
Brings his Artillery, but uſes it :
Which Word expounded to you, ſuch a Courteſy
Do you expect and ſudden.

Nov. jun. But he taſted the firſt Sweets, *Bellapert !*

Bellap. He wrong'd you ſhrewdly !
He toil'd to climb up to the *Phœnix'* Neſt,
And in his Prints leaves your Aſcent more eaſy.
I do not know, you that are perfect Criticks
In Women's Books, may talk of Maidenheads.

Nov. jun. But for her Marriage.——

Bellap. 'Tis a fair Protection
'Gainſt all Arreſts of Fear or Shame for ever.
Such as are fair, and yet not fooliſh, ſtudy
To have one at thirteen ; but they are mad
That ſtay till twenty. Then, Sir ! for the Pleaſure ;
To ſay Adultery's ſweeter, that is ſtale.
This only—Is not the Contentment more,
To ſay, this is my Cuckold, than my Rival.
More I could ſay—but briefly ſhe doats on you,

If it prove otherwise, spare not, poison me
With the next Gold you give me.

Enter Beaumelle.

Beaumel. How's this, Servant? Courting my Woman?
Bellap. As an Entrance to
The Favour of the Miftrefs : You are together
And I am perfect in my Cue.   [*Going.*
Beaumel. Stay *Bellapert.*
Bellap. In this I muft not, with your Leave, obey
            you.
Your Taylor and your Tire-woman wait without
And ftay my Counfel and Direction for
Your next Day's Dreffing.   I have much to do,
Nor will your Ladyfhip now, Time is precious,
Continue idle; this choice Lord will find
So fit employment for you.   [*Exit* Bellapert.
Beaumel. I fhall grow angry.
Nov. jun. Not fo; you have a Jewel in her, Madam!

Enter Bellapert.

Bellap. I had forgot to tell your Ladyfhip
The Clofet is private and your Couch ready;
And, if you pleafe that I fhall lofe the Key,
But fay fo, and 'tis done,   [*Exit* Bellapert.
Beaumel. You come to chide me, Servant ! and bring
            with you
Sufficient Warrant.   You will fay, and truly,
My Father found too much Obedience in me;
By being won too foon : Yet, if you pleafe
But to remember all my Hopes and Fortunes
Had Reference to his Liking, you will grant,
That, tho' I did not well towards you, I yet
Did wifely for myfelf.
   Nov. jun. With too much Fervor
I have fo long lov'd and ftill love you, Miftrefs;
To efteem that an Injury to me
Which was to you convenient ;—that is paft

My Help, is paſt my Cure. You yet may, Lady,
In Recompence of all my duteous Service,
(Provided that your Will anſwer your Power).
Become my Creditreſs.

    Beaumel. I underſtand you;
And for Aſſurance the Requeſt you make
Shall not be long unanſwered, pray you ſit,
And by what you ſhall hear, you'll eaſily find,
My Paſſions are much fitter to deſire
Than to be ſued to.

Enter Romont and Florimel.

    Flor. Sir, 'tis not Envy
At the Start my Fellow has got of me in
My Ladies good Opinion, that's the Motive
Of this Diſcovery; but due Payment
Of what I owe her Honour.

    Rom. So I conceive it.

    Flor. I have obſerv'd too much, nor ſhall my Silence
Prevent the Remedy——yonder they are,
I dare not be ſeen with you. You may do
What you think fit, which will be, I preſume,
The Office of a faithful and try'd Friend
To my young Lord.   [*Exit* Florimel.

    Rom. This is no Viſion: Ha!

    Nov. jun. With the next Opportunity.

    Beaumel. By this Kiſs, and this, and this.

    Nov. jun. That you would ever ſwear thus.

    Rom. If I ſeem rude, your Pardon, Lady! yours
I do not aſk: Come, do not dare to ſhew me
A Face of Anger, or the leaſt Diſlike;
Put on, and ſuddenly, a milder Look;
I ſhall grow rough elſe.

    Nov. jun. What have I done, Sir!
To draw this harſh unſavory Language from you?

    Rom. Done, Popinjay? Why, doſt thou think
        that, if
I e'er had dreamt that thou hadſt done me Wrong,
Thou ſhouldſt outlive it.

Beaumel. This is fomething more
Than my Lord's Friendfhip gives Commiffion for.
   Nov. jun. Your Prefence and the Place, makes him
      prefume
Upon my Patience.
   Rom. As if thou e'er wert angry
But with thy Taylor, and yet that poor Shred
Can bring more to the making up of a Man,
Than can be hop'd from thee: Thou art his Creature,
And, did he not each Morning new create thee,
Thou'dft ftink and be forgotten. I'll not change
One Syllable more with thee, until thou bring
Some Teftimony under good Mens Hands
Thou art a Chriftian. I fufpect thee ftrongly,
And will be fatisfied: 'Till which Time, keep from me.
The Entertainment of your Vifitation
Has made what I intended one " a Bufinefs.
   Nov. jun. So we fhall meet—Madam!
   Rom. Ufe that Leg again, and I'll cut off the other.
   Nov. jun. Very good.   [*Exit* Novall.
   Rom. So I refpect you,
Not for yourfelf, but in Remembrance of
Who is your Father, and whofe Wife you now are,
That I choofe rather not to underftand
Your nafty Scoff, than——
   Beaumel. What, you will not beat me,
If I expound it to you. Here's a Tyrant
Spares neither Man nor Woman.
   Rom. My Intents,
Madam, deferve not this; nor do I ftay
To be the Whetftone of your Wit: Preferve it
To fpend on fuch as know how to admire
Such colour'd Stuff. In me there is now fpeaks to you
As true a Friend and Servant to your Honour,
And one that will with as much Hazard guard it
As ever Man did Goodnefs.——But then, Lady!
You muft endeavour, not alone to be,
But to appear, worthy fuch Love and Service.

<hr>

11 That is, a Vifitation.

Beaumel. To what tends this ?

Rom. Why, to this Purpofe, Lady !
I do defire you fhould prove fuch a Wife
To *Charalois* (and fuch a one he merits)
As *Cæfar*, did he live, could not except at,
Not only innocent from Crime, but free
From all Taint and Sufpition.

Beaumel. They are bafe that judge me otherwife.

Rom. But yet be careful !
Detraction's a bold Monfter, and fears not
To wound the Fame of Princes, if it find
But any Blemifh in their Lives to work on :
But I'll be plainer with you : Had the People
Been learnt to fpeak, but what even now I faw,
Their Malice out of that would raife an Engine
To overthrow your Honour.   In my Sight,
With yonder painted Fool I frighted from you,
You us'd Familiarity beyond
A modeft Entertainment : You embrac'd him
With too much Ardour for a Stranger, and
Met him with Kiffes neither chafte nor comely :
But learn you to forget him, as I will
Your Bounties to him ; you will find it fafer
Rather to be uncourtly than immodeft.

Beaumel. This pretty Rag about your Neck fhews
        well,
And, being coarfe and little Worth, it fpeaks you
As terrible as thrifty.

Rom. Madam !

Beaumel. Yes.
And this ftrong Belt in which you hang your Honour,
Will outlaft twenty Scarfs.

Rom. What mean you, Lady ?

Beaumel. And all elfe about you Cap-a-pee,
So uniform in Spite of Handfomenefs,
Shews fuch a bold Contempt of Comelinefs,
That 'tis not ftrange your Laundrefs in the Leaguer
Grew mad with Love of you.

Vol. II.   P

Rom. Is my free Counsel
Answer'd with this ridiculous Scorn?

Beaumel. These Objects
Stole very much of my Attention from me;
Yet something I remember, to speak Truth,
Deliver'd gravely, but to little Purpose,
That almost would have made me swear some Curate
Had stol'n into the Person of *Romont*,
And, in the Praise of Good-wife Honesty,
Had read an Homily.

Rom. By this Hand.——

Beaumel. And Sword;
I will make up your Oath, 'twill want Weight else.
You're angry with me, and poor I laugh at it.
Do you come from the Camp, which affords only
The Conversation of cast Suburb Whores,
To set down to a Lady of my Rank
Limits of Entertainment?

Rom. Sure a Legion has possest this Woman.

Beaumel. One Stamp more would do well: Yet I de-
fire not
You should grow horn-mad till you have a Wife.
You are come to warm Meat, and perhaps clean Linen:
Feed, wear it, and be thankful. For me, know,
That tho' a thousand Watches were set on me,
And you the Master-spy, I yet would use
The Liberty that best likes me. I will revel,
Feast, kiss, embrace. Perhaps, grant larger Favours.
Yet such as live upon my Means, shall know
They must not murmur at it. If my Lord
Be now grown yellow, and has chose out you
To serve his Jealousy that Way; tell him this.
You've something to inform him.   [*Exit* Beaumelle.

Rom. And I will.
Believe it wicked one, I will. Hear, Heaven!
But, hearing, pardon me: If these Fruits grow
Upon the Tree of Marriage, let me shun it,
As a forbidden Sweet. An Heir and rich,
Young, beautiful—yet add to this—a Wife,
And I will rather choose a Spital Sinner

Carted an Age before, tho' three Parts rotten,
And take it for a Blessing, rather than
Be fetter'd to the hellish Slavery [12]
Of such an Impudence.

Enter Beaumont *with Writings.*

Beaum. Colonel! good Fortune
To meet you thus: You look sad, but I'll tell you
Something that shall remove it. O how happy
Is my Lord *Charalois* in his fair Bride!
Rom. A happy Man indeed!—pray you in what?
Beaum. I dare swear, you would think so good a
    Lady
A Dower sufficient.
Rom. No doubt.—But on.
Beaum. So fair, so chaste, so virtuous:—Indeed
All that is excellent.
Rom. Women have no Cunning to gull the World!
Beaum. Yet to all these, my Lord,
Her Father gives the full Addition of
All he does now possess in *Burgundy:*
These Writings to confirm it, are new seal'd,
And I most fortunate to present him with them;
I must go seek him out, can you direct me?
Rom. You'll find him breaking a young Horse.
Beaum. I thank you.   [*Exit* Beaumont.
Rom. I must do something worthy *Charalois'* Friend-
    ship:
If she were well inclin'd, to keep her so

☞ 12 In an Advertisement prefixed to *The Bondman,* which was revived in 1710, we are told that Mr. *Rowe* had revised the Works of *Massinger,* and did intend to publish them; I am apt to think this Assertion true, and that Mr. *Rowe* was a great Admirer of our Author, his excellent Play of *The Fair Penitent* being founded on the Tragedy now before us. The beautiful Scene between *Horatio* and *Califta* is evidently copied from the foregoing, as is that between *Altamont* and *Horatio* in the third Act where they quarrel, from the last Scene of this: The curious Reader may not be disagreeably amused in comparing many other similar Parts of these excellent Tragedies together.

Deferv'd hot Thanks : And yet, to ftay a Woman
Spurr'd headlong by hot Luft to her own Ruin,
Is harder than to prop a falling Tower
With a deceiving Reed.

Enter Rochfort.

Roch. Some one feek for me,
As foon as he returns.

Rom. Her Father ? ha !——
How if I break this to him ? Sure it cannot
Meet with an ill Conftruction. His Wifdom,
Made powerful by th' Authority of a Father,
Will warrant and give Privilege to his Counfels.
It fhall be fo—My Lord !

Roch. Your Friend, *Romont :*
Would you aught with me ?

Rom. I ftand fo engag'd
To your fo many Favours, that I hold it
A Breach in Thankfulnefs, fhould I not difcover,
Tho' with fome Imputation to myfelf,
All Doubts that may concern you.

Roch. The Performance
Will make this Proteftation worth my Thanks.

Rom. Then, with your Patience, lend me your At-
tention :
For what I muft deliver, whifper'd only,
You will with too much Grief receive.

Enter Beaumelle *and* Bellapert.

Beaumel. See, Wench !
Upon my Life as I forefpake, he's now
Preferring his Complaint : But be thou perfect,
And we will fit him.

Bellap. Fear not me, pox on him !
A Captain turn'd Informer againft Kiffing ?
Would he were hang'd up in his rufty Armour !
But, if our frefh Wits cannot turn the Plots
Of fuch a mouldy Murrion on itfelf ;

Rich Clothes, choice Fare, and a true Friend at a call,
With all the Pleasures the Night yields, forsake us.

 Roch. This in my Daughter ? Do not wrong her.

 Bellap. Now begin.
The Game's afoot, and we in Distance.

 Beaumel. 'Tis thy Fault, foolish Girl! pin on my
   Veil,
I will not wear those Jewels. Am I not
Already match'd beyond my Hopes ? Yet still
You prune and set me forth, as if I were
Again to please a Suitor.

 Bellap. 'Tis the Course
That our great Ladies take.

 Rom. A weak Excuse !

 Beaumel. Those that are better seen, in what concerns
A Lady's Honour and fair Fame condemn it.
You wait well : in your Absence, my Lord's Friend,
The understanding, grave and wise *Romont*——

 Rom. Must I be still her Sport ?   [*Aside.*

 Beaumel. Reprov'd me for it.
And he has travell'd to bring home a Judgment
Not to be contradicted. You will say
My Father, that owes more to Years than he,
Has brought me up to Musick, Language, Courtship,
And I must use them. True, but not t'offend,
Or render me suspected.

 Roch. Does your fine Story begin from this ?

 Beaumel. I thought a parting Kiss
From young *Novall* would have displeas'd no more
Than heretofore it hath done ; but I find
I must restrain such Favours now ; look therefore,
As you are careful to continue mine,
That I no more be visited. I'll endure
The strictest Course of Life that Jealousy
Can think secure enough, ere my Behaviour
Shall call my Fame in Question.

 Rom. Ten Dissemblers
Are in this subtle Devil. You believe this ?

Roch. So far, that if you trouble me again
With a Report like this, I shall not only
Judge you malicious in your Disposition,
But study to repent what I have done
To such a Nature.

Rom. Why, 'tis exceeding well.

Roch. And for you, Daughter, off with this; off
  with it;
I have that Confidence in your Goodness, I,
That I will not consent to have you live
Like to a Recluse in a Cloyster : Go,
Call in the Gallants, let them make you merry,
Use all fit Liberty.

Bellap. Blessing on you.
If this new Preacher with the Sword and Feather
Could prove his Doctrine for Canonical,
We should have a fine World.   [*Exit* Bellapert.

Roch. Sir, if you please
To bear yourself as fits a Gentleman,
The House is at your Service; but, if not,
Tho' you seek Company elsewhere, your Absence
Will not be much lamented——   [*Exit* Rochfort,

Rom. If this be
The Recompence of striving to preserve
A wanton Gigglet honest, very shortly
'Twill make all Mankind Pandars.—Do you smile,
Good Lady *Looseness ?* Your whole Sex is like you,
And that Man's mad that seeks to better any :
What new Change have you next ?

Beaumel. Oh, fear not you, Sir !
I'll shift into a Thousand, but I will
Convert your Heresy.

Rom. What Heresy ? speak !

Beaumel. Of keeping a Lady that is married,
From entertaining Servants.——

Enter Novall jun. Malotin, Liladam, Aymer, *and* Pontalier.

O, you're welcome.
Ufe any Means to vex him,
And then with Welcome follow me.   [*Exit* Beaumel.

   Nov. jun. You are tir'd
With your grave Exhortations, Colonel!

   Lilad. How is it? Faith, your Lordfhip may do well
To help him to fome Church-preferment: 'Tis
Now the Fafhion for Men of all Conditions,
However they have liv'd, to end that Way.

   Aymer. That Face would do well in a Surplice.

   Rom. Rogues, be filent—or—

   Pont. S'Death! will you fuffer this?

   Rom. And you, the Mafter Rogue, the Coward Rafcal,
I fhall be with you fuddenly.

   Nov. jun. Pontalier,
If I fhould ftrike him, I know I fhall kill him:
And therefore I would have thee beat him, for
He's good for nothing elfe.

   Lilad. His Back
Appears to me, as it would tire a Beadle.
And then he has a knotted Brow, would bruife
A Court-like Hand to touch it.

   Aymer. He looks like
A Currier when his Hide's grown dear.

   Pont. Take Heed he curry not fome of you.

   Nov. jun. Gads me! he's angry.

   Rom. I break no Jefts, but I can bread my Sword
About your Pates.

Enter Charalois *and* Beaumont.

   Lilad. Here's more.

   Aymer. Come, let's be gone!
We are beleaguer'd:

P 4

Nov. Jun. Look, they bring up their Troops.

Pont. Will you fit down with this Difgrace?
You are abus'd moft grofly.

Lilad. I grant you, Sir, we are; and you would have
      us
Stay, and be more abus'd,

Nov. jun. My Lord, I'm forry
Your Houfe is fo inhofpitable, we muft quit it.

      [*Exeunt. Manent* Charalois *and* Romont,

Char. Pr'ythee, *Romont*, what caus'd this Uproar?

Rom. Nothing.
They laugh'd and us'd their fcurvy Wits upon me.

Char. Come, 'tis thy jealous Nature: But I wonder
That you, which are an honeft Man and worthy,
Should fofter this Sufpition. No Man laughs,
No one can whifper, but thou apprehend'ft
His Conference and his Scorn reflects on thee.
For my Part, they fhould Scoff their thin Wits out,
So I not heard them; beat me, not being there.
Leave, leave thefe Fits to confcious Men, to fuch
As are obnoxious to thofe foolifh Things
As they can gibe at.

Rom. Well, Sir!

Char. Thou art known
Valiant without Defect, rightly defin'd,
Which is (as fearing to do Injury,
As tender to endure it) not a Brabbler,
A Swearer.

Rom. Pifh, pifh! what needs this, my Lord?
If I be known none fuch, how vainly you
Do caft away good Counfel? I have lov'd you,
And yet muft freely fpeak: So young a Tutor
Fits not fo old a Soldier as I am.
And I muft tell you, 'twas in your Behalf
I grew enrag'd thus; yet had rather die
Than open the great Caufe a Syllable further.

Char. In my Behalf? Wherein hath *Charalois*
Unfitly fo demean'd himfelf, to give

The leaſt Occaſion to the looſeſt Tongue
To throw Aſperſions on him ? Or ſo weakly
Protected his own Honour, as it ſhould
Need Defence from any but himſelf ?
They're Fools that judge me by my outward Seeming ;
Why ſhould my Gentleneſs beget Abuſe ?
The Lion is not angry that does ſleep,
Nor ever Man a Coward that can weep.
For God's Sake ſpeak the Cauſe.

 Rom. Not for the World.
Oh ! it will ſtrike Diſeaſe into your Bones,
Beyond the Cure of Phyſick ; drink your Blood,
Rob you of all your Reſt, contract your Sight,
Leave you no Eyes but to ſee Miſery,
And of your own ; nor Speech, but to wiſh thus,
Would I had periſh'd in the Priſon's Jaws,
From whence I was redeem'd ! 'Twill wear you old,
Before you have Experience in that Art
That Cauſes your Affliction.

 Char. Thou doſt ſtrike
A deathful Coldneſs to my Heart's high Heat,
And ſhrink'ſt my Liver like the *Calenture.*
Declare this Foe of mine, and Life's, that like
A Man I may encounter and ſubdue it.
It ſhall not have one ſuch Effect in me
As thou denounceſt : With a Soldier's Arm,
If it be Strength I'll meet it : If a Fault
Belonging to my Mind, I'll cut it off
With mine own Reaſon as a Scholar ſhould.
—Speak, tho' it make me monſtrous.

 Rom. I'll die firſt.
Farewell ! continue merry, and high Heaven
Keep your Wife chaſte.

 Char. Hum !—Stay and take this Wolf
Out of my Breaſt, that thou haſt lodg'd there, or
For ever loſe me.

 Rom. Loſe not, Sir, yourſelf,
And I will venture—ſo the Door is faſt.

         [*Locks the Door.*

Now, noble *Charalois,* collect yourſelf ;

Summon your Spirits; muster all your Strength
That can belong to Man ; sift Passion
From ev'ry Vein, and, whatsoe'er ensues,
Upbraid not me hereafter, as the Cause of
Jealousy, Discontent, Slaughter and Ruin :
Make me not Parent to Sin :—You will know
This Secret that I burn with.

   Char. Devil on't,
What should it be ? *Romont,* I hear you wish
My Wife's Continuance of Chastity.

   Rom. There was no Hurt in that.

   Char. Why ? do you know
A Likelihood or Possibility unto the contrary ?

   Rom. I know it not, but doubt it ; these the Grounds.
The Servant of your Wife now, young *Novall,*
The Son unto your Father's Enemy
(Which aggravates my Presumption the more)
I have been warn'd of, touching her ; nay, seen them
Tie Heart to Heart, one in another's Arms,
Multiplying Kisses, as if they meant
To pose Arithmetic, or whose Eyes would [13]
Be first burnt out with gazing on the other's.
I saw their mouths engender, and their Palms
Glew'd, as if Love had lock'd them ; their Words flow
And melt each other's, like two circling Flames,
Where Chastity, like a Phœnix, methought, burn'd,
But left the World nor Ashes nor an Heir.
Why stand you silent thus ? What cold dull Phlegm,
As if you had no Drop of Choler mix'd
In your whole Constitution, thus prevails,
To fix you now thus stupid, hearing this ?

   Char. You did not see him on my Couch within,
Like *George* a Horseback, on her, nor a-bed ?

---

    [13] *To pose Arithmetic, or whose Eyes would,* &c.

   This Passage, as it stands, is neither Sense nor Grammar ; for
the Verb *pose* cannot be applied to *Eyes.* There is certainly some
Word omitted, I therefore have here amended the Passage in the
Manner that appears to me the most natural.

    To pose Arithmetic, or *try* whose Eyes would. *M. M.*

Rom. No.

Char. Ha! ha!

Rom. Laugh you? E'en fo did your Wife,
And her indulgent Father.

Char. They were wife.
Would'ft have me be a Fool?

Rom. No, but a Man.

Char. There is no Dram of Manhood to fufpeét,
On fuch thin airy Circumftance as this;
Mere Compliment and Courtfhip. Was this Tale
The hideous Monfter which you fo conceal'd?
Away, thou curious Impertinent,
And idle Searcher of fuch lean nice Toys!
Go, thou feditious Sower of Debate!
Fly to fuch Matches, where the Bridegroom doubts
He holds not Worth enough to countervail
The Virtue and the Beauty of his Wife.
Thou buzzing Drone, that 'bout my Ears doft hum,
To ftrike thy rankling Sting into my Heart,
Whofe Venom, Time nor Medicine could affuage.
Thus do I put thee off, and, confident
In mine own Innocency and Defert,
Dare not conceive her fo unreafonable,
To put *Novall* in Balance againft me,
An Upftart, cran'd up to the Height he has.
Hence, Bufybody! thou'rt no Friend to me,
That muft be kept to a Wife's Injury.

Rom. Is't poffible?—Farewel fine honeft Man!
Sweet temper'd Lord, adieu! What Apoplexy
Hath knit Senfe up? Is this *Romont*'s Reward?
Bear Witnefs, the great Spirit of thy Father,
With what a healthful Hope I did adminifter
This Potion that hath wrought fo virulently!
I not accufe thy Wife of Aét, but would
Prevent her Precipice to thy Difhonour,
Which now thy tardy Sluggifhnefs will admit!
Would I had feen thee grav'd with thy great Sire,
Ere live to have Men's marginal Fingers point
At *Charalois*, as a lamented Story.
An Emperor put away his Wife for touching

Another Man; but thou wouldſt have thine taſted,
And keep her, I think. Phoh! I am a Fire
To warm a dead Man, that waſte out myſelf.
Blood!—What a Plague, a Vengeance, is't to me,
If you will be a Cuckold? Here I ſhew
A Sword's Point to thee; this Side you may ſhun,
Or that, the Peril; if you will run on,
I cannot help it.

Char. Didſt thou never ſee me
Angry, *Romont ?*

Rom. Yes, and purſue a Foe
Like Lightning.

Char. Pr'ythee ſee me ſo no more,
I can be ſo again.—Put up thy Sword,
And take thyſelf away, leſt I draw mine.

Rom. Come, fright your Foes with this, Sir? I am
       your Friend,
And dare ſtand by you thus.

Char. Thou'rt not my Friend;
Or being ſo, thou'rt mad.—I muſt not buy
Thy Friendſhip at this Rate; had I juſt Cauſe,
Thou know'ſt I durſt purſue ſuch Injury
Thro' Fire, Air, Water, Earth, nay, were they all
Shuffled again to *Chaos;* but there's none.
Thy Skill, *Romont,* conſiſts in Camps, not Courts,
Farewel, uncivil Man! let's meet no more.
Here our long Web of Friendſhip I untwiſt.
Shall I go whine, walk pale, and lock my Wife
For nothing, from her Birth's free Liberty,
That open'd mine to me? Yes; if I do——
The Name of Cuckold, then dog me with Scorn.
I am a *Frenchman,* no *Italian* born.   [*Exit.*

Rom. A dull *Dutch* rather:—Fall and cool my
      Blood!
Boil not in Zeal of thy Friend's Hurt ſo high,
That is ſo low, and cold himſelf in't! Woman,
How ſtrong art thou! how eaſily beguil'd!
How thou doſt rack us by the very Horns!
Now Wealth, I ſee, change Manners and the Man,

Something I muſt do mine own Wrath to aſſuage,
And note my Friendſhip to an After-age.

[*Exit.*

End of the Fourth Act.

ACT IV.   SCENE I.

Enter Novall *jun. as newly dreſſed, a* Taylor, Barber, Perfumer, Liladam, Aymer, *and Page.*

Novall *jun.*

MEND this a little: Pox! thou haſt burnt me, Oh! fie upon't!—O lard! he has made me ſmell, for all the World, like a Flax, or a red-headed Woman's Chamber: Powder, Powder, Powder.

Perf. Oh, ſweet Lord!

[Novall *ſits in a Chair, Barber orders his Hair, Perfumer gives Powder, Taylor ſets Cloaths.*

Page. That's his Perfumer.

Tayl. Oh, dear Lord!

Page. That's his Taylor.

Nov. jun. Monſieur *Liladam! Aymer!* how allow you the Model of theſe Cloaths?

Aymer. Admirably, admirably; oh ſweet Lord! aſſuredly it's Pity the Worms ſhould eat thee.

Page. Here's a fine Cell; a Lord, a Taylor, a Perfumer, a Barber, and a Pair of Monſieurs: Three to three, as little Wit in the one, as Honeſty in the other. S'foot I'll into the Country again, learn to ſpeak Truth, drink Ale, and converſe with my Father's Tenants; here I hear nothing all Day, but—upon my Soul! as I am a Gentleman, and an honeſt man!

Aymer. I vow and affirm, your Taylor muſt needs be an expert Geometrician; he has the Longitude, Latitude, Altitude, Profundity, every Dimenſion of your Body, ſo exquiſitely.—Here's a Lace laid as directly, as if Truth were a Taylor.

Page. That were a Miracle.

Lilad. With a Hair's Breadth's Error, there's a Shoulder-Piece cut, and the Baſe of a Pickadille [14] in *puncto.*

Aymer. You are right, Monſieur! his Veſtments ſit as if they grew upon him; or Art had wrought 'em on the ſame Loom, as Nature fram'd his Lordſhip; as if your Taylor were deeply read in Aſtrology, and had taken Meaſure of your honourable Body, with a *Jacob's* Staff, an *Ephimerides.*

Taylor. I am bound t'ye, Gentlemen!

Page. You are deceiv'd; they'll be bound to you: You muſt remember to truſt 'em none.

Nov. jun. Nay, 'faith, thou art a reaſonable, neat Artificer, give the Devil his Due.

Page. I, if he would but cut the Coat according to the Cloth ſtill.

Nov. jun. I now want only my Miſtreſs's Approbation, who is, indeed, the moſt polite punctual Queen of Dreſſing in all *Burgundy.* Pah, and makes all other young Ladies appear as if they came from Board laſt Week out of the Country; is't not true, *Liladam?*

Lilad. True, my Lord! as if any Thing your Lordſhip could ſay, could be otherwiſe than true.

Nov. jun. Nay, O my Soul, 'tis ſo, what fouler Object in the World, than to ſee a young, fair, handſome

---

☞ 14 A Pickadille *(Dutch)* the Hem about the Skirt of a Garment.

Pickadille is not derived from the *Dutch*, but from the *Spaniſh* Peccadillo, a Word adopted into the *Engliſh* Language; nor does it ſignify the Hem of a Garment, but a Ruff. The Puniſhment in old Times for ſlight Offences *(Peccadillos)* was to expoſe Criminals to public View, as we now do in the Pillory, with an indented Collar of Iron about their Necks. From the Nature of the Offences, for which this Puniſhment was inflicted, the inſtrument of it was called a Pickadille. This Name was afterwards given to a Ruff reſembling thoſe Collars. I have heard that the Street in *London*, called *Piccadilly*, obtained that Name from being the Place where this Machine was erected. *M. M.*

Beauty, unhandfomely dighted and incongruently ac-
couter'd ; or a hopeful Chevalier, unmethodically appointed, in the external Ornaments of Nature ? For,
even as the Index tells us the Contents of Stories, and
directs to the particular Chapters, even fo does the
outward Habit and fuperficial Order of Garments, (in
Man or Woman) give us a Tafte of the Spirit, and
demonftratively point (as it were a manual Note from
the Margin) all the internal Quality and Habiliment
of the Soul ; and there cannot be a more evident, pal-
pable, grofs Manifeftation of poor, degenerate, dung-
hilly Blood and Breeding, than a rude, unpolifh'd, dif-
order'd and flovenly Outfide.

Page. An admirable Lecture! oh, all you Gallants,
that hope to be faved by your Cloaths, edify, edify !

Aymer. By the Lard, fweet Lard ! thou deferv'ft a
Penfion o'the State.·

Page.—O' th' Taylors; two fuch Lords were able to
fpread Taylors o'er the Face of a whole Kingdom.

Nov. jun. 'Pox a this Glafs ! it flatters.—I could find
in my Heart to break it.

Page. O, fave the Glafs, my Lord ! and break their
Heads : They are the greater Flatterers, I affure you.

Aymer. Flatters, detracts, impairs.—Yet, put it by,
Left thou, dear Lord, *Narciffus*-like, fhould doat
Upon thyfelf, and die; and rob the World
Of Nature's Copy, that fhe works Form by.

Lilad. Oh ! that I were the Infanta Queen of *Europe!*
Who but thyfelf, fweet Lord, fhould marry me !

Nov. jun. I marry? Were there a Queen o'th' World,
    not I.
Wedlock? No, Padlock; Horfe-Lock; I wear Spurs
                       [*He capers.*
To keep it off my Heels; yet, my *Aymer* !
Like a free, wanton Jennet i'th' Meadows,
I look about, and neigh, take Hedge and Ditch,
Feed in my Neighbour's Paftures ; pick my Choice
Of all their fair maned Mares : But married once,
A Man is ftak'd or pounded, and cannot graze
Beyond his own Hedge.

Enter Pontalier *and* Malotin.

Pont. I have waited, Sir!
Three Hours to fpeak with you, and take it not well,
Such Magpies are admitted, whilft I dance
Attendance.

Lilad. Magpies? What d'ye take me for?

Pont. A long Thing with a moft unpromifing Face:

Aymer. I'll never afk him what he takes me for.

Malot. Do not, Sir!
For he'll go near to tell you.

Pont. Art not thou a Barber-Surgeon?

Barb. Yes, Sirrah! why?

Pont. My Lord is forely troubled with two Scabs.

Lilad. Aymer. Humph——

Pont. I prythee, cure him of 'em.

Nov. jun. Pifh! no more;
Thy Gall fure's overflown: Thefe are my Council,
And we were now in ferious Difcourfe.

Pont. Of Perfume and Apparel. Can you rife,
And fpend five Hours in Dreffing-Talk with thefe?

Nov. jun. Thould'ft have me be a Dog: Up, ftretch,
            and fhake,
And ready for all Day.

Pont. Sir! would you be
More curious in preferving of your Honour
Trim, 'twere more manly. I am come to wake
Your Reputation from this Lethargy
You let it fleep in; to perfuade, importune,
Nay, to provoke you, Sir! to call to Account
This Colonel *Romont*, for the foul Wrong,
Which, like a Burthen, he hath laid on you,
And, like a drunken Porter, you fleep under.
'Tis all the Town-Talk, and, believe Sir,
If your tough Senfe perfift thus, you're undone,
Utterly loft; you will be fcorn'd and baffled
By every Lacquey; feafon now your Youth
With one brave Thing, and it fhall keep the Odour
Even to your Death, beyond; and on your Tomb,

Scent like fweet Oils and Frankincenfe : Sir ! this Life
Which once you fav'd, I ne'er fince counted mine ;
I borrow'd it of you, and now will pay it ;
I tender you the Service of my Sword
To bear your challenge ; if you'll write, your Fate
I'll make mine own : Whate'er betide you, I,
That have liv'd by you, by your Side will die.

   Nov. jun. Ha! ha! wouldft ha' me challenge poor
       Romont :
Fight with clofe Breeches ? Thou may'ft think I dare
       not.
Do not miftake me, Coz : I'm very valiant ;
But Valour fhall not make me fuch an Afs.
What Ufe is there of Valour now-a-days ?
'Tis fure, or to be kill'd, or to be hang'd.
Fight thou as thy Mind moves thee ; 'tis thy Trade :
Thou haft nothing elfe to do. Fight with *Romont* ?
No, I'll not fight under a Lord.

   Pont. Farewell, Sir ! I pity you.
Such loving Lords walk their dead Honour's Graves,
For no Companions fit, but Fools and Knaves.
Come, *Malotin*.   [*Exeunt* Pontalier *and* Malotin.

         Enter Romont.

   Lilad. 'Sfoot, *Colbrand*, the low Giant.
   Aymer. He has brought a Battle in his Face, let's go.
   Page. Colbrand, d'ye call him ? He'll make fome of
you fmoke, I believe.
   Rom. By your Leave, Sirs !
   Aymer. Are you a Concert ? [15]

  ☞ 15 Aym. *Are you a Concert*, &c. *i. e.* Come you here to be
pay'd on. * —Thus in *Romeo*,
   Tyb. Mercutio, thou confort'ft with *Romeo*———
  Mer. Confort ! what doft thou make us Minftrels, if thou make
Minftrels of us, look to hear nothing but Difcords, &c.
                    Act 3, Scene 1.

  * This cannot poffibly be the Meaning, for a Concert is not *played upon*. M. M.

Rom. D'ye take me for
A Fidler ? [16] y'are deceiv'd :—Look.   I'll pay you.

[Kicks 'em.

Page. It feems. he knows you one, he bumfiddles
you fo.

Lilad. Was there ever fo bafe a Fellow ?

Aymer. A Rafcal !

Lilad. A moft uncivil Groom !

Aymer. Offer to kick a Gentleman in a Nobleman's
Chamber ? A-pox o' your Manners.

Lilad. Let him alone, let him alone, thou fhalt lofe
thy Aim, Fellow ! if we ftir againft thee, hang us.

Page. 'Sfoot, I think they have the better on him,
tho' they be kick'd, they talk fo.

Lilad. Let's leave the mad Ape.

Nov. jun. Gentlemen !

Lilad. Nay, my Lord ! we will not offer to difhonour
you fo much as to ftay by you, fince he's alone.

Nov. jun. Hark you.

Aymer. We doubt the Caufe, and will not difparage
you fo much as to take your Lordfhip's Quarrel in
Hand. Plague on him, how he has crumpled our
Bands.

Page. I'll e'en away with 'em, for this Soldier beats
Man, Woman and Child.

[Exeunt all but Novall *and* Romont.

Nov. jun. What mean you, Sir ? My People.—

Rom. Your Boy's gone,

[Locks the Door.

And Door's lock'd,—yet for no Hurt to you,
But Privacy : Call up your Blood again, Sir !
And therefore come without more Circumftance,
Tell me how far the Paffages have gone
'Twixt you and your fair Miftrefs *Beaumelle.*
Tell me the Truth, and, by my Hope of Heaven,
It never fhall go farther.

---

16 *D'ye take me for a Fidler,* &c.

By this and the following Speech of the Page, the Word Concert
was underftood to mean Inftruments play'd upon. D.

Nov. jun. Tell you ? Why, Sir ?
Are you my Confeffor ?

Rom. I will be your Confounder, if you do not.

[*Draws a Pocket Dagger.* [7]

Stir not, nor fpend your Voice.

Nov. jun. What will you do ?

Rom. Nothing but line your Brain-pan, Sir ! with
Lead,
If you not fatisfy me fuddenly,
I'm defperate of my Life, and command yours.

Nov. jun. Hold ! hold ! I'll fpeak.   I vow to Hea-
ven and you,
She's yet untouch'd, more than her Face and Hands.
I cannot call her innocent ; for, I yield,
On my folicitous Wooing fhe confented,
Where Time and Place met Opportunity
To grant me all Requefts.

Rom. But, may I build
On this Affurance ?

Nov. jun. As upon your Faith.

Rom. Write this, Sir ! nay, you muft.

[*Draws Inkhorn and Paper.*

Nov. jun. Pox of this Gun.

Rom. Withall, Sir ! you muft fwear; and put your
Oath
Under your Hand; (fhake not) ne'er to frequent
This Lady's Company ; nor ever fend
Token or Meffage, or Letter, to incline
This (too much prone already) yielding Lady.

Nov. jun. 'Tis done, Sir !

Rom. Let me fee, this firft is right ;
And here you wifh a fudden Death may light
Upon your Body, and Hell take your Soul,
If ever more you fee her but by Chance,
Much lefs allure her.   Now, my Lord ! your Hand.

Q 2

---

[7] *Romont*'s very next Speech, and the 20th Line of this fame
Page, fhews that this *Dagger* was a *Piftol.* M. M.

Nov. jun. My Hand to this?

Rom. Your Heart elſe, I aſſure you.

Nov. jun. Nay, there 'tis.

Rom. So, keep this laſt Article
Of your Faith given, and 'ſtead of Threat'nings, Sir!
The Service of my Sword and Life is yours :
But not a Word of it—'tis Fairies' Treaſure ;
Which, but reveal'd, brings on the Blabber's Ruin.
Uſe your Youth better, and this excellent Form
Heav'n hath beſtow'd upon you. So, good Morrow to
    your Lordſhip.   [*Exit.*

Nov. jun. Good Devil to your Rogueſhip. No
    Man's ſafe.——
I'll have a Cannon planted in my Chamber
Againſt ſuch roaring Rogues.

Enter Bellapert.

Bellap. My Lord, away !——
The Coach ſtays : Now have your Wiſh, and judge
If I have been forgetful.

Nov. jun. Ha !

Bellap. D'ye ſtand
Humming and hawing now !   [*Exit.*

Nov. jun. Sweet Wench, I come.
Hence Fear,
I ſwore,—that's all one ; my next Oath I'll keep
That I did mean to break, and then 'tis quit.
No Pain is due to Lover's Perjury :
If *Jove* himſelf laugh at it, ſo will I. [*Exit* Novall.

S C E N E II.

Enter Charalois *and* Beaumont.

Beaum. I grieve for the Diſtaſte
(Tho' I have Manners
Not to inquire the Cauſe) fall'n out between
Your Lordſhip and *Romont.*

Char. I love a Friend,
So long as he continues in the Bounds
Prescrib'd by Friendship; but, when he usurps
Too far what is proper to myself,
And puts the Habit of a Governor on,
I must and will preserve my Liberty.
But speak of something else, this is a Theme
I take no Pleasure in : What's this *Aymer ?*
Whose Voice for Song, and excellent Knowledge in
The chiefest Parts of Musick, you bestow
Such Praises on ?

Beaum. He is a Gentleman,
(For so his Quality speaks him) well receiv'd
Among our greatest Gallants ; but yet holds
His main Dependence from the young Lord *Novall.*
Some Tricks and Crochets he has in his Head,
As all Musicians have, and more of him
I dare not author : But, when you have heard him,
I may presume your Lordship so will like him,
That you'll hereafter be a Friend to Musick.

Char. I never was an Enemy to't, *Beaumont ;*
Nor yet do I subscribe to the Opinion
Of those old Captains, that thought nothing musical,
But Cries of yielding Enemies, Neighing of Horses,
Clashing of Armour, loud Shouts, Drums and Trum-
        pets :
Nor, on the other Side, in Favour of it,
Affirm the World was made by musical Discord,
Or that the Happiness of our Life consists
In a well-vary'd Note upon the Lute :
I love it to the Worth of it, and no farther.
—But, let us see this Wonder.

Beaum. He prevents my calling of him.

Enter Aymer.

Aymer. Let the Coach be brought
To the Back Gate, and serve the Banquet up :
Q 3

My good Lord *Charalois!* I think my House
Much honour'd in your Presence.

Char. To have Means
To know you better, Sir, has brought me hither
A willing Visitant; and you'll crown my Welcome
In making me a Witness to your Skill,
Which, crediting from others, I admire.

Aymer. Had I been one Hour sooner made acquainted.
With your Intent, my Lord, you should have found me
Better provided : Now, such as it is,
Pray you Grace with your Acceptance.

Beaum. You are modest.

Aymer. Begin the last new Air.

Char. Shall we not see them ?

Aymer. This little Distance from the Instruments
Will to your Ears convey the Harmony
With more Delight.

Char. I'll not contend.

Aymer. Y'are tedious,——
By this Means shall I with one Banquet please
Two Companies, those within, and these Gulls here.

[*Musick, and a Song above.*

Beaumel. within. Ha ! ha ! ha !

Char. How's this ? It is my Lady's Laugh, most
certain——
When I first pleas'd her, in this merry Language,
She gave me Thanks.

Beaum. How like you this ?

Char. 'Tis rare,——
Yet I may be deceiv'd, and should be sorry,
Upon uncertain Suppositions, rashly
To write myself in the black List of those
I have declaim'd against, and to *Romont.*

Aymer. I would he were well off.——Perhaps your
Lordship
Likes not these sad Tunes : I have a new Song,
Set to a lighter Note, may please you better ;
'Tis call'd *The Happy Husband.*

Char. Pray sing it.

Song below. At the End of the Song, Beaumelle *within.*

Beaumel. Ha! ha! 'tis fuch a Groom.——
Char. Do I hear this,
And yet ſtand doubtful ?   [*Exit* Charalois.
Aymer. Stay him !—I am undone,
And they difcover'd.
Beaum. What's the Matter ?
Aymer. Ah !
That Women, when they're well pleas'd, cannot hold,
But muſt laugh out.

Enter Noval jun. Charalois, Beaumelle, *and* Bellapert.

Nov. jun. Help! fave me ! Murther !. Murther !
Bellap. Undone for ever !
Char. Oh, my Heart !
Hold yet a little.—Do not hope to fcape
By Flight, it is impoffible : Tho' I might
On all Advantage take thy Life, and juſtly ;
This Sword, my Father's Sword, that ne'er was drawn
But to a noble Purpofe, fhall not now
Do th' Office of a Hangman ; I referve it
To right mine Honour, not for a Revenge
So poor, that tho' with thee it fhould cut off
Thy Family, with all that are ally'd
To thee in Luſt or Bafenefs, 'twere ſtill fhort of
All Terms of Satisfaction.—Draw.
Nov. jun. I dare not :
I have already done you too much Wrong
To fight in fuch a Caufe.
Char. Why ? dar'ſt thou neither
Be honeſt Coward, nor yet valiant Knave ?
In fuch a Caufe come, do not fhame thyfelf ;
Such whofe Blood's Wrongs, or Wrong done to them-
          felves
Could never heat, are yet in the Defence
Of their Whores, daring.—Look on her again.

You thought her worth the Hazard of your Soul,
And yet ſtand doubtful, in her Quarrel, to
Venture your Body.

    Beaum. No, he fears his Clothes
More than his Fleſh.

    Char. Keep from me :—Guard thy Life ;
Or, as thou haſt liv'd like a Goat, thou ſhalt
Die like a Sheep. [18]

    Nov. jun. Since there is no Remedy,
Deſpair of Safety now in me prove Courage!

                     [*They fight.* Navall *is ſlain.*

    Char. How ſoon weak Wrong's o'erthrown! Lend
        me your Hand,
Bear this to the Caroch—Come, you have taught me
To ſay, you muſt and ſhall : I wrong you not ;
Y' are but to keep Company you love.
—Is't done ? 'tis well.—Raiſe Officers ! and take Care,
All you can apprehend within the Houſe
May be forth-coming. Do I appear much mov'd ?

    Beaum. No, Sir.

    Char. My Griefs are now thus to be borne ;
Hereafter I'll find Time and Place to mourn.

                           [*Exeunt.*

SCENE III.

Enter Romont *and* Pontalier.

    Pont. I was bound to ſeek you, Sir!

    Rom. And, had you found me
In any Place but in the Street, I ſhould
Have done, not talk'd to you. Are you the Captain ?
The hopeful *Pontalier !* whom I have ſeen
Do in the Field ſuch Service, as then made you
Their Envy that commanded, here at Home
To play the Paraſite to a gilded Knave,
And, it may be, the Pandar ?

---

18 This is too vulgarly expreſſed to belong to *Maſſinger.* M. M.
  As groſs expreſſions are to be found in many Scenes of *Maſſinger.* D.

Pont. Without this,
I come to call you to Account for what
Is paft already.   I by your Example
Of Thankfulnefs to the dead General,
By whom you were rais'd, have practis'd to be fo
To my good Lord *Novall,* by whom I live ;
Whofe leaft Difgrace, that is or may be offer'd,
With all the Hazard of my Life and Fortunes,
I will make good on you or any Man
That has a Hand in't : and, fince you allow me
A Gentleman and a Soldier, there's no Doubt
You will except againft me.   You fhall meet
With a fair Enemy ; you underftand
The Right I look for and muft have.

　　Rom. I do ;
And with the next Day's Sun you fhall hear from me,
　　　　　　　　　　　　　　　　[Exeunt.

SCENE IV.

Enter Charalois *with a Cafket,* Beaumelle *and* Beau-
　　　　　　　mont.

　　Char. Pray bear this to my Father ; at his Leifure
He may perufe it : But with your beft Language
Intreat his inftant Prefence.   You have fworn
Not to reveal what I have done.
　　Beaum. Nor will I—but—
　　Char. Doubt me not.   By Heaven, I will do nothing
But what may ftand with Honour.—Pray you, leave me
　　　　　　　　　　　　　　[Exit Beaumont.
To my own Thoughts.—If this be to me, rife :
　　　　　　　　　　　　　　*[*Beaumel. *kneels.*
I am not worthy the looking on, but only
To feed Contempt and Scorn ; and that from you
Who with the Lofs of your fair Name have caus'd it,
Were too much Cruelty.
　　Beaumel. I dare not move you
To hear me fpeak.   I know my Fault is far

Beyond Qualification or Excuse;
That 'tis not fit for me to hope, or you
To think of Mercy; only I presume
To intreat you would be pleas'd to look upon
My Sorrow for it, and believe these Tears
Are the true Children of my Grief, and not
A Woman's Cunning.

 Char. Can you, *Beaumelle*,
Having deceived so great a Trust as mine,
Tho' I were all Credulity, hope again
To get Belief? No, no; if you look on me
With Pity, or dare practise any Means
To make my Sufferings less, or give just Cause
To all the World to think what I must do,
Was call'd upon by you, use other Ways;
Deny what I've seen, or justify
What you have done; and, as you desperately
Made Shipwreck of your Faith to be a Whore,
Use th' Arms of such a one and such Defence;
And multiply the Sin with Impudence.
Stand boldly up, and tell me to my Teeth,
That you have done but what's warranted
By great Examples, in all Places where
Women inhabit: Urge your own Deserts,
Or want in me of Merit: Tell me how
Your Dow'r from the low Gulf of Poverty,
Weigh'd up my Fortunes to what now they are:
That I was purchas'd by your Choice and Practice
To shelter you from Shame, that you might sin
As boldly as securely; that poor Men
Are married to those Wives that bring them Wealth,
One Day their Husbands, but Observers ever:
That when by this proud Usage you have blown
The Fire of my just Vengeance to the Height,
I then may kill you; and yet say, twas done
In Heat of Blood, and after die myself,
To witness my Repentance.

 Beaumel. O my Fate!
That never would consent that I should see
How worthy thou wert both of Love and Duty

Before I loſt you ; and my Miſery made
The Glaſs, in which I now behold your Virtue !
While I was good I was a Part of you,
And of two, by the virtuous Harmony
Of our fair Minds made one : But, ſince I wander'd
In the forbidden Labyrinth of Luſt,
What was inſeparable is by me divided.
With Juſtice, therefore, you may cut me off,
And from your Memory waſh the Remembrance
That e'er I was ; like to ſome vicious Purpoſe,
Which in your better Judgment, you repent of,
And ſtudy to forget.

    Char. O *Beaumelle !*
That you can ſpeak ſo well and do ſo ill !
But you had been too great a Bleſſing, if
You had continu'd chaſte : See how you force me
To this, becauſe mine Honour will not yield
That I again ſhould love you.

    Beaumel. In this Life
It is not fit you ſhould : Yet you ſhall find,
Tho' I was bold enough to be a Strumpet,
I dare not yet live one : Let thoſe fam'd Matrons
That are canoniz'd worthy of our Sex,
Tranſcend me in their Sanctity of Life,
I yet will equal them in dying nobly,
Ambitious of no Honour after Life,
But that, when I am dead, you will forgive me.

    Char. How Pity ſteals upon me ! ſhould I hear her
                              [*Knock within.*
But ten Words more, I were loſt.—One knocks, go in.
                              [*Exit* Beaumelle.
That to be merciful ſhould be a Sin !

        Enter Rochfort.

O, Sir, moſt welcome ! Let me take your Cloak,
I muſt not be deny'd.—Here are your Robes,
As you love Juſtice, once more put them on.
There is a Cauſe to be determin'd of
That does require ſuch an Integrity

As you have ever us'd.—I'll put you to
The Trial of your Conftancy and Goodnefs;
And look that you, that have been Eagle-ey'd
In other Mens Affairs, prove not a Mole
In what concerns yourfelf. Take you your Seat,
I will before you prefently.   [Exit.

   Roch. Angels guard me!
To what ftrange Tragedy does this Deftruction [19]
Serve for a Prologue?

Enter Charalois *with* Novall's *Body*, Beaumelle *and*
Beaumont.

   Char. So, fet it down before
The Judgment Seat, and ftand you at the Bar;
For me, I am the Accufer.
   Roch. Novall flain?
And *Beaumelle*, my Daughter, in the Place
Of one to be arraign'd?
   Char. O, are you touch'd?
I find that I muft take another Courfe.
                  [*He hoodwinks* Rochfort.
Fear nothing; I will only blind your Eyes,
For Juftice fhould do fo, when 'tis to meet
An Object that may fway her equal Doom
From what it fhould be aim'd at.—Good my Lord!
A Day of Hearing.
   Roch. It is granted, fpeak—You fhall have Juftice.
   Char. I then here accufe,
Moft equal Judge, the Prifoner, your fair Daughter,
For whom I ow'd fo much to you: Your Daughter,
So worthy in her own Parts, and that Worth
Set forth by yours, to whofe fo rare Perfections,
Truth witnefs with me, in the Place of Service
I almoft paid idolatrous Sacrifice,
To be a falfe Adultrefs.

---

   [19] ————————*Does this Deftruction,* &c.
  We fhould read *Induction. Rochfort* fpeaks thefe Words before
he could have feen the Body of *Novall*, or heard of his Death.
M. M.

Roch. With whom?

Char. With this *Novall*, here dead.

Roch. Be well advis'd,
And ere you fay Adultrefs again,
Her Fame depending on it, be moft fure
That fhe is one.

Char. I took them in the Act.
I know no Proof beyond it.

Roch. O my Heart!

Char. A Judge fhould feel no Paffions.

Roch. Yet, remember
He is a Man, and cannot put off Nature.
What Anfwer makes the Prifoner?

Beaumel. I confefs
The Fact I am charg'd with, and yield myfelf
Moft miferably guilty.

Roch. Heaven take Mercy
Upon your Soul, then: It muft leave your Body.——
Now free mine Eyes: I dare unmov'd look on her,
And fortify my Sentence with ftrong Reafons.
Since that the politick Law provides that Servants,
To whofe Care we commit our Goods, fhall die,
If they abufe our Truft; what can you look for,
To whofe Charge this moft hopeful Lord gave up
All he receiv'd from his brave Anceftors,
Or he could leave to his Pofterity?
His Honour: wicked Woman! in whofe Safety
All his Life's Joys and Comforts were lock'd up,
Which thy Luft, a Thief, hath now ftolen from him;
And therefore——

Char. Stay, juft Judge.—May not what's loft
By her one Fault (for I am charitable,
And charge her not with many) be forgotten
In her fair Life hereafter?

Roch. Never, Sir!
The Wrong that's done to the chafte married Bed,
Repentant Tears can never expiate;
And be affur'd to pardon fuch a Sin,
Is an Offence as great as to commit it.

Char. I may not then forgive her?

Roch. Nor she hope it :
Nor can she wish to live. No Sun shall rise,
But ere it set shall shew her ugly Lust
In a new Shape, and every one more horrid :
Nay, ev'n those Prayers, which with such humble Fer-
vour
She seems to send up yonder, are beat back ;
And all Suits which her Penitence can proffer,
As soon as made, are with Contempt thrown off
From all the Courts of Mercy.

Char. Let her die then. [*He kills her.*
Better prepar'd I'm sure I could not take her,
Nor she accuse her Father as a Judge
Partial against her.

Beaumel. I approve his Sentence,
And kiss the Executioner : My Lust
Is now run from me in that Blood in which
It was begot and nourish'd. [*Dies.*

Roch. Is she dead then ?

Char. Yes, Sir, this is her Heart-blood, is it not ?
I think it be.

Roch. And you have kill'd her ?

Char. True, and did it by your Doom.

Roch. But I pronounc'd it
As a Judge only, and a Friend to Justice,
And zealous in Defence of your wrong'd Honour,
Broke all the Ties of Nature ; and cast off
The Love and soft Affection of a Father.
I, in your Cause, put on a Scarlet Robe
Of red-dy'd Cruelty ; but, in Return,
You have advanc'd for me no Flag of Mercy.
I look'd on you as a wrong'd Husband ; but
You clos'd your Eyes against me as a Father.
O *Beaumelle !* my Daughter !

Char. This is Madness.

Roch. Keep from me.—Could not one good Thought
rise up,
To tell you that she was my Age's Comfort,
Begot by a weak Man, and born a Woman,
And could not, therefore, but partake of Frailty ?

Or wherefore did not Thankfulnefs ftep forth,
To urge my many Merits, which I may
Object unto you, fince you prove ungrateful;
Flinty-hearted *Charalois?*

  Char. Nature does prevail above your Virtue.

  Roch. No; it gives me Eyes,
To pierce the Heart of your Defign againft me.
I find it now; it was my 'State was aim'd at,
A nobler Match was fought for, and the Hours
I liv'd, grew tedious to you: My Compaffion
Towards you hath render'd me moft miferable,
And foolifh Charity undone myfelf.
But there's a Heaven above, from whofe juft Wreak
No Mifts of Policy can hide Offenders.

Enter Novall fen. *with Officers.*

  Nov. fen. Force ope the Doors.—O Monfter! Can-
     nibal!
Lay hold on him—My Son! my Son!—O *Rochfort!*
'Twas you gave Liberty to this bloody Wolf
To worry all our Comforts.——But this is
No Time to quarrel; now give your Affiftance
For the Revenge.

  Roch. Call it a fitter Name.
—Juftice for innocent Blood.

  Char. Tho' all confpire
Againft that Life which I am weary of,
A little longer yet I'll ftrive to keep it,
To fhew, in Spite of Malice and their Laws,
His Plea muft fpeed, that hath an honeft Caufe.

                   [*Exeunt.*

End of the Fourth Act.

ACT V.   SCENE I.

Enter Liladam, *Taylor and Officers.*

Liladam.

WHY, 'tis both most unconscionable and un-
        timely,
T' arrest a Gallant for his Cloaths, before
He has worn them out : Besides, you said you ask'd
My Name in my Lord's Bond but for Form only,
And now you'll lay me up for't.   Do not think
The taking Measure of a Customer
By a Brace of Varlets, tho' I rather wait
Never so patiently, will prove a Fashion
Which any Courtier or Inns-of-court-man
Would follow willingly.
    Taylor. There I believe you.
But, Sir! I must have present Monies, or
Assurance, to secure me when I shall————
Or I will see to your coming forth.
    Lilad. Plague on't !
You have provided for my Entrance in :
That coming forth you talk of, concerns me.
What shall I do ? You've done me a Disgrace
In the Arrest, but more in giving Cause
To all the Street to think I cannot stand
Without these two Supporters for my Arms :
Pray you, let them loose me : For their Satisfaction
I will not run away.
    Taylor. For theirs you will not ;
But for your own you would : Look to him, Fellows !
    Lilad. Why do you call them Fellows ? Do not
        wrong
Your Reputation, as you are merely
A Taylor, faithful, apt to believe in Gallants.
You're a Companion at a Ten Crown Supp-

For Cloth of Bodkin, and may with one Lark
Eat up three Manchets, and no Man obferve you,
Or call your Trade in Queftion for't. But, when
You ftudy your Debt-book, and hold Correfpondence
With Officers of the Hanger, and leave Swordfmen,
The Learned conclude, the Taylor and Serjeant,
In the Expreffion of a Knave or Thief,
To be fynonymous. Look, therefore, to it!
And let us part in Peace. I would be loth
You fhould undo yourfelf.

Enter Old Novall *and* Pontalier.

Taylor. To let you go
Were the next Way. But, fee! here's your old Lord;
Let him but give his Word I fhall be paid,
And you are free.
  Lilad. 'Slid! I'll put him to't:
I can be but denied: or—what fay you?
His Lordfhip owing me three Times your Debt;
If you arreft him at my Suit, and let me
Go run before, to fee the Action enter'd,
'Twould be a witty Jeft.
  Taylor. I muft have Earneft.—
I cannot pay my Debts fo.
  Pont. Can your Lordfhip
Imagine, while I live, and wear a Sword,
Your Son's Death fhall be unreveng'd?
  Nov. fen. I know not
One Reafon why you fhould not do like others:
I am fure, of all the Herd that fed upon him,
I cannot fee in any, now he's gone,
In Pity or in Thankfulnefs, one true Sign
Of Sorrow for him.
  Pont. All his Bounties yet
Fell not in fuch unthankful Ground: 'Tis true,
He had Weakneffes, but fuch as few are free from.
And, tho' none footh'd them lefs than I, for now
To fay that I forefaw the Dangers that

Would rife from cherifhing them, were but untimely,
I yet could wifh the Juftice that you feek for
In the Revenge, had been trufted to me,
And not the uncertain Iffue of the Laws:
It has robb'd me of a noble Teftimony
Of what I durft do for him.—But, however,
My forfeit Life redeem'd by him, tho' dead,
Shall do him Service.

    Nov. fen. As far as my Grief
Will give me Leave, I thank you.

    Lilad. O, my Lord!
Oh my good Lord! deliver me from thefe Furies.

    Pont. Arrefted? This is one of them, whofe bafe
And abject Flattery help'd to dig his Grave:
He is not worth your Pity nor my Anger.—
Go to the Bafket, and repent.

    Nov. fen. Away!—I only know now to hate thee
        deadly:
I will do nothing for thee.

    Lilad. Nor you, Captain?

    Pont. No, to your Trade again; put off this Cafe,
It may be, the difcovering what you were,
When your unfortunate Mafter took you up,
May move Compaffion in your Creditor.
Confefs the Truth.

                [*Exit* Novall fen. *and* Pontalier.
    Lilad. And, now I think on't better,
I will: Brother, your Hand, your Hand, fweet Brother.
I'm of your Sect, and my Gallantry but a Dream,
Out of which thefe two fearful Apparitions
Againft my Will have wak'd me. This rich Sword
Grew fuddenly out of a Taylor's Bodkin;
Thefe Hangers from my Vails and Fees in Hell;
And where, as now this Beaver fits, full often
A thrifty Cap, compos'd of Broad-cloth Lifts,
Near-'kin unto the Cufhion where I fat
Crofs-legg'd, and yet ungarter'd, hath been feen;
Our Breakfafts, famous for the butter'd Loaves,
I have with Joy been oft acquainted with;
And therefore ufe a Confcience, tho' it be

Forbidden in our Hall towards other Men,
To me that, as I have been, will again
Be of the Brotherhood.

    Officer. I know him now:
He was a 'Prentice to *Le Robe* at *Orleance.*

    Lilad. And from thence brought by my young Lord,
        now dead,
Unto *Dijon*; and with him, till this Hour,
Have been receiv'd here for a compleat Monsieur.
Nor wonder at it: for but tythe our Gallants,
Even those of the first Rank, and you will find
In every ten, one, peradventure two,
That smell rank of the Dancing-school or Fiddle.
The Pantofle or Pressing-iron :—But hereafter
We'll talk of this. I will surrender up
My Suits again; there cannot be much Loss.
'Tis but the turning of the Lace, with one
Addition more you know of, and what wants
I will work out.

    Taylor. Then here our Quarrel ends :
The Gallant is turn'd Taylor, and all Friends.

[Exeunt.

S C E N E II.

Enter Romont and Beaumont.

    Rom. You have them ready.

    Beaum. Yes; and they will speak
Their Knowledge in this Cause, when thou think'st fit
To have them call'd upon.

    Rom. 'Tis well; and something
I can add to their Evidence, to prove
This brave Revenge, which they would have call'd
        Murther,
A noble Justice.

R 2

Beaum. In this you express
(The Breach, by my Lord's Want of you, now made
     up)
A faithful Friend.

Rom. That Friendship's rais'd on Sand,
Which every sudden Gust of Discontent,
Or flowing of our Passions, can change,
As if it ne'er had been :—But do you know
Who are to sit on him?

Beaum. Monsieur *Du Croy*,
Assisted by *Charmi.*

Rom. The Advocate,
That pleaded for the Marshal's Funeral,
And was check'd for it by *Novall.*

Beaum. The same.

Rom. How fortunes that?

Beaum. Why, Sir, my Lord *Novall*,
Being the Accuser, cannot be the Judge;
Nor would griev'd *Rochfort*, but Lord *Charalois*
(However he might wrong him by his Power,)
Should have an equal Hearing.

Rom. By my Hopes
Of *Charalois*'s Aquittal, I lament
That reverend old Man's Fortune.

Beaum. Had you seen him,
As to my Grief I have, now promise Patience,
And ere it was believ'd, tho' spake by him
That never breaks his Word, enrag'd again
So far as to make War upon those Hairs,
Which not a barbarous *Scythian* durst presume
To touch, but with a superstitious Fear,
As something sacred ;—and then curse his Daughter;
But with more frequent Violence himself,
As if he had been guilty of her Fault,
By being incredulous of your Report,
You would not only judge him worthy Pity,
But suffer with him.—But here comes the Prisoner;

Enter Charalois, *with Officers.*

I dare not ftay to do my Duty to him ;
Yet, reft affur'd, all poffible Means in me
To do him Service, keeps you Company.
   Rom. It is not doubted.   [*Exit* Beaumont.
   Char. Why, yet, as I came hither,
The People, apt to mock Calamity,
And tread on the opprefs'd, made no Horns at me,.
Tho' they are too familiar I deferve them.
And, knowing too what Blood my Sword hath drunk,
In Wreak of that Difgrace ; they yet forbear
To fhake their Heads, or to revile me for
A Murtherer ; they rather all put on
(As for great Loffes the old *Romans* us'd)
A general Face of Sorrow, waited on
By a fad Murmur breaking thro' their Silence,
And no Eye but was readier with a Tear
To witnefs 'twas fhed for me; than I could
Difcern a Face made up with Scorn againft me.
Why fhould I then, tho' for unufual Wrongs
I chofe unufual Means to right thofe Wrongs,
Condemn myfelf, as over-partial
In my own Caufe.—*Romont ?*
   Rom. Beft Friend, well met !
By my Heart's Love to you, and join to that
My Thankfulnefs that ftill lives to the dead,
I look upon you now with more true Joy,
Than when I faw you married.
   Char. You have Reafon
To give you Warrant for't. My falling off
From fuch a Friendfhip, with the Scorn that anfwered
Your too prophetick Counfel, may well move you
To think your meeting me, going to my Death,
A fit Encounter for that Hate which juftly
I have deferv'd from you.
   Rom. Shall I ftill, then,
Speak Truth, and be ill underftood ?

Char. You are not.
I'm confcious I have wrong'd you, and allow me
Only a moral Man, to look on you,
Whom foolifhly I have abus'd and injur'd,
Muft of Neceffity be more terrible to me,
Than any Death the Judges can pronounce
From the Tribunal which I am to plead at.

Rom. Paffion tranfports you.

Char. For what I have done
To my falfe Lady, or *Novall*, I can
Give fome apparent Caufe; but, touching you,
In my Defence, Child-like, I can fay nothing,
But I am forry for't; a poor Satisfaction!
And yet, miftake me not; for it is more
Than I will fpeak, to have my Pardon fign'd
For all I ftand accus'd of.

Rom. You much weaken
The Strength of your good Caufe, fhould you but
        think,
A Man for doing well could entertain
A Pardon, were it offer'd. You have given
To blind and flow-pac'd Juftice, Wings and Eyes,
To fee and overtake Impieties,
Which from a cold Proceeding had receiv'd
Indulgence or Protection,

Char. Think you fo?

Rom. Upon my Soul, nor fhould the Blood you
        challenge
And took to cure your Honour, breed more Scruple
In your foft Confcience, than if your Sword
Had been fheath'd in a Tygrefs or She-Bear,
That in their Bowels would have made your Tomb.
To injure innocence is more than Murther:
But when inhuman Lufts transform us, then
As Beafts we are to fuffer, not like Men,
To be lamented. Nor did *Charalois* ever
Perform an Act fo worthy the Applaufe
Of a full Theatre of perfect Men,
As he hath done in this: The Glory got
By overthrowing outward Enemies,

Since Strength and Fortune are main Sharers in it,
We cannot, but by Pieces, call our own :
But, when we conquer our inteſtine Foes,
Our Paſſions bred within us, and of thoſe
The moſt rebellious Tyrant, powerful Love,
Our Reaſon ſuffering us to like no longer
Than the fair Object, being good, deſerves it,
That's a true Victory; which, were great Men
Ambitious to atchieve, by your Example
Setting no Price upon the Breach of Faith,
But Loſs of Life, 'twould fright Adultery
Out of their Families; and make Luſt appear
As loathſome to us in the firſt Conſent,
As when 'tis waited on by Puniſhment.

    Char. You have confirm'd me. Who would love a
        Woman
That might enjoy, in ſuch a Man, a Friend ?
You've made me know the Juſtice of my Cauſe,
And mark'd me out the Way how to defend it.

    Rom. Continue to that Reſolution conſtant,
And you ſhall, in Contempt of their worſt Malice,
Come off with Honour.—Here they come.

    Char. I am ready.

S C E N E III. [20]

Enter Du Croy, Charmi, Rochfort, Novall *ſen.* Pontalier, *and* Beaumont.

    Nov. ſen. See, equal Judges, with what Confidence
The cruel Murtherer ſtands, as if he would
Out-face the Court and Juſtice !

☞ 20 Scene 3. The enſuing Scene is moſt finely written, as is indeed the whole Act. The Misfortune of the good old generous *Rochfort*, and the pious *Charalois*'s continued Round of Sorrows muſt be very affecting to every Heart, that is capable of being touched with Pity and Tenderneſs.

Roch. But look on him,
And you shall find (for still methinks I do,
Tho' Guilt hath dy'd him black) something good in
   him,
That may perhaps work with a wiser Man,
Than I have been, again to set him free
And give him all he has.
 Charm. This is not well.
I would you had liv'd so, my Lord! that I,
Might rather have continu'd your poor Servant,
Than sit here as your Judge.
 Du Croy. I am sorry for you.
 Roch. In no Act of my Life I have deserv'd
This Injury from the Court, that any here
Should thus uncivilly usurp on what
Is proper to me only.
 Du Croy. What Distaste
Receives my Lord?
 Roch. You say you are sorry for him:
A Grief in which I must not have a Partner:
'Tis I alone am sorry, that when I raised
The Building of my Life, for seventy Years,
Upon so sure a Ground, that all the Vices,
Practis'd to ruin Man, tho' brought against me,
Could never undermine, and no Way left
To send these grey Hairs to the Grave with Sorrow,
Virtue, that was my Patroness, betray'd me:
For, entring, nay, possessing this young Man,
It lent him such a powerful Majesty
To grace whate'er he undertook, that freely
I gave myself up with my Liberty,
To be at his disposing: Had his Person,
Lovely I must confess, or far-fam'd Valour,
Or any other seeming Good, that yet
Holds a near Neighbourhood with Ill, wrought on me,
I might have borne it better; But, when Goodness
And Piety itself in her best Figure
Were brib'd to my Destruction, can you blame me,
Tho' I forget to suffer like a Man,
Or rather act a Woman?

Beaum. Good my Lord!

Nov. fen. You hinder our Proceeding.

Charmi. And forget
The Parts of an Accuſer.

Beaum. 'Pray you, remember
To uſe the Temper, which to me you promis'd.

Roch. Angels themſelves muſt break, *Beaumont!* that
  promiſe,
Beyond the Strength and Patience of Angels.
But I have done :—My good Lord! pardon me
A weak old Man; and pray add to that
A miſerable Father ; yet be careful
That your Compaſſion of my Age, nor his,
Move you to any Thing, that may miſ-become
The Place on which you ſit.

Charmi. Read the Indictment.

Char. It ſhall be needleſs ; I myſelf, my Lords!
Will be my own Accuſer, and confeſs
All they can charge me with : nor will I ſpare
To aggravate that Guilt with Circumſtance,
They ſeek to load me with : Only I pray,
That, as for them you will vouchſafe me Hearing,
I may not be deny'd it for myſelf,
When I ſhall urge by what unanſwerable Reaſons
I was compell'd to what I did, which yet,
Till you have taught me better, I repent not.

Roch. The Motion's honeſt.

Charmi. And 'tis freely granted.

Char. Then I confeſs, my Lords! that I ſtood bound,
When, with my Friends, ev'n Hope itſelf had left me,
To this Man's Charity for my Liberty ;
Nor did his Bounty end there, but began :
For, after my Enlargement, cheriſhing
The Good he did, he made me Maſter of
His only Daughter and his whole Eſtate :
Great Ties of Thankfulneſs, I muſt acknowledge,
Could any one, feed by you, preſs this further?
But yet conſider, my moſt honour'd Lords!
If to receive a Favour, make a Servant,
And Benefits are Bonds to tie the Taker

To the Imperious Will of him that gives,
There's none but Slaves will receive Courtefies,
Since they muſt fetter us to our Diſhonours.
Can it be call'd Magnificence in a Prince,
To pour down riches with a liberal Hand,
Upon a poor Man's Wants, if that muſt bind him,
To play the foothing Paraſite to his Vices?
Or any Man, becauſe he ſav'd my Hand,
Preſume my Head and Heart are at his Service?
Or, did I ſtand engag'd to buy my Freedom
(When my Captivity was honourable)
By making myſelf here, and Fame hereafter,
Bondſlaves to Men's Scorn and calumnious Tongues?
Had his fair Daughter's Mind been like her Feature,
Or, for ſome little Blemiſh, I had fought
For my Content elſewhere, waſting on others
My Body and her Dowry; my Forehead then
Deſerv'd the Brand of baſe Ingratitude:
But if obſequious Uſage, and fair Warning
To keep her Worth my Love, could not preſerve her
From being a Whore, and yet no cunning one,
So to offend, and yet the Fault kept from me;
What ſhould I do? Let any free-born Spirit
Determine truly, if that Thankfulneſs,
Choice Form, with the whole World given for a Dowry,
Could ſtrengthen ſo an honeſt Man with Patience,
As with a willing Neck to undergo
The inſupportable Yoke of Slave or Wittal.

 Charmi. What Proof have you ſhe did play falſe,
   beſides
Your Oath?
 Char. Her own Confeſſion to her Father.
I aſk him for a Witneſs.
 Roch. 'Tis moſt true.
I would not willingly blend my laſt Words
With an Untruth.
 Char. And then to clear myſelf,
That his great Wealth was not the Mark I ſhot at,
But that I held it, when fair *Beaumelle*
Fell from her Virtue, like the fatal Gold

Which *Brennus* took from *Delphos*, whose Poſſeſſion
Brought with it Ruin to himſelf and Army.
Here's one in Court, *Beaumont*, by whom I ſent
All Grants and Writings back which made it mine,
Before his Daughter dy'd by his own Sentence,
As freely as unaſk'd he gave it to me.

 Beaum. They are here to be ſeen.
 Charmi. Open the Caſket.——
Peruſe that Deed of Gift.
 Rom. Half of the Danger
Already is diſcharged : The other Part
As bravely, and you are not only free,
But crown'd with Praiſe for ever.
 Du Croy. 'Tis apparent.
 Charmi. Your 'State, my Lord, again is yours.
 Roch. Not mine ;
I am not of the World : If it can proſper,
(And yet, being juſtly got, I'll not examine
Why it ſhould be ſo fatal) do you beſtow it
On pious Uſes : I'll go ſeek a Grave.
And yet, for Proof, I die in Peace, your Pardon
I aſk ; and, as you grant it me, may Heaven,
Your Conſcience, and theſe Judges, free you from
What you are charg'd with, So farewell for ever.——
        [*Exit* Rochfort.

 Novall. ſen. I'll be mine own Guide. Paſſion, nor
   Example
Shall be my Leaders. I have loſt a Son,
A Son, grave Judges, I require his Blood
From his accurſed Homicide.
 Charmi. What Reply you,
In your Defence, for this ?
 Char. I but attended
Your Lordſhip's Pleaſure.—For the Fact, as of
The former, I confeſs it ; but with what
Baſe Wrongs I was unwillingly drawn to it,
To my few Words there are ſome other Proofs
To witneſs this for Truth. When I was married
(For there I muſt begin) the ſlain *Novall*
Was to my Wife, in Way of our *French* Courtſhip,

A most devoted Servant; but yet aimed at
Nothing but Means to quench his wanton Heat,
His Heart being never warm'd by lawful Fires
As mine was, Lords; and tho', on these Presumptions,
Join'd to the Hate between his House and mine,
I might, with Opportunity and Ease,
Have found a Way for my Revenge, I did not;
But still he had the Freedom as before,
When all was mine; and told that he abus'd it
With some unseemly Licence, by my Friend,
My approv'd Friend, *Romont*, I gave no Credit
To the Reporter, but reprov'd him for it,
As one uncourtly and malicious to him.
What could I more, my Lords? Yet, after this,
He did continue in his first Pursuit,
Hotter than ever, and at length obtained it;
But, how it came to my most certain Knowledge,
For the Dignity of the Court, and my own Honour,
I dare not say.

 Nov. sen. If all may be believ'd
A passionate Prisoner speaks, who is so foolish
That durst be wicked, that will appear guilty?
No, my grave Lords: In his Impunity
But give Example unto jealous Men
To cut the Throats they hate, and they will never
Want Matter or Pretence for their bad Ends.

 Charmi. You must find other Proofs, to strengthen
   these
But mere Presumptions.——

 Du Croy. Or we shall hardly
Allow your Innocence.

 Char. All your Attempts
Shall fail on me, like brittle Shafts on Armour,
That break themselves; or like Waves against a Rock,
That leave no Sign of their ridiculous Fury
But Foam and Splinters; my Innocence like these
Shall stand triumphant, and your Malice serve
But for a Trumpet to proclaim my Conquest:
Nor shall you, tho' you do the worst Fate can,
Howe'er condemn, affright an honest Man.

Rom. May it pleafe the Court, I may be heard.

Nov. fen. You come not
To rail again ? But do—You fhall not find
Another *Rochfort.*

Rom. In *Novall* I cannot.
But I come furnifhed with what will ftop
The Mouth of his Confpiracy againft the Life
Of innocent *Charalois.* Do you know this Character ?

Nov. fen. Yes, 'tis my Son's.

Rom. May it pleafe your Lordfhips, read it,
And you fhall find there, with what Vehemency
He did folicit *Beaumelle;* how he had got
A Promife from her to enjoy his Wifhes;
How after he abjur'd her Company,
And yet—(but that 'tis fit I fpare the Dead)
Like a damn'd Villain, as foon as recorded,
He brake that Oath;—to make this manifeft,
Produce his Bawds and her's.

Enter Aymer, Florimel, *and* Bellapert.

Charmi. Have they took their Oaths ?

Rom. They have, and, rather than endure the Rack,
Confefs the Time, the Meeting, nay the Act;
What would you more ? Only this Matron made
A free Difcovery to a good End;
And therefore I fue to the Court fhe may not
Be plac'd in the black Lift of the Delinquents.

Pont. I fee by this, *Novall's* Revenge needs me;
And I fhall do.——

Charmi. 'Tis evident——

Nov. fen. That I
Till now was never wretched : Here's no Place
To curfe him or my Stars.   [*Exit* Novall *fen.*

Charmi. Lord *Charalois !*
The Injuries you have fuftain'd, appear
So worthy of the Mercy of the Court,
That, notwithftanding you have gone beyond
The Letter of the Law, they yet acquit you.

Pont. But, in *Novall,* I do condemn him—thus.

             [*Stabs him.*

 Char. I'm flain.

 Rom. Can I look on ? Oh, murd'rous Wretch !
Thy Challenge now I anfwer.—So die with him,

           [*Stabs* Pontalier.

 Charmi. A Guard ! difarm him !

 Rom. I yield up my Sword
Unforc'd—Oh, *Charalois !*

 Char. For Shame, *Romont !*
Mourn not for him that dies as he hath liv'd;
Still conftant and unmov'd : What's fall'n upon me,
Is by Heav'ns Will ; becaufe I made myfelf
A Judge in my own Caufe without their Warrant :
But he, that lets me know thus much in Death,
With all good Men—forgive me.   [*Dies.*

 Pont. I receive
The Vengeance, which my Love, not built on Virtue,
Has made me worthy of.   [*Dies.*

 Charmi. We're taught
By this fad Precedent, how juft foever
Our Reafons are to remedy our Wrongs,
We're yet to leave them to their Will and Power,
That to that Purpofe have Authority.
For you, *Romont,* altho' in your Excufe
You may plead what you did was in Revenge
Of the Difhonour done unto the Court :
Yet, fince from us you had not Warrant for it,
We banifh you the State : For thefe, they fhall,
A they are found guilty or innocent,
Or be fet free, or fuffer Punifhment.   [*Exeunt.*

F I N I S:

 This is by far the beft of thofe Plays in which our Author was affifted by any other Perfon ; and it is evident that his Stile unites
more naturally with that of *Field,* than it does with *Decker's,* who
joined with him in writing the *Virgin Martyr* ; yet ftill a critical
Reader will perceive that *Rochfort* and *Charalois* fpeak a different
Language in the Second and Third Acts, from that which they

ſpeak in the Firſt and laſt, which are undoubtedly *Maſſinger*'s; as is alſo Part of the Fourth Act, though not the Whole of it.

Rowe has formed from the *Fatal Dowry* his Tragedy of the *Fair Penitent*, which is frequently exhibited on the preſent Stage, and is a popular Performance: yet ſurely it is much inferior to its Original, both with reſpect to the Language, and to the Conduct of it.

The gentle *Altamont*, though the principal in the Play, is rather an inſipid, unintereſting Character; there is nothing that prepoſſeſſes us very ſtrongly in his Favour, and if we wiſh he ſhould ſucceed in the Combat with *Lothario*, it ariſes from our reflecting on the Juſtice of his Cauſe, not from any perſonal Intereſt we feel for him: nor do we commiſerate the good *Sciolto*, more than we ſhould any other Parent expoſed to the ſame Degree of Diſtreſs.——But the pious *Charalois* takes ſuch Hold of our Affections in the very firſt Scene, that we ſympathize with him in all the Changes of his Fortune; and every Heart muſt bleed for the venerable *Rochfort*, when he falls a Victim to his Love of Virtue.

Why are we more ſtrongly affected by the deplorable Fate of *Rochfort* and *Charalois*, than we are by that of *Sciolto* and *Altamont?* Becauſe, as *Horace* judiciouſly obſerves,

> *Segnius irritant animos demiſſa per aures*
> *Quamque quæ oculis ſubjecta fidelibus.*

We know nothing, either of *Altamont*'s Goodneſs, or of *Sciolto*'s generous Conduct towards him, but from a ſhort and cold Narration, not ſufficiently pointed to engage the Attention of the Audience, or to make any deep Impreſſion on them; whereas the Spectators themſelves are Witneſſes to the filial Piety of the noble *Charalois*, and to the immediate Effect that the Admiration of his Virtue operates on the juſt and generous Mind of the amiable *Rochfort*.

The Character of *Lothario* is preferable to that of Young *Novall*, whom *Maſſinger* repreſents as too contemptible; and *Califta*, in my Opinion, is rather an Improvement on that of *Beaumelle:* but the brave *Romont* is of a much more noble and generous Nature than the ſententious *Horatio:* The former, when he hears of *Charalois*' Misfortunes, forgetting the Inſults he had received from him, flies inſtantly to his Relief, and will not liſten to the ſlighteſt Apology; but the ſtern *Horatio*, though he ſees his poor Friend plunged in the Abyſs of Miſery, perſeveres in his Reſentment, and remains inexorable till he lays him at his Feet reduced to the moſt abject State of Submiſſion.——Yet to this Defect in the Character of *Horatio*, we owe the moſt affecting Scene in that Play. *M. M.*

* * The Editor's Critique on *The Fatal Dowry* is in general very judicious, and it cannot fail of meriting the Approbation of every candid Reader.

Maſſinger is, however, ſo licentious in his Language, and ſo different ſometimes from his uſual flow of graceful and majeſtick Harmony, even in thoſe Plays which are written entirely by himſelf, that we cannot with any Degree of Certainty fix the Inequality of Style in this Tragedy upon *Field*.

Rowe, in his *Fair Penitent*, has borrowed not only the Fable and Character of *The Fatal Dowry*, but has stolen from thence some of *Maſſinger's* moſt ſtriking Sentiments.—*Lothario* is in my Judgment *Rowe's* Maſterpiece. The Outline of this too-agreeable Libertine is exact, the Colouring rich, and the Finiſhing high; the Whole is written in a Taſte ſuperior to all the Characters this Author has brought on the Stage.

I am ſorry to differ from the Editor's Opinion of the principal Lady in *The Fair Penitent*.—*Beaumelle*, in the Original Play (if we make Allowances for ſome coarſe and free Expreſſions, the Growth of the Times,) is a far more conſiſtent and affecting Part than *Califta*, who is bold, inſolent, and haughty, even to the laſt.—Her Behaviour in the 3d Act of the Play, where ſhe endeavours to provoke her Hufband and his Friend to a Quarrel, is more conformable to the hardened Impudence of the Strumpet, than the Feelings of a young unhappy Lady, whoſe high Birth and poliſhed Education ſhould have taught her a very different Conduct.   *D.*

THE

EMPEROR of the EAST.

A

TRAGI-COMEDY.

To the Right Honourable, and my Especial
Good Lord,

J O H N Lord M O H U N,

Baron of OKEHAMPTON, &c.

My Good Lord,

*L ET my Presumption in stiling you so (having never de--
served it in my Service) from the Clemency of your
noble Disposition, find Pardon. The Reverence due to the
Name of Mohun, long since honoured in three Earls of So-
merset, and eight Barons of Munster, may challenge from
all Pens a deserved Celebration. And the rather in respect
those Titles were not purchased, but conferred, and continued
in your Ancestors, for many virtuous, noble, and still living
Actions; nor ever forfeited or tainted, but when the Iniquity
of those Times laboured the Depression of approved Goodness,
and in wicked Policy held it fit that Loyalty and Faith, in
taking Part with the true Prince, should be degraded and
mulcted. But this admitting no farther Dilation in this
Place, may your Lordship please, and with all possible Brevity, to understand the Reasons why I am, in humble Thankfulness, ambitious to shelter this Poem under the Wings of
your Honourable Protection. My worthy Friend, Mr. Aston
Cockain, your Nephew, to my extraordinary Content, delivered to me, that your Lordship, at your vacant Hours,
sometimes vouchsafed to peruse such Trifles of mine as have
passed the Press, and not alone warranted them in your
gentle Suffrage, but disdained not to bestow a Remembrance
of your Love, and intended Favour to me. I profess to
the World, I was exalted with the Bounty, and with good
Assurance, it being so rare in this Age to meet with one
Noble Name, that, in Fear to be censured of Levity and*

*Weakness, dares express itself a Friend or Patron to con-
temned Poetry*. Having, therefore, no Means else left me
to witness the Obligation, in which I stand most willingly
bound to your Lordship, I offer this Tragi-Comedy to your
gracious Acceptance, no Way despairing, but that with a
clear Aspect, you will deign to receive it (it being an Induction to my future Endeavours) and that in the List of
those, that to your Merit truly admire you, you may descend
to number*

Your Lordship's

Faithful Honourer,

PHILIP MASSINGER.

---

* That this noble Lord not only favoured Poetry, but wrote
himself, appears from Sir *Aston Cockayn's* Letter to his Lordship in
Verse. See *Cockain's* Poems, Page 80.

PROLOGUE at the BLACK-FRYERS.

BUT that imperious Cuſtom warrants it,
   Our Author with much Willingneſs would omit
This Preface to his new Work.   He hath found
(And ſuffer'd for't) many are apt to wound
His Credit in this Kind : and, whether he .
Expreſs himſelf fearful, or peremptory,
He cannot 'ſcape their Cenſures who delight
To miſapply whatever he ſhould write.
'Tis his hard Fate.   And tho' he will not ſue,
Or baſely beg ſuch Suffrages, yet to you
Free and ingenuous Spirits, he doth now,
In me preſent his Service, with his Vow
He hath done his beſt ; and, tho' he cannot glory,
In his Invention, (this Work being a Story,
Of reverend Antiquity) he doth hope
In the Proportion of it, and the Scope,
You may obſerve ſome Pieces drawn like one
Of a ſtedfaſt Hand, and with the whiter Stone
To be mark'd in your fair Cenſure.   More than this
I am forbid to promiſe, and it is
With the moſt 'till you confirm it : ſince we know
Whate'er the Shaft be, Archer, or the Bow
From which 'tis ſent, it cannot hit the White
Unleſs your Approbation guide it right.

PROLOGUE at COURT.

AS ever (Sir) you lent a gracious Ear
  To oppreſs'd Innocence, now vouchſafe to hear
A ſhort Petition. At your Feet, in me,
The Poet kneels, and to your Majeſty
Appeals for Juſtice. What we now preſent,
When firſt conceiv'd, in his Vote and Intent,
Was ſacred to your Pleaſure; in each Part
With his beſt of Fancy, Judgment, Language, Art,
Faſhion'd and form'd ſo, as might well, and may
Deſerve a Welcome, and no vulgar Way.
He durſt not (Sir) at ſuch a ſolemn Feaſt
Lard his grave Matter with one ſcurrilous Jeſt;
But labour'd that no Paſſage might appear,
But what the Queen without a Bluſh might hear:
And yet this poor Work ſuffer'd by the Rage,
And Envy of ſome *Catos* of the Stage:
Yet ſtill he hopes this Play, which then was ſeen
With ſore Eyes, and condemn'd out of their Spleen,
May be by you, the ſupreme Judge, ſet free,
And rais'd above the Reach of Calumny.

EMPEROR of the EAST.

Dramatis Personæ.

THEODOSIUS the Younger.

PAULINUS, a Kinsman to the Emperor.
PHILANAX, Captain of the Guard.
PATRIARCH.
TIMANTUS,
CHRYSAPIUS, } Eunuchs of the Emperor's Chamber.
GRATIANUS,
CLEON, a Traveller, Friend to PAULINUS.
Informer.
Projector.
Master of the Manners.
Mignion of the Suburbs.
Countryman.
Chirurgeon.
Empirick.

PULCHERIA, the Protectress.
ATHENAIS, a strange Virgin, after, the Empress.
ARCADIA,
FLACCILLA, } the young Sisters of the Emperor.

Servants.
Mutes.

The Scene, Constantinople.

THE

EMPEROR of the EAST.

ACT I.   SCENE I.*

Paulinus *and* Cleon,

Paulinus.

IN your fix Years Travel, Friend, no doubt, you've
    met with
Many and rare Adventures, and obferv'd
The Wonders of each Climate, varying in
The Manners and the Men, and fo return,
For the future Service of your Prince and Country,
In your Underftanding better'd,
  Cleon. Sir, I have made of it
The beft Ufe in my Power, and hope my Gleanings,
After the full Crop others reap'd before me,
Shall not, when I am call'd on, altogether
Appear unprofitable : Yet I left
The Miracle of Miracles in our Age
At Home behind me ; every where abroad
Fame with a true tho' prodigal Voice, deliver'd
Such Wonders of *Pulcheria* the Princefs,
To the Amazement, nay Aftonifhment rather
Of fuch as heard it, that I found not one,

---

* The Plot of this Play is founded on the Hiftory of *Theodofius*
the younger. See *Socrates*, Lib. 7. *Theodoret*, L, 5, *&c.*

In all the States and Kingdoms that I pafs'd thro'
Worthy to be her fecond.

Paul. She, indeed, is
A perfect Phœnix, and difdains a Rival.
Her infant Years, as you know, promis'd much :
But grown to Ripenefs fhe tranfcends, and makes
Credulity her Debtor.   I will tell you
In my blunt Way, to entertain the Time
Until you have the Happinefs to fee her,
How in your Abfence fhe hath borne herfelf,
And with all poffible Brevity, tho' the Subject
Is fuch a fpacious Field, as would require
An Abftract of the pureft Eloquence
(Deriv'd from the moft famous Orators
The Nurfe of Learning, *Athens,* fhew'd the World)
In that Man, that fhould undertake to be
Her true Hiftorian.

Cleon. In this you fhall do me
A fpecial Favour.

Paul. Since *Arcádius'* Death,
Our late great Mafter, the Protection of
The Prince his Son, the fecond *Theodofius,*
By a general Vote and Suffrage of the People ;
Was to her Charge affign'd, with the Difpofure
Of his fo many Kingdoms.   For his Perfon,
She hath fo train'd him up in all thofe Arts
That are both great and good, and to be wifhed
In an imperial Monarch, that the Mother
Of the *Gracchi,* grave *Cornelia (Rome* ftill boafts of)
The wife *Pulcheria* but nam'd, muft be
No more remember'd.   She, by her Example,
Hath made the Court a kind of Academy,
In which true Honour is both learn'd and practis'd,
Her private Lodgings a chafte Nunnery,
In which her Sifters, as Probationers, hear
From her their Sovereign Abbefs, all the Precepts
Read in the School of Virtue.

Cleon. You amaze me.

Paul. I fhall, ere I conclude: For here the Wonder
Begins, not ends.   Her Soul is fo immenfe,

And her ſtrong Faculties ſo apprehenſive,
To ſearch into the Depth of deep Deſigns,
And of all Natures, that the Burthen, which
To many Men were inſupportable,
To her is but a gentle Exerciſe,
Made by the frequent Uſe familiar to her.

Cleon. With your good Favour, let me interrupt you.
Being as ſhe is in every Part ſo perfect,
Methinks that all Kings of our Eaſtern World
Should become Rivals for her.

Paul. So they have;
But to no Purpoſe. She, that knows her Strength
To rule and govern Monarchs, ſcorns to wear
On her free Neck the ſervile Yoke of Marriage.
And for one looſe Deſire, envy itſelf
Dares not preſume to taint her. *Venus'* Son
Is blind indeed, when he but gazes on her.
Her Chaſtity being a Rock of Diamonds,
With which encounter'd, his Shafts fly in Splinters,
His flaming Torches in the living Spring
Of her Perfections quenched: And, to crown all;
She's ſo impartial when ſhe ſits upon
The high Tribunal, neither ſway'd with Pity,
Nor aw'd by Fear, beyond her equal Scale,
That 'tis not Superſtition to believe
Aſtrea once more lives upon the Earth,
Pulcheria's Breaſt her Temple.

Cleon. You have given her
An admirable Character.

Paul. She deſerves it,
And ſuch is the commanding Power of Virtue,
That from her vicious enemies it compels
Pæans of Praiſe as a due Tribute to her.
                                    [*Solemn loud Muſick.*

Cleon. What means this ſolemn Muſick?

Paul. It uſhers
The Emperor's Morning Meditation,
In which *Pulcheria* is more than aſſiſtant.
'Tis worth your Obſervation, and you may

Collect from her Expence of Time this Day,
How her Hours for many Years have been dispos'd of.
   Cleon. I am all Eyes and Ears.

Enter after a Strain of Musick, Philanax, Timantus, Patriarch, Theodosius, Pulcheria, Flaccilla *and* Arcadia, *followed by* Chrysapius *and* Gratianus, *Informer,*
   Servants, and Officers.

   Pulch. Your Patience, Sir.
Let those corrupted Ministers of the Court,
Which you complain of, our Devotions ended,
Be cited to appear. For the Ambassadors
Who are importunate to have Audience,
From me you may assure them, that To-morrow
They shall in publick kiss the Emperor's Robe,
And we in private with our soonest Leisure
Will give 'em Hearing. Have you especial Care too
That free Access be granted unto all
Petitioners. The Morning wears.—Pray you on, Sir;
Time lost is ne'er recover'd.
       [*Exeunt* Theodosius, Pulcheria, *and the Train.*
   Paul. Did you note
The Majesty she appears in?
   Cleon. Yes, my good Lord;
I was ravish'd with it.
   Paul. And then with what Speed
She orders her Dispatches, not one daring
To interpose; the Emperor himself
Without Reply, putting in Act whatever
She is pleas'd t' impose upon him.
   Cleon. Yet there were some
That in their sullen Looks rather confessed
A forc'd Constraint to serve her, than a Will
To be at her Devotion: What are they?
   Paul. Eunuchs of the Emperor's Chamber, that
      repine
The Globe and awful Scepter should give Place
Unto the Distaff, for as such they whisper

A Woman's Government, but dare not yet
Exprefs themfelves.

Cleon. From whence are the Ambaffadors
To whom fhe promis'd Audience?

Paul. They are
Employ'd by divers Princes, who defire
Alliance with our Emperor, whofe Years now,
As you fee, write him Man. One would advance
A Daughter to the Honour of his Bed;
A fecond his fair Sifter: To inftruct you
In the Particulars would afk longer time
Than my own Defigns give Way to. I have Letters
From fpecial Friends of mine, that to my Care
Commend a ftranger Virgin, whom this Morning
I purpofe to prefent before the Princefs:
If you pleafe, you may accompany me.

Cleon. I'll wait on you.   [*Exeunt.*

SCENE II.

*Informer and Officers bringing in the Projector, the Suburbs
Minion, and the Mafters of the Habit and Manners.*

Informer. Why fhould you droop, or hang your work-
    ing Heads?
No Danger is meant to you; pray bear up,
For aught I know you're cited to receive
Preferment due to your Merits.

Projector. Very likely:
In all the Projects I have read and practis'd,
I never found one Man compell'd to come
Before the Seat of Juftice under Guard,
To receive Honour.

Informer. No? It may be you are
The firft Example. Men of Qualities,
As I've deliver'd you to the Protectrefs,
Who knows how to advance them, can't conceive
A fitter Place to have their Virtues publifh'd,
Than in open Court. Could you hope that the Princefs,

Knowing your precious Merits, will reward 'em
In a private Corner? No; you know not yet
How you may be exalted.

   Suburbs Minion. To the Gallows.

   Informer. Fie

Nor yet deprefs'd to the Gallies; in your 'Names
You carry no fuch Crimes: Your fpecious Titles
Cannot but take her—Prefident of the Projectors!
What a Noife it makes? The Mafter of the Habit!
How proud would fome one Country be that I know
To be your firft Pupil? Minion of the Suburbs,
And now and then admitted to the Court,
And honour'd with the Stile of Squire of Dames,
What Hurt is in it? One Thing I muft tell you,
As I am the State-fcout, you may think me an In-
      former.

   Mafter of the Habit. They are Synonimous.

   Informer. Conceal nothing from her
Of your good Parts, 'twill be better for you;
Or if you fhould, it matters not, fhe can conjure,
And I am her ubiquitary Spirit,
Bound to obey her—You have my Inftructions,
Stand by, here's better Company.

Enter Paulinus, Cleon, *and* Athenais, *with a Petition.*

   Athen. Can I hope, Sir,
Opprefled Innocence fhall find Protection,
And Juftice among Strangers, when my Brothers,
Brothres of one Womb, by one Sire begotten,
Trample on my Afflictions?

   Paul. Forget them,
Remembring thofe may help you.

   Athen. They have robb'd me
Of all Means to prefer my juft Complaint
With any promifing Hope to gain a Hearing,
Much lefs Redrefs: Petitions not fweetened
With Gold, are but unfavory, oft refufed;
Or, if receiv'd, are pocketed, not read.
A Suitor's fwelling Tears by the glowing Beams

Of cholerick Authority are dry'd up,
Before they fall ; or, if feen, never pitied.
What will become of a forfaken Maid ?
My flatt'ring Hopes are too weak to encounter
With my ftrong Enemy, Defpair, and 'tis
In vain t' oppofe her.

   Cleon. Cheer her up ; fhe faints, Sir.

   Paul. This argues Weaknefs, tho' your Brothers
      were
Cruel beyond Expreffion, and the Judges
That fentenc'd you corrupt; you fhall find here
One of your own Fair Sex to do you right,
Whofe Beams of Juftice, like the Sun, extend
Their Light and Heat to Strangers, and are not
Municipal or confin'd.

   Athen. Pray you do not feed me
With airy Hopes, unlefs you can affure me
The great *Pulcheria* will defcend to hear
My miferable Story, it were better
I died without her Trouble.

   Paul. She is bound to it
By the fureft Chain, her natural Inclination
To help th' afflicted ; nor fhall long Delays
(More terrible to miferable Suitors
Than quick Denials) grieve you.   Dry your fair Eyes;
This Room will inftantly be fanctify'd
With her blefs'd Prefence ; to her ready Hand
Prefent your Grievances, and reft affur'd
You fhall depart contented.

   Athen. You breathe in me
A fecond Life.

   Informer. Will your Lordfhip pleafe to hear
Your Servant a few Words ?

   Paul. Away, you Rafcal !
Did I ever keep fuch Servants ?

   Informer. If your Honefty
Would give you Leave, it would be for your Profit.

   Paul. To make Ufe of an Informer ? Tell me in what
Can you advantage me ?

Informer. In the firſt Tender
Of a freſh Suit never begg'd yet,

    Paul. What's your Suit, Sir?

    Informer. 'Tis feaſible:—Here are three arrant Knaves
Diſcover'd by my Art:

    Paul. And thou the Arch-knave;
The great devour the leſs:

    Informer. And with good Reaſon;
I muſt eat one a Month, I cannot live elſe.

    Paul. A notable Cannibal? But, ſhould I hear thee,
In what do your Knaves concern me?

    Informer. In the begging
Of their Eſtates.

    Paul. Before they are condemn'd?

    Informer. Yes, or arraign'd, your Lordſhip may
        ſpeak too late elſe.
They are your own, and I will be content
With the fifth Part of a Share.

    Paul. Hence, Rogue!

    Informer. Such Rogues
In this Kind will be heard and cheriſh'd too.
Fool that I was to offer ſuch a Bargain,
To a ſpic'd Conſcience Chapman—But I care not;
What he diſdains to taſte others will ſwallow.

                       [*Loud Muſick.*

Enter Theodoſius, Pulcheria, *and the Train.*

    Cleon. They are returned from the Temple.

    Paul. See, ſhe appears;
• What think you now?

    Athen. A cunning Painter, thus,
Her Veil ta'en off, and awful Sword and Balance
Laid by, would picture Juſtice.

    Pulch. When you pleaſe,
You may intend thoſe royal Exerciſes
Suiting your Birth and Greatneſs: I will bear
The Burthen of your Cares, and, having purged
The Body of your Empire of ill Humours,
Upon my Knees ſurrender it.

Chryf. Will you ever
Be aw'd thus like a Boy?
    Grat. And kifs the Rod
Of a proud Miftrefs?
    Timan. Be what you were born, Sir.
    Phila. Obedience and Majefty never lodg'd
In the fame Inn.
    Theod. No more; he never learned
The right Way to command, that ftopp'd his Ears
To wife Directions.
    Pulch. Read o'er the Papers
I left upon my Cabinet; two Hours hence
I will examine you.
    Flac. We fpend our Time well.
Nothing but praying and poring on a Book;
It ill agrees with my Conftitution, Sifter.
    Arcad. Would I had been born fome mafqu'ing La-
        dy's Woman,
Only to fee ftrange Sights, rather than live thus.
    Flac. We are gone, forfooth; there is no Remedy,
        Sifter.   [*Exeunt* Arcadia *and* Flaccilla.
    Grat. What hath his Eye found out?
    Timan. 'Tis fix'd upon
That Stranger Lady.
    Chryf. I am glad yet that
He dares look on a Woman.
    [*All this Time the Informer kneeling to* Pulcheria, *and
        delivering Papers.*
    Theod. Philanax,
What is that comely Stranger?
    Phila. A Petitioner.
    Chryf. Will you hear her Cafe, and difpatch her in
        your Chamber?
I'll undertake to bring her.
    Theod. Bring me to
Some Place where I may look on her Demeanour.
—'Tis a lovely Creature!
    Chryf. There's fome Hope in this yet.
        [*Exeunt* Theodofius, Patriarch, *and the Train.*

Pulch. Now, you have done your Parts:

Paul. Now Opportunity courts you,
Prefer your Suit.

Athen. As low as Mifery
Can fall, for Proof of my Humility,
A poor diftreffed Virgin bows her Head,
And lays hold on your Goodnefs, the laft Altar]
Calamity can fly to for Protection.
Great Minds erect their never-failing Trophies
On the firm Bafe of Mercy; but to triumph
Over a Suppliant, by proud Fortune captiv'd,
Argues a Baftard Conqueft—'tis to you
I fpeak, to you, the fair and juft *Pulcheria*,
The Wonder of the Age, your Sex's Honour;
And, as fuch, deign to hear me. As you have
A Soul moulded from Heaven, and do defire
To have it made a Star there, make the Means
Of your Afcent to that celeftial Height
Virtue wing'd with brave Action. They draw near
The Nature, and the Effence of the Gods,
Who imitate their Goodnefs.

Pulch. If you were
A Subject of the Empire, which your Habit
In every Part denies——

Athen. O fly not to
Such an Evafion; whate'er I am,
Being a Woman, in Humanity
You are bound to right me, tho' the Difference
Of my Religion may feem to exclude me
From your Defence (which you would have confin'd)
The moral Virtue, which is general,
Muft know no Limits—By thefe bleffed Feet
That pace the Paths of Equity, and tread boldly
On the ftiff Neck of tyrannous Oppreffion,
By thefe Tears by which I bathe 'em, I conjure you
With Pity to look on me.

Pulch. Pray you, rife.
And, as you rife, receive this Comfort from me.
Beauty fet off with fuch fweet Language never
Can want an Advocate; and you muft bring

More than a guilty Caufe if you prevail not.
Some Bufinefs long fince thought upon, difpatched,
You fhall have Hearing, and, as far as Juftice
Will warrant me, my beft Aids.

Athen. I do defire
No ftronger Guard; my Equity needs no Favour.

Pulch. Are thefe the Men?

Projector. We were, an't like your Highnefs,
The Men, the Men of Eminence and Mark,
And may continue fo, if it pleafe your Grace.

Mafter. This Speech was well projected.   [*Afide.*

Pulch. Does your Confcience
(I will begin with you) whifper unto you
What here you ftand accus'd of? Are you named
The Prefident of Projectors?

Informer. Juftify it, Man,
And tell her in what thou'rt ufeful.

Project. That's apparent;
And, if you pleafe, afk fome about the Court,
And they will tell you, to my rare Inventions
They owe their Bravery, perhaps Means to purchafe,
And cannot live without me. I, alas!
Lend out my labouring Brains to Ufe, and fometimes
For a Drachma in the Pound,—the more the Pity.
I am all Patience, and endure the Curfes
Of many, for the Profit of one Patron.

Pulch. I do conceive the reft—What is the Second?

Informer. The Minion of the Suburbs.

Pulch. What hath he
To do in *Conftantinople?*

Min. I fteal in now and then,
As I am thought ufeful; marry, there I am call'd
The Squire of Dames, or Servant of the Sex,
And by the Allowance of fome fportful Ladies
Honour'd with that Title.

Pulch. Spare your Character,
You're here decipher'd—Stand by with your Compeer.
What is the Third? A Creature I ne'er heard of;

T 2

The Master of the Manners and the Habit?
You have a double Office.

   Master. In my Actions
I make both good; for by my Theorems
Which your polite and terser Gallants practise,
I refine the Court, and civilize
Their barbarous Natures. I have in a Table
With curious Punctuality set down
To a Hair's Breadth, how low a new-stamp'd Courtier
May vail to a Country Gentleman, and, by
Gradation, to his Merchant, Mercer, Draper,
His Linen-man and Taylor.

   Pulch. Pray you, discover
This hidden Mystery.

   Master. If the 'foresaid Courtier
(As it may chance sometimes) find not his Name
Writ in the Citizen's Books with a State-hum
He may salute 'em after three Days waiting:
But, if he owe them Money, that he may
Preserve his Credit, let him in Policy never
Appoint a Day of Payment: so they may hope still:
But, if he be to take up more, his Page
May attend 'em at the Gate, and usher 'em
Into his Cellar, and when they are warm'd with Wine,
Conduct 'em to his Bedchamber, and tho' then
He be under his Barber's Hands, as soon as seen,
He must start up to embrace 'em, vail thus low;
Nay, tho' he call 'em Cousins, 'tis the better,
His Dignity no Way wrong'd in't.

   Paul. Here's a fine Knave!

   Pulch. Does this Rule hold without Exception, Sir-
      rah;
For Courtiers in General?

   Master. No, dear Madam;
For one of the last Edition, and for him
I have compos'd a Dictionary, in which
He is instructed, how, when, and to whom
To be proud or humble; at what times of the Year
He may do a good Deed for itself, and that is
Writ in Dominical Letters; all Days else

Are his own, and of those Days the several Hours
Mark'd out, and to what Use.

Pulch. Shew us your Method;
I'm strangely taken with it.

Master. 'Twill deserve
A Pension, I hope. First a strong Cullis
In his Bed, to heighten Appetite: Shuttle-cock
To keep him in Breath when he rises; Tennis-Courts
Are chargeable, and the riding of great Horses
Too boist'rous for my young Courtier; let the old ones
I think not of, use it; next his Meditation
How to court his Mistress, and that he may seem witty,
Let him be furnish'd with confederate Jests
Between him and his Friend, that, on Occasion,
They may vent 'em mutually: What his Pace and
    Garb
Must be in the Presence, then the Length of his Sword,
The Fashion of the Hilt—what the Blade is
It matters not, 'twere Barbarism to use it,
Unless to shew his Strength upon an Andiron;
So, the sooner broke, the better.

Pulch. How I abuse
This precious Time! Projector, I treat first
Of you and your Disciples; you roar out,
All is the King's, his Will above his Laws;
And that fit Tributes are too gentle Yokes
For his poor Subjects; whisp'ring in his Ear,
If he would have their Fear, no Man should dare
To bring a Sallad from his Country Garden,
Without the paying Gabel; kill a Hen,
Without Excise: and that, if he desire
To have his Children, or his Servants wear
Their Heads upon their Shoulders, you affirm
In Policy, 'tis fit the Owner should
Pay for 'em by the Poll; or, if the Prince want
A present Sum, he may command a City
Impossibilities, and for Non-performance,
Compel it to submit to any Fine
His Officers shall impose. Is this the Way

To make our Emperor happy? Can the Groans
Of his Subjects yield him Musick? Must his Thresh-
   olds
Be wash'd with Widows and wrong'd Orphans' Tears,
Or his Power grow contemptible?

Project. I begin
To feel myself a Rogue again.

Pulch. But you are
The Squire of Dames, devoted to the Service
Of gamesome Ladies, the hidden Mystery
Discover'd, their close Bawd; thy slavish Breath
Fanning the Fires of Lust, the Go-between
This Female and that wanton Sir; your Art
Can blind a jealous Husband, and, disguis'd
Like a Millener or Shoemaker, convey
A Letter in a Pantofle or Glove
Without Suspicion: nay, at his Table,
In a Case of Picktooths. You instruct 'em how
To parley with their Eyes, and make the Temple
A Mart of Looseness; to discover all
Thy subtile Brokages, were to teach in Publick
Those private Practices, which are, in Justice,
Severely to be punish'd.

Minion. I am cast;
A Jury of my Patronesses cannot quit me.

Pulch. You are Master of the Manners and the Ha-
   bit;
Rather the Scorn of such as would live Men,
And not, like Apes, with servile Imitation
Study prodigious Fashions. You keep
Intelligence abroad, that may instruct
Our giddy Youth at home what new-found Fashion
Is now in Use, swearing he's most complete
That first turns Monster. Know, Villains, I can thrust
This Arm into your Hearts, strip off the Flesh
That covers your Deformities, and shew you
In your Nakedness. Now, tho' the Law
Call not your Follies Death, you are for ever

Baniſh'd my Brother's Court.—Away with 'em;
I will hear no Reply.

[Exeunt Informer, Officers and Priſoners.

The Curtains drawn above, Theodoſius *and his Eunuchs
diſcovered.*

Paul. What think you now?
Cleon. That I am in a Dream; or that I ſee
A ſecond *Pallas.*
Pulch. Theſe remov'd, to you
I clear my Brow: Speak without Fear, ſweet Maid,
Since with a mild Aſpect and ready Ear,
I ſit prepar'd to hear you.
Athen. Know, great Princeſs,
My Father, tho' a *Pagan,* was admired ·
For his deep Search into thoſe hidden Studies,
Whoſe Knowledge is deny'd to common Men;
The Motion, with the divers Operations
Of the ſuperior Bodies, by his long
And careful Obſervation, were made
Familiar to him; all the ſecret Virtues
Of Plants and Simples, and in what Degree
They were uſeful to Mankind, he could diſcourſe of;
In a Word, conceive him as a Prophet honour'd
In his own Country. But being born a Man,
It lay not in him to defer the Hour
Of his approaching Death, tho' long foretold:
In this ſo fatal Hour he call'd before him
His two Sons and myſelf, the deareſt Pledges
Lent him by Nature, and with his right Hand
Bleſſing our ſeveral Heads, he thus began:
Chryſ. Mark his Attention.
Phila. Give me Leave to mark too.
Athen. " If I could leave my Underſtanding to you,
" It were ſuperfluous to make Diviſion
" Of whatſoever elſe I can bequeath you:
" But, to avoid Contention, I allot
" An equal Portion of my Poſſeſſions

T 4

" To you, my Sons ; but unto thee, my Daughter,
" My Joy, my Darling (pardon me, tho' I
" Repeat his Words) if my prophetick Soul
" Ready to take her Flight, can truly guefs at
" Thy future Fate, I leave thee ftrange Affurance
" Of the Greatnefs thou art born to, unto which
" Thy Brothers fhall be proud to pay their Service :——
 Paul. And all Men elfe that honour Beauty.
 Theod. Ha !
 Athen. " Yet, to preprre thee for certain Fortune,
" And that I may from prefent Wants defend thee,
" I leave ten thoufand Crowns"——which faid, being
   call'd
To th' Fellowfhip of our Duties, he expir'd,
And with him all Remembrance of the Charge
Concerning me, left by him to my Brothers.
 Pulch. Did they detain your Legacy ?
 Athen. And ftill do,
His Afhes were fcarce quiet in his Urn,
When, in Derifion of my future Greatnefs,
They thruft me out of Doors, denying me
One fhort Night's Harbour,
 Pulch. Weep not,
 Athen. I defire,
By your Perfuafion or commanding Power,
The Reftitution of mine own ; or that,
To keep my Frailty from Temptation,
In your Compaffion of me, you would pleafe
I, as a Handmaid, may be entertain'd
To do the meaneft Offices to all fuch
As are honour'd in your Service,
 Pulch. Thou art welcome,
What is thy Name ?
 Athen. The forlorn *Athenais.*
 Pulch. The Sweetnefs of thy Innocence ftrangely
  takes me,

     [Takes her up, and kiffes her,
Forget thy Brothers Wrongs ; for I will be
In my Care a Mother, in my Love a Sifter to thee ;

And, were it poſſible thou could'ſt be won
To be of our Belief——
    Paul. May it pleaſe your Excellence,
That is an eaſy Taſk, I, tho' no Scholar,
Dare undertake it ; clear Truth cannot want
Rhetorical Perſuaſions.
    Pulch. 'Tis a Work,
My Lord, will well become you.—Break up the Court;
May your Endeavours proſper.
    Paul. Come, my Fair One;
I hope, my Convert.
    Athen. Never : I will die
As I was born.
    Paul. Better you ne'er had been.   [*Exeunt.*
    Phila. What does your Majeſty think of?——The
        Maid's gone.
    Theod. She's wondrous fair, and in her Speech ap-
        pear'd
Pieces of Scholarſhip.
    Chryſ. Make Uſe of her Learning
And Beauty together ; on my Life ſhe will be proud
To be ſo converted.
    Theod. From foul Luſt Heaven guard me.
                             [*Exeunt,*

The End of the Firſt Act.

ACT II, SCENE I.

Philanax, Timantus, Chryſapius, and *Gratianus,*

Philanax.

WE only talk, when we ſhould do,
    Timan. I'll ſecond you ;
Begin, and when you pleaſe.
    Grat. Be conſtant in it,

Chryſ. That Reſolution which grows cold To-day,
Will freeze To-morrow.

Grat. 'Slight, I think ſhe'll keep him
Her Ward for ever, to herſelf engroſſing
The Diſpoſition of all the Favours
And Bounties of the Empire.

Chryſ. We, that by
The Nearneſs of our Service to his Perſon,
Should raiſe this Man, or pull down that, without
Her Licence, hardly dare prefer a Suit,
Or, if we do, 'tis croſs'd.——

Phila. You are troubled for
Your proper Ends; my Aims are high and honeſt,
The Wrong that's done to Majeſty I repine at:
I love the Emperor, and 'tis my Ambition
To have him know himſelf, and to that Purpoſe
I'll run the Hazard of a Check,

Grat. And I
The Loſs of my Place.

Timan. I will not come behind,
Fall what can fall.

Chryſ. Let us put on ſad Aſpects
To draw him on; charge home, we'll fetch you off,
Or lie dead by you.

Enter Theodoſius.

Theod. How's this? Clouds in the Chamber,
And the Air clear abroad!

Phila. When you, our Sun,
Obſcure your glorious Beams, poor we, that borrow
Our little Light from you, cannot but ſuffer
A general Eclipſe.

Timan. Great Sir, 'tis true;
For, 'till you pleaſe to know and be yourſelf,
And freely dare diſpoſe of what's your own
Without a Warrant, we are falling Meteors,
And not fix'd Stars.

Chryſ. The pale-fac'd Moon, that ſhould
Govern the Night, uſurps the Rule of Day,

And still is at the Full, in Spite of Nature,
And will not know a Change.

Theod. Speak you in Riddles?
I am no *Oedipus,* but your Emperor,
And as such would be instructed.

Phila. Your Command
Shall be obey'd: 'Till now, I never heard you
Speak like yourself; and may that Power, by which
You are so, strike me dead, if what I shall
Deliver as a faithful Subject to you,
Hath Root or Growth from Malice, or base Envy.
Of your Sister's Greatness, I could honour in her
A Power subordinate to yours; but not
As 'tis predominant.

Timan. Is it fit that she,
In her birth your Vassal, should command the Knees
Of such as should not bow but to yourself?

Grat. She with Security walks upon the Heads
Of the Nobility; the Multitude,
As to a Deity, offering Sacrifice
For her Grace and Favour.

Chrys. Her proud Feet ev'n wearied
With the Kisses of Petitioners.

Grat. While you,
To whom alone such Reverence is proper,
Pass unregarded by her.

Timan. You have not yet
Been Master of one Hour of your whole Life.

Chrys. Your Will and Faculties kept in more Awe
Than she can do her own.

Phila. And as a Bondman,
(O let my Zeal find grace, and Pardon from you,
That I descend so low) you are design'd
To this or that Employment, suiting well
A private Man, I grant, but not a Prince.
To be a perfect Horseman; or to know
The Words of the Chace; or a fair Man of Arms;
Or to be able to pierce to the Depth,
Or write a Comment on th' obscurest Poets,
I grant are Ornaments; but your main Scope

Should be to govern Men, to guard your own,
If not enlarge your Empire.

Chryf. You are built up
By th' curious Hand of Nature to revive
The Memory of *Alexander*; or by
A profperous Succefs in your brave Actions,
To rival *Cæfar.*

Timan. Rouze yourfelf, and let not
Your Pleafures be a Copy of her Will.

Phila. Your Pupil Age is paft, and manly Actions
Are now expected from you.

Grat. Do not lofe
Your Subjects Hearts.

Timan. What is't to have the Means
To be magnificent, and not exercife
The boundlefs Virtue?

Grat. You confine yourfelf
To that which ftrict Philofophy allows of,
As if you were a private Man.

Timan. No Pomp
Or glorious Shows of Royalty, rend'ring it
Both lov'd and terrible.

Grat. 'Slight, you live, as it
Begets fome Doubt, whether you have, or not,
Th' Abilities of a Man.

Chryf. The Firmament
Hath not more Stars than there are feveral Beauties
Ambitious at the Height to impart their dear,
And fweeteft Favours to you.

Grat. Yet you have not
Made Choice of one, of all the Sex, to ferve you,
In a phyfical Way of Courtfhip.

Theod. But that I would not
Begin the Expreffion of my being a Man,
In Blood, or ftain the firft white Robe I wear
Of Abfolute Power, with a fervile Imitation
Of any tyrannous Habit, my juft Anger
Prompts me to make you in your Suff'rings feel,
And not in Words to inftruct you, that the Licence

Of the loose and saucy Language you now practised,
Hath forfeited your Heads.

 Grat. How's this?   [*Aside.*

 Phila. I know not
What the Play may prove; but I assure you that
I do not like the Prologue.   [*Aside.*

 Theod. O the miserable
Condition of a Prince; who, tho' he vary
More Shapes than *Proteus* in his Mind and Manners,
He cannot win an universal Suffrage.
From the many-headed Monster, Multitude.
Like *Æsop*'s foolish Frogs, they trample on him,
As a senseless Block, if his Government be easy:
And, if he prove a Stork, they croak and rail
Against him as a Tyrant.—I'll put off
That Majesty, of which you think I have
Nor Use nor Feeling; and, in arguing with you,
Convince you with strong Proofs of common Reason,
And not with Absolute Power, against which, Wretches,
You are not to dispute. Dare you, that are
My Creatures, by my prodigal Favours fashion'd,
Presuming on the Nearness of your Service,
Set off with my familiar Acceptance,
Condemn my Obsequiousness to the wise Directions
Of an incomparable Sister, whom all Parts
Of our World, that are made happy in Knowledge
Of her Perfections, with Wonder gaze on?
And yet you that were only born to eat
The Blessings of our Mother Earth, that are
Distant but one Degree from Beasts (since Slaves
Can claim no larger Privilege) that know
No farther than your sensual Appetites
Or wanton Lust have taught you, undertake
To give your Sovereign Laws to follow that
Your Ignorance marks out to him?   [*Walks by.*

 Grat. How were we
Abus'd in our Opinion of his Temper! [*Aside.*

 Phil. We had forgot 'tis found in Holy Writ,
That Kings Hearts are inscrutable.   [*Aside.*

Timan. I ne'er read it;
My Study lies not that Way.   [*Aside.*
· *Phila.* By his Looks
The Tempeſt ſtill increaſes.   [*Aside.*
  Theod. Am I grown
So ſtupid in your Judgments, that you dare
With ſuch Security offer Violence
To Sacred Majeſty ? Will you not know
The Lion is a Lion, tho' he ſhew not
His rending Paws, or fill th' affrighted Air
With the Thunder of his Roarings ? ——You bleſs'd
          Saints !
How am I trenched on ? Is that Temperance
So famous in your cited *Alexander,*
Or *Roman Scipio,* a Crime in me ?
Cannot I be an Emperor, unleſs
Your Wives and Daughters bow to my proud Luſts ?
And 'cauſe I raviſh not their faireſt Buildings
And fruitful Vineyards, or what is deareſt,
From ſuch as are my Vaſſals, muſt you conclude
I do not know the awful Power and Strength
Of my Prerogative ? Am I cloſe-handed,
Becauſe I ſcatter not among you that
I muſt not call mine own ? Know, you Court-leeches,
A Prince is never ſo magnificent
As when he's ſparing to enrich a Few
With th' Injuries of Many.   Could your Hopes
So groſly flatter you, as to believe
I was born and train'd up as an Emperor, only
In my Indulgence to give Sanctuary,
In their unjuſt Proceedings, to the Rapine
And Avarice of my Grooms ?
    Phila. In the true Mirror
Of your Perfections, at length we ſee
Our own Deformities.
    Timan. And not once daring
To look upon that Majeſty we now ſlighted——
    Chryſ. With our Faces thus glu'd to the Earth, we
          beg
Your gracious Pardon.

Grat. Offering our Necks
To be trod on, as a Punishment for our late
Presumption, and a willing Testimony
Of our Subjection.

Theod. Deserve our Mercy
In your better Life hereafter, you shall find,
Tho' in my Father's Life I held it Madness
To usurp his Power, and in my Youth disdain'd not
To learn from the Instructions of my Sister,
I'll make it good to all the World, I am
An Emperor; and ev'n this Instant grasp
The Scepter, my rich Stock of Majesty
Entire, no Scruple wasted.

Phila. If these Tears
I drop proceed not from my Joy to hear this,
May my Eye-balls follow 'em.

Timan. I will shew myself
By your sudden Metamorphosis, transform'd
From what I was.

Grat. And ne'er presume to ask
What fits not you to give.

Theod. Move in that Sphere,
And my Light with full Beams shall shine upon you.
Forbear this slavish Courtship; 'tis to me
In a kind idolatrous.

Phila. Your gracious Sister.

Enter Pulcheria *and Servant.*

Pulch. Has he converted her?
Serv. And, as such, will
Present her, when you please.
Pulch. I am glad of it.
Command my Dresser to adorn her with
The Robes that I gave Order for.
Serv. I shall.
Pulch. And let those precious Jewels I took last
Out of my Cabinet, if't be possible,
Give Lustre to her Beauties; and, that done,
Command her to be near us.

Serv. 'Tis a Province
I willingly embrace.   [*Exit Servant.*

Pulch. O my dear Sir,
You have forgot your Morning Taſk, and therefore
With a Mother's Love I come to reprehend you,
But it ſhall be gently.

Theod. 'Twill become you, tho'
You ſaid with reverend Duty. Know hereafter,
If my Mother liv'd in you, howe'er her Son,
Like you ſhe were my ſubject.

Pulch. How?

Theod. Put off
Amazement; you will find it. Yet I'll hear you
At Diſtance, as a Siſter, but no longer
As a Governeſs, I aſſure you.

Grat. This is put home.   [*Aſide.*
Timan. Beyond our Hopes.   [*Aſide.*
Phila. She ſtands, as if his Words
Had powerful Magick in 'em.   [*Aſide.*

Theod. Will you have me
Your Pupil ever? The Down on my Chin
Confirms I am a Man; a Man of Men;
The Emperor! that knows his Strength.

Pulch. Heaven grant
You know it not too ſoon.

Theod. Let it ſuffice
My Wardſhip's out. If your Deſign concerns us
As a Man, and not a Boy, with our Allowance
You may deliver it.

Pulch. A ſtrange Alteration!
But I will not contend. [*Aſide.*] Be as you wiſh, Sir,
Your own Diſpoſer; uncompell'd I cancel
All Bonds of my Authority.   [*Kneels.*

Theod. You in this
Pay your due Homage; which perform'd, I thus
Embrace you as a Siſter, no Way doubting
Your Vigilance for my Safety as my Honour;
And what you now come to impart, I reſt
Moſt confident, points at one of them.

Pulch. At both,

And not alone the prefent, but the future
Tranquility of your Mind : Since in the Choice
Of her you are to heat with holy Fires,
And make the Confort of your Royal Bed,
The certain Means of glorious Succeffion,
With the true Happinefs of our human Being,
Are wholly comprehended.

    Theod. How ? a Wife?

Shall I become a Votary to *Hymen*,
Before my Youth hath facrific'd to *Venus ?*
'Tis fomething with the fooneft—Yet, to fhew,
In Things indifferent, I am not averfe
To your wife Counfels, let me firft furvey
Thofe Beauties, that, in being a Prince, I know
Are Rivals for me. You will not confine me
To your Election ; I muft fee, dear Sifter
With mine own Eyes.

    Pulch. 'Tis fit, Sir—Yet, in this,

You may pleafe to confider, abfolute Princes
Have, or fhould have, in Policy, lefs free Will
Than fuch as are their Vaffals. For you muft,
As you are an Emperor, in this high Bufinefs,
Weigh with due Providence, with whom Alliance
May be moft ufeful for the Prefervation
Or Increafe of your Empire.

    Theod. I approve not

Such Compofitions for our moral Ends,
In what is in itfelf divine, nay more,
Decreed in Heav'n. Yet, if our Neighbour Princes,
Ambitious of fuch Nearnefs, fhall prefent
Their deareft Pledges to me (ever referving
The Caution of mine own Content) I'll not
Contemn their courteous Offers.

    Pulch. Bring in the Pictures.

                     [*Two Pictures brought in.*

    Theod. Muft I then judge the Subftances by the
        Shadows ?

The Painters are moft envious, if they want

Good Colours for Preferment. Virtuous Ladies
Love this Way to be flatter'd, and accuse
The Workman of Detraction, if he add not
Some Grace they cannot truly call their own.
Is't not so, *Gratianus?* You may challenge
Some Interest in the Science.

 Grat. A Pretender
To the Art, I truly honour; and subscribe
To your Majesty's Opinion.

 Theod. Let me see——
Cleanthe, Daughter to the King of *Epirus*
Ætatis suæ, the fourteenth: Ripe enough,
And forward too, I assure you. Let me examine
The Symmetries. If Statuaries could
By the Foot of *Hercules* set down punctually
His whole Dimensions, and the Countenance be
The Index of the Mind, this may instruct me,
With th' Aids of that I've read touching this Subject
What she is inward. The Colour of her Hair,
(If it be, as this does promise,) pale and faint,
And not a glitt'ring white. Her brow, so so.
The Circles of her Sight, too much contracted;
Juno's fair Cow-eyes by old *Homer* are
Commended to their Merit; here's a sharp Frost,
I' th' Tip of her Nose, which by the Length assures me
Of Storms at Midnight, if I fail to pay her
The Tribute she expects.—I like her not:
What is the other?

 Chrys. How hath he commenc'd
Doctor in this so sweet and secret Art,
Without our Knowledge?   [*Aside.*

 Timan. Some of his forward Pages
Have robbed us of the Honour.   [*Aside.*

 Phila. No such Matter;
He has the Theory only, not the Practice.   [*Aside.*

 Theod. Amasia, Sister to the Duke of *Athens;*
Her Age eighteen, descended lineally
From *Theseus,* as by her Pedigree
Will be made apparent—Of his lusty Kindred,

And lofe fo much Time ? 'Tis ftrange !—As I live, fhe
 hath
A philofophical Afpect : There is
More Wit than Beauty in her Face, and, when
I court her, it muft be in Tropes, and Figures,
Or fhe will cry *abfurd.* She will have her Clenches
To cut off any Fallacy I can hope
To put upon her, and expect I fhould
Ever conclude in Syllogifms, and thofe true ones
In parte & toto, or fhe'll tire me with
Her tedious Elocutions in the Praife
Of the Increafe of Generation, for which
Alone the Sport, in her Morality,
Is good and lawful, and to be often practis'd
For fear of miffing.—Fie on't, let the Race
Of *Thefeus* be match'd with *Ariftotles,*
I'll none of her.

   Pulch. You are curious in your Choice, Sir,
And hard to pleafe ; yet, if that your Confent
May give Authority to it, I'll prefent you
With one, that if her Birth and Fortunes anfwer'd
The Rarities of her Body and her Mind,
Detraction durft not tax her.

   Theod. Let me fee her,
Tho' wanting thofe Additions, which we can
Supply from our Store : it is in us
To make Men rich and noble : but, to give
Legitimate Shapes and Virtues, does belong
To the Great Creator of 'em, to whofe Bounties
Alone 'tis proper, and in this difdains
An Emperor for his Rival.

   Pulch. I applaud
This fit Acknowledgment, fince Princes then
Grow lefs than common Men, when they contend
With Him, by whom they are fo.

Enter Paulinus, Cleon, Athenais, *newly habited.*

Theod. I confess it.

Pulch. Not to hold you in Suspense, Behold the Virgin
Rich in her natural Beauties, no Way borrowing
Th' adulterate Aids of Art.   Peruse her better;
She's worth your serious View.

Phila. I am amaz'd too:
I never saw her Equal.

Grat. How his Eye
Is fix'd upon her!

Timan. And, as she were a Fort,
He'd suddenly surprize, he measures her
From the Bases to the Battlements.

Chrys. Ha! now I view her better,
I know her; 'tis the Maid that not long since
Was a Petitioner: her Bravery
So alters her, I had forgot her Face.

Phila. So has the Emperor.

Paul. She holds out yet,
And yields not to th' Assault.

Cleon. She's strongly guarded
In her Virgin Blushes.

Paul. When you know, fair Creature,
It is the Emperor that honours you
With such a strict Survey of your sweet Parts,
In Thankfulness you cannot but return
Due Reverence for the Favour.

Athen. I was lost
In my Astonishment at the glorious Object,
And yet rest doubtful whether he expects,
Being more than Man, my Adoration,
(Since sure there is Divinity about him:)
Or will rest satisfy'd, if my humble Knees
In Duty thus bow to him.

Theod. Ha! it speaks.

Pulch. She is no Statue, Sir.

Theod. Suppose her one,
And that she had nor Organs, Voice, nor Heat,

Moſt willingly I would reſign my Empire,
So it might be to After-times recorded
That I was her *Pygmalion*, tho', like him,
I doated on my Workmanſhip, without Hope too
Of having *Cytherea* ſo propitious
To my Vows or Sacrifice, in her Compaſſion
To give it Life or Motion.

    Pulch. Pray you, be not rapt ſo,
Nor borrow from imaginary Fiction
Impoſſible Aids. She's Fleſh and Blood, I aſſure you;
And, if you pleaſe to honour her in the Trial,
And be your own Security, as you'll find
I fable not, ſhe comes in a noble Way
To be at your Devotion.

    Chryſ. 'Tis the Maid
I offer'd to your Highneſs; her chang'd Shape
Conceal'd her from you:

    Theod. At the firſt I knew her;
And a ſecond Firebrand *Cupid* brings, to kindle
My Flames almoſt put out: I am too cold,
And play with Opportunity.—May I taſte then
The Nectar of her Lip?—I do not give it
The Praiſe it merits: Antiquity is too poor
To help me with a Simile to expreſs her.
Let me drink often from this living Spring,
To nouriſh new Invention.

    Pulch. Do not ſurfeit
In over-greedily devouring that
Which may without Satiety feaſt you often.
From the Moderation in receiving them,
The choiceſt Viands do continue pleaſing
To the moſt curious Palates. If you think her
Worth your Embraces, and the ſovereign Title
Of the *Grecian* Empreſs——

    Theod. If? How much you ſin,
Only to doubt it; the Poſſeſſion of her
Makes all that was before moſt precious to me
Common and cheap, in this you've ſhewn yourſelf
A provident Protectreſs. I already

Grow weary of the absolute Command
Of my so numerous Subjects, and desire
No Sov'reignty but here, and write down gladly
A Period to my Wishes.

Pulch. Yet, before
It be too late, consider her Condition;
Her Father was a *Pagan*, she herself
A new-converted Christian.

Theod. Let me know
The Man to whose religious Means I owe
So great a Debt.

Paul. You are advanc'd too high, Sir,
To acknowledge a Beholdingness, 'tis discharg'd,
And I, beyond my Hopes, rewarded, if
My Service please your Majesty.

Theod. Take this Pledge
Of our assured Love. Are there none here
Have Suits to prefer? On such a Day as this
My Bounty's without Limit. O my dearest,
I will not hear thee speak; whatever in
Thy Thoughts is apprehended, I grant freely.
Thou wouldst plead thy Unworthiness; be thyself
(The Magazine of Felicity,) in thy Lowness.
Our Eastern Queens, at their full Height, bow to thee,
And are, in their best Trim, thy Foils and Shadows.
Excuse the Violence of my Love, which cannot
Admit the least Delay. Command the Patriarch
With Speed to do his Holy Office for us,
That, when we are made one——

Pulch. You must forbear, Sir;
She is not yet baptiz'd.

Theod. In the same Hour
In which she is confirmed in our Faith,
We mutually will give away each other,
And both be Gainers; we'll hear no Reply
That may divert us. On

Pulch. You may hereafter
Please to remember to whose Furtherance
You owe this Height of Happiness.

Athen. As I was
Your Creature when I firſt petition'd you,
I will continue ſo, and you ſhall find me,
Tho' an Empreſs, ſtill your Servant.

    [*All exit but* Philanax, Gratianus *and* Timantus.

  Grat. Here's a Marriage
Made up o' th' ſudden !

  Phila. I repine not at
The fair Maid's Fortune—tho' I fear the Princeſs
Had ſome peculiar End in't.

  Timan. Who's ſo ſimple
Only to doubt it ?

  Grat. It is too apparent,
She hath preferr'd a Creature of her own,
By whoſe Means ſhe may ſtill keep to herſelf
The Government of the Empire.

  Timan. Whereas if
The Emperor had eſpous'd ſome Neighbour Queen,
Pulcheria, with all her Wiſdom, could not
Keep her Pre-eminence.

  Phila. Be it as it will,
'Tis not now to be alter'd,—Heaven, I ſay,
Turn all to th' beſt !

  Grat. Are we come to praying again ?

  Phil. Leave thy Prophaneſs.

  Grat. Would it leave me.
I am ſure I thrive not by it.

  Timan. Come to the Temple.

  Grat. Ev'n where you will—I know not what to
    think on't.

End of the Second Act.

ACT III. SCENE I.

Enter Paulinus *and* Philanax.

Paulinus.

NOR this, nor th' Age before us, ever look'd on
  The like Solemnity.
  Phila. A sudden Fever
Kept me at home.   Pray you, my Lord, acquaint me
With the Particulars.
  Paul. You may presume,
No Pomp nor Ceremony could be wanting,
Where there was Privilege to command, and Means
To cherish rare Inventions.
  Phila. I believe it;
But the Sum of all, in brief.
  Paul. Pray you, so take it;
Fair *Athenais,* not long since a Suitor,
And almost in her Hopes forsaken, first
Was christen'd, and the Emperor's Mother's Name,
Eudoxia, as he will'd, impos'd upon her;
Pulcheria, the ever-matchless Princess,
Assisted by her reverend Aunt *Maria,*
Her God-mothers.
  Phila. And who the Masculine Witness?
  Paul. At the new Empress' Suit I had the Honour;
—For which I must ever serve her,
  Phila. 'Twas a Grace
With Justice you may boast of.
  Paul. The Marriage follow'd;
And, as 'tis said, the Emperor made bold
To turn the Day to Night; for to Bed they went

As foon as they had din'd, and there are Wagers
Laid by fome merry Lords, he hath already
Begot a Boy upon her.

Phila. That is yet
To be determin'd of; but I am certain
A Prince, fo foon in his Difpofition alter'd,
Was never heard nor read of.

Paul. But of late,
Frugal and fparing, now nor Bounds nor Limits
To his magnificent Bounties. He affirm'd,
Having receiv'd more Bleffings by his Emprefs
Than he could hope, in Thankfulnefs to Heaven
He cannot be too prodigal to others.
Whatever's offer'd to his Royal Hand
He figns without perufing it.

Phila. I am here
Injoin'd to free all fuch as lie for Debt,
The Creditors to be paid out of his Coffers.

Paul. And I all Malefactors that are not
Convicted or for Treafon or foul Murther;
Such only are excepted;

Phila. 'Tis a rare Clemency!

Paul. Which we muft not difpute, but put in Practice. [*Exeunt.*

SCENE II.

*Loud Mufick, Shouts within: Heaven preferve the Emperor,
Heaven blefs the Emprefs. Then in State,* Chryfapius,
Patriarch. Paulinus, Theodofius, Athenais, Pulcheria, *her two young Sifters bearing up* Athenais's Train,
follozwed by Philanax, Gratianus, Timantus, Suitors,
prefenting Petitions, the Emperor fealing them. Pulcheria *appears troubled.*

Pulch. Sir, by your own Rules of Philofophy,
You know Things violent laft not. Royal Bounties
Are great and gracious, while they are difpens'd
With Moderation; but, when their Excefs
In giving Giant-bulks to others, take from

The Prince's juſt Proportion, they loſe
The Name of Virtues, and, their Natures chang'd,
Grow the moſt dangerous Vices.

 Theod. In this, Siſter,
Your Wiſdom is not circular; they that ſow
In narrow Bounds, cannot expect in Reaſon
A Crop beyond their Ventures; what I do
Diſperſe I lend, and will with Uſury
Return unto my Heap. I only then
Am rich, and happy (tho' my Coffers ſound
With Emptineſs) when my glad Subjects feel,
Their Plenty and Felicity is my Gift;
And they will find, when they with Cheerfulneſs
Supply not my Defects, I being the Stomach
To th' politick Body of the State, the Limbs
Grow ſuddenly faint and feeble. I could urge
Proofs of more Fineneſs in their Shape and Language;
But none of greater Strength.—Diſſuade me not;
What we will, we will do; yet, to aſſure you
Your Care does not offend us, for an Hour
Be happy in the Converſe of my beſt
And deareſt Comfort—May you pleaſe to licence
My Privacy ſome few Minutes?   [*To* Athenais.
 Athen. Licence, Sir?
I have no Will but is deriv'd from yours,
And that ſtill waits upon you; nor can I
Be left with ſuch Security with any
As with the gracious Princeſs, who receives
Addition, tho' ſhe be all Excellence,
In being ſtil'd your Siſter.
 Theod. O ſweet Creature!
Let me be cenſur'd fond and too indulgent,
Nay, tho' they ſay uxorious, I care not;
Her Love and ſweet Humility exact
A Tribute far above my Power to pay
Her matchleſs Goodneſs. [*Aſide.*] Forward.
     [*Exeunt* Theodoſius *and the Train.*
 Pulch. Now you find
Your dying Father's Prophecy, that foretold
Your preſent Greatneſs, to the full accompliſh'd.

For the poor Aids and Furtherance I lent you,
I willingly forget.

Athen. Ev'n that binds me
To a more ftrict Remembrance of the Favour;
Nor fhall you, from my foul Ingratitude,
In any Circumftance, ever find Caufe
T'upbraid me with your Benefit.

Pulch. I believe fo.
Pray you, give us leave—What now I muft deliver
Under the deepeft Seal of Secrecy,
Tho' it be for your Good, will give Affurance
Of what is look'd for, if you not alone
Hear, but obey my Counfels.

Atehn. They muft be
Of a ftrange Nature, if with zealous Speed
I put 'em not in Practice.

Pulch. 'Twere Impertinence
To dwell on Circumftances, fince the Wound
Requires a fudden Cure; efpecially
Since you, that are the happy Inftrument
Elected to it, tho' young, in your Judgment
Write far above your Years, and may inftruct
Such as are more experienc'd.

Athen. Good Madam,
In this I muft oppofe you, I am well
Acquainted with my Weaknefs, and it will not
Become your Wifdom, by which I am rais'd
To this titulary Height, that fhould correct
The Pride and overweening of my Fortune,
To play the Parafite to it, in afcribing
That Merit to me, unto which I can
Pretend no Intereft—Pray you, excufe
My bold Simplicity, and to my Weight
Defign me where you pleafe, and you fhall fiad
In my Obedience, I am ftill your Creature.

Pulch. 'Tis nobly anfwer'd, and I glory in
The Building I have rais'd. Go on, fweet Lady,
In this your virtuous Progrefs.—But to the Point;
You know, nor do I envy it, you have
Aquir'd that Power which, not long fince, was mine,

In governing the Emperor, and muſt uſe
The Strength you hold in the Heart of his Affections,
For his private, as the publick Preſervation,
To which there is no greater Enemy
Than his exorbitant Prodigality,
Howe'er his Sycophants and Flatterers call it
Royal Magnificence ; and, tho' he may
Urge what's done for your Honour, muſt not be
Curb'd, or be controul'd by you, you cannot in
Your Wiſdom but conceive, if that the Torrent
Of his violent Bounties be not ſtopp'd or leſſen'd,
It will prove moſt pernicious.   Therefore, Madam,
Since 'tis your Duty, as you are his Wife,
To give him ſaving Counſels, and in being
Almoſt his Idol, may command him to
Take any Shape you pleaſe, with a powerful Hand,
To ſtop him in his Precipice to Ruin.

   Athen. Avert it, Heaven !

   Pulch. Heaven is moſt gracious to you, Madam,
In chooſing you to be the Inſtrument
Of ſuch a pious Work.   You ſee he ſigns
What Suit ſoever is preferr'd, not once
Enquiring what it is, yielding himſelf
A Prey to all.   I would, therefore, have you, Lady,
As I know you will, to adviſe him, or command him,
As he would reap the Plenty of your Favours,
To uſe more Moderation in his Bounties ;
And that, before he gives, he would conſider
The what, to whom, and wherefore.

   Athen. Do you think
Such Arrogance, or Uſurpation rather
Of what is proper, and peculiar
To ev'ry private Huſband, and much more
To him an Emperor, can rank with th' Obedience
And Duty of a Wife ? Are we appointed
In our Creation (let me reaſon with you)
To rule, or to obey ? Or, 'cauſe he loves me
With a kind Impotence, muſt I tyrannize
Over his Weakneſs ? Or abuſe the Strength
With which he arms me, to his Wrong ? Or, like

A proftituted Creature, merchandize
Our mutual Delight for Hire? Or to
Serve mine own fordid Ends ? In vulgar Nuptials
Priority is exploded, tho' there be
A Difference in the Parties ; and fhall I,
His Vaffal, from Obfcurity rais'd by him
To this fo eminent Light, [a] prefume t' appoint him
To do, or not to do, this, or that ? When Wives
Are well accommodated by their Hufbands
With all Things both for Ufe, and Ornament,
Let them fix there, and never dare to queftion
Their Wills or Actions.   For myfelf, I vow,
Tho' now my Lord would rafhly give away
His Scepter and imperial Diadem,
Or if there could be any Thing more precious,
I would not crofs it ;—but I know this is
But a Trial of my Temper, and as fuch
I do receive it ; or, if't be otherwife,
You are fo fubtil in your Arguments,
I dare not ftay to hear them.

   Pulch. Is't ev'n fo ?
I've Power o'er thefe, yet, and command their Stay,
To hearken, nearer to me.

   1 *Sifter.* We are charg'd
By the Emperor, our Brother, to attend
The Emprefs' Service.

   2 *Sifter.* You are too mortify'd, Siftet,
(With Reverence I fpeak it) for young Ladies
To keep you Company.   I am fo tir'd
With your tedious Exhortations, Doctrines,
Ufes of your religious Morality,

----

   [a] *To this fo eminent Light.*

Thus we read in the old Copies, which I have here followed, tho'
I think it ought to be

   To this fo eminent Height.

Light is the right Reading, and is oppofed to Obfcurity in the
Line preceding. *M. M.*

That, for my Health-fake, I muſt take the Freedom
To enjoy a little of thoſe Pleaſures
That I was born to.

   1 *Siſter.* When I come to your Years,
I'll do as you do; but, till then, with your Pardon,
I'll loſe no more Time. I have not learn'd to dance
     yet,
Nor ſing, but holy Hymns, and thoſe to vile Tunes too;
Nor to diſcourſe but of Schoolmen's Opinions.
How ſhall I anſwer my Suitors? Since, I hope,
Ere long I ſhall have many, without Practice
To write, and ſpeak ſomething that's not deriv'd
From the Fathers of Philoſophy.

   2 *Siſt.* We ſhall ſhame
Our Breeding, Siſter, if we ſhould go on thus.

   1 *Siſter.* 'Tis for your Credit that we ſtudy
How to converſe with Men; Women with Women
Yields but a barren Argument.

   2 *Siſter.* She frowns——
But you'll protect us, Madam?

   Athen. Yes, and love
Your ſweet Simplicity.

   1 *Siſt.* But, when we are enter'd,
We ſhall go on a good round Pace.

   Athen. I'll leave you, Madam.

   1 *Siſter.* And we; our Duties with you.
          [*Exeunt* Athenais *and the young Ladies.*

   Pulch. On all Hands
Thus ſlighted? No Way left? Am I grown ſtupid
In my Invention? Can I make no Uſe
Of the Emperor's Bounties?——Now 'tis thought: with-
     in there.

           Enter Servant.

   Serv. Madam.
   Pulch. It ſhall be ſo:——Nearer; your Ear
Draw a Petition to this End.
   Serv. Beſides
The Danger to prefer it, I believe
'Twill ne'er be granted.

Pulch. How's this ? Are you grown,
From a Servant my Director ? Let me hear
No more of this. Difpatch, I'll mafter him

[*Exit Servant.*

At his own Weapon.

Enter Theodofius, Favorinus, Philanax, Timantus, *and*
Gratianus.

Theod. Let me underftand it,
If yet there be ought wanting that may perfect
A general Happinefs.

Favor. The People's Joy
In Seas of Acclamations flow in
To wait on yours.

Phila. Their Love with Bounty levied,
Is a fure Guard : Obedience, forc'd from Fear,
Paper Fortification, which in Danger
Will yield to the Impreffion of a Reed,
Or of itfelf fall off.

Theod. True, *Philanax.*
And by that certain Compafs we refolve
To fteer our Barque of Government.

Enter Servant with the Petition.

Pulch. 'Tis well.

Theod. My deareft and my all-deferving Sifter,
As a Petitioner kneel ? It muft not be.
Pray you rife ; altho' your Suit were half my Empire,
'Tis freely granted.

Pulch. Your Alacrity
To give hath made a Beggar ; yet, before
My Suit is by your facred Hand and Seal
Confirm'd, 'tis neceflary you perufe
The Sum of my Requeft.

Theod. We will not wrong
Your Judgment, in conceiving what 'tis fit
For you to afk, and us to grant, fo much,
As to proceed with Caution, give me my Signet,

With Confidence I fign it, and here vow
By my Father's Soul, but with your free Confent,
It is irrevocable.

Timan. What if fhe now,
Calling to Memory how often we
Have crofs'd her Government, in Revenge hath made
Petition for our Heads ?

Grat. They muft even off then;
No Ranfom can redeem us.

Theod. Let thofe Jewels
So highly rated by the *Perfian* Merchants
Be bought, and as a Sacrifice from us
Prefented to *Eudoxia,* fhe being only
Worthy to wear 'em.   I am angry with
The unrefiftable Neceffity
Of my Occafions and important Cares,
That fo long keep me from her.

                [*Exeunt* Theodofius *and the Train.*

Pulch. Go to the Emprefs,
And tell her on the fudden I am fick,
And do defire the Comfort of a Vifit,
If fhe pleafe to vouchfafe it.   From me ufe
Your humbleft Language.—But, when once I have her
                [*Exit Servant.*

In my Poffeffion, I will rife and fpeak
In a higher Strain : Say it raife Storms, no matter.
Fools judge by the Event, my Ends are honeft.
                [*Exeunt.*

SCENE III.

Theodofius, Timantus, *and* Philanax.

Theod. What is become of her ? Can fhe that carries
Such glorious Excellence of Light about her
Be any where conceal'd ?

Phila. We have fought her Lodgings,
And all we can learn from the Servants, is,
She, by your Majefty's Sifters waited on,

The Attendance of her other Officers,
By her exprefs Command, deny'd,——

Theod. Forbear
Impertinent Circumftances,——whither went fhe ? Speak.

Phila. As they guefs, to the Laurel Grove.

Theod. So flightly guarded !
What an Earthquake I feel in me ! and, but that
Religion affures the contrary,
The Poets Dreams of luftful Fawns and Satyrs,
Would make me fear I know not what.

Enter Favorinus.

Favor. I have found her,
An it pleafe your Majefty.

Theod. Yes, it doth pleafe me.
But why return'd without her ?

Favor. As fhe made
Her fpeedieft Approaches to your Prefence,
A Servant of the Princefs's, *Pulcheria,*
Encounter'd her. What 'twas he whifper'd to her
I'm ignorant ; but, hearing it, fhe ftarted,
And will'd me to excufe her Abfence from you
The third Part of an Hour.

Theod. In this fhe takes
So much of my Life from me ; yet, I'll bear it
With what Patience I may ; fince 'tis her Pleafure,
Go back, my *Favorinus,* and intreat her
Not to exceed a Minute.

Timant. Here's ftrange Fondnefs ! 　　　　　[*Exeunt.*

S C E N E IV.

Pulcheria. *Servants.*

Pulch. You're certain fhe will come ?

Serv. She is already
Enter'd your outward Lodgings.

Pulch. No Train with her?

Serv. Your Excellency's Sifters only.

Pulch. 'Tis the better.
See the Doors strongly guarded, and deny
Accefs to all, but with our fpecial Licence:
Why doft thou ftay? Shew your Obedience;
Your Wifdom now is ufelefs.   [*Exeunt Servants.*

Enter Athenais, Arcadia, *and* Flaccilla.

Flac. She is fick, fure;
Or, in fit Reverence to your Majefty,
She had waited you at the Door.

Arcad. 'Twould hardly be

[Pulcheria *walking by.*

Excus'd, in civil Manners, to her Equal:
But with more difficulty to you, that are
So far above her.

Athen. Not in her Opinion;
She hath been too long accuftom'd to Command
T' acknowledge a Superior.

Arcad. There fhe walks.

Flac. If fhe be not fick of the Sullens, I fee not
The leaft Infirmity in her.

Athen. This is ftrange!

Arcad. Open your Eyes: The Emprefs. ——

Pulch. Reach that Chair:
Now, fitting thus at Diftance, I'll vouchfafe
To look upon her.

Arcad. How, Sifter? Pray you awake.
Are you in your Wits?

Flac. Grant, Heaven, your too much Learning
Does not conclude in Madnefs.

Athen. You intreated
A Vifit from me.

Pulch. True, my Servant us'd
Such Language: But now, as a Miftrefs, I
Command your Service.

Athen. Service?

Arcad. She's ftark mad, fure.

Pulch. You'll find I can difpofe of what's mine own
Without a Guardian.

Athen. Follow me:—I will fee you
When your frantick Fit is o'er. I do begin
To be of your Belief.

Pulch. It will deceive you.
Thou fhalt not ftir from hence.—Thus, as mine own,
I feize upon thee.

Flac. Help, help! Violence
Offer'd to the Emprefs' Perfon!

Pulch. 'Tis in vain:
She was an Emprefs once; but, by my Gift:
Which, being abus'd, I do recall my Grant.
You are read in Story; call to Remembrance
What the great *Hector's* Mother, *Hecuba,*
Was to *Ulyffes, Ilium* fack'd.

Athen. A Slave.

Pulch. To me thou art fo.

Athen. Wonder and Amazement
Quite overwhelm me: How am I transform'd?
How have I loft my Liberty?   [*Knocking without.*

Enter Servant.

Pulch. Thou fhalt know
Too foon, no Doubt.—Who's that, that with fuch
            Rudenefs,
Beats at the Door?

Serv. The Prince *Paulinus,* Madam,
Sent from the Emperor to attend upon
The gracious Emprefs.

Arcad. And who is your Slave now?

Flac. Sifter, repent in Time, and beg Pardon
For your Prefumption.

Pulch. —It is refolv'd:
From me return this Anfwer to *Paulinus*;
She fhall not come; fhe's mine; the Emperor hath
No Intereft in her.   [*Exit Servant.*

Athen. Whatsoe'er I am
You take not from your Power o'er me, to yield
A Reason for this Usage.

Pulch. Tho' my Will is
Sufficient: to add to thy Affliction,
Know, Wretched Thing, 'tis not thy Fate, but Folly,
Hath made thee what thou art: 'Tis some Delight
To urge my Merits to one so ungrateful;
Therefore with Horror hear it. When thou wert
Thrust as a Stranger from thy Father's House,
Expos'd to all Calamities that Want
Could throw upon thee; thine own Brothers' Scorn,
And in thy Hopes, as by the World, forsaken,
My Pity, the last Altar that was left thee;
I heard thy *Syren* Charms, with Feeling heard them,
And my Compassion made mine Eyes vie Tears
With thine, dissembling Crocodile! and when Queens
Were emulous for thy Imperial Bed,
The Garments of thy Sorrows cast aside,
I put thee in a Shape as would have forc'd
Envy from *Cleopatra*, had she seen thee.
Then, when I knew my Brother's Blood was warm'd
With youthful Fires, I brought thee to his Presence:
And how my deep Designs, for thy good plotted,
Succeeded to my Wishes, is apparent,
And needs no Repetition.

Athen. I am conscious
Of your so many and unequall'd Favours,
But find not how I may accuse myself
For any Facts committed, that with Justice
Can raise your Anger to this Height against me.

Pulch. Pride and Forgetfulness would not let thee
see that,
Against which now thou canst not close thy Eyes.
What Injury could be equal to thy late
Contempt of my good Counsel, when I urg'd
The Emperor's prodigal Bounties, and intreated
That you would use your Power to give 'em Limits,
Or, at the least, a due Consideration
Of such as su'd, and for what, ere he sign'd it?

In Oppofition, you brought againft me
Th' Obedience of a Wife, that Ladies were not,
Being well accommodated by their Lords,
To queftion, but much lefs to crofs, their Pleafures;
Nor would you, tho' the Emperor were refolv'd
To give away his Scepter, hinder it,
Since 'twas done for your Honour, covering with
Falfe Colours of Humility your Ambition.

  Athen. And is this my Offence?

  Pulch. As wicked Counfel
Is ftill moft hurtful unto thofe that give it;
Such as deny to follow what is good,
In Reafon, are the firft that muft repent it.
When I pleafe, you fhall hear more; in the mean Time,
Thank your own wilful Foily that hath chang'd you
From an Emprefs to a Bondwoman.

  Theod. Force the Doors:
Kill thofe that dare refift.

Enter Theodofius, Paulinus, Philanax, Chryfapius,
        and Gratianus.

  Athen. Dear Sir, redeem me.

  Flac. O fuffer not, for your own Honour's Sake,
The Emprefs, you late fo lov'd, to be made
A Prifoner in the Court.

  Arcad. Leap to his Lips,
You'll find them the beft Sanctuary.

  Flac. And try then,
What Intereft my reverend Sifter hath
To force you from 'em.

  Theod. What ftrange May-game's this?
Tho' done in Sport, how ill this Levity
Becomes your Wifdom?

  Pulch. I am ferious, Sir,
And have done nothing but what you in Honour,
And as you are yourfelf an Emperor,
Stand bound to juftify.

Theod. Take heed; put not thefe
Strange Trials on my Patience,
   Pulch. Do not you, Sir,
Deny your own Act; as you are a Man,
And ſtand on your own Bottom, 'twill appear
A childiſh Weakneſs to make void a Grant,
Sign'd by your Sacred Hand and Seal, and ſtrengthen'd
With a religious Oath, but with my Licence
Never to be recall'd. For ſome few Minutes
Let Reafon rule your Paſſion, and in this,
                      [Delivers the Deed.
Be pleas'd to read my Intereſt. You will find there,
What you in me call Violence, is Juſtice,
And that I may make Uſe of what's mine own,
According to my Will. 'Tis your own Gift, Sir;
And what an Emperor gives, ſhould ſtand as firm
As the Celeſtial Poles upon the Shoulders
Of *Atlas*, or his Succeſſor in that Office
The great *Alcides*.
   Theod. Miſeries of more Weight,
Than 'tis feign'd they ſupported, fall upon me!
What hath my Raſhneſs done? In this Tranſaction
Drawn in expreſs and formal Terms, I have
Giv'n and conſign'd into your Hands, to uſe
And obſerve, as you pleaſe, my dear *Eudoxa*.
It is my Deed, I do confeſs it is,
And, as I am myſelf, not to be cancell'd :
But yet you may ſhew Mercy—and you will,
When you conſider that there is no Beauty
So perfect in a Creature, but is ſoil'd
With ſome unbeſeeming Blemiſh. You have labour'd
To build me up a complete Prince; 'tis granted :
Yet, as I am a Man, like other Monarchs,
I have Defects and Frailties; my Facility
To ſend Petitioners with pleas'd Looks from me,
Is all I can be charg'd with, and it will
Become your Wiſdom, (ſince 'tis in your Power)
In Charity to provide, I fail no further
Or in my Oath or Honour.

Pulch. Royal Sir,
This was the Mark I aim'd at, and I glory
At the length you fo conceive it : 'Twas a Weaknefs
To meafure by your own Integrity
The Purpofes of others.   I have fhewn you,
In a true Mirror, what Fruit grows upon
The Tree of hoodwink'd.Bounty, and what Dangers
Precipitation in the managing
Your great Affairs produceth.

Theod. I embrace it
As a grave Advertifement, and vow hereafter
Never to fign Petitions at this Rate.

Pulch. For mine, fee, Sir, 'tis cancell'd ; on my
          Knees
I re-deliver what I now begg'd from you.
                              [*Tears the Deed.*
She is my fecond Gift.

Theod. Which if I part from
'Till Death divorce us——   [*Kiffing* Athenais.

Athen. So, Sir——   .

Theod. Nay, Sweet, chide not :
I am punifh'd in thy Looks ; defer the reft,
'Till we're more private.

Pulch. I afk Pardon too,
If, in my perfonated Paffion, I
Appear'd too harfh and rough.

Athen. 'Twas gentle Language,
What I was then confider'd.

Pulch. O dear Madam,
It was Decorum in the Scene.

Athen. This Trial,
When I was *Athenais,* might have pafs'd ;
But as I am the Emprefs——

Theod. Nay, no Anger,
Since all Good was intended.
              [*Exeunt* Theodofius, Athenais, Arcadia,
                    and Flaccilla.

X 4

Pulch. Building on
That certain Base, I fear not what can follow.
　　　　　　　　　　　　　　　　　[*Exit* Pulcheria.
　　Paul. These are strange Devices, *Philanax.*
　　Phila. True, my Lord.
May all turn to the best !
　　Grat. The Emperor's Looks
Promis'd a Calm.
　　Chryf. But the vex'd Empress' Frowns
Presag'd a second Storm.
　　Paul. I am sure I feel one
In my Leg already.
　　Phila. Your old Friend, the Gout?
　　Paul. My forc'd Companion, *Philanax.*
　　Chryf. To your Rest.
　Paul. Rest, and forbearing Wine, with a temperate
　　　　Diet,
Tho' many Mountebanks pretend the Cure of't,
I've found my best Physicians.
　　Phila. Ease to your Lordship.　　　　　[*Exeunt.*

The End of the Third Act.

A C T IV. S C E N E I.

Athenais and *Chryfapius.*

Athenais.

MAKE me her Property ?
　　Chryf. Your Majesty
Hath just Cause of Distaste ; and your Resentment
Of the Affront in the Point of Honour cannot
But meet a fair Construction.
　　Athen. I have only
The Title of an Empress, but the Power

Is by her ravish'd from me.   She surveys
My Actions as a Governess, and calls
My not obferving all that she directs,
Folly and Difobedience.

   Chryf. Under Correction
With Grief I've long obferv'd it; and, if you
Stand pleas'd to fign my Warrant, I'll deliver
In my unfeign'd Zeal and Defire to ferve you,
(Howe'er I run the Hazard of my Head for't,
Should it arrive at the Knowledge of the Princefs)
Not alone, the Reafons why Things are thus carried,
But give into your Hands the Power to clip
The Wings of her Command.

   Athen. Your Service this Way
Cannot offend me.

   Chryf. Be you pleas'd to know then,
(But ftill with Pardon, if I am too bold)
Your too much Sufferance imps the broken Feathers
Which carry her to this proud Height, in which
She with Security foars, and ftill tow'rs o'er you:
But, if you would employ the Strength you hold
In the Emperor's Affections, and remember
The Orb you move in fhould admit no Star elfe,
You never would confefs the managing
Of State Affairs to her alone are proper,
And you fit by a Looker on.

   Athen. I would not,
If it were poffible I could attempt
Her Diminution, without a Taint
Of foul Ingratitude in myfelf.

   Chryf. In this
The Sweetnefs of your Temper does abufe you;
And you call that a Benefit to yourfelf
Which fhe for her own Ends conferr'd upon you.
'Tis yielded fhe gave Way to your Advancement :
But for what Caufe ? that fhe might ftill continue
Her abfolute Sway and Swing o'er the whole State;
And that fhe might to her Admirers vaunt,
The Emprefs was her Creature, and the Giver
To be preferr'd before the Gift,

Athen. It may be.

Chryſ. Nay, 'tis moſt certain : Whereas, would you
    pleaſe
In a true Glaſs to look upon yourſelf,
And view without Detraction your own Merits,
Which all Men wonder at, you would find that Fate,
Without a ſecond Cauſe, appointed you
To the ſupremeſt Honour. For the Princeſs,
She hath reign'd long enough, and her Remove
Will make your Entrance free to the Poſſeſſion
Of what you were born to ; and, but once reſolve
To build upon her Ruins, leave the Engines
That muſt be us'd to undermine her Greatneſs
To my Proviſion.

    Athen. I thank your Care :
But a Deſign of ſuch Weight muſt not be
Raſhly determin'd of ; it will exact
A long and ſerious Conſultation from me.
In the mean Time, *Chryſapius,* reſt aſſur'd
I live your thankful Miſtreſs.   [*Exit* Athenais.

    Chryſ. Is this all ?
Will the Phyſick that I miniſter'd work no further ?
I've play'd the Fool ; and, leaving a calm Port,
Embark'd myſelf on a rough Sea of Danger.
In her Silence lies my Safety, which how can I
Hope from a Woman ? But the Die is thrown,
And I muſt ſtand the Hazard.

Enter Theodoſius, Philanax, Timantus, Gratianus, *and*
    Huntſmen.

    Theod. Is *Paulinus*
So tortur'd with his Gout ?

    Phila. Moſt miſerably, Sir.
And it adds much to his Affliction, that
The Pain denies him Power to wait upon
Your Majeſty.

    Theod. I pity him.——He is
A wond'rous honeſt Man, and what he ſuffers,
I know, will grieve my Empreſs.

Timan. He, indeed, is
Much bound to her gracious Favour.

Theod. He deferves it;
She cannot find a Subject upon whom
She better may confer it.—Is the Stag
Safe lodg'd?

Grat. Yes, Sir, and the Hounds and Huntfmen
ready.

Phila. He will make you royal Sport. He is a Deer
Of ten [3] at the leaft.

Enter Countryman with an Apple.

Grat. Whither will this Clown?

Timan. Stand back.

Count. I would zee the Emperor. Why fhould you
Courtiers
Scorn a poor Countryman? We zweat at the Plough
To vill your Mouths, you and your Curs might ftarve
elfe.
We prune the Orchards, and you cranch the Fruit;
Yet ftill y'are fnarling at us.

Theod. What's the Matter?

Count. I would look on thy fweet Face.

Timan. Unmannerly Swain!

Count. Zwain? Tho' I am a Zwain, I have a Heart,
yet,
As ready to do Service for my Leg, [4]
As any Princock, Peacock of you all.
Zookers! had I one of you zingle, with this Twig
I would fo veeze you,

Timan. Will your Majefty
Hear this rude Language?

Theod. Yes, and hold it as
An Ornament, not a Blemifh. O *Timantus!*
Since that dread Power, by whom we are, difdains not

---

3 *A Deer of ten.* Is a Deer that has ten Branches to his Horns,
which they have at Three Years old. *M. M.*

4 My Liege is the Word intended by the Speaker, but I fuppofe
it is mifpelt on Purpofe. *M. M.*

With an open Ear to hear Petitions from us,
Eaſy Acceſs in us, his Deputies,
To the meaneſt of our Subjects, is a Debt
Which we ſtand bound to pay.

   Count. By my Granam's Ghoſt
'Tis a wholeſome Zaying; our Vicar could not mend it
In the Pulpit on a Zunday.

   Theod. What's thy Suit Friend?

   Count. Zute? I would laugh at that. Let the Court
        beg from thee,
What the poor Country gives. I bring a Preſent
To thy good Grace, which I can call mine own,
And look not, like theſe gay Volk, for a Return
Of what they venture. Have I giv'nt you, ha!

   Chryſ. A perilous Knave.

   Count. Zee here a dainty Apple. [*Preſents the Apple.*
Of mine own grafting; zweet and zownd, I aſſure thee.

   Theod. It is the faireſt Fruit I ever ſaw.
Thoſe golden Apples in the *Heſperian* Orchards
So ſtrangely guarded by the watchful Dragon,
As they requir'd great *Hercules* to get 'em;
Or thoſe with which *Hippomenes* deceiv'd
Swift-footed *Atalanta*, when I look
On this, deſerve no Wonder. You behold
The poor Man and his Preſent with Contempt;
I to their Value prize both; He, that could
So aid weak Nature by his Care and Labour,
As to compel a Crab-tree ſtock to bear
A precious Fruit of this large Size and Beauty,
Would by his Induſtry change a petty Village
Into a populous City, and from that
Erect a flouriſhing Kingdom. Give the Fellow,
For an Encouragement to his future Labours,
Ten *Attick* Talents.

   Count. I will weary Heaven
With my Prayers for your Majeſty. [*Exit Countryman.*

   Theod. *Philanax,*
From me preſent this Rarity to the rareſt
And beſt of Women. When I think upon
The boundleſs Happineſs that from her flows to me,

In my Imagination I am rapt
Beyond myfelf.—But I forget our Hunting,
To the Foreft for the Exercife of my Body;
But for my Mind, 'tis wholly taken up
In the Contemplation of her matchlefs Virtues.

[Exeunt.

S C E N E II.

Athenais, Pulcheria, Arcadia, *and* Flaccilla.

Athen. You fhall know there's a Difference, between us.

Pulch. There was, I'm certain, not long fince, when
you
Kneel'd a Petitioner to me; then you were happy
To be near my Feet; and do you hold it, now,
As a Difparagement that I fide you, Lady?

Athen. Since you refpect me only as I was,
What I am fhall be remember'd.

Pulch. Does the Means
I practis'd, to give good and faving Counfels
To th' Emperor, and your new-ftamp'd Majefty
Still ftick in your Stomach?

Athen. 'Tis not yet digefted,
In troth it is not. Why, good Governefs,
Tho' you are held for a grand Madam, and yourfelf
The firft that overprize it, I ne'er took
Your Words for *Delphian* Oracles, nor your Actions
For fuch Wonders as you make 'em,—there is one,
When fhe fhall fee her Time, as fit and able
To be made Partner of the Emperor's Cares,
As your wife felf, and may with Juftice challenge
A nearer Intereft.—You have done your Vifit,
So, when you pleafe, you may leave me.

Pulch. I'll not bandy
Words with your Mightinefs, proud one, only this,

You carry too much Sail for your fmall Bark;
And that, when you leaft think upon't, may fink you.
[*Exit.* Pulcheria.

Flac. I am glad fhe's gone.

Arcad. I fear'd fhe would have read
A tedious Lecture to us.

Enter Philanax *with the Apple.*

Phila. From the Emperor.
This rare Fruit to the rareft.

Athen. How, my Lord?

Phila. I ufe his Language, Madam; and that Truft,
Which he impos'd on me, difcharg'd, his Pleafure
Commands my prefent Service.   [*Exit* Philanax.

Athen. Have you feen
So fair an Apple?

Flac. Never.

Arcad. If the Tafte
Anfwer the Beauty.

Athen. Prettily begg'd:—you fhould have it;
But that you eat too much cold Fruit, and that
Changes the frefh Red in your Cheeks to Palenefs.

Enter Servant.

I've other Dainties for you; you come from
Paulinus; how is't with that truly noble
And honeft Lord? My Witnefs at the Fount;
In a Word, the Man to whofe blefs'd Charity
I owe my Greatnefs. How is't with him?

Serv. Spiritly,
In his Mind; but, by the raging of his Gout,
In his Body much diftemper'd; that you pleas'd
To inquire his Health, took off much from his Pain;
His glad Looks did confirm it.

Athen. Do his Doctors
Give him no Hope?

Serv. Little; they rather fear,
By his continual burning, that he ſtands
In Danger of a Fever.

Athen. To him again,
And tell him that I heartily wiſh it lay
In me to eaſe him, and from me deliver
This choice Fruit to him; you may ſay to that,
I hope it will prove phyſical.

Serv. The good Lord
Will be o'erjoy'd with the Favour.

Athen. He deſerves more.   [*Exeunt.*

SCENE III.

Paulinus brought in a Chair, and Chirurgeon.

Chirurg. I've done as much as Art can do, to ſtop
The violent Courſe of your Fit, and I hope you feel it.
How does your Honour?

Paul. At ſome Eaſe, I thank you:
I would you could aſſure Continuance of it,
For the Moiety of my Fortune.

Chirurg. If I could cure
The Gout, my Lord, without a Philoſopher's Stone]
I ſhould ſoon purchaſe, it being a Diſeaſe,
In poor Men very rare, and in the rich
The Cure impoſſible, your many Bounties
Bid me prepare you for a certain Truth,
And to flatter you were diſhoneſt.

Paul. Your plain dealing
Deſerves a Fee. Happy are poor Men;
If ſick with the Exceſs of Heat or Cold,
Caus'd by neceſſitous Labour, not looſe Surfeits,
They, when ſpare Diet, or kind Nature fail
To perfect their Recovery, ſoon arrive at
Their Reſt in Death; but, on the contrary,
The Great and Noble are expos'd as Preys
To the Rapine of Phyſicians; and they,
In ling'ring out what is remedileſs,

Aim at their Profit, not the Patient's Health.
A thousand Trials and Experiments
Have been put upon me, and I forc'd to pay dear
For my Vexation; but I am resolv'd,
(I thank your honest Freedom) to be made
A Property no more for Knaves to work on.
—What have you there?

Enter Cleon *with a Parchment Roll.*

 Cleon. The Triumphs of an Artsman
O'er all Infirmities, made authentical
With the Names of Princes, Kings and Emperors
That were his Patients.
 Paul. Some Empirick.
 Cleon. It may be so; but he swears, within three
  Days
He will grub up your Gout by th' Roots, and make you
  able
To march ten Leagues a Day in complete Armour.
 Paul. Impossible.
 Cleon. Or, if you like not him——
 Chirurg. Hear him, my Lord, for your Mirth; I will
  take Order
They shall not wrong you.
 Paul. Usher in your Monster.
 Cleon. He is at Hand, march up: Now speak for
  yourself.

Enter Empirick.

 Empir. I come not, Right Honourable, to your Presence, with any base and sordid End of Reward; the Immortality of my Fame is the White I shoot at, the Charge of my most curious and costly Ingredients defray'd, amounting to some seventeen thousand Crowns —a Trifle in respect of Health—writing your noble Name in my Catalogue, I shall acknowledge myself amply satisfy'd.
 Chirurg. I believe so.

Empir. For your own Sake, I moſt heartily wiſh, that you had now all the Diſeaſes, Maladies and Infirmities upon you, that were ever remember'd by old *Galen, Hippocrates,* or the latter, and more admired *Paracelſus.*

Paul. For your good Wiſh I thank you.

Empir. Take me with you; I beſeech your good Lordſhip. I urg'd it, that your Joy, in being certainly and ſuddenly free from them, may be the greater, and my not to be parallell'd Skill the more remarkable. The Cure of the Gout's a Toy; without Boaſt be it ſaid; my Cradle-practice; the Cancer, the Fiſtula, the Dropſy, Conſumption of Lungs and Kidneys, Hurts in the Brain, Heart, or Liver, are Things worthy my Oppoſition; but in the Recovery of my Patients I ever overcome them.—But to your Gout—

Paul. I, marry, Sir; that cur'd, I ſhall be apter To give Credit to the reſt.

Empir. Suppoſe it done, Sir.

Chirur. And the Means you uſe, I beſeech you.

Empir. I will do it in the plaineſt Language, and diſcover my Ingredients. Firſt, my *boteni Terebinthina,* of *Cypris,* my Manna, *ros 'cœlo,* coagulated with *vetulos ovorum,* vulgarly Yolks of Eggs, with a little Cyath, or Quantity of my potable Elixir, with ſome few Scruples of Saſſafras and Guacum, ſo taken every Morning and Evening, in the Space of three Days, purgeth, cleanſeth, and diſſipateth the inward Cauſes of the virulent Tumor.

Paul. Why do you ſmile?

Chirur. When he hath done, I will reſolve you.

Empir. For my exterior Applications, I have theſe Balſumunguentulums, extracted from Herbs, Plants, Roots, Seeds, Gums, and a Million of other Vegetables, the principal of which are Uliſſipona, or Serpentaria, Sophia, or Herba Conſolidarum, Parthenion, or Commanilla Romana, Mumia tranſmarina, mixed with my plumbum Philoſophorum, and mater metallorum, *cum oſſa paraleli, eſt univerſale medicamentum in podagra.*

Cleon. A conjuring Balfamum.

Empir. This applied warm upon the pained place, with a Feather of Struthio cameli, or a Bird of Para-dife, which is every where to be had, fhall expulfe this tartarous, vifcous, anatheos, and malignant Dolor.

Chirur. An excellent Receipt ! but does your Lord-fhip know what it is good for ?

Paul. I would be inftructed.

Chirur. For the Gonorrhœa, or, if you will hear it In a plainer Phrafe, the Pox.

Empir. If it cure his Lordfhip
Of that, by the Way, I hope, Sir, 'tis the better.
My Medicine ferves for all Things, and the Pox, Sir,
Tho' falfely nam'd the Sciatica, or Gout,
Is the more Catholick Sicknefs.

Paul. Hence with the Rafcal !
Yet hurt him not ; he makes me fmile, and that
Frees him from Punifhment. [*They thruft off the* Empir.

Chirur. Such Slaves as this
Render our Art contemptible.

Enter Servant.

Serv. My good Lord——

Paul. So foon return'd ?

Serv. And with this Prefent from
Your great and gracious Miftrefs, with her Wifhes
It may prove phyfical to you.

Paul. In my Heart
I kneel, and thank her Bounty. Dear Friend *Cleon,*
Give him the Cupboard of Plate in the next Room.
For a Reward.   [*Exeunt* Cleon *and the Servant.*
Moft glorious Fruit ; but made
More precious by her Grace and Love that fent it.
To touch it only, coming from her Hand,
Makes me forget all Pain. A Diamond
Of this large Size, though it would buy a Kingdom,
Hew'd from the Rock, and laid down at my Feet ;
Nay, tho' a Monarch's Gift, will hold no Value,
Compar'd with this—And yet, ere I prefume

To taſte it, tho', ſans Queſtion, it is
Some heavenly Reſtorative, I in Duty
Stand bound to weigh my own Unworthineſs.
Ambroſia is Food only for the Gods;
And not by human Lips to be prophan'd.
I may adore it as ſome holy Relique
Deriv'd from thence, but impious to keep it
In my Poſſeſſion; the Emperor only
Is worthy to enjoy it.—Go, good *Cleon*,

Enter Cleon.

And (ceaſe this Admiration at this Object)
From me preſent this to my Royal Maſter,
I know it will amaze him, and excuſe me
That I am not myſelf the Bearer of it.
That I ſhould be lame now, when with Wings of Duty
I ſhould fly to the Service of this Empreſs!
Nay, no Delays, good *Cleon*.
  Cleon. I am gone, Sir.   [*Exeunt.*

S C E N E IV.

Enter Theodoſius, Chryſapius, Timantus *and* Gratianus.

  Chryſ. Are you not tir'd, Sir!
  Theod. Tir'd? I muſt not ſay ſo,
However, tho' I rode hard. To a Huntſman,
His Toil is his Delight, and to complain
Of Wearineſs, would ſhew as poorly in him,
As if a General ſhould grieve for a Wound
Receiv'd upon his Forehead, or his Breaſt,
After a glorious Victory, lay by
Theſe Accoutrements for the Chace.

Enter Pulcheria.

  Pulch. You are well return'd, Sir,
From your princely Exerciſe.
                    Y 2

Theod. Sister, to you
I owe the Freedom, and the Use of all
The Pleasures I enjoy. Your Care provides
For my Security, and the Burthen, which
I should alone sustain, you undergo,
And, by your painful Watchings, yield my Sleeps
Both sound and sure. How happy am I in
Your Knowledge of the Art of Government!
And, credit me, I glory to behold you
A Partner, and no Subject of my Empire.

Pulch. My Vigilance, since it hath well succeeded,
I'm confident you allow of—yet it is not
Approv'd by all.

Theod. Who dares repine at that
Which hath our Suffrage?

Pulch. One that too well knows
The Strength of her Abilities can better
My weak Endeavours.

Theod. In this you reflect
Upon my Empress?

Pulch. True; for, as she is
The Consort of your Bed, 'tis fit she share in
Your Cares and absolute Power.

Theod. You touch a String
That sounds but harshly to me, and I must
In a Brother's Love advise you, that hereafter
You would forbear to move it. Since she is
In her pure Self a Harmony of such Sweetness,
Compos'd of Duty, chaste Desires, her Beauty
(Tho' it might tempt a Hermit from his Beads)
The least of her Endowments. I am sorry
Her holding the first Place, since that the second
Is proper to yourself, calls on your Envy.
She err? It is impossible in a Thought,
And, much more, speak or do what may offend me.
In other Things I would believe you, Sister:
But, tho' the Tongues of Saints and Angels tax'd her
Of any Imperfection, I should be
Incredulous.

Pulch. She is yet a Woman, Sir.

Theod. The Abftraft of what's excellent in the Sex :
But to their Mulcts and Frailties a mere Stranger :
—I'll die in this Belief.

Enter Cleon *with the Apple.*

Cleon. Your humbleft Servant,
The Lord *Paulinus,* as a Witnefs of
His Zeal and Duty to your Majefty,
Prefents you with this Jewel.
  Theod. Ha !
  Cleon. It is
Preferr'd by him——
  Theod. Above his Honour ?
  Cleon. No, Sir ;
I would have faid his Patrimony.
  Theod. 'Tis the fame.
  Cleon. And he intreats, fince Lamenefs may excufe
His not prefenting it himfelf, from me
(Tho' far unworthy to fupply his Place)
You would vouchfafe to accept it.
  Theod. Farther off ;
You've told your Tale : Stay you for a Reward ?
—Take that.   ı   [*Strikes him.*
  Pulch. How's this ?
  Chryf. I never faw him mov'd thus.
  Theod. We muft not part fo, Sir—A Guard upon
       him.

Enter Guard.

Theod. May I not vent my Sorrows in the Air,
Without Difcovery ? Forbear the Room !
                  [*They all go afide.*
Yet be within Call—What an Earthquake I feel in me !
And on the fudden my whole Fabrick totters.
My Blood within me turns, and thro' my Veins
Parting with natural Rednefs I difcern it,
Chang'd to a fatal Yellow. What an Army

Of hellifh Furies, in the horrid Shapes
Of Doubts and Fears, charge on me! Rife to my
          Refcue,
Thou ftout Maintainer of a chafte Wife's Honour,
The Confidence of her Virtues; be not fhaken
With the Wind of vain Surmifes; much lefs fuffer
The Devil Jealoufy to whifper to me
My curious Obfervation of that
I muft no more remember,—Will it not be?
Thou uninvited Gueft, ill-manner'd Monfter,
I charge thee, leave me! wilt thou force me to
Give Fuel to that Fire I would put out?
The Goodnefs of my Memory proves my Mifchief,
And I would fell my Empire, could it purchafe
The dull Art of Forgetfulnefs.—Who waits there?

  Timan. Moft facred Sir,

  Theod. Sacred as 'tis accurs'd ⁵,
Is proper to me. Sirrah, upon your Life,
Without a Word concerning this, command
                              [*Exit* Timantus,
Eudoxia to come to me.—Would I had
Ne'er known her by that Name, my Mother's Name!
Or that, for her own Sake, fhe had continued
Poor *Athenais* ftill;—No Intermiffion?
Wilt thou fo foon torment me? Muft I read
Writ in the Table of my Memory,
To warrant my Sufpicion, how *Paulinus*
('Tho' ever thought a Man averfe to Women).
Firft gave her Entertainment? Made her Way
For Audience to my Sifter; then I did
Myfelf obferve how he was ravifh'd with
The gracious Delivery of her Story,
(Which was, I grant, the Bait that firft took me too)
She was his Convert; what the Rhetorick was
He us'd, I know not; and, fince fhe was mine
In private as in publick, what a Mafs

---

5 *Sacratus*, in *Latin*, means accurfed; to this *Theodofius* alludes,
when he fays, that *Sacred, as it is accurfed*, is proper to him. *M. M.*

Of Grace and Favours hath fhe heap'd upon him!
And but to-day this fatal Fruit—She's come.

Enter Timantus, Athenais, Flaccilla, *and* Arcadia.

Can fhe be guilty?

Athen. You feem troubl'd, Sir;
My Innocence makes me bold to afk the Caufe,
That I may eafe you of it.—No Salute,
After four long Hours' Abfence?

Theod. Prithee, forgive me.　　　　[*Kiffes her.*
Methinks I find *Paulinus* on her Lips,
And the frefh Nectar that I drew from thence
Is on the fudden pall'd. [*Afide.*] How have you fpent
Your Hours fince I laft faw you?

Athen. In the Converfe
Of your fweet Sifters.

Theod. Did not *Philanax*,
From me deliver you an Apple?

Athen. Yes, Sir;
Heaven! how you frown! Pray you, talk of fomething
　　　elfe:
Think not of fuch a Trifle.

Theod. How! a Trifle?
Does any Toy from me prefented to you,
Deferve to be fo flighted? Do you value
What's fent, and not the Sender?—From a Peafant
It had deferv'd your Thanks.

Athen. And meets from you, Sir,
All poffible Refpect.

Theod. I priz'd it, Lady,
At a higher Rate than you believe, and would not
Have parted with it, but to one I did
Prefer before myfelf.

Athen. It was, indeed,
The faireft that I ever faw.

Theod. It was?
And it had Virtues in it, my *Eudoxia*,
Not vifible to the Eye.

Athen. It may be fo, Sir.

Theod. What did you with it,—tell me punctually;
I look for a ftrict Accompt.

Athen. What fhall I anfwer?

Theod. Do you ftagger? Ha!

Athen. No, Sir, I have eaten it.
It had the pleafant Tafte. I wonder that
You found it not in my Breath.

Theod. I'faith, I did not,
And it was wond'rous ftrange.

Athen. Pray you, try again.

Theod. I find no Scent of't here. You play with me.
You have it ftill?

Athen. By your facred Life and Fortune,
An Oath I dare not break; I've eaten it.

Theod. Do you know how this Oath binds?

Athen. Too well to break it.

Theod. That ever Man, to pleafe his brutifh Senfe,
Should flave his Underftanding to his Paffions,
And, taken with foon fading White and Red,
Deliver up his credulous Ears to hear
The Magick of a *Syren,* and from thefe
Believing there ever was, is, or can be
More than a feeming Honefty in bad Woman.

Athen. This is ftrange Language, Sir.

Theod. Who waits? Come all.
—Nay, Sifter not fo near; being of the Sex,
I fear you are infected too.

Pulch. What mean you?

Theod. To fhow you a Miracle, a Prodigy,
Which *Africk* never equall'd:——Can you think [6]
This Mafterpiece of Heaven, this precious Vellum,

☞ 6 ————————*Can you think*
This Mafterpiece of Heaven, &c.

Thus in *Othello:*

Was this fair Paper, this moft godly Book,
Made to write Whore upon?

Act 4. Scene 9.

Of such a Purity and Virgin Whiteness,
Could be defign'd to have Perjury and Whoredom,
In capital Letters writ upon't ?

Putch. Dear Sir.

Theod. Nay, add to this, an Impudence beyond
All proftituted Boldnefs.   Art not dead yet ?'
Will not the Tempefts in thy Confcience rend thee
As fmall as Atoms ? That there may no Sign
Be left thou ever wert fo ? Wilt thou live
'Till thou art blafted with the dreadful Lightning
Of pregnant and unanfwerable Proofs
Of thy adulterous twines ? Die yet, that I
With my Honour may conceal it.

Athen. Would long fince
The *Gorgon* of your Rage had turn'd me Marble.
Or, if I have offended——

Theod. If !——good Angels !——
But I am tame.   Look on this dumb Accufer.

                                [*Shewing the Apple.*

Athen. Oh, I am loft !   [*Afide.*

Theod. Did ever Cormorant
Swallow his Prey, and then digeft it whole,
As fhe hath done this Apple ? *Philanax,*
As 'tis, from me prefented it.   The good Lady
Swore fhe had eaten it ; yet, I know not how,
It came intire unto *Paulinus'* Hands,
And I from him receiv'd it ; fent in Scorn,
Upon my Life, to give me a clofe touch
That he was weary of thee.   Was there nothing
Left thee to fee him, to give Satisfaction
To thy infatiate Luft, but what was fent
As a dear Favour from me ? How have I finn'd
In my Dotage on this Creature ? But to her
I've liv'd as I was born, a perfect Virgin.
Nay, more, I thought it not enough to be
True to her Bed, but that I muft feed high,
To ftrengthen my Abilities to cloy
Her rav'nous Appetite, little fufpecting
She would defire a Change.

Athen. I never did, Sir.

Theod. Be dumb; I will not waſte my Breath in taxing
Thy baſe Ingratitude. How I have rais'd thee
Will by the World be, to thy Shame, ſpoke often.
But for that Ribawd, who held in my Empire
The next Place to myſelf, ſo bound unto me
By all the Ties of Duty and Allegiance,
He ſhall pay dear for't, and feel what it is
In a Wrong of ſuch high Conſequence to pull-down
His Lord's ſlow Anger on him. *Philanax,*
He's troubl'd with the Gout; let him be cur'd
With a violent Death, and in the other World,
Thank his Phyſician.

Phila. His Cauſe unheard, Sir?

Pulch. Take Heed of Raſhneſs.

Theod. Is what I command
To be diſputed?

Phila. Your Will ſhall be done, Sir;
But that I am the Inſtrument——

Theod. Do you murmur?

[*Exit* Philanax *with the Guard.*

What couldſt thou ſay, if that my Licence ſhould
Give Liberty to thy Tongue? Thou would'ſt die? I am not

[Athenais *kneeling, points to* Theodoſius' *Sword.*

So to be reconcil'd.—See me no more:
The Sting of Conſcience ever knawing on thee,
A long Life be thy Puniſhment. [*Exit* Theodoſius.

Flac. O ſweet Lady.
How I could weep for her!

Arcad. Speak, dear Madam, ſpeak.
Your Tongue, as you are a Woman, while you live,
Should be ever moving; at the leaſt, the laſt Part
That ſtirs about you.

Pulch. Tho' I ſhould, ſad Lady,
In Policy rejoice, you as a Rival
Of my Greatneſs are remov'd, Compaſſion,
Since I believe you innocent, commands me
To mourn your Fortune; credit me I will urge

All Arguments I can allege that may
Appeafe the Emperor's Fury.

Arcad. I will grow too,
Unto my Knees, unlefs he bid me rife,
And fwear he will forgive you.

Flac. And repent too :
All this Pother for an Apple ?

        [*Exeunt* Pulcheria, Arcadia, *and* Flaccilla.

Chryf. Hope, dear Madam,
And yield not to Defpair.   I'm ftill your Servant,
And never will forfake you ; tho' a-while
You leave the Court and City, and give Way
To th' violent Paffions of the Emperor.
Repentance in his Want of you will foon find him,
In the mean Time I'll difpofe of you, and omit
No Opportunity that may invite him
To fee his Error.

Athen. Oh !   [*Wringing her Hands,*
Chryf. Forbear, for Heav'n's Sake :

The End of the Fourth Act.

A C T   V,   S C E N E   I.

Philanax, Paulinus, *Guard, and Executioners.*

Paulinus.

THIS is moft barbarous ! how have you loft
    All Feeling of Humanity, as Honour,
In your Confent alone, to have me us'd thus ?
But to be, as you are a Looker on,
Nay, more, a principal Actor in't (the Softnefs
Of your former Life confider'd) almoft turns me
Into a fenfelefs Statue,

Phila. Would, long since,
Death, by some other Means, had made you one,
That you might be less sensible of what
You have, or are to suffer

Paul. Am to suffer?
Let such, whose Happiness and Heaven depend
Upon their present Being, fear to part with
A Fort, they cannot long hold; mine to me is
A Charge that I am weary of, all Defences
By Pain and Sickness batter'd;—yet, take Heed,
Take Heed, Lord *Philanax*, that, for private Spleen,
Or any false conceived Grudge against me,
(Since in one Thought of Wrong to you, I am
Sincerely innocent) you do not that
My Royal Master must in Justice punish,
If so you pass to your own Heart thorough mine,
The Murther, as it will come out, discover'd.

Phila. I murther you, my Lord? Heav'n witness
for me
With the restoring of your Health, I wish you
Long Life and Happiness: For myself, I am
Compell'd to put in Execution that
Which I would fly from; 'tis the Emperor,
The high incensed Emperor's Will commands
What I must see perform'd.

Paul. The Emperor?
Goodness and Innocence guard me! Wheels nor Racks
Can force into my Memory the Remembrance
Of the least Shadow of Offence, with which
I ever did provoke him; tho' belov'd,
(And yet the People's Love is short and fatal)
I never courted popular Applause;
Feasted the Men of Action, or labour'd
By prodigal Gifts to draw the needy Soldier,
The Tribunes, or Centurions to a Faction,
Of which I would rise up the Head against him.
I hold no Place of Strength, Fortress or Castle
In my Command, that can give Sanctuary
To Mal-contents, or countenance Rebellion.
I've built no Palaces to face the Court,

Nor do my Followers' Bravery shame his Train ;
And, tho' I cannot blame my Fate for Want,
My competent Mean of Life deserves no Envy.
In what, then, am I dangerous ?

Phila. His Displeasure
Reflects on none of those Particulars
Which you have mention'd, tho' some jealous Princes
In a Subject cannot brook 'em.

Paul. None of these ?
In what, then, am I worthy his Suspicion ?
But it may, nay it must be, some Informer,
To whom my Innocence appear'd a Crime,
Hath poison'd his late good opinion of me.
'Tis not to die, but, in the Censure of
So good a Master, guilty, that afflicts me,

Phila. There is no Remedy.

Paul. No?—I have a Friend yet,
Could the Strictness of your Warrant give Way to it,
To whom the State I stand in now deliver'd,
That by fair Intercession for me would
So far prevail, that, my Defence unheard,
I should not, innocent or guilty, suffer,
Without a fit Distinction.

Phila. These false Hopes,
My Lord, abuse you, What Man, when condemn'd,
Did ever find a Friend ? or who dares lend
An Eye of Pity to that Star-cross'd Subject
On whom his Sovereign frowns ?

Paul. She that dares plead
For Innocence without a Fee ; the Empress,
My great and gracious Mistress.

Phila. There's your Error.
Her many Favours, which you hop'd should make you,
Prove your Undoing. She, poor Lady, is
Banish'd for ever from the Emperor's Presence,
And his confirm'd Suspicion, to his Wrong,
That you have been over-familiar with her,
Dooms you to Death. I know you understand me.

Paul. Over-familiar ?

Phila. In fharing with him
Thofe fweet and fecret Pleafures of his Bed,
Which can admit no Partner.

Paul. And is that
The Crime for which I am to die? Of all
My num'rous Sins, was there not one of Weight
Enough to fink me, if he borrow'd not
The Colour of a Guilt I never faw,
To paint my Innocence in a deform'd
And monftrous Shape? But that it were prophane
To argue Heav'n of Ignorance or Injuftice,
I now fhould tax it. Had the Stars that reign'd
At my Nativity fuch curfed Influence,
As not alone to make me miferable,
But, in the Neighbourhood of her Goodnefs to me,
To force Contagion upon a Lady,
Whofe purer Flames were not inferior
To theirs when they fhine brighteft? To die for her,
Compar'd with what fhe fuffers, is a Trifle.
By her Example warn'd, let all great Women
Hereafter throw Pride and Contempt on fuch
As truly ferve 'em, fince a Retribution
In lawful Courtefies is now ftil'd Luft,
And to be thankful to a Servant's Merits
Is grown a Vice, no Virtue.

Phila. Thefe Complaints
Are to no Purpofe: Think on the long Flight
Your better Part muft make.

Paul. She is prepar'd:
Nor can the freeing of an Innocent
From the Emperor's furious Jealoufy, hinder her.
It fhall out, 'tis refolv'd, but to be whifper'd
To you alone. What a folemn Preparation
Is made here to put forth an Inch of Taper
In itfelf almoft extinguifh'd? Mortal Poifon?
The Hangman's Sword, the Halter?

Phila. 'Tis left to you
To make Choice of which you pleafe.

Paul. Any will ferve
To take away my Gout and Life together.
I would not have have the Emperor imitate
Rome's Monfter, *Nero,* in that cruel Mercy
He fhew'd to *Seneca.* When you have difcharg'd
What you are trufted with, and I have giv'n you
Reafons beyond all Doubt or Difputation,
Of the Emprefs's and my Innocence; when I am dead,
(Since 'tis my Mafter's Pleafure, and high Treafon
In you not to obey it) I conjure you,
By the Hopes you have of Happinefs hereafter,
Since mine in this World are now parting from me,
That you would win the young Man to Repentance
Of the Wrong done to his chafte Wife *Eudoxia* ;
And if perchance he fhed a Tear for what
In his Rafhnefs he impos'd on his true Servant,
So it cure him of future Jealoufy,
'Twill prove a precious Balfam, and find me
When I am in my Grave.—Now, when you pleafe,
For I am ready.

 Phila. His Words work ftrangely on me,
And I would do—but I know not what to think on't.
            [*Exeunt.*

SCENE II.

Enter Pulcheria, Flaccilla, Arcadia, Timantus, Gratianus *and* Chryfapius.

 Pulch. Still in his fullen Mood? No Intermiffion
Of his melancholy Fit?

 Timan. It rather, Madam,
Increafes, than grows lefs.

 Grat. In the next Room
To his Bed-chamber we watch'd; for he by Signs
Gave us to underftand, he would admit
Nor Company, nor Conference.

 Pulch. Did he take
No Reft, as you could guefs?

Chryf. Not any, Madam ;
Like a *Numidian* Lion, by the Cunning
Of the defp'rate Huntfman taken in a Toil,
And forc'd into a fpacious Cage, he walks
About his Chamber, we might hear him gnafh
His Teeth in Rage ; which open'd, hollow Groans
And Murmurs iffu'd from his Lips, like Winds
Imprifon'd in the Caverns of the Earth
Striving for Liberty ; and fometimes throwing
His Body on his Bed, then on the Ground,
And with fuch Violence, that we more than fear'd,
And ftill do, if the Tempeft of his Paffions
By your Wifdom be not laid, he will commit
Some Outrage on himfelf.

Pulch. His better Angel,
I hope, will ftay him from fo foul a Mifchief ;
Nor fhall my Care be wanting.

Timan. Twice I heard him
Say, Falfe *Eudoxia !* how much art thou
Unworthy of thefe Tears ! Then figh'd, and ftraight
Roar'd out, *Paulinus !* was his gouty Age
To be preferr'd before my Strength and Youth ?
Then groan'd again, fo many Ways expreffing
Th' Afflictions of a tortur'd Soul, that we,
Who wept in vain for what we could not help,
Were Sharers in his Suff'rings.

Pulch. Tho' your Sorrow
Is not to be condemn'd, it takes not from
The Burthen of his Miferies. We muft practife
With fome frefh Object, to divert his Thoughts
From that they're wholly fix'd on.

Chryf. Could I gain
The Freedom of Accefs, I would prefent him
                              [*A Paper deliver'd.*
With this Petition. Will your Highnefs pleafe
To look upon it : You will foon find there
What my Intents and hopes are.

Enter Theodofius.

Grat. Ha! 'tis he.

Pulch. Stand clofe,
And give way to his Paffions; 'tis not fafe
To ftop them in their violent Courfe, before
They've fpent themfelves.

Theod. I play the Fool, and am
Unequal to myfelf; Delinquents are
To fuffer, not the Innocent. I have done
Nothing, which will not hold Weight in the Scale
Of my impartial Juftice; neither feel
The Worm of Confcience upbraiding me
With one black Deed of Tyranny; wherefore, then,
Should I torment myfelf? Great *Julius* would not
Reft fatisfy'd that his Wife was free from Fact,
But, only for Sufpicion of a Crime,
Su'd a Divorce; nor was the *Roman* Rigour
Cenfur'd as cruel: And ftill the wife *Italian,*
That knows the Honour of his Family
Depends upon the Purity of his Bed,
For a Kifs, nay, wanton Look, will plough up Mif-
    chief,
And fow the Seeds of his Revenge in Blood.
And fhall I, to whofe Power the Law's a Servant,
That ftand accountable to none, for what
My Will calls an Offence, being compell'd,
And on fuch Grounds to raife an Altar to
My Anger; tho', I grant, 'tis cemented
With a loofe Strumpet's and Adulterer's Gore,
Repent the Juftice of my Fury? No,
I fhould not: Yet ftill my Excefs of Love,
Fed high in the Remembrance of her choice
And fweet Embraces, would perfuade me that
Connivance or Remiffion of her Fault,
Made warrantable by her true Submiffion
For her Offence, might be excufable,

Did not the Cruelty of my wounded Honour
With an open Mouth deny it.

 Pulch. I approve of
Your good Intention, and I hope 'twill prosper.

         [*To* Chrysapius.

—He now seems calm. Let us upon our Knees
Encompass him. Most Royal Sir——

 Flac. Sweet Brother——

 Arcad. As you're our Sovereign, by the Ties of Nature
You're bound to be a Father in your Care
To us poor Orphans.

 Timant. Shew Compassion, Sir,
Unto yourself.

 Grat. The Majesty of your Fortune
Should fly above the Reach of Grief.

 Chrys. And 'tis
Impair'd, if you yield to it.

 Theod. Wherefore pay you
This Adoration to a sinful Creature?
I'm Flesh and Blood, as you are; sensible
Of Heat and Cold; as much a Slave unto
The Tyranny of my Passions, as the meanest
Of my poor Subjects. The proud Attributes,
By oil-tongu'd Flattery impos'd upon us,
As sacred, glorious, high, invincible,
The Deputy of Heaven, and in that
Omnipotent, with all false Titles else,
Coin'd to abuse our Frailty, tho' compounded,
And by the Breath of Sycophants apply'd,
Cure not the least Fit of an Ague in us.
We may give poor Men Riches; confer Honours
On Undeservers; raise, or ruin such
As are beneath us, and, with this puff'd up,
Ambition would persuade us to forget
That we are Men: But He that sits above us,
And to whom, at our utmost Rate, we are
But pageant-properties, derides our Weakness.
In me, to whom you kneel, 'tis most apparent.
Can I call back Yesterday, with all their Aids
That bow unto my Scepter? Or restore

My Mind to that Tranquility and Peace
It then enjoy'd?——Can it make *Eudoxia* chaste?
Or vile *Paulinus* honeft?

 Pulch. If I might,
Without Offence, deliver my Opinion——
 Theod. What would you fay?
 Pulch. That, on my Soul, the Emprefs
Is innocent.
 Chryf. The good *Paulinus* guiltlefs.
 Grat. And this fhould yield you Comfort.
 Theod. In being guilty
Of an Offence, far, far tranfcending that
They ftand condemn'd for. Call you this a Comfort,
Suppofe it could be true? A Corrofive rather;
Not to eat our dead Flefh, but putrify
What yet is found. Was Murther ever held
A Cure for Jealoufy? or the crying Blood
Of Innocence, a Balm to take away
Her feft'ring Anguifh;——As you do defire
I fhould not do a Juftice on myfelf,
Add to the Proofs by which *Paulinus* fell,
And not take from 'em; in your Charity
Sooner believe that they were falfe, than I
Unrighteous in my Judgment? Subjects Lives
Are not their Prince's Tennis-balls, to be bandy'd
In Sport away. All that I can endure
For them, if they were guilty, is an Atom
To the Mountain of Affliction I pull'd on me,
Should they prove Innocent.
 Chryf. For your Majefty's Peace
I more than hope they were not. The falfe Oath
Took by the Emprefs, and for which fhe can
Plead no Excufe, convicted her, and yields
A fure Defence for your Sufpicion of her.
And yet, to be refolv'd, fince ftrong Doubts are
More grievous, for the moft Part, than to know
A certain Lofs.——
 Theod. 'Tis true, *Chryfapius*;
Were there a poffible Means.

Chryf. 'Tis offer'd to you,
If you pleafe to embrace it.   Some few Minutes
Make Truce with Paffion ; and but read, and follow
What's there projected, you fhall find a Key
Will make your Entrance eafy to difcover
Her fecret Thoughts ; and then, as in your Wifdom
You fhall think fit, you may determine of her,
And reft confirm'd, whether *Paulinus* died
A Villain or a Martyr.

    Theod. It may do ;
Nay, fure it muft : Yet, howfoever it fall,
I am moft wretched ; which Way in my Wifhes
I fafhion the Event, I'm fo diftracted
I cannot yet refolve on.—Follow me ;
Tho' in my Name all Names are comprehended,
I muft have Witneffes, in what Degree
I have done Wrong or fuffer'd.

    Pulch. Hope the beft, Sir.   [*Exeunt.*

S C E N E III.

A fad Song.   Athenais in Sack-cloth ; her Hair loofe.

Athen. **WHY** art thou *flow,* thou *Reft of Trouble,*
      Death,
    To ftop a Wretch's Breath,
That calls on thee, and offers her fad Heart
    A Prey unto thy Dart ?
I am nor young nor fair ; be, therefore, bold.
    Sorrow hath made me old.
Deform'd and wrinkled ; all that I can crave,
    Is Quiet in my Grave.
Such as live happy, hold long Life a Jewel ;
    But to me thou art cruel ;
If thou end not my tedious Mifery,
    And I foon ceafe to be.
Strike, and ftrike home, then ; Pity unto me,
    In one fhort Hour's Delay is Tyranny.

Thus, like a dying Swan, to a sad Tune
I sing my own Dirge; would a Requiem follow,
Which in my Penitence I despair not of,
(This brittle Glass of Life already broken
With Misery) the long and quiet Sleep
Of Death would be most welcome.—Yet, before
We end our Pilgrimage, 'tis fit that we
Should leave Corruption, and foul Sins behind us.
But with wash'd Feet and Hands, the Heathens dare not
Enter their prophane Temples; and for me
To hope my Passage to Eternity
Can be made easy, 'till I have shook off
The Burthen of my Sins in free Confession,
Aided with Sorrow and Repentance for 'em,
Is against Reason. 'Tis not laying by
My royal Ornaments, or putting on
This Garment of Humility and Contrition;
The throwing Dust and Ashes on my Head;
Long Fasts to tame my proud Flesh, that can make
Atonement for my Soul; that must be humbled,
All outward Signs of Penitence else are useless.
Chrysapius did assure me he would bring me
A holy Man, from whom (having discover'd
My secret crying Sins) I might receive
Full Absolution.—And he keeps his Word.

Enter Theodosius *like a Friar, with* Chrysapius.

Welcome, most Reverend Sir! upon my Knees
I entertain you.
    Theod. Noble Sir, forbear
The Place; the sacred Office that I come for
                         [*Exit* Chrysapius.
Commands all Privacy.—My penitent Daughter,
Be careful, as you wish Remission from me,
That, in Confession of your Sins, you hide not
One Crime, whose pond'rous Weight, when you would
      make
Your Flights above the Firmament, may sink you.

A foolish Modesty in concealing aught
Is now far worse than Impudence to profess
And justify your Guilt; be, therefore, free:
So may the Gates of Mercy open to you.

Athen. First then, I ask a Pardon, for my being
Ingrateful to Heav'n's Bounty.

Theod. A good Entrance.

Athen. Greatness comes from Above; and I, rais'd
       to it
From a low Condition, sinfully forgot
From whence it came, and, looking on myself
In the false Glass of Flattery, I receiv'd it
As a Debt due to my Beauty, not a Gift
Or Favour from the Emperor.

Theod. 'Twas not well.

Athen. Pride waited on Unthankfulness, and no more
Rememb'ring the Compassion of the Princess,
And the Means she us'd to make me what I was,
Contested with her, and with sore Eyes seeing
Her greater Light as it dimm'd mine, I practis'd
To have it quite put out.

Theod. A great Offence;
But, on Repentance, not unpardonable.
Forward.

Athen. O Father!—what I now must utter,
I fear, in the Delivery will destroy me,
Before you have absolv'd me.

Theod. Heav'n is gracious,
Out with it.

Athen. Heav'n commands us to tell Truth.
Yet I, most sinful Wretch—forswore myself.

Theod. On what Occasion?

Athen. Quite forgetting that
An innocent Truth can never stand in need
Of a guilty Lie, being on the sudden ask'd
By the Emperor, my Husband, for an Apple
Presented by him, I swore I had eaten it;
When my griev'd Conscience too well knows I sent it
To comfort sick *Paulinus*, being a Man
I truly lov'd and favour'd.

Theod. A cold Sweat,
Like the Juice of Hemlock, bathes me.   [*Afide.*

Athen. And from this
A furious Jealousy getting Possession
Of the good Emperor's Heart, in his Rage he doom'd
The innocent Lord to die, my Perjury
The fatal Cause of Murder.

    Theod. Take heed, Daughter,
You niggle not with your Conscience and Religion,
In stiling him an Innocent from your Fear,
And Shame to accuse yourself. The Emperor
Had many Spies upon you, saw such Graces,
Which Virtue could not warrant, shower'd upon him;
Glances in publick, and more liberal Favours
In your private Chamber-meetings, making Way
For foul Adultery; nor could he be
But sensible of the Compact pass'd between you,
To the Ruin of his Honour.

    Athen. Hear me, Father:
I look'd for Comfort; but, in this you come
To add to my Afflictions.

    Theod. Cause not you
Your own Damnation, in concealing that
Which may, in your Discovery, find Forgiveness.
Open your Eyes; set Heaven or Hell before you.
In the revealing of the Truth, you shall
Prepare a Palace for your Soul to dwell in,
Stor'd with celestial Blessings; whereas, if
You palliate your Crime, and dare beyond,
Playing with Lightning, in concealing it,
Expect a dreadful Dungeon, fill'd with Horror,
And never-ending Torments.

    Athen. May they fall
Eternally upon me, and increase,
When that which we call Time hath lost its Name!
May Lightning cleave the Centre of the Earth
And I sink quick, before you have absolv'd me,
Into the bottomless Abyss, if ever
In one unchaste Desire, nay, in a Thought

I wrong'd the Honour of the Emperor's Bed.
I do deserve, I grant, more than I suffer,
In that, my Fervor and Desire to please him,
In my holy Meditations, press'd upon me,
And would not be kept out; now to dissemble
(When I shall suddenly be insensible
Of what the World speaks of me) were mere madness:
And, tho' you are incredulous, I presume,
If, as I kneel now; my Eyes swol'n with Tears,
My Hands heav'd up thus, my stretch'd Heart-strings
   ready
To break asunder, my incensed Lord
(His Storm of Jealousy blown o'er) should hear me,
He would believe I lied not.
 Theod. Rise, and see him,   [*Discovers himself.*
On his Knees, with Joy affirm it.
  Athen. Can this be?
  Theod. My Sisters, and the rest there,—all bear Wit-
   ness,

Enter Pulcheria, Arcadia, Flaccilla, Chrysapius, Gratianus, Timantus, *and* Philanax.

In freeing this incomparable Lady
From the Suspicion of Guilt, I do
Accuse myself, and willingly submit
To any Penance she in Justice shall
Please to impose upon me.
  Athen. Royal Sir,
Your ill Opinion of me's soon forgiven.
  Pulch. But how you can make Satisfaction to
The poor *Paulinus*, he being dead, in Reason
You must conclude impossible.
  Theod. And in that
I am most miserable; The Ocean
Of Joy, which in your Innocence flow'd high to me,
Ebbs in the Thought of my unjust Command,
By which he died. O *Philanax* (as thy Name
Interpreted speaks thee) thou hast ever been
A Lover of the King, and thy whole Life

Can witnefs thy Obedience to my Will,
In putting that in Execution which
Was trufted to thee; fay but, yet, this once,
Thou haft not done what rafhly I commanded,
And that *Paulinus* lives, and thy Reward
For not performing that which I enjoin'd thee,
Shall centuple whatever yet thy Duty
Or Merit challeng'd from me.

 Phila. 'Tis too late, Sir.
He's dead; and, when you know he was unable
To wrong you in the Way that you fufpected,
You'll wifh it had been otherwife.

 Theod. Unable?

 Phila. I am fure he was an Eunuch, and might
   fafely
Lie by a Virgin's Side; at four Years made one;
Tho', to hold Grace with Ladies, he conceal'd it.
—The Circumftances and the Manner how
You may hear at better Leifure.

 Theod. How! an Eunuch?
The more the Proofs are that are brought to clear thee,
My beft *Eudoxia,* the more my Sorrows.

 Athen. That I am innocent?

 Theod. That I am guilty
Of Murther, my *Eudoxia.* I will build
A glorious Monument to his Memory;
And, for my Punifhment, live and die upon it,
And never more converfe with Men.

Enter Paulinus,

 Paul. Live long, Sir!
May I do fo to ferve you! and, if that
I live does not difpleafe you, you owe for it
To this good Lord.

 Theod. Myfelf, and all that's mine.——

 Phila. Your Pardon is a Payment.

 Theod. I am rapt
With Joy beyond myfelf. Now, my *Eudoxia,*

My Jealoufy puff'd away thus, in this Breath
I fcent the natural Sweetnefs.   [*Kiffes her.*

    Arcad. Sacred Sir,
I'm happy to behold this, and prefume,
Now you are pleas'd, to move a Suit, in which
My Sifter is join'd with me.

    Theod. Pr'ythee fpeak it;
For I have vow'd to hear before I grant;
I thank your good Inftructions.   [*To* Pulcheria.

    Arcad. 'Tis but this, Sir.
We have obferv'd the falling out and in
Between the Hufband and the Wife fhews rarely;
Their Jars and Reconcilements ftrangely take us.

    Flac. Anger and Jealoufy that conclude in Kiffes
Is a fweet War, in footh.

    Arcad. We therefore, Brother,
Moft humbly beg you would provide us Hufbands,
That we may tafte the Pleafure of't.

    Flac. And with Speed, Sir;
For fo your Favour's doubled.

    Theod. Take my Word,
I will with all Convenience; and not blufh
Hereafter to be guided by your Counfels:
I will deferve your Pardon.   *Philanax*
Shall be remember'd, and magnificent Bounties
Fall on *Chryfapius:* My Grace on all.
Let *Cleon* be deliver'd and rewarded.
My Grace on all, which as I lend to you,
Return your Vows to Heaven, that it may pleafe
(As it is gracious) to quench in me
All future Sparks of burning Jealoufy.

EPILOGUE.

WE'VE Reafon to be doubtful, whether he,
On whom (forc'd to it by Neceffity)
The Maker did confer his Emp'ror's Part,
Hath giv'n you Satisfaction, in his Art
Of Action and Delivery; 'tis fure Truth
The Burden was too heavy for his Youth [7]
To undergo.—But in his Will, we know,
He was not wanting, and fhall ever owe,
With his, our Service, if your Favours deign
To give him Strength, hereafter to fuftain
A greater Weight. It is your Grace that can
In your Allowance of this, write him Man
Before his Time : which, if you pleafe to do,
You make the Player and the Poet too.

[7] *The Burden was too heavy for his Youth.*

The Intent of this Epilogue is to apologize for fome young Actor, who performed the Part of the *Emperor*, and of whofe Abilities they were fomething doubtful.

THE

MAID of HONOUR.

A

TRAGI-COMEDY.

Sir FRANCIS FOLIAMBE, Knt. and Bart,

AND TO

Sir THOMAS BLAND, Knt.

THAT you have been and continued so for many Years, since you vouchsafed to own me, Patrons to me and my despised Studies, I cannot but with all humble Thankfulness acknowledge: And living, as you have done, inseparable in your Friendship (notwithstanding all Differences, and Suits in Law arising between you) I held it as impertinent, as absurd, in the Presentment of my Service in this Kind, to divide you. A free Confession of a Debt in a meaner Man, is the amplest Satisfaction to his Superiors; and I heartily wish, that the World may take Notice, and from myself, that I had not to this Time subsisted, but that I was supported by your frequent Courtesies and Favours. When your serious Occasions will give you Leave, you may please to peruse this Trifle, and peradventure find something in it that may appear worthy of your Protection. Receive it, I beseech you, as a Testimony of his Duty, who, while he lives, resolves to be

Truly and sincerely devoted to your Service,

PHILIP MASSINGER.

Dramatis Personæ.

ROBERTO, King of *Sicily.*

FERDINAND, Duke of *Urbin.*

BERTOLDO, the King's natural Brother, a Knight of *Malta.*

GONZAGA, a Knight of *Malta,* General to the Dutchess of *Siena.*

ASTUTIO, a Counsellor of State.

FULGENTIO, the Minion of *Roberto.*

ADORNI, a Follower of *Camiola*'s Father.

AMBASSADOR, from the Duke of *Urbin.*

SIGNIOR SYLLI, a foolish Self-lover.

ANTHONIO,
GASPARO, } Two Rich Heirs, City-bred.

PIERIO, a Colonel to *Gonzaga.*

RODERIGO,
IACOMO, } Captains to *Gonzaga.*

DRUSO,
LIVIO, } Captains to Duke *Ferdinand.*

PAULO, a Priest, *Camiola*'s Confessor.

AURELIA, Dutchess of *Siena.*

CAMIOLA, the Maid of Honour.

CLARINDA, her Woman.

Scout, Soldiers, Servants, Gaoler, Dwarf, Mutes.

MAID of HONOUR.

ACT I. SCENE I.

The Presence Chamber.

Astutio *and* Adorni.

Adorni.

GOOD Day to your Lordship !
   Astutio. Thanks, *Adorni.*
  Adorni. May I presume to ask if the Ambassador
Employ'd by *Ferdinand,* the Duke of *Urbin,*
Hath Audience this Morning ?

Enter Fulgentio.

  Astutio. 'Tis uncertain,
For, tho' a Counsellor of State, I am not
Of the Cabinet Council. But there's one, if he please,
That may resolve you.
  Adorni. I will move him Sir.
  Fulgen. If you've a Suit, shew Water, I am blind
    else.
  Adorni. A Suit, yet of a Nature, not to prove
The Quarry that you hawk for : If your Words
Are not like *Indian* Wares, and every Scruple,
To be weigh'd and rated, one poor Syllable,
Vouchsaf'd in Answer of a fair Demand,
Cannot deserve a Fee.

Fulgen. It feems you're ignorant;
I neither fpeak nor hold my Peace for nothing:
And yet, for once, I care not if I anfwer
One fingle Queftion, *gratis.*
  Adorni. I much thank you.
Hath the Ambaffador Audience, Sir, To-day?
  Fulgen. Yes.
  Adorni. At what Hour?
  Fulgen. I promis'd not fo much.
A Syllable you begg'd; my Charity gave it.
Move me no further.   [*Exit* Fulgentio.
  Aftutio. This you wonder at?
With me, 'tis ufual.
  Adorni. Pray you, Sir, what is he?
  Aftutio. A Gentleman, yet no Lord.   He hath fome
       Drops
Of the King's Blood running in his Veins, deriv'd
Some ten Degrees off.   His Revenue lies
In a narrow Compafs, the King's Ear; and yields him
Every Hour a fruitful Harveft.   Men may talk
Of three Crops in a Year in the *Fortunate Iflands.*
Or Profit made by Wool: But, while there are Suitors,
His Sheep-fhearing, nay, fhaving to the Quick
Is in every Quarter of the Moon, and conftant.
In the Time of truffing a Point, he can undo
Or make a Man.   His Play or Recreation
Is to raife this up, or pull down that; and, tho'
He never yet took Orders, makes more Bifhops
In *Sicily,* than the Pope himfelf.

     Enter Bertoldo, Gafparo, Anthonio, *and a Servant.*

  Adorni. Moft ftrange!
  Aftutio. The Prefence fills.   He in the *Malta* Habit
Is the natural Brother of the King—a By-blow.
  Adorni. I underftand you.
  Gafp. 'Morrow to my Uncle.
  Anth. And my late Guardian.   But at length I have
The Reins in my own Hands.

Aſtutio. Pray you uſe 'em well,
Or you'll too late repent it.

Bert. With this Jewel
Preſented to *Camiola,* prepare
This Night a Viſit for me. I ſhall have *[Exit Servant.*
Your Company, Gallants, I perceive, if that
The King will hear of War.

Anth. Sir, I have Horſes
Of the beſt Breed in *Naples,* fitter far
To break a Rank than crack a Lance, and are
In their Career of ſuch incredible Swiftneſs
They out-ſtrip Swallows.

Bert. And ſuch may be uſeful
To run away with, ſhould we be defeated.
You're well provided, Signior ?

Anth. Sir, excuſe me.
All of their Race by Inſtinct know a Coward,
And ſcorn the Burthen. They come on like Lightning;
Founder'd in a Retreat.

Bert. By no means back 'em ;
Unleſs you know your Courage ſympathize
With the Daring of your Horſe.

Anth. My Lord, this is bitter.

Gaſp. I will raiſe me a Company of Foot;
And, when at puſh of Pike I am to enter
A Breach, to ſhew my Valour, I have brought me
An Armour Cannon-proof.

Bert. You will not leap, then,
O'er an Out-work in your Shirt ?

Gaſp. I do not like
Activity that Way.

Bert. You had rather ſtand
A Mark to try their Muſkets on ?

Gaſp. If I do
No Good, I'll do no Hurt.

Bert. 'Tis in you, Signior,
A Chriſtian Reſolution and becomes you ;
But I will not diſcourage you.

Anth. You are, Sir,
A Knight of *Malta*, and, as I have heard,
Have ferv'd againſt the *Turk.*

Bert. 'Tis true.

Anth. Pray you, ſhew us
The Difference between the City-Valour,
And Service in the Field.

Bert. 'Tis ſomewhat more
Than roaring in a Tavern or a Brothel,
Or to ſteal a Lanthorn from a ſleeping Watch;
Then burn their Halberts; or, ſafe guarded by
Your Tenant's Sons, to carry away a Maypole
From a Neighbour-Village. You will not find, there,
Your Maſters of Dependencies to take up
A drunken Brawl, or, to get you the Names
Of valiant Chevaliers, Fellows that will be,
For a Cloak with thrice-dy'd Velvet, and a caſt Suit,
Kick'd down the Stairs. A Knave with half a Breech,
                    there,
And no Shirt (being a Thing ſuperfluous,
And worn out of his Memory) if you bear not
Yourſelves both in, and upright with a provant
                    Sword,
Will flaſh your Scarlets, and your Pluſh a new Way;
Or with the Hilts thunder about your Ears
Such Muſick as will make your Worſhips dance
To the doleful Tune of *Lachryma.*

Gaſp. I muſt tell you
In private, as you are my princely Friend,
I do not like ſuch Fidlers.

Bert. No? They are uſeful
For your Initiation; I remember you,
When you came firſt to the Court, and talk'd of nothing
But your Rents and your Entradas, ever chiming
The Golden Bells in your Pockets, you believ'd
The taking of the Wall as a Tribute due to
Your gaudy Cloaths; and could not walk at Midnight
Without a cauſeleſs Quarrel, as if Men
Of coarſer Outſides were in Duty bound

To fuffer your Affronts : But, when you had been
Cudgel'd well,. twice or thrice, and from the Doctrine
Made profitable Ufes, you concluded
The Sov'reign Means to teach irregular Heirs
Civility, with Conformity of Manners,
Were two or three found Beatings.

   Anth. I confefs
They did much Good upon me.

   Gafp. And on me ;—the Principles that they read
     were found.

   Bert. You'll find
The like Inftructions in the Camp.

   Aftutio. The King ——

A Flourifh.

Enter Roberto, Fulgentio, Ambaffador, *and Attendants.*

   Rober. We fit prepared to hear.

   Ambaff. Your Majefty
Hath been long fince familiar, I doubt not,
With th' defp'rate Fortunes of my Lord ; and Pity
Of the much that your Confederate hath fuffer'd
(You being his laft Refuge) may perfuade you
Not alone to compaffionate, but to lend
Your Royal Aids to ftay him in his Fall
To certain Ruin. He, too late, is confcious
That his Ambition to encroach upon
His Neighbour's Territories, with the Danger of
His Liberty, nay, his Life, hath brought in Queftion
His own Inheritance : But Youth and Heat
Of Blood, in your Interpretation, may
Both plead and mediate for him. I muft grant it
An Error in him, being deny'd the Favours
Of the fair Princefs of *Siena* (tho'
He fought her in a noble Way) t' endeavour
To force Affection by Surprifal of
Her principal Seat, *Siena.*

Rober. Which now proves
The Seat of his Captivity, not Triumph.
Heav'n is still just.

Ambass. And yet that justice is
To be with Mercy temper'd, which Heav'n's Deputies
Stand bound to minister. The injur'd Dutchess
By Reason taught, as Nature,¹ could not, with
The Reparation of her Wrongs, but aim at
A brave Revenge; and my Lord feels too late
That Innocence will find Friends. The great *Gonzaga*,
The Honour of his Order—(I must praise
Virtue, tho' in an Enemy) He whose Fights
And Conquests hold one Number, rallying up
Her scatter'd Troops before we could get Time
To victual, or to man the conquer'd City,
Sat down before it; and, presuming that
'Tis not to be reliev'd, admits no Parley,
Our Flags of Truce hung out in vain: Nor will he
Lend an Ear to Composition, but exacts
With th' rend'ring up the Town, the Goods, and Lives
Of all within the Walls, and of all Sexes
To be at his Discretion.

Rober. Since Injustice
In your Duke meets this Correction, can you press us,
With any seeming Argument of Reason,
In foolish Pity to decline his Dangers,
To draw 'em on Our Self? Shall We not be
Warn'd by his Harms? The League proclaim'd be-
             tween us,
Bound neither of us farther than to aid
Each other, if by foreign Force invaded;
And so far in my Honour I was ty'd.
But, since, without our Counsel, or Allowance,
He hath took Arms, with his good Leave, he must
Excuse us, if we steer not on a Rock
We see, and may avoid. Let other Monarchs
Contend to be made glorious by proud War,
And with the Blood of their poor Subjects purchase

---

¹ Means here, as well as Nature. *M. M.*

Increase of Empire, and augment their Cares
In keeping that which was by wrongs extorted,
Gilding unjust Invasions with the trim
Of glorious Conquests; We, that would be known
The Father of our People in our Study
And Vigilance for their Safety, must not change
Their Plough-shares into Swords, and force them from
The secure Shade of their own Vines to be
Scorch'd with the Flames of War, or, for our Sport,
Expose their Lives to Ruin.

Ambass. Will you, then,
In his Extremity forsake your Friend?

Rober. No; but preserve Our Self.

Bert. Cannot the Beams
Of Honour thaw your icy Fears?

Rober. Who's that?

Bert. A kind of Brother, Sir; howe'er, your Sub-
ject,
Your Father's Son, and one who blushes that
You are not Heir to his brave Spirit and Vigour,
As to his Kingdom.

Rober. How's this?

Bert. Sir, to be
His living Chronicle, and to speak his Praise,
Cannot deserve your Anger.

Rober. Where's your Warrant
For this Presumption?

Bert. Here, Sir, in my Heart.
Let Sycophants, that feed upon your Favours,
Stile Coldness in you Caution, and prefer
Your Ease before your Honour; and conclude
To eat and sleep supinely, is the End
Of Human Blessings: I must tell you, Sir,
Virtue, if not in Action, is a Vice, [2]
And, when we move not forward, we go backward;

A a 4

Nor is this Peace (the Nurse of Drones and Cowards)
Our Health, but a Disease.

Gasp. Well urg'd, my Lord.

Anth. Perfect what is so well begun,

Ambass. And bind
My Lord your Servant.

Rober. Hair brain'd Fool! What Reason
Canst thou infer to make this Good?

Bert. A thousand,
Not to be contradicted. But consider
Where your Command lies? 'Tis not, Sir, in *France,*
Spain, Germany, Portugal, but in *Sicily;*
An Island, Sir. Here are no Mines of Gold
Or Silver to enrich you; No Worm spins
Silk in her Womb, to make Distinction
Between you and a Peasant in your Habits.
No Fish lives near our Shores, whose Blood can dye
Scarlet or Purple; all that we possess,
With Beasts we have in common: 'Nature did
Design us to be Warriors, and to break thro'
Our Ring the Sea, by which we are environ'd;
And we by Force must fetch in what is wanting,
Or precious to us. Add to this, we are
A populous Nation, and increase so fast,
That, if we by our Providence are not sent
Abroad in Colonies, or fall by the Sword,
Not *Sicily* (tho' now it were more fruitful
Than when 'twas stil'd the Granary of great *Rome)*
Can yield our num'rous Fry Bread: We must starve,
Or eat up one another.

The Poets have many Passages similar to this. Thus *Shakespeare*

———— If our Virtues
Did not go forth of us, 'twere all alike
As if we had them not.
                                        Measure for Measure, Act 1. Scene 2.

And *Horace* tells us, Virtue concealed is of little Consequence.

   Paulum sepultæ distat inertiæ
   Celata virtus.

Adorni. The King hears
With much Attention. [*Aside.*

Aſlutio. And ſeems mov'd with what
Bertoldo hath deliver'd. [*Aside.*

Bert. May you live long, Sir,
The King of Peace, ſo you deny not us
The Glory of the War ; let not our Nerves
Shrink up with Sloth, nor, for Want of Employment,
Make younger Brothers Thieves : 'Tis their Sword, Sir,
Muſt ſow and reap their Harveſt. If Examples
May move you more than Arguments, look on *Eng-
         land,* [1]
The Empreſs of the *European* Iſles,
And unto whom alone ours yields Precedence,
When did ſhe flouriſh ſo, as when ſhe was
The Miſtreſs of the Ocean ? Her Navies
Putting a Girdle round about the World,
When the *Iberian* quak'd, her Worthies nam'd ;
And the fair *Fleur de Lis* grew pale, ſet by
The Red Roſe and the White. Let not our Armour
Hung up, or our unrigg'd *Armada* make us
Ridiculous to the late poor Snakes our Neighbours
Warm'd in our Boſoms, and to whom again
We may be terrible ; while we ſpend our Hours
Without Variety, confin'd to Drink,
Dice, Cards, or Whores. Rouze us, Sir, from the
         Sleep
Of Idleneſs, and redeem our mortgag'd Honours.
Your Birth, and juſtly, claims my Father's Kingdoms ;
But his heroic Mind deſcends to me :
—I will confirm ſo much.

Adorni. In his Looks he ſeems
To break ope *Janus'* Temple.

☞ 3 ————— *Look on* England,
The Empreſs of European *Iſles.*

All our old Poets have celebrated their Country, neither is *Maſſinger* wanting : As the Paſſages ſimilar to this are well known, I
ſhall forbear ſetting them down here.

Aſtutio. How theſe Younglings
Take Fire from him!

Adorni. It works an Alteration
Upon the King.

Anth. I can forbear no longer:
War, War, my Sovereign!

Fulgen. The King appears
Reſolv'd, and does prepare to ſpeak.

Rober. Think not
Our Counſel's built upon ſo weak a Baſe,
As to be overturn'd, or ſhaken with
Tempeſtuous Winds of Words. As I, my Lord,
Before reſolv'd you, I will not engage
My Perſon in this Quarrel; neither preſs
My Subjects to maintain it: Yet, to ſhew
My Rule is gentle, and that I've Feeling of
Your Maſter's Sufferings, ſince the Gallants, weary
Of the Happineſs of Peace, deſire to taſte
The bitter Sweets of War, we do conſent
That, as Adventurers and Volunteers
(No Way compell'd by us) they may make Trial
Of their boaſted Valours.

Bert. We deſire no more.

Rober. 'Tis well; and, but my Grant in this, expect
         not
Aſſiſtance from me. Govern as you pleaſe
The Province you make Choice of; for, I vow
By all Things ſacred, if that thou miſcarry
In this raſh Undertaking, I will hear it
No otherwiſe than as a ſad Diſaſter,
Fall'n on a Stranger; nor will I eſteem
That Man my Subject, who, in thy Extremes,
In Purſe or Perſon aids thee. Take your Fortune:
You know me; I have ſaid it. So, my Lord,
You have my whole Anſwer.

Ambaſſ. My Prince pays
In me his Duty.

Rober. Follow me, *Fulgentio,*
And you, *Aſtutio.*

         [*Exeunt* Roberto, Fulgentio, Aſtutio *and Attendants.*

Gafp. What a Frown he threw
At his Departure on you.

Bert. Let him keep
His Smiles for his State-Catamite; I care not.

Anth. Shall we aboard to-night?

Ambaff. Your Speed, my Lord,
Doubles the Benefit.

Bert. I have a Bufinefs
Requires Difpatch.—Some two Hours hence I'll meet
you.   [*Exeunt.*

SCENE II.

Camiola's *Houfe.*

Enter Signior Sylli, *walking fantaftically before, followed
by* Camiola *and* Clarinda.

Camiola. Nay, Signior, this is too much Ceremony
In my own Houfe.

Sylli. What's gracious abroad,
Muft be in private practis'd.

Clar. For your Mirth-fake,
Let him alone, he has been all this Morning
In Practice with a peruk'd Gentleman Ufher,
To teach him his true Amble and his Poftures
          [Sylli *walking by, and practifing his Poftures,*
When he walks before a Lady.

Sylli. You may, Madam,
Perhaps, believe that I in this ufe Art,
To make you doat upon me by expofing
My more than moft rare Features to your View,
But I, as I have ever done, deal fimply;
A Mark of fweet Simplicity, ever noted
I' th' Family of the *Syllies.* Therefore, Lady,
Look not with too much Contemplation on me;
If you do, you are i' th' Suds.

Camiola. You are no Barber?

Sylli. Fie! no, not I; but my good Parts have drawn
More loving Hearts out of fair Ladies Bellies,
Than the whole Trade have done Teeth.

    Camiola. Is't possible?

    Sylli. Yes, and they live too; marry, much condoling
The Scorn of their *Narcissus,* as they call me,
Because I love myself.

    Camiola. Without a Rival.
What Philtres or Love-powders do you use
To force Affection? I see nothing in
Your Person, but I dare look on, yet keep
My own poor Heart still.

    Sylli. You are warn'd—be arm'd;
And do not lose the Hope of such a Husband,
In being too soon enamour'd.

    Clar. Hold in your Head,
Or you must have a Martingale.

    Sylli. I have sworn
Never to take a Wife, but such a one
(O may your Ladyship prove so strong!) as can
Hold out a Month against me.

    Camiola. Never fear it;
Tho' your best taking Part, your Wealth, were trebled,
I would not woo you. But, since in your Pity
You please to give me Caution, tell me what
Temptations I must fly from.

    Sylli. The first is,
That you ne'er hear me sing; for I'm a Syren.
If you observe, when I warble, the Dogs howl,
As ravish'd with my Ditties, and you will
Run mad to hear me.

    Camiola. I will stop my Ears,
And keep my little Wits.

    Sylli. Next, when I dance,
And come aloft thus, cast not a Sheep's Eye
Upon the Quiv'ring of my Calf.

    Camiola. Proceed, Sir.

Sylli. But on no Terms (for 'tis a main Point) dream
    not
O' th' Strength of my Back, tho' 'twill bear a Burthen
With any Porter.

    Camiola. I mean not to ride you.

    Sylli. Nor I your little Ladyſhip, 'till you have
Perform'd the Covenant.—Be not taken with
My pretty Spider-fingers; nor my Eyes,
That twinkle on both Sides.

    Camiola. Was there ever ſuch   [*One knocks.*
A Piece of Motley heard of!—Who's that; you may
    ſpare
The Catalogue of my Dangers.   [*Exit* Clarinda.

    Sylli. No, good Madam;
I have not told you half.

    Camiola. Enough, good Signior;
If I eat more of ſuch Sweet-meats, I ſhall ſurfeit.

Enter Clarinda.

Who is't?

    Clar. The Brother of the King.

    Sylli. Nay, ſtart not.
The Brother of the King! Is he no more?
Were it the King himſelf, I'd give him Leave
To ſpeak his Mind to you, for I'm not jealous;
And, to aſſure your Ladyſhip of ſo much,
I'll uſher him in, and, that done—hide myſelf.
    [*Exit* Sylli.

    Camiola. Camiola, if ever, now be conſtant:
This is, indeed, a Suitor, whoſe ſweet Preſence,
Courtſhip, and loving Language, would have ſtagger'd
The chaſte *Penelope;* and, to increaſe
The Wonder, did not Modeſty forbid it,
I ſhould aſk that from him he ſues me for.
And yet my Reaſon, like a Tyrant, tells me
I muſt not give nor take it.

Enter Sylli *and* Bertoldo.

Sylli. I muſt tell you,
You loſe your Labour. 'Tis enough to prove it,
Signior *Sylli* came before you ; and you know,
Firſt come, firſt ſerv'd : Yet, you ſhall have my Coun-
         tenance
To parley with her ; and I'll take ſpecial Care
That none ſhall interrupt you.
   Bert. You are courteous.
   Sylli. Come, Wench, wilt thou hear Wiſdom ?
                             [Steps aſide.

   Clar. Yes, from you, Sir.
   Bert. If forcing this ſweet Favour from your Lips,
                              [Kiſſeth her.
Fair Madam, argue me of too much Boldneſs,
When you are pleas'd to underſtand, I take
A parting Kiſs, if not excuſe, at leaſt
'Twill qualify th' Offence.
   Camiola. A parting Kiſs, Sir ?
What Nation, envious of the Happineſs
Which *Sicily* enjoys in your ſweet Preſence,
Can buy you from her ? or what Climate yield
Pleaſures tranſcending thoſe which you enjoy here,
Being both belov'd and honour'd ? the North-Star,
And Guider of all Hearts ; and, to ſum up
Your full Accompt of Happineſs in a Word,
The Brother of the King.
   Bert. Do you, alone,
And with an unexampled Cruelty,
Enforce my Abſence, and deprive me of
Thoſe Bleſſings, which you with a poliſh'd Phraſe
Seem to inſinuate that I do poſſeſs,
And yet tax me as being guilty of
My wilful Exile ? What are Titles to me ?
Or popular Suffrage ? or my Nearneſs to
The King in Blood ? or fruitful *Sicily,*
Tho' it confeſs'd no Sovereign but myſelf ;
When you, that are the Eſſence of my Being,

The Anchor of my Hopes, the real Subſtance
Of my Felicity, in your Diſdain
Turn all to fading and deceiving Shadows ?
   Camiola. You tax me without Cauſe.
   Bert. You muſt confeſs it.
But, anſwer Love with Love, and ſeal the Contraƈt
In the uniting of our Souls, how gladly
(Tho' now I were in Aƈtion, and aſſur'd,
Following my Fortune, that plum'd Viƈtory
Would make her glorious ſtand upon my Tent)
Would I put off my Armour, in my Heat
Of Conqueſt, and, like *Anthony,* purſue
My *Cleopatra !* Will you yet look on me
With an Eye of Favour ?
   Camiola. Truth bear Witneſs for me,
That, in the Judgment of my Soul, you are
A Man ſo abſolute, and circular
In all thoſe wiſh'd-for Rarities, that may take
A Virgin captive, that, tho' at this Inſtant
All ſcepter'd Monarchs of our Weſtern World
Were Rivals with you, and *Camiola* worthy
Of ſuch a Competition, you alone
Should wear the Garland.
   Bert. If ſo, what diverts
Your Favour from me ?
   Camiola. No Mulƈt in yourſelf ;
Or in your Perſon, Mind or Fortune.
   Bert. What then ?
   Camiola. The Conſciouſneſs of mine own Wants.—
     Alas ! Sir, 4

☞ 4 ————————*Alas, Sir !*
   We are not Parallels ; *but,* like Lines divided,
   Can ne'er meet in one Center.

  This ſeems badly expreſſed. Parallels are the only Lines that
cannot meet in a Center ; for all Lines divided with any Angle towards each other, muſt meet ſomewhere, if continued both Ways.

  We are not Parallels, means merely *we are not alike ; we are not
Equals ;* the Expreſſion is common, and is uſed again in the
Page of this Volume.

We are not Parallels; but, like Lines divided,
Can ne'er meet in one Center.   Your Birth, Sir,
(Without Addition) were an ample Dowry
For one of fairer Fortunes; and this Shape,
Were you ignoble, far above all Value:
To this so clear a Mind, so furnish'd with
Harmonious Faculties, moulded from Heaven,
That, tho' you were *Therſites* in your Features,
Of no Descent, and *Irus* in your Fortunes,
Ulyſſes-like, you'd force all Eyes and Ears
To love, but seen; and, when heard, wonder at
Your matchleſs Story.   But, all theſe bound up
Together in one Volume, give me Leave
With Admiration to look upon 'em;
But not preſume, in my own flatt'ring Hopes,
I may, or can, enjoy 'em.
   Bert. How you ruin
What you would seem to build up! I know no
Diſparity between us; you're an Heir
Sprung from a noble Family; fair, rich, young,
And ev'ry Way my Equal.
   Camiola. Sir, excuſe me, ⁵

―――――――――――True, I do;
But you and he, Sir, are not Parallels.

By *Lines divided, Maſſinger* does not mean, as the Editor ſuppo-
ſes, Lines inclined to each other in any Angle; but the divided
Parts of the ſame right Line which never can meet in one Center.
M. M.

☞ 5 ―――――――――Sir, *excuſe me,*
   One airy with Proportion ne'er diſcloſes
   The Eagle and the Wren.

This Paſſage is ſomewhat difficult. *Camiola* is ſhewing how un-
likely it was, that *Bertoldo* ſhould condeſcend to marry her, becauſe
of the Diſparity of their Birth; and ſhe ſays, " One who is puffed
up with an high Opinion of his own Birth, and the Equality there
ought to be in Marriages: *One airy with Proportion*, will never
ſtoop ſo low as *Bertoldo* muſt, to marry her: The Eagle might as
well vouchſafe to court the Wren."

One airy with Proportion, ne'er [7] difclofes
The Eagle and the Wren : Tiffue and Frize,
In the fame Garment, monftrous : But, fuppofe
That what's in you exceffive, were diminifh'd,
And my Defert fupply'd, the ftrongeft Bar,
Religion, ftops our Entrance. You are, Sir,
A Knight of *Malta,* by your Order bound
To a fingle Life : You cannot marry me ;
And, I affure myfelf, you are too noble
To feek me (tho' my Frailty fhould confent)
In a bafe Path.

 Bert. A Difpenfation, Lady,
Will eafily abfolve me.

 Camiola. O take heed, Sir !
When what is vow'd to Heav'n is difpens'd with,
To ferve our Ends on Earth, a Curfe muft follow,
And not a Bleffing.

 Bert. Is there no Hope left me ?

 Camiola. Nor to myfelf, but is a Neighbour to
Impoffibility. True Love fhould walk
On equal Feet ; in us it does not, Sir.
But reft affur'd, excepting this, I fhall be
Devoted to your Service.

 Bert. And this is your
Determinate Sentence ?

 Camiola. Not to be revok'd.

 Bert. Farewel ! then, faireft Cruel ! All Thoughts in
  me
Of Women perifh ! Let the glorious Light
Of noble War extinguifh Love's divine Taper,
That only lends me Light to fee my Folly !
Honour, be thou my ever-living Miftrefs,
And fond Affection as thy Bond-flave ferve thee !

       [Exit Bertoldo.

---

7 *Difclofes,* we fhould read *enclofes,* and the Meaning is this : The
Airy that is fit for an Eagle cannot be equally fit for a Wren. If it
be proportion'd to the one, it can bear no Proportion to the other.
M. M.

Camiola. How foon my Sun is fet! (He being abfent)
Never to rife again! What a fierce Battle
Is fought between my Paffions!—Methinks
We fhould have kifs'd at Parting.

Sylli. I perceive
He has his Anfwer.—Now muft I ftep in
To comfort her. You have found, I hope, fweet Lady,
Some Difference between a Youth of my Pitch,
And this Bug-bear, *Bertoldo.* Men are Men,
The King's Brother is no more: Good Parts will do it,
When Titles fail.—Defpair not; I may be
In Time intreated.

Camiola. Be fo now, to leave me.
Lights for my Chamber.—O my Heart!
                                [*Exeunt* Camiola *and* Clarinda.

Sylli. She now,
I know, is going to Bed to ruminate
Which Way to glut herfelf upon my Perfon;
But, for my Oath-fake, I will keep her hungry!
And, to grow full myfelf, I'll ftrait to Supper.
                                                [*Exit.*

The End of the Firft Act.

ACT II. SCENE I.

The Palace at Palermo.

Enter Roberto, Fulgentio *and* Aftutio.

Roberto.

EMBARK'D to-night, do you fay?
    Fulgen. I faw him aboard, Sir.
Rober. And without taking of his Leave?
Aftutio. 'Twas ftrange!

Rober. Are we grown fo contemptible?

Fulgen. 'Tis far from me, Sir, to add Fuel to your Anger,
That in your ill Opinion of him burns
Too hot already; elfe, I fhould affirm
It was a grofs Neglect.

Rober. A wilful Scorn
Of Duty and Allegiance; you give it
Too fair a Name.—But we fhall think on't. Can you
Guefs what the Numbers were that follow'd him
In his defperate Action?

Fulgen. More than you think, Sir.
All ill-affected Spirits in *Palermo*,
Or to your Government or Perfon, with
The turbulent Sword-men; fuch whofe Poverty forc'd 'em
To wifh a Change, are gone along with him;
Creatures devoted to his Undertakings,
In Right or Wrong; and, to exprefs their Zeal,
And Readinefs to ferve him, ere they went,
Prophanely took the Sacrament on their Knees,
To live and die with him.

Rober. O moft impious!
Their Loyalty to us forgot?

Fulgen. I fear fo.

Aftutio. Unthankful as they are!

Fulgen. Yet this deferves not
One troubled Thought in you, Sir; with your Pardon,
I hold that their Remove from hence, makes more
For your Security than Danger.

Rober. True;
And, as I'll fafhion it, they fhall feel it too.
Aftutio, you fhall prefently be difpatch'd
With Letters writ, and fign'd with your own Hand,
To the Duchefs of *Siena*, in Excufe
Of thefe Forces fent againft her. If you fpare
An Oath to give it Credit, that we never
Confented to it, fwearing for the King,
Tho' falfe, it is no Perjury.

Aſtutio. I know it.
They are not fit to be State Agents, Sir,
That, without Scruple of their Conſcience, cannot
Be prodigal in ſuch Trifles.

 Fulgen. Right, *Aſtutio.*

 Rober. You muſt, beſide, from us take ſome Inſtruc-
   tions,
To be imparted as you judge 'em uſeful,
To the General *Gonzaga.* Inſtantly
Prepare you for your Journey.

 Aſtutio. With the Wings
Of Loyalty and Duty.   *[Exit* Aſtutio.

 Fulgen. I am bold to put your Majeſty in Mind——

 Rober. Of my Promiſe,
And Aids, to further you in your am'rous Project
To the fair and rich *Camiola :* There's my Ring ;
Whatever you ſhall ſay that I intreat,
Or can command by Pow'r, I will make good.

 Fulgen. Ever your Majeſty's Creature.

 Rober. Venus prove propitious to you !
            [Exit Roberto.

 Fulgen. All ſorts to my Wiſhes.
Bertoldo was my Hindrance. He remov'd,
I now will court her in the Conqu'ror's Stile ;
" Come, See, and Overcome."——Boy !

Enter Page.

 Page. Sir, your Pleaſure !

 Fulgen. Haſte to *Camiola ;* bid her prepare
An Entertainment ſuitable to a Fortune
She could not hope for. Tell her, I vouchſafe
To honour her with a Viſit.

 Page. 'Tis a Favour
Will make her proud.

 Fulgen. I know it.

 Page. I am gone, Sir.   *[Exit Page.*

 Fulgen. Intreaties fit not me ; a Man in Grace
May challenge Awe and Privilege, by his Place.
           [Exit Fulgentio.

SCENE II.

Camiola's *Houſe*.

Enter Sylli, Adorni *and* Clarinda.

Adorni. So melancholick, ſay you?
Clar. Never given
To ſuch Retirement.
Adorni. Can you gueſs the Cauſe?
Clar. If it hath not its Birth and Being from
The brave *Bertoldo*'s Abſence, I confeſs
'Tis paſt my Apprehenſion.
Sylli. You are wide. I, in my Underſtanding,
Pity your Ignorance.—Yet, if you will
Swear to conceal it, I will let you know
Where her Shoe wrings her.
Clar. I vow, Signior,
By my Virginity.
Sylli. A perilous Oath,
In a Waiting Woman of Fifteen! and is, indeed,
A Kind of Nothing.
Adorni. I'll take one of Something,
If you pleaſe to miniſter it.
Sylli. Nay, you ſhall not ſwear:
I had rather take your Word; for, ſhould you vow,
" Damn me, I'll do this," you are ſure to break.
Adorni. I thank you, Signior; but reſolve us——
Sylli. Know, then,
Here walks the Cauſe. She dares not look upon me;
My Beauties are ſo terrible and inchanting,
She can't endure my Sight.
Adorni. There I believe you.
Sylli. But the Time will come (be comforted) when
          I will
Put off this Vizor of Unkindneſs to her,

And fhew an amorous and yielding Face:
And, until then, tho' *Hercules* himfelf,
Defire to fee her, he had better eat
His Club than pafs the Threfhold; for I'll be
Her *Cerberus* to guard her.

    Adorni. A good Dog!

    Clar. Worth twenty Porters.

           Enter Page.

    Page. Keep you open Houfe here?
No Groom t'attend a Gentleman? O, I fpy one,

    Sylli. He means not me, I am fure.

    Page. You, Sirrah! Sheep's-head,
With a Face cut on a Cat-ftick, Do you hear?
You Yeoman-phewterer, conduct me to
The Lady of the Manfion; or my Poignard
Shall difembogue thy Soul.

    Sylli. O terrible!
Difembogue? I talk'd of *Hercules,* and here is one
Bound up in *decimo-fexto.*

    Page. Anfwer, wretch.

    Sylli. Pray you, little Gentleman, be not fo furious;
The Lady keeps her Chamber.

    Page. And we prefent?
Sent in an Embaffy to her? But here is
Her Gentlewoman: Sirrah! hold my Cloak,
While I take a Leap at her Lips. Do it, and neatly;
Or, having firft tripp'd up thy Heels, I'll make
Thy Back my Footftool.   [*Page kiffes* Clarinda.

    Sylli. Tamerlane in little!
Am I turn'd *Turk?* What an Office am I put to!

    Clar. My Lady, gentle Youth, is indifpos'd.

    Page. Tho' fhe were dead and buried, only tell her,
The great Man in the Court, the brave *Fulgentio,*
Defcends to vifit her, and it will raife her
Out of the Grave for Joy.

Enter Fulgentio.

Sylli Here comes another !
The Devil, I fear in his Hóliday Clothes.
Page. So foon !
My Part is at an End then.   Cover my Shoulders ;
When I grow great, thou fhalt ferve me.
Fulgen. Are you, Sirrah,
An Implement of the Houfe ?
Sylli. Sure he will make
A Joint-ftool of me !
Folgen. Or, if you belong
To the Lady of the Place, command her hither.
· *Adorni.* I do not wear her Livery ; yet acknowledge
A Duty to her.   And as little bound
To ferve your peremptory Will, as fhe is
To obey your Summons.   'Twill become you, Sir,
To wait her Leifure ; then, her Pleafure known,
You may prefent your Duty.
Fulgen. Duty, Slave ?
I'll teach you Manners.
Adorni. I'm paft Learning ; make not
A Tumult in the Houfe.
Fulgen. Shall I be brav'd thus ?   [*They draw.*
Sylli. O I am dead ! and now I fwoon.
Clar. Help ! Murther !   [*Falls on his Face.*
Page. Recover, Sirrah ! the Lady's here.

Enter Camiola.

Sylli. Nay, then
I am alive again, and I'll be valiant.
Camiola. What Infolence is this ?   *Adorni,* Hold,
Hold, I command you.
Fulgen. Saucy Groom !
Camiola. Not fo, Sir ;
However, in his Life, he had Dependence
Upon my Father.   Put on your Hat.

Fulgen. In my Prefence, without Leave?

Sylli. He has mine, Madam?

Camiola. And I muſt tell you, Sir, and in plain Language,

Howe'er your glitt'ring Outſide promiſe Gentry,
The Rudeneſs of your Carriage and Behaviour
Speaks you a coarſer Thing.

Sylli. She means a Clown, Sir:
I am her Interpreter, for want of a better.

Camiola. I am a Queen in mine own Houſe; nor muſt you
Expect an Empire here.

Sylli. Sure, I muſt love her
Before the Day, the pretty Soul's ſo valiant.

Camiola. What are you? And what would you with me?

Fulgen. Proud one,
When you know what I am, and what I came for,
And may, on your Submiſſion, proceed to,
You in your Reaſon muſt repent the Coarſeneſs
Of my Entertainment.

Camiola. Why, fine Man, what are you?

Fulgen. A Kinſman of the King's.

Camiola. I cry you Mercy!
For his Sake, not your own. But, grant you are ſo,
'Tis not impoſſible but a King may have
A Fool to his Kinſman,—no Way meaning you, Sir,

Fulgen. You have heard of *Fulgentio.*

Camiola. Long ſince, Sir;
A Suit-broker in Court. He has, the worſt
Report, among good Men, I ever heard of,
For Bribery and Extortion: In their Prayers,
Widows and Orphans curſe him for a Canker
And Caterpillar in the State. I hope, Sir,
You're not the Man; much leſs employ'd by him
As a Smock-agent to me.

Fulgen. I reply not
As you deſerve, being aſſur'd you know me,
Pretending Ignorance of my Perſon, only

To give me a Taste of your Wit: 'Tis well and courtly;
I like a sharp Wit well.

Sylli. I can't endure it!
Nor any of the *Syllies.*

Fulgen. More I know too,
This harsh Induction must serve as a Foil
To the well-tun'd Observance and Respect
You will hereafter pay me, being made
Familiar with my Credit with the King,
And that, (contain your Joy) I deign to love you.

Camiola. Love me? I am not rapt with it.

Fulgen. Hear it again
I love you honestly—Now you admire me.

Camiola. I do, indeed, it being a Word so seldom
Heard from a Courtier's Mouth: But, pray you, deal
　　　　plainly,
Since you find me simple, what might be the Motives
Inducing you to leave the Freedom of
A Batchelor's Life, on your soft Neck to wear,
The stubborn Yoke of Marriage? And, of all
The Beauties in *Palermo,* to choose me,
Poor me? That is the main Point you must treat of.

Fulgen. Why, I will tell you. Of a little Thing
You are a pretty Piece, indifferently fair too;
And, like a new rigg'd Ship both tight, and yare
Well truss'd to bear. Virgins of Giant Size
Are Sluggards at the Sport: But, for my Pleasure,
Give me a neat well-timber'd Gamester like you;
Such need no Spurs,—the Quickness of your Eye
Assures an active Spirit.

Camiola. You're pleasant, Sir;
Yet I presume that there was one Thing in me
Unmention'd yet, that took you more than all
Those Parts you have remember'd.

Fulgen. What?

Camiola. My Wealth, Sir.

Fulgen. You're in the right: without that, Beauty is
A Flower worn in the Morning, at Night trod on:
But Beauty, Youth, and Fortune meeting in you,
I will vouchsafe to marry you.

Camiola. You fpeak well ;
And, in Return, excufe me, Sir, if I
Deliver Reafons why, upon no Terms,
I'll marry you ; I fable not.

   Sylli. I'm glad
To hear this ; I began to have an Ague.   [*Afide.*

   Fulgen. Come, your wife Reafons.

   Camiola. Such as they are, pray you, take them.
Firft, I am doubtful whether you are a Man,
Since, for your Shape trimm'd up in a Lady's Dreffing,
You might pafs for a Woman: Now I love
To deal on Certainties.   And, for the Fairnefs
Of your Complexion, which you think will take me,
The Colour, I muft tell you, in a Man
Is weak and faint, and never will hold out
If put to Labour.   Give me the lovely brown.
A thick curl'd Hair of the fame Dye; broad Shoulders ;
A brawny Arm full of Veins ; a Leg without
An artificial Calf ;—I fufpect yours ;
But let that pafs.

   Sylli. She means me all this while,
For I have every one of thofe good Parts,
O *Sylli !* fortunate *Sylli !*

   Camiola. You are mov'd, Sir.

   Fulgen. Fie ! no; go on.

   Camiola. Then, as you are a Courtier,
A grac'd one too, I fear you have been too forward ;
And fo much for your Perfon.   Rich you are,
Devilifh rich, as 'tis reported, and fure have
The Aids of *Satan*'s little Fiends to get it ;
And what is got upon his Back, muft be
Spent you know where ; the Proverb's ftale.   One
         Word more,
And I have done.

   Fulgen. I'll eafe you of the Trouble,
Coy and difdainful.

   Camiola. Save me, or elfe he'll beat me.

   Fulgen. No, your own Folly fhall ; and, fince you
      put me

To my laſt Charm, look upon this and tremble.
[*Shews the King's Ring.*

Camiola. At the Sight of a fair Ring? The King's, I
take it:
I have ſeen him wear the like: If he hath ſent it
As a Favour to me——

Fulgen. Yes, 'tis very likely;
His dying Mother's Gift, priz'd at his Crown.
By this he does command you to be mine;
By his Gift you are ſo:—You may yet redeem all.

Camiola. You are in a wrong Account ſtill. Tho'
the King may
Diſpoſe of my Life and Goods, my Mind's mine own,
And never ſhall be your's. The King (Heav'n bleſs him!)
Is good and gracious, and, being in himſelf
Abſtemious from baſe and goatiſh Looſeneſs,
Will not compel, againſt their Wills, chaſte Maidens,
To dance in his Minion's Circles. I believe,
Forgetting it, when he waſh'd his Hands, you ſtole it
With an Intent to awe me. But you are cozen'd;
I'm ſtill myſelf and will be.

Fulgen. A proud Haggard,
And not to be reclaim'd! Which of your Grooms,
Your Coachman, Fool, or Footman, miniſters
Night-phyſick to you?

Camiola. You're foul-mouth'd,

Fulgen. Much fairer
Than thy black Soul; and ſo I will proclaim thee.——

Camiola. Were I a Man thou durſt not ſpeak this.

Fulgen. Heaven
So proſper me, as I reſolve to do it
To all Men, and in every Place,—ſcorn'd by
A Tit of Ten-pence? [*Exit* Fulgentio *and his Page.*

Sylli. Now I begin to be valiant:
Nay, I will draw my Sword. O for a Butcher! *

☞ 8 ———— *O for a Butcher!*
Do a Friends Part, &c.

This is a true Picture of a Fop. He is here drawn in his proper
Features—A Coward. Nothing could be more abjectly fearful, than

·Do a Friend's Part; 'Pray you, carry him the Length
    of't.
I give him three Years and a Day to match my Toledo;
And then we'll fight like Dragons.

    Adorni. Pray, have Patience.

    Camiola. I may live to have Vengeance: My *Bertoldo*
Would not have heard this.

    Adorni. Madam.——

    Camiola. 'Pray you, ſpare
Your Language; Pr'thee Fool, make me merry:

    Sylli. That is my Office ever.

    Adorni. I muſt do,
Not talk; this glorious Gallant ſhall hear from me.

                        [*Exeunt.*

SCENE III.

The Caſtle at Siena.

The Chambers diſcharg'd. A Flouriſh as to an Aſſault.
Gonzaga, Pierio, Roderigo, Jacomo, *and Soldiers.*

    Gonz. Is the Breach made aſſaultable?

    Pierio. Yes, and the Moat
Fill'd up; the Cannoneer hath done his Parts,
We may enter ſix a-breaſt.

    Roder. There's not a Man
Dares ſhew himſelf upon the Wall,

this our Bravado, when in Danger: But, now his Enemy is gone,
he ſwaggers about moſt courageouſly. *Now I begin to be valiant;* nay,
I will draw my Sword. O for a Butcher! The bloody cruel Temper * of one: He wiſhes he could act like one of them. Then
turning to *Adorni* with the ſame intrepid Reſolution, he ſays, *Do a
Friend's Part; pray you, carry him the Length of't,* &c.

            * *O for a Butcher! The bloody cruel Temper,* &c.

    It is impoſſible that the Words ſhould convey the Senſe that the Editor attri-
butes to them.. It is a difficult Paſſage, and my Conjecture may poſſibly be er-
roneous, but I ſhould read it thus:

        Nay I will draw my Sword: O for a Bout! Here
        Do a Friend's Part, &c. M. M.

Jacomo. Defeat not
The Soldiers hoped-for Spoil.
 Pierio. If you, Sir,
Delay the Affault, and the City be given up
To your Difcretion, you in Honour cannot
Ufe the Extremity of War, but, in
Compaffion to 'em, you to us prove cruel.
 Jacomo. And an Enemy to yourfelf.
 Roder. A Hindrance to
The brave Revenge you've vow'd.
 Gonz. Temper your Heat,
And lofe not, by too fudden Rafhnefs, that
Which, be but patient, will be offer'd to you.
Security ufhers Ruin ; proud Contempt
Of an Enemy, three Parts vanquifh'd, with Defire
And Greedinefs of Spoil, hath often wrefted
A certain Victory from the Conqu'ror's Gripe.
Difcretion is the Tutor of the War,
Valour the Pupil ; and, when we command
With Lenity, and our Direction's follow'd
With Chearfulnefs, a profp'rous End muft crown
Our Works well undertaken.
 Roder. Ours are finifh'd.
 Pierio. If we make Ufe of Fortune.
 Gonz. Her falfe Smiles
Deprive you of your Judgments. The Condition
Of our Affairs exacts a double Care.
And like bifronted *Janus*, we muft look
Backward, as forward. Tho' a flatt'ring Calm
Bids us urge on, a fudden Tempeft rais'd,
Not fear'd, much lefs expected, in our Rear
May foully fall upon us, and diftract us
To our Confufion.

Enter Scout.

Our Scout ! what brings
Thy ghaftly Looks and fudden Speed ?
 Scout. Th' Affurance
Of a new Enemy.

I

Gonz. This I forefaw and fear'd.
What are they ? Know'ft thou ?

Scout. They are, by their Colours,
Sicilians, bravely mounted, and the Brightnefs
Of their Rich Armours doubly gilded with
Reflection of the Sun.

Gonz. From *Sicily* ?
The King in League! No War proclaim'd! 'Tis foul:
But this muft be prevented, not difputed.
Ha! how is this ? Your Oftrich plumes that but
E'en now, like Quills of Porcupine feem'd to threaten
The Stars, drop at the Rumour of a Shower;
And like to captive Colours fweep the Earth:
Bear up; but, in great Dangers, greater Minds
Are never proud. Shall a few loofe Troops, untrain'd
But in a cuftomary Oftentation
Prefented as a Sacrifice to your Valours,
Caufe a Dejection in you.

Pierio. No Dejection.

Roder. However ftartl'd, where you lead we'll follow.

Gonz. 'Tis bravely faid. We will not ftay their
                Charge,
But meet 'em Man to Man, and Horfe to Horfe.
Pierio, in our Abfence hold our Place,
And with our Footmen, and thofe fickly Troops,
Prevent a Sally. I in mine own Perfon,
With part of the Cavalry, will bid
Thefe Hunters welcome to a bloody Breakfaft:
But I lofe Time.

Pierio. I'll to my Charge.   [*Exit* Pierio.

Gonz. And we
To ours: I'll bring you on.

Jacomo. If we come off,
It's not amifs; if not, my 'State is fettl'd.

                              [*Exeunt, Alarm.*

SCENE IV. Siena.

Ferdinand, Drufo, and Livio *above.*

Ferd. No Aids from *Sicily?* Hath Hope forfook us?
And that vain Comfort to Affliction, Pity,
By our vow'd Friend deny'd us? We can nor live
Nor die with Honour : Like Beafts in a Toil
We wait the Leifure of the bloody Hunter,
Who is not fo far reconcil'd to us,
As in one Death to give a Period
To our Calamities; but in delaying
The Fate we cannot fly from, ftarv'd with Wants,
We die this Night to live again To-morrow,
And fuffer greater Torments.

Drufo. There is not
Three Days Provifion for every Soldier,
At an Ounce of Bread a Day, left in the City.

Liv. To die the Beggar's Death, with Hunger made
Anatomies while we live, cannot but crack
Our Heart-ftrings with Vexation.

Ferd. Would they would break,
Break altogether! How willingly, like *Cato*,
Could I tear out my Bowels, rather than
Look on the Conqueror's infulting Face;
But that Religion, and the horrid Dream ⁹
To be fuffer'd in th' other World, denies it.
What News with thee?

Enter Soldier.

Sold. From the Turret of the Fort,
By the rifing Clouds of Duft, thro' which, like Lightning,
The Splendour of bright Arms fometimes break thro',
I did defcry fome Forces making towards us;

9 ————————*And the horrid Dream,* &c.

An imitation of *Shakefpeare's Hamlet,* Act 3d.

————————To die! to fleep!
To fleep, perchance to dream! Ay, this is the Rub
That makes Calamity of fo long Life——— *D.*

And, from the Camp, as emulous of their Glory,
The General, (for I know him by his Horfe)
And bravely feconded, encounter'd 'em.
Their Greetings were too rough for Friends; their
             Swords,
And not their Tongues, exchanging Courtefies.
By this the main Battalias are join'd;
And, if you pleafe to be Spectators of
The horrid Iffue, I will bring you where,
As in a Theatre, you may fee their Fates
In purple Gore prefented.
    Ferd. Heav'n, if yet
Thou art appeas'd for my Wrong done to *Aurelia*,
Take Pity of my Miferies!—Lead the Way, Friend.
                            [*Exeunt.*

SCENE V.

Before the Caftle of Siena.

A long Charge, after a Flourifh for Victory.

Gonzaga, Jacomo, *and* Roderigo *wounded.* Bertoldo,
    Gafparo, *and* Anthonio *Prifoners.*

    Gonz. We have 'em yet, tho' they coft us dear. This
           was
Charg'd home and bravely follow'd. Be yourfelves
True Mirrors to each other's Worth; and, looking
With noble Emulation on his Wounds
(The glorious Liv'ry of triumphant War)
                    [*To* Jacomo *and* Roderigo.
Imagine thefe with equal Grace appear
Upon yourfelf. The bloody Sweat you've fuffer'd
In this laborious, nay, toilfome Harveft,
Yields a rich Crop of Conqueft, and the Spoil,
Moft precious Balfam to a Soldier's Hurts,
Will eafe and cure 'em. Let me look upon
                    [*To* Gafparo *and* Anthonio.

The Prifoners Faces. Oh, how much transform'd
From what they were! O *Mars !* were thefe Toys fa-
fhion'd
To undergo the Burthen of thy Service?
The Weight of their defenfive Armour bruis'd
Their weak effem'nate Limbs, and would have forc'd
'em
In a hot Day without a Blow to yield.

 Anth. This Infultation fhews not manly in you.

 Gonz. To Men I had forborn it; you are Women,
Or, at the beft, loofe Carpet-knights. What Fury
Seduc'd you to exchange your Eafe in Court
For Labour in the Field? Perhaps, you thought
To charge thro' Duft and Blood an armed Foe,
Was but like graceful running at the Ring
For a wanton Miftrefs' Glove, and the Encounter
A foft Impreffion on her Lips. But you
Are gaudy Butterflies, and I wrong myfelf
In parl'ing with you.

 Gafp. Væ victis ! now we prove it.

 Roder. But here's one fafhion'd in another Mould,
And made of tougher Metal.

 Gonz. True; I owe him
For this Wound bravely given.

 Bert. O that Mountains
Were heap'd upon me, that I might expire
A Wretch no more remember'd!

 Gonz. Look up, Sir,
To be o'ercome deferves no Shame. If you
Had fallen ingloriously, or could accufe
Your want of Courage in Refiftance, 'twere
To be lamented: But, fince you perform'd
As much as could be hop'd for from a Man,
(Fortune his Enemy) you wrong yourfelf
In this Dejection. I am honour'd in
My Victory o'er you; but to have thefe
My Prifoners, is, in my true Judgment, rather
Captivity than a Triumph. You fhall find
Fair Quarter from me, and your many Wounds

(Which I hope are not mortal) with such Care
Look'd to and cur'd, as if your nearest Friend
Attended on you.

 Bert. When you know me better,
You will make void this Promise: can you call me
Into your Memory?

 Gonz. The brave *Bertoldo!*
A Brother of our Order! by St. *John,*
(Our holy Patron) I am more amaz'd,
Nay, thunderstruck with thy Apostacy
And *Precipice* from the most solemn Vows
Made unto Heaven, when this, the glorious Badge
Of our Redeemer was conferr'd upon thee
By the great Master, than if I had seen
A reprobate *Jew,* an Atheist, *Turk,* or *Tartar*
Baptiz'd in our Religion.

 Bert. This I look'd for,
And am resolv'd to suffer.

 Gonz. Fellow-Soldiers,
Behold this Man, and, taught by his Example,
Know that 'tis safer far to play with Lightning,
Than trifle in Things sacred.—In my Rage, [*Weeps.*
I shed these at the Funeral of his Virtue,
Faith and Religion—why, I will tell you;
He was a Gentleman so train'd up, and fashion'd
For noble Uses, and his Youth did promise
Such Certainties, more than Hopes, of great Atchieve-
   ments,
As if the Christian World had stood oppos'd
Against the *Ottoman* Race to try the Fortune
Of one Encounter, this *Bertoldo* had been,
(For his Knowledge to direct, and matchless Courage
To execute) without a Rival, by the
Votes of good Men chosen General,
As the prime Soldier and most deserving
Of all that wear the Cross; which now, in Justice,
I thus tear from him.

 Bert. Let me die with it
Upon my Breast.

 Gonz. No; by this thou wert sworn
On all Occasions, as a Knight, to guard

Weak Ladies from Oppreſſion, and never
To draw thy Sword againſt 'em; whereas thou,
In Hope of Gain or Glory, when a Princeſs,
And ſuch a Princeſs as *Aurelia* is,
Was diſpoſſeſs'd by Violence, of what was
Her true Inheritance, againſt thine Oath
Haſt to thy uttermoſt labour'd to uphold
Her falling Enemy. But thou ſhalt pay
A heavy Forfeiture, and learn too late,
Valour, employ'd in an ill Quarrel, turns
To Cowardice, and Virtue then puts on
Foul Vice's Vizard. This is that which cancels
All Friendſhip's Bands between us.——Bear 'em off;
(I will hear no Reply) and let the Ranſom
Of theſe, for they are yours, be highly rated.
In this I do but right, and let it be
Stil'd Juſtice, and not wilful Cruelty.   *[Exeunt.*

The End of the Second Act.

ACT III. SCENE I.

Before the Walls of Siena.

Gonzaga, Aſtutio, Roderigo, *and* Jacomo.

Gonzaga.

WHAT I have done, Sir, by the Law of Arms
I can and will make good.
Aſtutio. I've no Commiſſion
To expoſtulate the Act. Theſe Letters ſpeak
The King my Maſter's Love to you, and his
Vow'd Service to the Dutcheſs, on whoſe Perſon
I am to give Attendance.
  Gonz. At this Inſtant,
She's at *Pienza :* You may ſpare the Trouble

Of riding thither; I have advertised her
Of our Success, and on what humble Terms
Siena stands : Tho' presently I can
Possess it, I defer it, that she may
Enter her own, and, as she please, dispose of
The Prisoners and the Spoil.

    Astutio. I thank you, Sir.
I' the mean Time, if I may have your Licence,
I have a Nephew, and one once my Ward ;
For whose Liberties and Ransoms I would gladly
Make Composition.

    Gonz. They are, as I take it,
Call'd *Gasparo* and *Anthonio.*

    Astutio. The same, Sir.

    Gonz. For them you must treat with these : But, for
        Bertoldo,
He is mine own : If the King will ransom him,
He pays down fifty thousand Crowns ; if not
He lives and dies my Slave.

    Astutio. Pray you a Word——
The King will rather thank you to detain him,
Than give one Crown to free him.

    Gonz. At his Pleasure.
I'll send the Prisoners under Guard : My Business
Calls me another Way.   [*Exit* Gonzaga.

    Astutio. My Service waits you.
Now, Gentlemen, do not deal like Merchants with me,
But noble Captains ; you know, in great Minds,
Posse, & nolle, nobile.

    Roder. Pray you, speak
Our Language.

    Jacomo. I find not, in my Commission,
An Officer's bound to speak or understand
More than his Mother-tongue.

    Roder. If he speak that
After Midnight, 'tis remarkable.

    Astutio. In plain Terms, then,
Anthonio is your Prisoner ; *Gasparo,* yours.

    Jacomo. You are i' the right.

Aſtutio. At what Sum do you rate
Their ſeveral Ranſoms?

Roder, I muſt make my Market
As the Commodity coſt me.

Aſtutio. As it coſt you?
You did not buy your Captainſhip? Your Deſert,
I hope, advanc'd you.

Roder. How? It well appears
You are no Soldier. Deſert in theſe Days?
Deſert may make a Serjeant to a Colonel,
And it may hinder him from riſing higher;
But, if it ever get a Company
(A Company; pray you, mark me) without Money,
Or private Service done for the General's Miſtreſs,
With a Commendatory Epiſtle from her,
I will turn Lancepeſade.

Jacomo. Pray you, obſerve, Sir:
I ſerv'd two 'Prenticeſhips, juſt fourteen Years,
Trailing the puiſſant Pike; and half ſo long
Had the Right-hand File; and I fought well, 'twas
    ſaid, too:
But I might have ſerv'd, and fought, and ſerv'd till
    Doomſday,
And ne'er have carried a Flag, but for the Legacy
A buckſome Widow of threeſcore bequeath'd me,
And that too, my Back knows, I labour'd hard for,
But was better paid.

Aſtutio. Y're merry with yourſelves:
But this is from the Purpoſe.

Roder. To the Point then.
Pris'ners are not ta'en every Day; and, when
We have 'em, we muſt make the beſt Uſe of 'em.
Our Pay is little to the Part[10] we ſhould bear,
And that ſo long a coming, that 'tis ſpent

---

10 ——————*Part we ſhould bear.*

The Author in all Probability wrote *Port,* meaning that a
Captain's Pay did not anſwer his Expences, and the manner of
living which his rank obliged him to ſupport. *D.*

Before we have it, and hardly wipes off Scores
At the Tavern and th' Ordinary.

Jacomo. You may add too,
Our Sport took up on Trust.

Roder. Peace, thou Smock-vermin !
Discover Commanders Secrets ? In a Word, Sir,
We have enquir'd, and find our Pris'ners rich :
Two thousand Crowns a-piece our Companies cost us ;
And so much each of us will have, and that
In present Pay.

Jacomo. It is too little : Yet,
Since you have said the Word, I am content;
But will not go a Gazet less. "

Astutio. Since you are not
To be brought lower, there is no evading :
I'll be your Pay-master.

Roder. We desire no better.

Astutio. But not a Word of what's agreed between us,
'Till I have school'd my Gallants.

Jacomo. I am dumb, Sir.

Enter a Guard: Bertoldo, Anthonio, *and* Gasparo *in Irons.*

Bert. And where remov'd now ? Hath the Tyrant found out
Worse Usage for us ?

Anth. Worse it cannot be..
My Greyhound has fresh Straw, and Scraps in his Kennel ;
But we have neither.

Gasp. Did I ever think
To wear such Garters on Silk Stockings ? Or

☞ 11 *But will not go a* Gazet *less.*

From the Word *Gazetta*, a Farthing, *Massinger* makes Use of the same Word, and to the same Purpose, in the first Scene of the *Guardian.*

Gazetta is a *Venetian* Coin ; and being the Price paid for the first Newspapers that were printed, they obtained from thence the Name of Gazettes. *M. M.*

That my too curious Appetite, that turn'd
At the Sight of Godwits, Pheafant, Partridge, Quails,
Larks, Wood-cocks, collar'd Salmon, as coarfe Diet,
Would leap at a mouldy Cruft ?

Anth. And go without it ;
So oft as I do? Oh! how have I jeer'd
The City Entertainment !   A huge Shoulder
Of glorious Ram Mutton, feconded
With a Pair of tame Cats, or Conies, a Crab-tart
With a worthy Loin of Veal and valiant Capon,
Mortify'd to grow tender.—Thefe I fcorn'd
From their plentiful Horn of Abundance, tho' invited :
But now I could carry my own Stool to a Tripe,
And call their Chitterlings Charity, and blefs the Foun-
   der.

Bert. O that I were no farther fenfible
Of my Miferies than you are! You, like Beafts,
Feel only Stings of Hunger, and complain not
But when you're empty : But your narrow Souls
(If you have any) cannot comprehend
How infupportable the Torments are,
Which a free and noble Soul, made captive, fuffers :
Moft miferable Men ! and what am I, then,
That envy you ? Fetters, tho' made of Gold,
Exprefs bafe Thraldom, and all Delicates
Prepar'd by *Midian* Cooks for Epicures,
When not our own, are bitter ; Quilts, fill'd high
With Goffemore and Rofes, cannot yield
The Body foft Repofe, the Mind kept waking
With Anguifh and Affliction.

Aftutio. My good Lord——

Bert. This is no Time nor Place for Flatt'ry, Sir :
Pray you, ftile me as I am, a Wretch, forfaken
Of the World, as myfelf.

Aftutio. I would it were
In me to help you.

Bert. If that you want Power, Sir,
Lip-Comfort cannot cure me.—Pray you, leave me
To mine own private Thoughts.

Aſtutio. My valiant Nephew!   [*Walks by.*
And my more than warlike Ward! I am glad to ſee you
After your glorious Conqueſts. Are theſe Chains
Rewards for your good Service? If they are,
You ſhould wear 'em on your Necks (ſince they are
    maſſey)
Like Aldermen of the Ward.

    Anth. You jeer us too.

    Gaſp. Good Uncle, name not (as you are a Man of
    Honour)
That fatal Word of War; the very Sound of it
Is more dreadful than a Cannon.

    Anth. But redeem us
From this Captivity, and I'll vow hereafter
Never to wear a Sword, or cut my Meat
With a Knife that has an Edge or Point. I'll ſtarve firſt,

    Gaſp. I will cry Brooms or Cat's Meat in *Palermo*;
Turn Porter, carry Burthens; any Thing,
Rather than live a Soldier.

    Aſtutio. This ſhould have
Been thought upon before. At what Price, think you,
Your two wiſe heads are rated?

    Anth. A Calve's Head is
More worth than mine; I'm ſure it had more Brains in't,
Or I had ne'er come here.

    Roder. And I will eat it
With Bacon. if I have not ſpeedy Ranſom.

    Anth. And a little Garlick too, for your own Sake,
    Sir;
'Twill boil in your Stomach elſe.

    Gaſp. Beware of mine,
Or th' Horns may choak you. I am marry'd, Sir.

    Anth. You ſhall have my Row of Houſes near the
    Palace.

    Gaſp. And my Villa.—All——

    Anth. All that we have.   [*To* Aſtutio.

    Aſtutio. Well, have more Wit hereafter: For this
    Time
You're ranſom'd.

    Jacomo. Off with their Irons.

Roder. Do, do :

If you are ours again, you know your Price.

Anth. Pray you, difpatch us : I fhall ne'er believe
I am a Freeman, 'till I fet my Foot
In *Sicily* again, and drink *Palermo*,
And in *Palermo* too.

Aftutio. The Wind fits fair,
You fhall aboard To-night : With the rifing Sun
You may touch upon the Coaft. But take your Leaves
Of the late General, firft.

Gafp. I will be brief.

Anth. And I.—My Lord, Heaven keep you.

Gafp. Yours, to ufe
In the Way of Peace ; but, as your Soldiers, never.

Anth. A Pox of War ! No more of War !

Bert. Have you

[*Exeunt* Roderigo, Jacomo, Anthonio, *and* Gafparo.
Authority to loofe their Bonds, yet leave
The Brother of your King, whofe Worth difdains
Comparifon with fuch as thefe, in Irons ?
If Ranfom may redeem them, I have Lands,
A Patrimony of mine own affign'd me
By my deceafed Sire, to fatisfy
Whate'er can be demanded for my Freedom.

Aftutio. I wifh you had, Sir ; but the King, who
        yields
No Reafon for his Will, in his Difpleafure
Hath feiz'd on all you had ; nor will *Gonzaga*,
Whofe Pris'ner now you are, accept of lefs
Than fifty thoufand Crowns.

Bert. I find it now,
That Mifery never comes alone. But, grant
The King is yet inexorable, Time
May work him to a Feeling of my Suff'rings.
I've Friends that fwore their Lives and Fortunes were
At my Devotion, and among the reft
Yourfelf, my Lord, when, forfeited to the Law
For a foul Murther, and in cold Blood done,
I made your Life my Gift, and reconcil'd you
To this incenfed King, and got your Pardon.

—Beware Ingratitude. I know you're rich,
And may pay down the Sum.

Aſtutio. I might, my Lord ;
But pardon me.

Bert. And will *Aſtutio* prove, then,
To pleaſe a paſſionate Man, the King's no more,
Falſe to his Maker and his Reaſon, which
Commands more than I aſk ? O Summer-Friendſhip,
Whoſe flatt'ring Leaves that ſhadow'd us in
Our Proſperity, with the leaſt Guſt drop off
In th' Autumn of Adverſity ! How like
A Priſon is to a Grave ! When dead, we are
With ſolemn Pomp brought thither ; and our Heirs,
(Maſking their Joy in falſe diſſembled Tears)
Weep o'er the Hearſe ; but Earth no ſooner covers
The Earth brought thither, but they turn away
With inward Smiles, the Dead no more remember'd.
So, enter'd in a Priſon.——

Aſtutio. My Occaſions
Command me hence, my Lord.

Bert. Pray you, leave me, do ;
And tell the cruel King that I will wear
Theſe Fetters, till my Fleſh and they are one
Incorporated Subſtance. In myſelf,
As in a glaſs, I'll look on human Frailty,
And curſe the Height of royal Blood : ſince I,
In being born near to *Jove*, am near his Thunder.

                      [Exit Aſtutio.
Cedars once ſhaken with a Storm, their own
Weight grubs their Roots out.—Lead me where you
        pleaſe ;
I am his, not Fortune's Martyr, and will die
The great Example of his Cruelty.

                      [Exit with the Guard.

SCENE II.

A Grove near the Palace at Palermo.

Adorni. He undergoes my Challenge, and contemns
    it,
And threatens me with the late Edict made
'Gainst Duellists, that Altar Cowards fly to. [12]
But I, that am engag'd, and nourish in me
A higher Aim than fair *Camiola* dreams of,
Must not fit down thus. In the Court I dare not
Attempt him; and in Publick he's fo guarded
With a Herd of Parafites, Clients, Fools and Suitors,
That a Musket cannot reach him.—My Defigns
Admit of no Delay. This is her Birth-day,
Which with a fit and due Solemnity
Camiola celebrates; and on it, all fuch
As love to ferve her, ufually prefent
A tributary Duty. I'll have fomething
To give, if my Intelligence prove true,
Shall find Acceptance. I'm told, near this Grove
Fulgentio every Morning makes his Markets
With his Petitioners. I may prefent him
With a fharp Petition.——Ha! 'tis he: my Fate
Be ever blefs'd for't.

Enter Fulgentio.

Fulgen. Command fuch as wait me,
Not to prefume, at the leaft for half an Hour,
To prefs on my Retirements.

<hr>

☞ 12 *'Gainst Duellifts, then, &c.*

Fulgentio put up his Challenge, and, inftead of accepting it,
threatened him with the Law againft Duels. This *Adorni* would
reprefent as bafe Treatment. A Man of Courage he fuppofes would
not have taken the Advantage of fuch a Law. *That Altar,* that
was a Sanctuary Cowards only would fly to. The Senfe here
plainly requires the Alteration I have made of, *that* for *then,* which
in the former Reading was fcarce intelligible.

I take *the* to be the right Reading, which might eafily be miftak-
en for *then.* D.

Page. I will fay, Sir, you are at your Prayers,
Fulgen. That will not find Belief;
Courtiers have fomething elfe to do.—Be gone, Sir.
Challeng'd! 'tis well. And by a Groom! ftill better.
Was this Shape made to fight? I have a Tongue yet,
Howe'er no Sword, to kill him; and what Way
This Morning I'll refolve of.   [*Exit* Fulgentio.
    Adorni. I fhall crofs ...
Your Refolution, or fuffer for you.   [*Exit* Adorni.

SCENE III.

, Camiola's *Houfe.*

Camiola : *divers Servants with Prefents,*

Enter Sylli *and* Clarinda.

Sylli. What are all thefe?
Clar. Servants with feveral Prefents,
And rich ones too.
    1 *Serv.* With her beft Wifhes, Madam,
Of many fuch Days to you, the Lady *Petula*
Prefents you with this Fan.
    2 *Serv.* This Diamond
From your Aunt *Honoria.*
    3 *Serv.* This Piece of Plate
From your Uncle, old *Vincentio,* with your Arms
Graven upon it.
    Camiola. Good Friends! they are too
Munificent in their Love and Favour to me.
Out of my Cabinet return fuch Jewels
As this directs you; for your Pains;—and yours;—
Nor muft you be forgotten. Honour me
With the drinking of a Health.
    1 *Serv.* Gold, on my Life!
    2 *Serv.* She fcorns to give bafe Silver.
    3 *Serv.* Would fhe had been
Born every Month in the Year!

1 *Serv.* Month.? every Day.

2 *Serv.* Shew such another Maid.

3 *Serv.* All Happiness wait you.

Sylli. I'll see your Will done.

[*Exeunt* Sylli, Clarinda, *and Servants.*

Enter Adorni *wounded.*

Camiola. How! *Adorni* wounded!

Adorni. A Scratch got in your Service, else not worth
Your Observation; I bring not, Madam,
In Honour of your Birth-day, antique Plate,
Or Pearl, for which the savage *Indian* dives
Into the Bottom of the Sea; nor Diamonds
Hewn from steep Rocks with Danger: Such as give
To those that have what they themselves want, aim at
A glad Return with Profit: Yet, despise not
My Off'ring at the Altar of your Favour;
Nor let the Lowness of the Giver lessen
The Height of what's presented. Since it is
A precious Jewel, almost forfeited,
And, dimm'd with Clouds of Infamy, redeem'd,
And, in its natural Splendor, with Addition,
Restor'd to the true Owner.

Camiola. How is this?

Adorni. Not to hold you in Suspense, I bring you,
Madam,
Your wounded Reputation cur'd; the Sting
Of virulent Malice, fest'ring your fair Name,
Pluck'd out and trod on: That proud Man, that was
Deny'd the Honour of your Bed, yet durst
With his untrue Reports strumpet your Fame,
Compell'd by me, hath giv'n himself the Lye,
And in his own Blood wrote it.—You may read
Fulgentio subscrib'd.

Camiola. I am amaz'd!

Adorni. It does deserve it, Madam. Common Service
Is fit for Hinds, and the Reward proportion'd

To their Conditions. Therefore, look not on me
As a Follower of your Father's Fortunes, or
One that fubfifts on.yours.—You frown.! my Service
Merits not this Afpect.

∴.*Camiola.* Which of my Favours,
I might fay Bounties, hath begot and nourifh'd
This more than rude Prefumption? Since you had
An Itch to try your defp'rate Valour, wherefore
Went you not to the War? Couldft thou fuppofe
My.Innocence could ever.fall fo low
As to have Need of thy.rafh Sword to guard it
Againft malicious Slander? O how much
Thofe Ladies are deceiv'd and cheated, when . .
The Clearnefs and Integrity of their Actions
Do·not defend themfelves, and ftand.fecure
On their own Bafes? Such as in·a Colour
Of feeming Service give Protection to 'em,
Betray their own Strengths. Malice, fcorn'd, puts out
Itfelf; but argu'd,.gives·a kind of Credit
To a falfe Accufation. In this,
This your moft memorable Service, you believ'd
You did me Right; but you have wrong'd me more
In your Defence of my undoubted Honour,
Than falfe *Fulgentio* could. .

Adorni. I am forry what
Was fo well intended, is fo ill receiv'd.

Enter Clarinda.

Yet, under your Correction, you wifh'd
Bertoldo had been prefent.

Camiola. True, I did:
But he and you, Sir, are not Parallels,
Nor muft you think yourfelf fo.

Adorni. I am what
You'll pleafe to have me.

·*Camiola.* If *Bertoldo* had
Punifh'd *Fulgentio's* Infolence, it had fhown
His Love to her, whom in his Judgment he
Vouchfaf'd to make his Wife; a Height, I hope,

Which you dare not afpire to. The fame Actions
Suit not all Men alike :—But I perceive
Repentance in your Looks. For this Time, leave me:
I may forgive, perhaps forget, your Folly :
Conceal yourfelf till this Storm be blown over.
You will be fought for ; yet, if my Eftate
       [*Gives him her Hand to kifs.*
Can hinder it, fhall not fuffer in my Service.

 Adorni. This is fomething yet, tho' I .mifs'd the
  Mark I fhot at.   [*Exit* Adorni.

 Camiola. This Gentleman is of a noble Temper ;
And I too harfh, perhaps, in my Reproof :
Was I not, *Clarinda ?*

 Clar. I am not to cenfure
Your Actions, Madam : but there are a thoufand
Ladies, and of good Fame, in fuch a Caufe,
Would be proud of fuch a Servant.

 Camiola. It may be ;

     Enter a Servant.

Let me offend in this Kind.
Why uncall'd for ?

 Serv. The Signiors, Madam, *Gafparo* and *Antonio,*
(Selected Friends of the renown'd *Bertoldo*)
Put afhore this Morning.

 Camiola. Without him ?

 Serv. I think fo.

 Camiola. Never think more then.

 Serv. They have been at Court.
Kifs'd the King's Hand ; and, their firft Duties done
To him, appear ambitious to tender
To you their fecond Service.

 Camiola. Wait 'em hither.   [*Exit Servant.*
Fear, do not rack me ! Reafon, now, if ever,
Hafte with thy Aids, and tell me, fuch a Wonder
As my *Bertoldo* is, with fuch Care fafhion'd,
Muft not, nay, cannot, in Heav'n's Providence

Enter Anthonio, Gasparo, *and Servant.*

So soon miscarry; pray you, forbear; ere you
Take the Privilege, as Strangers, to salute me,
(Excuse my Manners) make me first understand,
How it is with *Bertoldo?*

Gasp. The Relation
Will not, I fear, deserve your Thanks.

Anth. I wish
Some other should inform you.

Camiola. Is he dead?
You see, tho' with some Fear, I dare enquire it.

Gasp. Dead? Would that were the worst, a Debt
were paid then;
Kings in their Birth owe Nature.

Camiola. Is there aught
More terrible than Death?

Anth. Yes, to a Spirit
Like his; cruel Imprisonment, and that
Without the Hope of Freedom.

Camiola. You abuse me:
The royal King cannot, in Love to Virtue
(Tho' all Springs of Affection were dry'd up)
But pay his Ransom.

Gasp. When you know what 'tis,
You will think otherwise—No less will do it
Than fifty thousand Crowns.

Camiola. A petty Sum;
The Price weigh'd with the Purchase; fifty thousand?
To the King 'tis nothing. He that can spare more
To his Minion for a Masque, cannot but ransom
Such a Brother at a Million—You wrong
The King's Magnificence.

Anth. In your Opinion;
But 'tis most certain. He does not alone
In himself refuse to pay it; but forbids
All other Men.

Camiola. Are you sure of this?

Gaſp. You may read
The Edict to that Purpoſe, publiſh'd by him:
That will reſolve you.

Camiola. Poſſible? Pray you, ſtand off;
If I do not mutter Treaſon to myſelf,
My Heart will break: Yet I will not curſe him; [*Aſide.*
He is my King—The News you have deliver'd,
Makes me weary of your Company; we'll ſalute
When we meet next. I'll bring you to the Door.
—Nay, pray you, no more Compliments.

Gaſp. One thing more,
And that's ſubſtantial: Let your *Adorni*
Look to himſelf.

Anth. The King is much incens'd
Againſt him for *Fulgentio.*

Camiola. As I am
For your Slowneſs to depart.

Both. Farewel, ſweet Lady!
[*Exeunt* Gaſparo *and* Anthonio.

Camiola. O more than impious Times! when not
alone
Subordinate Miniſters of Juſtice are
Corrupted and ſeduc'd, but Kings themſelves
(The greater Wheels by which the leſſer move)
Are broken and disjointed! could it be elſe,
A King, to ſooth his politick Ends, ſhould ſo far
Forſake his Honour, as at once to break
Th' Adamant Chains of Nature and Religion,
To bind up Atheiſm, as a Defence [13]
To his Dark Counſels? Will it ever be?
That to deſerve too much is dangerous,

☞ [13] *To bind up Atheiſm,* &c.

This appears to me to be falſe; I would read,

To *bring* up Atheiſm, &c.

To *bind* is certainly preferable to the propoſed Amendment; but I ſee nothing Atheiſtical in the King's Conduct, according to the preſent Uſe of that Word. *M. M.*

And Virtue, when too eminent, a Crime?
Muft She ferve Fortune ftill? Or, when ftripp'd of
Her gay and glorious Favours, lofe the Beauties
Of her own natural Shape? O my *Bertoldo!*
Thou only Sun in Honour's Sphere, how foon
Art thou eclips'd and darken'd! not the Nearnefs
Of Blood prevailing on the King; nor all
The Benefits to the gen'ral Good difpens'd
Gaining a Retribution! but that
To owe a Courtefy to a fimple Virgin
Would take from thy deferving, I find in me
Some Sparks of Fire, which, fann'd with Honour's
          Breath,
Might rife into a Flame, and in Men darken
Their ufurp'd Splendor. Ha! my Aim is high,
And, for the Honour of my Sex, to fall fo,
Can never prove inglorious.—'Tis refolv'd:
Call in *Adorni.*

Clar. I am happy in
Such Employment, Madam.   [*Exit* Clarinda.

Camiola. He's a Man,
I know, that at a reverend Diftance loves me,
And fuch are ever faithful.   What a Sea
Of melting Ice I walk on! what ftrange Cenfures
Am I to undergo! but good Intents
Deride all future Rumours.

          Enter Clarinda *and* Adorni.

Adorni. I obey
Your Summons, Madam.
     Camiola. Leave the Place, *Clarinda:*
One Woman, in a Secret of fuch Weight,
Wife Men may think too much.   Nearer, *Adorni.*
                              [*Exit* Clarinda.
I warrant it with a Smile.
     Adorni. I cannot afk
Safer Protection, what's your Will?
     Camiola. To doubt
Your ready Defire to ferve me, or prepare you

With the Repetition of former Merits,
Would, in my Diffidence, wrong you : But I will,
And without Circumstance, in the Trust that I
Impose upon you, free you from Suspicion.

Adorni. I foster none of you.

Camiola. I know you do not,
You are *Adorni*, by the Love you owe me.——

Adorni. The surest Conjuration.

Camiola. Take me with you.——
Love born of Duty ; but advance no further.
You are, Sir, as I said, to do me a Service,
To undertake a Task, in which your Faith,
Judgment, Discretion—in a Word, your all
That's good, must be engag'd ; nor must you study
In the Execution, but what may make
For th' Ends I aim at.

Adorni. They admit no Rivals.

Camiola. You answer well.—You have heard of *Ber-*
          toldo's
Captivity, and the King's Neglect ; the Greatness
Of his Ransom, fifty thousand Crowns, *Adorni* ;
Two Parts of my Estate.

Adorni. To what tends this ?

Camiola. Yet I so love the Gentleman (for to you
I will confess my Weakness) that I purpose
Now, when he is forsaken by the King,
And his own Hopes, to ransom, and receive him
Into my Bosom as my lawful Husband,

              [Adorni *starts, and seems troubled.*
Why change you Colour ?

Adorni. 'Tis in Wonder of
Your Virtue, Madam.

Camiola. You must therefore to
Siena for me, and pay to *Gonzaga*
This Ransom for his Liberty ; you shall
Have Bills of Exchange along with you. Let him
          swear
A solemn Contract to me, for you must be

My principal Witnefs, if he fhould—But why
Do I entertain thefe Jealoufies? You will do this?
   Adorni. Faithfully, Madam.—But not live long af-
      ter.   [*Afide.*
   Camiola. One Thing I had forgot.—Befides his Free-
      dom,
He may want Accommodations; furnifh him
According to his Birth. And from *Camiola*
Deliver this Kifs, printed on your Lips   [*Kiffes him.*
Seal'd on his Hand.—You fhall not fee my Blufhes;
I'll inftantly difpatch you.   [*Exit* Camiola.
   Adorni. I'm half-hang'd
Out of the Way already.—Was there ever
Poor Lover fo employ'd? againft himfelf
To make Way for his Rival. I muft do it.
Nay, more, I will. If Loyalty can find
Recompence beyond Hope or Imagination,
Let it fall on me in the other World,
As a Reward; for in this I dare not hope it.   [*Exit.*

End of the Third Act.

ACT IV. SCENE I.

The Camp.

Enter Gonzaga, Pierio, Roderigo, *and* Jacomo.

Gonzaga.

YOU'VE feiz'd upon the Citadel, and difarm'd
    All that could make Refiftance?
   Pierio. Hunger had
Done that, before we came; nor was the Soldier
Compell'd to feek for Prey; the famifh'd Wretches,

In Hope of Mercy, as a Sacrifice offer'd
All that was worth the taking.

Gonz. You proclaim'd,
On Pain of Death, no Violence fhould be offer'd
To any Woman ?

Roder. But it needed not;
For Famine had fo humbled 'em, and took off
The Care of their Sex's Honour, that there was not
So coy a Beauty in the Town, but would
For half a mouldy Bifket fell herfelf
To a poor Befognion, [14], and without fhrieking.

Gonz. Where is the Duke of *Urbin* !

Jacomo. Under Guard,
As you directed.

Gonz. See the Soldiers fet
In Rank and File ; and, as the Dutchefs paffes,
Bid 'em vail their Enfigns ; and charge 'em, on their
   Lives,
Not to cry Whores.

Jacomo. The Devil cannot fright 'em
From their military Licence ; tho' they know
They are her Subjects, and will part with Being
To do her Service ; yet, fince fhe's a Woman,
They will touch at her Breech with their Tongues—
   and that is all
That they can hope for.
   [*A Shout, and a general Cry within,* Whores !
   Whores !

Gonz. O the Devil ! they are at it.
Hell ftop their brawling Throats.——Again ! make
   up
And cudgel them into Jelly.

Roder. To no Purpofe,
Tho' their Mothers were there,
They would have the fame Name for 'em.
       [*Exeunt.*

[14] Bifogni, in *Italian*, fignifies a Recruit. *M. M.*

SCENE II.

Before the Walls of Siena.

Enter Roderigo, Jacomo, Pierio, Gonzaga, *and* Aurelia, *(under a Canopy.)* Aſtutio *preſents her with Letters.* Loud Muſick. *She reads the Letters.*

Gonz. I do beſeech your Highneſs not to aſcribe
To th' Want of Diſcipline, the barbarous Rudeneſs
Of the Soldier, in his Prophanation of
Your ſacred Name and Virtues.

Aurelia. No, Lord General,
I've heard my Father ſay oft, 'twas a Cuſtom
Uſual i' th' Camp ; nor are they to be puniſh'd
For Words, that have in Fact deſerv'd ſo well.
Let the one excuſe the other.

All. Excellent Princeſs !

Aurelia. But for theſe Aids from *Sicily* ſent againſt us
To blaſt our Spring of Conqueſt in the Bud :
I cannot find, my Lord Ambaſſador,
How we ſhould entertain't but as a Wrong,
With Purpoſe to detain us from our own ;
Howe'er the King endeavours, in his Letters,
To mitigate th' Affront.

Aſtutio. Your Grace hereafter
May hear from me ſuch ſtrong Aſſurances
Of his unlimited Deſires to ſerve you,
As will, I hope, drown in Forgetfulneſs
The Mem'ry of what's paſt.

Aurelia. We ſhall take Time
To ſearch the Depth of't further, and proceed
As our Council ſhall direct us.

Gonz. We preſent you
With the Keys of the City ; all Lets are remov'd ;
Your Way is ſmooth and eaſy ; at your Feet
Your proudeſt Enemy falls.

Aurelia. We thank your Valours:
A Victory without Blood is twice atchiev'd,
And the Difpofure of it, to us tender'd,
The greateft Honour. Worthy Captains, Thanks !
My Love extends itfelf to all.

    [*A Guard made.* Aurelia *paffes thro' them.* Loud
      Mufick.

Gonz. Make Way there.   [*Exeunt.*

S C E N E III.

A Prifon.

Enter Bertoldo, *with a fmall Book, in Fetters, and Jailor.*

Bert. 'Tis here determin'd (great Examples, arm'd
With Arguments, produc'd to make it good)
That neither Tyrants, nor the wrefted Laws ;
The People's frantick Rage, fad Exile, Want,
Nor, that which I endure, captivity,
Can do a wife Man any Injury.
Thus *Seneca,* when he wrote it, thought.—But then
Felicity courted him ; his Wealth exceeding
A private Man's ; happy in the Embraces
Of his chafte Wife *Paulina* ; his houfe full
Of Children, Clients, Servants, flatt'ring Friends,
Soothing his Lip-pofitions, and created
Prince of the Senate, by the general Voice,
At his new Pupil's Suffrage : Then, no doubt,
He held, and did believe, this. But no fooner
The Prince's Frowns and Jealoufies had thrown him
Out of Security's Lap, and a Centurion
Had offer'd him what Choice of Death he pleas'd ;
But told him, die he muft : when ftraight the Armour
Of his fo boafted Fortitude, fell off,
                    [*Throws away the Book.*
Complaining of his Frailty. Can it then
Be cenfur'd womanifh Weaknefs in me, if,

Thus clogg'd with Irons, and the Period
To close up all Calamities deny'd me,
(Which was presented *Seneca*) I wish
I ne'er had Being; at least, never knew
What Happiness was; or argue with Heav'ns Justice,
Tearing my Locks, and in defiance throwing
Dust in the Air? or, falling on the Ground, thus
With my Nails and Teeth to dig a Grave, or rend
The Bowels of the Earth, my Step-mother,
And not a natural Parent? or thus practise
To die, and, as I were insensible,
Believe I had no Motion?   [*Lies on his Face.*

Enter Gonzaga, Adorni, *and Jailor.*

Gonz. There he is:
I'll not enquire by whom his Ransom's paid,
I'm satisfy'd that I have it; nor alledge
One Reason to excuse his cruel Usage,
As you may interpret it; let it suffice
It was my Will to have it so.—He is yours, now,
Dispose of him as you please.   [*Exit* Gonzaga.
  Adorni. Howe'er I hate him,
As one preferr'd before me, being a Man,
He does deserve my Pity. Sir,—he sleeps,
Or is he dead? Would he were a Saint in Heaven;
'Tis all the Hurt I wish him. But, I was not
                                        [*Kneels by him.*
Born to such Happiness.—No, he breathes—Come near,
And, if't be possible, without his Feeling,
Take off his Irons.—So, now leave us private.
                                  [*His Irons taken off.*
He does begin to stir, and as transported [*Exit Jailor.*
With a joyful Dream.—How he stares! and feels his
         Legs,
As yet uncertain whether it can be
True or fantastical.
  Bert. Ministers of Mercy,
Mock not Calamity.—Ha! 'tis no Vision!
Or, if it be, the happiest that ever

Appear'd to finful Flefh!—Who's here? His Face
Speaks him *Adorni!* but fome glorious Angel,
Concealing its Divinity in his Shape,
Hath done this Miracle, it being not an Act
For wolfifh Man.   Refolve me, if thou look'ft for
Bent Knees in Adoration?

   Adorni. O forbear, Sir!
I am *Adorni,* and the Inftrument
Of your Deliverance; but the Benefit
You owe another.

   Bert. If he has a Name,
As foon as fpoken, 'tis writ on my Heart,
I am his Bondman.

   Adorni. To the Shame of Men,
This great Act is a Woman's.

   Bert. The whole Sex
For her Sake muft be deify'd.   How I wander
In my imagination, yet cannot
Guefs who this Phœnix fhould be!

   Adorni. 'Tis *Camiola.*

   Bert. Pray you fpeak it again!   There's Mufick in
      her Name!
Once more, I pray you, Sir!

   Adorni. Camiola,
The Maid of Honour.

   Bert. Curs'd Atheift that I was,
Only to doubt it could be any other;
Since fhe alone, in th' Abftract of herfelf,
That fmall, but ravifhing Subftance, comprehends
Whatever is or can be wifh'd in the
Idea of a Woman.   O what Service,
Or Sacrifice of Duty can I pay her,
If not to live and die her Charity's Slave?
Which is refolv'd already.

   Adorni. She expects not
Such a Dominion o'er you: Yet, ere I
Deliver her Demands, give me your Hand:
On this, as fhe enjoin'd me, with my Lips
I print her Love and Service, by me fent you.

   Bert. I am overwhelm'd with Wonder!

Adorni. You muſt now —
(Which is the Sum of all that ſhe deſires)
By a ſolemn Contract bind yourſelf, when ſhe
Requires it, as a Debt due for your Freedom,
To marry her.

Bert. This does engage me further;
A Payment ? An Increaſe of Obligation !
To marry her ?—'Twas my *nil ultra,* ever !
The End of my Ambition ! O. that now
The Holy Man, ſhe preſent, were prepar'd
To join our Hands, but with that Speed my Heart
Wiſhes mine Eyes might ſee her.

Adorni. You muſt ſwear this.

Bert. Swear it ? Collect all Oaths and Imprecations,
Whoſe leaſt Breach is Damnation ; and thoſe
Miniſter'd to me in a Form more dreadful ;
Set Heav'n and Hell before me, I will take 'em :
Falſe to *Camiola ?* Never.—Shall I now
Begin my Vows to you ?

Adorni. I am no Churchman ;
Such a one muſt file it on Record. You are free ;
And, that you may appear like to yourſelf
(For ſo ſhe wiſh'd) there's Gold with which you may
Redeem your Trunks and Servants, and whatever
Of late you loſt. I have found out the Captain
Whoſe Spoil they were.—His Name is *Roderigo.*

Bert. I know him.

Adorni. I have done my Part.

Bert. So much, Sir,
As I am ever yours for't. Now, methinks,
I walk in Air !—Divine *Camiola !*——
But Words cannot expreſs thee. I'll build to thee
An Altar in my Soul, on which I'll offer
A ſtill increaſing Sacrifice of Duty.   [*Exit* Bertoldo.

Adorni. What will become of me now is apparent !
Whether a Poniard or a Halter be
The neareſt Way to Hell (for I muſt thither,
After I've kill'd myſelf) is ſomewhat doubtful.
This *Roman* Reſolution of Self-Murther,
Will not hold Water at the high Tribunal,

When it comes to be argu'd ; my good Genius
. Prompts me to this Confideration. He
That kills himfelf to avoid Mifery, fears it,
And, at the beft, fhews but a baftard Valour.
This Life's a Fort committed to my Truft,
Which I muft not yield up till it be forc'd.
—Nor will I. He's not valiant that dares die,
But he that boldly bears Calamity.

S C E N E IV.

Siena. *A Flourifh.*

Enter Pierio, Roderigo, Jacomo, Gonzaga, Aurelia,
Ferdinand, Aftutio, *and Attendants.*

Aurelia. A Seat here for the Duke. It is our Glory
To overcome with Courtefies, not Rigour;
The lordly *Roman,* who held it the Height
Of human Happinefs to have Kings and Queens
To wait by his triumphant Chariot-wheels
In his infulting Pride, depriv'd himfelf
Of drawing near the Nature of the Gods,
Beft known for fuch, in being merciful.
Yet, give me Leave, but ftill with gentle Language,
And with the Freedom of a Friend, to tell you,
To feek by Force, what Courtfhip could not win,
Was harfh, and never taught in Love's mild School.
Wife Poets feign that *Venus'* Coach is drawn
By Doves and Sparrows, not by Bears and Tygers.
Ferd. I fpare the Application,—In my Fortune
Heav'n's Juftice hath confirm'd it; yet, great Lady,
Since my Offence grew from Excefs of Love,
And not to be refifted, having paid too,
With Lofs of Liberty (the Forfeiture
Of my Prefumption) in your Clemency
It may find Pardon.
Aurelia. You fhall have juft Caufe
To fay it hath. The Charge of the long Siege

Defray'd, and the Lofs my Subjects have fuftain'd
Made good, (fince fo far I muft deal with Caution)
You have your Liberty.

Ferd. I could not hope for
Gentler Conditions.

Aurelia. My Lord *Gonzaga*,
Since my coming to *Siena*, I've heard much of
Your Pris'ner, brave *Bertoldo*.

Gonz. Such an one,
Madam, I had.

Aftutio. And have ftill, Sir, I hope.

Gonz. Your Hopes deceive you.—He is ranfom'd,
    Madam.

Aftutio. By whom, I pray you, Sir?

Gonz. You had beft enquire
Of your Intelligencer: I am no Informer.

Aftutio. I like not this.   [*Afide.*

Aurelia. He is, as 'tis reported,
A goodly Gentleman, and of noble Parts,
A Brother of your Order.

Gonz. He was, Madam,
'Till he, againft his Oath, wrong'd you, a Princefs,
Which his Religion bound him from.

Aurelia. Great Minds,
For Trial of their Valours, oft maintain
Quarrels that are unjuft; yet without Malice;
And fuch a fair Conftruction I make of him.
I would fee that brave Enemy.

Gonz. My Duty
Commands me to feek for him.

Aurelia. Pray you do:
And bring him to our Prefence.   [*Exit Gonzaga.*

Aftutio. I muft blaft
His Entertainment. [*Afide.*] May it pleafe your Ex-
    cellency,
He is a Man debauch'd, and for his Riots
Caft off by th' King my Mafter; and that, I hope, is
A Crime fufficient.

Ferd. To you, his Subjects,
That like as your King likes ——

Aurelia. But not to Us;
We muſt weigh wjth our own Scale.

Enter Gonzaga, Bertoldo *richly habited, and* Adorni.

This is he, ſure!! .
How ſoon mine Eye had found him!—What a Port
He bears! how well his Bravery becomes him!.
A Priſ'ner! nay, a princely Suitor, rather!
But I'm too ſudden.
    Gonz. Madam, 'twas his Suit,
Unſent for, to preſent his Service to you,.
Ere his Departure.
    Aurelia. With what Majeſty
He bears himſelf!
    Aſtutio. The Devil, I think, ſupplies him.
Ranſom'd? and thus rich, too!
    Aurelia. You ill deſerve
                [Bertoldo *kneeling, kiſſes her Hand.*
The Favour of our Hand—(We are not well:
Give Us more Air.)   [*She deſcends ſuddenly.*
    Gonz. What ſudden Qualm is this?
    Aurelia. —That lifted yours againſt me.
    Bert. Thus, once more,
I ſue for Pardon.
    Aurelia. Sure his Lips are poiſon'd,
And, thro' theſe Veins, force Paſſage to my Heart,
Which is already ſeiz'd upon.   [*Aſide.*
    Bert. I wait, Madam,
To know what your Commands are; my Deſigns
Exact me in another Place.
    Aurelia. Before
You have our Licence to depart? If Manners,
Civility of Manners cannot teach you
T' attend our Leiſure, I muſt tell you, Sir,
That you are ſtill our Priſoner; nor had you
Commiſſion to free him.
    Gonz. How's this, Madam?
    Aurelia. You were my Subſtitute, and wanted Power,
Without my Warrant, to diſpoſe of him.

I will pay back his Ranſom ten Times over,
Rather than quit my Intereſt.

    Bert. This is
Againſt the Law of Arms.

    Aurelia. But not of Love: [*Aſide.*
Why, hath your Entertainment, Sir, been ſuch
In your Reſtraint, that, with the Wings of Fear,
You would fly from it.

    Bert. I know no Man, Madam,
Enamour'd of his Fetters, or delighting
In Cold or Hunger, or that would in Reaſon
Prefer Straw in a Dungeon, before
A Down Bed in a Palace.

    Aurelia. How!—Come nearer;
Was his Uſage ſuch?

    Gonz. Yes; and it had been worſe,
Had I foreſeen this.

    Aurelia. O thou miſ-ſhap'd Monſter!
In thee it is confirm'd, that ſuch as have
No Share in Nature's Bounties, know no Pity
To ſuch as have 'em. Look on him with my Eyes,
And anſwer then, whether this were a Man
Whoſe Cheeks of lovely Fulneſs ſhould be made
A Prey to meagre Famine? or theſe Eyes,
Whoſe every Glance ſtore *Cupid*'s empty'd Quiver,
To be dimm'd with tedious Watching; or theſe Lips,
Theſe ruddy Lips, of whoſe freſh Colour, Cherries
And Roſes were but Copies, ſhould grow pale
For Want of Nectar? or theſe Legs that bear
A Burthen of more Worth, than is ſupported
By *Atlas*' weary'd Shoulders, ſhould be cramp'd
With the Weight of Iron? Oh, I could dwell ever
On this Deſcription!

    Bert. Is this in Deriſion
Or Pity of me?

    Aurelia. In your Charity
Believe me innocent. Now you are my Priſoner,
You ſhall have fairer Quarter; you will ſhame
The Place where you have been, ſhould you now
        leave it

Before you are recover'd. I'll conduct you
To more convenient Lodgings, and it shall be
My Care to cherish you. Repine who dare;
It is our Will. You'll follow me?

Bert. To the Centre,
Such a *Sibylla* guiding me.

[*Exeunt* Aurelia *and* Bertoldo.

Gonz. Who speaks first?

Ferd. We stand, as we had seen *Medusa*'s Head!

Pierio. I know not what to think, I'm so amaz'd!

Roder. Amaz'd! I'm thunderstruck!

Jacomo. We are enchanted.
And this is some Illusion.

Adorni. Heav'n forbid!
In dark Despair it shews a Beam of Hope.
Contain thy Joy, *Adorni.*

Astutio. Such a Princess,
And of so long experienc'd Reservedness,
Break forth, and on the sudden, into Flashes
Of more than doubted Looseness!

Gonz. They come again,
—Smiling, as I live: His Arm circling her Waist—
—I shall run mad:—Some Fury hath possess'd her.
If I speak, I may be blasted. Ha! I'll mumble
A Prayer or two, and cross myself, and then,
Tho' the Devil fart Fire, have at him.

Enter Bertoldo *and* Aurelia.

Aurelia. Let not, Sir,
The Violence of my Passion nourish in you
An ill Opinion; or, grant my Carriage
Out of the Road and Garb of private Women,
'Tis still done with Decorum. As I am
A Princess, what I do is above Censure,
And to be imitated.

Bert. Gracious Madam,
Vouchsafe a little Pause; for I am so rapt
Beyond myself, that, 'till I have collected

My ſcatter'd Faculties, I cannot tender
My Reſolution.

 Aurelia. Conſider of it,
I will not be long from you.

[Bertoldo walking by, muſing.

 Gonz. Pray I cannot,
This curſed Object ſtrangles my Devotion :
I muſt ſpeak, or I burſt. Pray you, fair Lady,
If you can, in Courteſy direct me to
The chaſte *Aurelia.*

 Aurelia. Are you blind ? Who are we ?

 Gonz. Another kind of Thing. Her blood was go-
  vern'd
By her Diſcretion, and not rul'd her reaſon :
The Reverence and Majeſty of *Juno*
Shin'd in her Looks, and, coming to the camp,
Appear'd a ſecond *Pallas.* I can ſee
No ſuch Divinities in you : If I
Without Offence may ſpeak my Thoughts, you are,
As 'twere, a wanton *Helen.*

 Aurelia. Good ; ere long
You ſhall know me better.

 Gonz. Why, if you are *Aurelia,*
How ſhall I diſpoſe of the Soldier ?

 Aſtutio. May it pleaſe you
To haſten my Diſpatch ?

 Aurelia. Prefer your Suits
Unto *Bertoldo* ; we will give him Hearing,
And you'll find him your beſt Advocate. [*Exit* Aurelia.

 Aſtutio. This is rare !

 Gonz. What are we come to ?

 Roder. Grown up in a Moment
A Favourite !

 Ferd. He does take State already.

 Bert. No, no, it cannot be !—yet, but *Camiola,*
There is no Step between me and a Crown :
—Then my Ingratitude ! a Sin in which
All Sins are comprehended ! aid me, Virtue,
Or I am loſt. [*Aſide.*

Gonz. May it please your Excellence——
—Second me, Sir.

Bert. Then my so horrid Oaths,
And hell-deep Imprecations made against it.   [*Aside.*

Astutio. The King, your Brother, will thank you for
          th' Advancement
Of his Affairs——

Bert. And yet who can hold out
Against such Batteries, as her Power and Greatness
Raise up against my weak Defences !   [*Aside.*

Gonz. Sir,

Enter Aurelia.

Do you dream waking ?—Slight, she's here again.
¹⁵ Walks she on woollen Feet !

Aurelia. You dwell too long
In your Deliberation, and come
With a Cripple's Pace to that which you should fly to.

Bert. It is confess'd : Yet, why should I, to win
From you, that hazard all to my poor nothing,
By false Play send you off a Loser from me ?
I'm already too too much engag'd
To th' King my Brother's Anger ; and who knows
But that his Doubts and politick Fears, should you
Make me his Equal, may draw War upon
Your Territories ; were that Breach made up,
I should with Joy embrace, what now I fear
To touch but with due Rev'rence.

Aurelia. That Hind'rance
Is easily remov'd.   I owe the King
For a royal Visit, which I straight will pay him ;
And having first reconcil'd you to his Favour,
A Dispensation shall meet with us.

Bert. I am wholly yours.

¹⁵ Bert. *Walks she on woollen Feet !*

These Words are certainly Part of *Gonzaga's* Speech, who is sur-
prized at the sudden Return of *Aurelia* ; they would come strangely
from *Bertoldo* in the midst of his Meditations. *M. M.*

Aurelia. On this Book seal it.

Gonz. What Hand and Lip too? Then the Bargain's
    sure,
You've no Employment for me?

Aurelia. Yes, *Gonzaga*;
Provide a royal Ship.

Gonz. A Ship? Saint *John*!
Whither are we bound, now?

Aurelia. You shall know hereafter,
My Lord, your Pardon, for my too much trenching
Upon your Patience.

Adorni. Camiola.   [*Whispers to* Bertoldo.

Aurelia. How do you?

Bert. Indisposed; but I attend you.   [*Exeunt.*

Adorni. The heavy Curse that waits on Perjury,
And foul Ingratitude, pursue thee, ever!
Yet why from me this? In this Breach of Faith
My Loyalty finds Reward! what poisons him,
Proves Mithridate to me. I have perform'd
All she commanded punctually; and now,
In the clear Mirrour of my Truth, she may
Behold his Falsehood. O that I had Wings
To bear me to *Palermo!* this, once known,
Must change her Love into a just Disdain,
And work her to Compassion of my Pain.   [*Exit.*

SCENE II.   *Camiola's House.*

Enter Sylli, Camiola, *and* Clarinda, *at several Doors.*

Sylli. Undone! undone!—poor I, that whilome was
The Top and Ridge of my House, am, on the sudden,
Turn'd to the pitifullest Animal
O' th' Lineage of the *Syllies!*

Camiola. What's the Matter?

Sylli. The King—break Girdle, break!

Camiola. Why, what of him?

Sylli. Hearing how far you doated on my Person,
Growing envious of my Happiness, and knowing

His Brother, nor his Favourite *Fulgentio*,
Could get a ſheep's Eye from you, I being preſent,
Is come himſelf a Suitor, with the Awl
Of his Authority to bore my Noſe,
And take you from me—Oh, oh, oh!

 Camiola. Do not roar ſo :
The King?

 Sylli. The King : Yet loving *Sylli* is not
So ſorry for his own, as your Misfortune ;
If the King ſhould carry you, or you bear him,
What a Loſer ſhould you be ? He can but make you
A Queen, and what a ſimple Thing is that
To th' being my lawful Spouſe. The World can never
Afford you ſuch a Huſband.

 Camiola. I believe you.
But how are you ſure the King is ſo inclin'd?
Did not you dream this?

 Sylli. With theſe Eyes I ſaw him
Diſmiſs his Train, and lighting from his Coach,
Whiſper *Fulgentio* in the Ear.

 Camiola. If ſo,
I gueſs the Buſineſs.

 Sylli. It can be no other,
But to give me the Bob, that being a Matter
Of main Importance.—Yonder they are; I dare not

    Enter Roberto *and* Fulgentio.

Be ſeen, I am ſo deſperate ! if you forſake me,
Send me Word, that I may provide a Willow Garland,
To wear, when I drown myſelf. O *Sylli, Sylli.!*
           [*Exit crying.*

 Ful. It will be worth your Pains, Sir, to obſerve
The Conſtancy and Bravery of her ſpirit.
Tho' great Men tremble at your Frowns, I dare
Hazard my Head, your Majeſty, ſet off
With Terror, cannot fright her.

 Rober. May ſhe anſwer
My Expectation.

 Fulgen. There ſhe is.

      E e 2

Cam. My Knees thus
Bent to the Earth (while my Vows are fent upward
For the Safety of my Sov'reign) pay the Duty
Due for fo great an Honour, in this Favour
Done to your humbleſt Hand-maid.

Rober. You miſtake me,
I come not, Lady, that you may report
The King, to do you Honour, made your Houſe [16]
(He being there) his Court ; but to correct
Your ſtubborn Diſobedience.   A Pardon
For that, could you obtain it, were well purchas'd
With this Humility.

Camiola. A Pardon, Sir ?
'Till I am conſcious of an Offence,
I will not wrong my Innocence to beg one.
What is my Crime, Sir ?

Rober. Look on him I favour,
You ſcorn'd and neglected.

Camiola. Is that all, Sir ?

Rober. No, Minion ; tho' that were too much. How
            can you
Anſwer the ſetting on your deſp'rate Bravo
To murder him ?

Camiola. With your Leave, I muſt not kneel, Sir,
While I reply to this : But thus riſe up
In my Defence, and tell you as a Man
(Since when you are unjuſt, the Deity
Which you may challenge as a King, parts from you)
'Twas never read in Holy Writ, or moral,
That Subjects on their Loyalty were oblig'd
To love their Sov'reign's Vices ; your Grace, Sir,
To ſuch an Undeſerver is no Virtue.

Fulgen. What think you now, Sir ?

Camiola. Say you ſhould love Wine,
You being the King, and 'cauſe I am your Subject,
Muſt I be ever drunk ? Tyrants, not Kings,
By Violence, from humble Vaſſals force
The Liberty of their Souls.   I could not love him.

---

[16] Courts make not Kings, but Kings Courts. DENHAM.

And to compel Affection, as I take it,
Is not found in your Prerogative.

Rober. Excellent Virgin!
How I admire her Confidence! [*Aside.*

Camiola. He complains
Of Wrong done him : But, be no more a King,
Unlefs you do me Right. Burn your Decrees,
And of your Laws and Statutes make a Fire,
To thaw the frozen Numbnefs of Delinquents,
If he efcape unpunifh'd. Do your Edicts
Call it Death in any Man that breaks into
Another's Houfe to rob him, tho' of Trifles ;
And fhall *Fulgentio*, your *Fulgentio* live ?
Who hath committed more than Sacrilege
In the Pollution of my clear Fame
By his malicious Slanders.

Rober. Have you done this ?
Anfwer truly on your Life.

Fulgen. In the Heat of Blood
Some fuch Thing I reported.

Rober. Out of my Sight!
For I vow, if by true Penitence thou win not
This injur'd Lady to fue out thy Pardon,
Thy Grave is digg'd already.

Fulgen. By my own Folly
I've made a fair Hand of't. [*Exit* Fulgentio.

Rober. You fhall know, Lady,
While I wear a Crown, Juftice fhall ufe her Sword
To cut Offenders off, tho' neareft to us.

Camiola. I : now you fhew whofe Deputy you are,
If now I bathe your Feet with Tears, it cannot
Be cenfur'd Superftition.

Rober. You muft rife.
Rife in our Favour and Protection ever : [*Kiffes her.*

Camiola. Happy are Subjects! when the Prince is ftill
Guided by Juftice, not his paffionate Will. [*Exeunt.*

End of the Fourth Act.

ACT V.   SCENE I.

Camiola's *House.*

Enter Camiola *and* Sylli.

Camiola.

YOU see how tender I am of the Quiet
        And Peace of your Affection, and what great
        ones
I put off in your Favour.
    Sylli. You do wisely,
Exceeding wisely ! and, when I have said,
I thank you for't, be happy.
    Camiola. And good Reason,
In having such a Blessing.
    Sylli. When you have it,
But the Bait is not yet ready. Stay the Time,
While I triumph by myself.—King, by your Leave,
I have wip'd your royal Nose without a Napkin ;
You may cry Willow, Willow ! for your Brother,
I'll only say go by. For my fine Favourite,
He may graze where he please ; his Lips may water
Like a Puppy's o'er a frumenty Pot, while *Sylli*
Out of his two-leav'd Cherry-stone Dish drinks *Nectar !*
I cannot hold out any longer ; Heav'n forgive me,
'Tis not the first Oath I have broke, I must take
A little for Preparative.   [*Offers to kiss and embrace her.*
    Camiola. By no Means.
If you forswear yourself we shall not prosper.
I'll rather lose my Longing.
    Sylli. Pretty Soul !
How careful it is of me ! let me buss yet,

Thy little dainty Foot for't: That, I'm sure, is
Out of my Oath.

Camiola. Why, if thou canst dispense with't
So far, I'll not be scrupulous; such a Favour
My amorous Shoemaker steals.

Sylli. O most rare Leather! [*Kisses her Shoe often.*
I do begin at the lowest, but in time
I may grow higher.

Camiola. Fie! you dwell too long there;
Rise, prithee rise.

Sylli. O, I am up already.

Enter Clarinda *hastily.*

Camiola. How I abuse my Hours!——What News
  with thee, now?

Clar. Off with that gown, 'tis mine; mine by your
  Promise;
Signior *Adorni* is return'd! now upon Entrance;
Off with it, off with it, Madam.

Camiola. Be not so hasty:
When I go to Bed, 'tis thine.

Sylli. You have my Grant too;
But, do you hear, Lady, tho' I give Way to this,
You must hereafter ask my Leave, before
You part with Things of Moment.

Camiola. Very good;
When I'm yours, I'll be govern'd.

Sylli. Sweet Obedience!

Enter Adorni.

Camiola. You're well return'd.

Adorni. I wish that the Success
Of my Service had deserv'd it.

Camiola. Lives *Bertoldo?*

Adorni. Yes, and return'd with Safety.

Camiola. 'Tis not then
In the Power of Fate to add to, or take from

E e 4

My perfect Happineſs: And yet he ſhould
Have made me his firſt Viſit.

   Adorni. So I think too;
But he——

   Sylli. Durſt not appear, I being preſent:
That's his Excuſe, I warrant you.

   Camiola. Speak, where is he?
With whom? Who hath deſerv'd more from him? Or
Can be of equal Merit? In this
Do not except the King.

   Adorni. He's at the Palace
With the Dutcheſs of *Siena.* One Çoach brought 'em
       thither,
Without a third. He's very gracious with her,
You may conceive the reſt.

   Camiola. My jealous Fears
Make me to apprehend.

   Adorni. Pray you, diſmiſs
Signior Wiſdom, and I'll make relation to you
Of the Particulars.

   Camiola. Servant, I would have you
To haſte unto the Court.

   Sylli. I will outrun
A Footman for your Pleaſure.

   Camiola. There obſerve
The Dutcheſs' Train and Entertainment.

   Sylli. Fear not,
I will diſcover all that is of Weight
To the Liveries of her Pages and her Footmen.
This is fit Employment for me.   [*Exit* Sylli.

   Camiola. Gracious with
The Dutcheſs! ſure, you ſaid ſo?

   Adorni. I will uſe
All poſſible Brevity to inform you, Madam,
Of what was truſted to me, and diſcharg'd
With Faith and loyal Duty.

   Camiola. I believe it;
You ranſom'd him, and ſupply'd his Wants—imagine
That is already ſpoken; and what Vows
Of Service he made to me, is apparent;

His Joy of me, and Wonder too, perfpicuous;
Does not your Story end fo?
    Adorni. Would the End
Had anfwered the Beginning—In a Word,
Ingratitude and Perjury at the Height,
Cannot exprefs him.
    Camiola. Take Heed.
    Adorni. Truth is arm'd,
And can defend itfelf. It muft out, Madam,
I faw (the Prefence full) the amorous Dutchefs
Kifs and embrace him, on his Part accepted
With equal Ardour, and their willing Hands
No fooner join'd, but a Remove was publifh'd,
And put in Execution.
    Camiola. The Proofs are
Too pregnant.—*O Bertoldo!*
    Adorni. He's not worth
Your Sorrow, Madam.
    Camiola. Tell me, when you faw this,
Did not you grieve, as I do now, to hear it?
    Adorni. His Precipice from Goodnefs raifing mine,
And ferving as a Foil to fet my Faith off,
I had little Reafon.
    Camiola. In this you confefs
The Devilifh Malice of your Difpofition.
As you were a Man, you ftood bound to lament it,
And not in Flattery of your falfe Hopes
To glory in it. When good Men purfue
The Path mark'd out by Virtue, the bleffed Saints
With Joy look on it, and Seraphic Angels
Clap their celeftial Wings in heav'nly Plaudits,
To fee a Scene of Grace fo well prefented,
The Fiends, and Men made up of Envy, mourning;
Whereas now, on the contrary, as far
As their Divinity can partake of Paffion,
With me they weep, beholding a fair Temple,
Built in *Bertoldo*'s Loyalty, turn'd to Afhes
By the Flames of his Inconftancy, the damn'd
Rejoicing in the Object.—'Tis not well
In you, *Adorni.*

Adorni. What a Temper dwells
In this rare Virgin?—Can you pity him   [*Aside.*
That hath shewn none to you?

Camiola. I must not be
Cruel by his Example. You, perhaps,
Expect now I should seek Recovery
Of what I have lost by Tears, and with bent Knees
Beg his Compassion. No; my tow'ring Virtue,
From the Assurance of my Merit, scorns
To stoop so low. I'll take a nobler Course;
And, confident in the Justice of my Cause,
(The King his Brother, and new Mistress Judges)
Ravish him from her Arms—You have the Contract
In which he swore to marry me?

Adorni. 'Tis here, Madam.

Camiola. He shall be, then, against his Will my Hus-
            band,
And when I have him, I'll so use him—Doubt not,
But that, your Honesty being unquestion'd;
This Writing with your Testimony clears all.

Adorni. And buries me in the dark Mists of Error.

Camiola. I'll presently to Court; pray you, give Or-
            der
For my Coach.

Adorni. A Cart for me were fitter,
To hurry me to th' Gallows.   [*Exit* Adorni.

Camiola. O false Men! !
Inconstant! perjur'd! My good Angel, help me
In these my Extremities!

Enter Sylli.

Sylli. If you ever will see a brave Sight,
Lose it not now. *Bertoldo* and the Dutchess
Are presently to be married. There's such Pomp
And Preparation.

Camiola. If I marry, 'tis
This Day, or never.

Sylli. Why, with all my Heart;
Tho' I break this, I'll keep the next Oath I make,
And then it is quit.

Camiola. Follow me to my Cabinet;
You know my Confeffor, Father *Paulo?*

Sylli. Yes: Shall he
Do the Feat for us?

Camiola. I will give in Writing
Directions to him, and attire myself.
Like a Virgin-bride, and fomething I will do
That fhall deferve Men's Praife and Wonder too.

Sylli. And I, to make all know I am not fhallow,
Will have my Points of Cochineal and Yellow.
[Exeunt,

SCENE II,

The Palace at Palermo,

Loud Mufick.

Enter Roberto, Bertoldo, Aurelia, Aftutio, Gonzaga,
Roderigo, Iacomo, Pierio, *and* Bifhop, *with Atten-*
dants.

Rober. Had our Divifion been greater, Madam,
Your Clemency, (the Wrong being done to you)
In Pardon of it, like the Rod of Concord,
Muft make a perfect Union, once more
With a brotherly Affection we receive you
Into our Favour. Let it be your Study
Hereafter to deferve this Bleffing, far
Beyond your Merit.

Bert. As the Princefs' Grace
To me is without Limit, my Endeavours,
With all Obfequioufnefs to ferve her Pleafures,
Shall know no Bounds: nor will I, being made
Her Hufband, forget the Duty that
I owe her as a Servant.

Aurelia. I expect not
But fair Equality, fince I well know,
If that Superiority be due,

'Tis not to me. When you are made my Confort,
All the Prerogatives of my high Birth cancell'd,
I'll practife the Obedience of a Wife,
And freely pay it. Queens themfelves, if they
Make Choice of their Inferiors, only aiming
To feed their fenfual Appetites, and to reign
Over their Hufbands, in fome Kind commit
Authoriz'd Whoredom, nor will I be guilty
In my Intent of fuch a Crime.

Gonz. This done,
As it is promis'd, Madam, may well ftand for
A Precedent to great Women : But, when once
The griping Hunger of Defire is cloy'd,
(And the poor Fool, advanc'd, brought on his Knees)
Moft of your Eagle-breed, I'll not fay all,
(Ever excepting you) challenge again,
What in hot Blood they parted from.

Aurelia. You are ever
An Enemy of our Sex, but you, I hope, Sir,
Have better Thoughts,

Bert. I dare not entertain
An ill one of your Goodnefs.

Rober. To my Power
I will enable him, to prevent all Danger
Envy can raife againft your Choice. One Word more
Touching the Articles,

Enter Fulgentio, Camiola, Sylli, *and* Adorni.

Fulgen. In you alone
Lie all my Hopes ; you can or kill or fave me ;
But pity in you will become you better,
(Tho' I confefs in Juftice 'tis deny'd me)
Than too much Rigour.

Camiola. I will make your Peace
As far as it lies in me ; but muft firft
Labour to right myfelf.

Aurelia. Or add or alter
What you think fit. In him I have my all,
Heav'n make me thankful for him.

Rober. On to the Temple.

Camiola. Stay, royal Sir, and, as you are are a King,
Erect one [17] here, in doing Justice to
An injur'd Maid.

Aurelia. How's this?

Bert. O I am blasted!

Rober. I have giv'n some Proof, sweet Lady, of my
Promptness
To do you Right, you need not therefore doubt me;
And rest assur'd, that this great Work dispatch'd,
You shall have Audience, and Satisfaction
To all you can demand.

Camiola. To do me Justice
Exacts your present Care, and can admit
Of no Delay. If ere my Cause be heard,
In Favour of your Brother, you go on, Sir,
Your Scepter cannot right me. He's the Man,
The guilty Man whom I accuse, and you
Stand bound in Duty, as you are Supreme,
To be impartial. Since you are a Judge,
As a Delinquent look on him, and not
As on a Brother: Justice painted blind,
Infers, her Ministers are oblig'd to hear
The Cause and Truth, the Judge determine of it;
And not sway'd or by Favour or Affection,
By a false Gloss or wrested Comment, alter
The true Intent and Letter of the Law.

Roberto. Nor will I, Madam.

Aurelia. You seem troubl'd, Sir.

Gonz. His Colour changes too.

Camiola. The Alteration
Grows from his Guilt. The Goodness of my Cause
Begets such Confidence in me, that I bring
No hir'd Tongue to plead for me, that with gay
Rhetorical Flourishes may palliate
That which, stripp'd naked, will appear deform'd.
I stand here mine own Advocate; and my Truth,
Deliver'd in the plainest Language, will

17 That is, a Temple. *M. M.*

Make good itfelf; nor will I, if the King
Give Suffrage to it, but admit of you,
My greateft Enemy, and this Stranger Prince,
To fit Affiftants with him.

    Aurelia. I ne'er wrong'd you.

    Camiola. In your Knowledge of the Injury, I believe it;
Nor will you in your Juftice, when you are
Acquainted with my Intereft in this Man
Which I lay Claim to.

    Rober. Let us take our Seats,
What is your Title to him?

    Camiola. By this Contract,
Seal'd folemnly before a reverend Man,
I challenge him for my Hufband.

    Sylli. Ha! was I
Sent for the Friar for this? O *Sylli! Sylli!*

    Rober. This Writing is
Authentical.

    Aurelia. But done in the Heat of Blood,
(Charm'd by her Flatt'ries, as, no doubt, he was)
To be difpens'd with.

    Ferd. Add this, if you pleafe,
The Diftance and Difparity between
Their Births and Fortunes.

    Camiola. What can Innocence hope for,
When fuch as fit her Judges, are corrupted!
Difparity of Birth or Fortune urge you?
Or *Syren* Charms? or, at his beft, in me,
Wants to deferve him? Call fome few Days back,
And, as he was, confider him, and you
Muft grant him my Inferior. Imagine
You faw him now in Fetters, with his Honour,
His Liberty loft; with her black Wings Defpair
Circling his Miferies, and this *Gonzaga*
Trampling on his Afflictions; the great Sum
Propofed for his Redemption; the King
Forbidding Payment of it; his near Kinfmen,
With his protefting Followers and Friends,
Falling off from him; by the whole World forfaken;

Dead to all Hope, and buried in the Grave
Of his Calamities; and then weigh duly
What she deserv'd (whose Merits now are doubted)
That, as his better Angel, in her Bounties
Appear'd unto him, his great Ransom paid;
His Wants, and with a prodigal Hand, supply'd;
Whether, then, being my manumised Slave,
He ow'd not himself to me?

Aurelia. Is this true?

Rober. In his Silence 'tis acknowledg'd.

Gonz. If you want
A Witness to this Purpose, I'll depose it.

Camiola. If I have dwelt too long on my Deservings
To this unthankful Man, pray you pardon me;
The Cause requir'd it. And, tho' now I add
A little, in my Painting, to the Life,
His barbarous Ingratitude, to deter
Others from Imitation, let it meet with
A fair Interpretation. This Serpent,
Frozen to Numbness, was no sooner warm'd
In the Bosom of my Pity and Compassion,
But, in Return, he ruin'd his Preserver;
The Prints, the Irons had made in his Flesh,
Still ulcerous; but all that I had done,
My Benefits (in Sand, or Water written)
As they had never been, no more remember'd:
And on what Ground, but his ambitious Hopes
To gain this Dutchess' Favour.

Aurelia. Yes; the Object
(Look on it better, Lady) may excuse
The Change of his Affection.

Camiola. The Object?
In what? forgive me, Modesty, if I say
You look upon your Form in the false Glass
Of Flattery and Self-love, and that deceives you.
That you were a Dutchess, as I take it, was not
Character'd on your Face, and, that not seen,
For other Feature, make all these, that are
Experienc'd in Women, Judges of 'em;

And, if they are not Parasites, they must grant,
For Beauty without Art, tho' you storm at it,
I may take the Right-hand File.

  Gonz. Well said, i' faith!
I see fair Women on no Terms will yield
Priority in Beauty.

  Camiola. Down, proud Heart!
Why do I rise up in Defence of that,
Which, in my cherishing of it, hath undone me!
No, Madam, I recant;—You are all Beauty,
Goodness and Virtue; and poor I not worthy
As a Foil to set you off; enjoy your Conquest;
But do not tyrannize. Yet, as I am
In my Lowness from your Height, you may look on
    me,
And in your Suffrage to me, make him know
That, tho' to all Men else I did appear
The Shame and Scorn of Women, [18] He stands bound
To hold me as [19] her Masterpiece.

  Rober. By my Life,
You've shewn yourself of such an abject Temper,
So poor, and low-condition'd, as I grieve for
Your Nearness to me.

  Ferd. I am chang'd in my
Opinion of you, Lady, and profess
The Virtues of your Mind, an ample Fortune
For an absolute Monarch.

☞ 18 —————————*I did appear*
    The Shame and Scorn of Women.

  This is the Reading of all the Old Copies, but I imagine it is false,
and that we ought to read

—————————————— I did appear
  The Shame and Scorn of *Nature.*

  What strengthens this Supposition, is the Line following, which
makes the Sense entire.

  19 If we read *a* instead of *her* in the last of these Lines, there
will be no Need of any other Alteration. *M. M.*

Gonz. Since you are refolv'd
To damn yourfelf, in your forfaking of
Your noble Order for a Woman, do it
For this. You may fearch thro' the World, and meet
    not
With fuch another *Phænix*.

   Aurelia. On the Sudden
I feel all Fires of Love quench'd in the Water
Of Compaffion.—Make your Peace; you have
My free Confent; for here I do difclaim
All Int'reft in you : And, to further your
Defires, fair Maid, compos'd of Worth and Honour,
The Difpenfation procur'd by me,
Freeing *Bertoldo* from his Vow, makes Way
To your Embraces.

   Bert. Oh, how have I ftray'd,
And wilfully, out of the noble Track
Mark'd me by Virtue ! 'Till now, I was never
Truly a Prifoner. To excufe my late
Captivity, I might alledge the Malice
Of Fortune; you, that conquer'd me, confeffing
Courage in my Defence was no Way wanting.
But now I have furrender'd up my Strengths
Into the Power of Vice, and on my Forehead
Branded with mine own Hand, in capital Letters,
Difloyal and ingrateful. Tho' barr'd from
Human Society, and hifs'd into
Some Defart ne'er yet haunted with the Curfes
Of Men and Women, fitting as a Judge
Upon my guilty Self, I muft confefs
It juftly falls upon me; and one Tear,
Shed in Compaffion of my Suff'rings, more
Than I can hope for.

   Camiola. This Compunction
For th' Wrong that you have done me, tho' you fhould
Fix here, and your Sorrow move no farther,
Will, in refpect I lov'd once, make thefe Eyes
Two Springs of Sorrow for you.

Bert. In your Pity
My Cruelty shews more monstrous : Yet I am not,
Tho' most ingrateful, grown to such a Height
Of Impudence, as in my Wishes only
To ask your Pardon.   If, as now I fall
Prostrate before your Feet, you will vouchsafe
To act your own Revenge, treading upon me
As a Viper eating thro' the Bowels of
Your Benefits, to whom, with Liberty,
I owe my Being, 'twill take from the Burthen
That now is insupportable.

 Camiola. Pray you, rise ;
As I wish Peace and Quiet to my Soul,
I do forgive you heartily.   Yet, excuse me,
Tho' I deny myself a Blessing that,
By the Favour of the Dutchess seconded,
With your Submission is offer'd to me,
Let not the Reason I alledge for't grieve you,
You have been false once.—I have done : and if,
When I am married (as this Day I will be)
As a perfect Sign of your Atonement with me,
You wish me Joy, I will receive it for
Full Satisfaction of all Obligations
In which you stand bound to me.

 Bert. I will do it,
And, what's more, in Despite of Sorrow, live
To see myself undone, beyond all Hope
To be made up again.

 Sylli. My Blood begins
To come to my Heart again.

 Camioli. Pray you, Signior *Sylli,*
Call in the holy Friar.   He's prepar'd
For finishing the Work.

 Sylli. I knew I was
The Man.   Heaven make me thankful !

 Rober. Who is this ?

 Astutio. His Father was the great Banker of *Palermo* :
And this the Heir of his great Wealth.—His Wisdom
Was not hereditary.

 Sylli. Tho' you know me not,
Your Majesty owes me a round Sum ; I have

A Seal or two to witnefs; yet, if you pleafe
To wear my Colours, and dance at my Wedding,
I'll never fue you.

 Rober. And I'll grant your Suit.

 Sylli. Gracious *Madona,* noble General,
Brave Captains and my quondam Rivals wear 'em,
Since I am confident you dare not harbour
A Thought, but that Way current.   [*Exit.*

 Aurelia. For my Part,
I cannot guefs the Iffue.

Enter Sylli *with the Friar.*

 Sylli. Do your Duty,
And with all Speed you can, you may difpatch us.

 Paulo. Thus, as a principal Ornament to the Church,
I feize her.

 All. How!

 Rober. So young, and fo religious!

 Paulo. She has forfook the World.

 Sylli. And *Sylli* too?
I fhall run mad.

 Rober. Hence with the Fool! proceed, Sir.
           [Sylli *thruft off.*

 Paulo. Look on this Maid of Honour, now
Truly honour'd in her Vow
She pays to Heaven : Vain Delight
By Day, or Pleafure of the Night,
She no more thinks of : This fair Hair
(Favours for great Kings to wear)
Muft now be fhorn. Her rich Array
Chang'd into a homely grey.
The Dainties with which fhe was fed,
And her proud Flefh pampered,
Muft not be tafted ; from the Spring,
For Wine, cold Water we will bring,
And with Fafting mortify
The Feafts of Senfuality.
Her Jewels, Beads ; and fhe muft look
Not in a Glafs, but holy Book ;

To teach her the ne'er-erring Way
To Immortality.   O may
She, as she purposes to be
A Child new-born to Piety,
Persevere in it, and good Men,
With Saints and Angels say, Amen!

Camiola. This is the Marriage! this the Port to which
My Vows must steer me! Fill my spreading Sails
With the pure Wind of your Devotions for me,
That I may touch the secure Haven, where
Eternal Happiness keeps her Residence,
Temptations to Frailty never ent'ring.
I am dead to the World, and thus dispose
Of what I leave behind me, and, dividing
My 'State into three Parts, I thus bequeath it.
The first to the fair Nunnery, to which
I dedicate the last, and better Part
Of my frail Life ; a second Portion
To pious Uses ; and the third to thee,
Adorni, for thy true and faithful Service.
And, ere I take my last Farewel, with Hope
To find a Grant, my Suit to you is, that
You would, for my Sake, pardon this young Man,
And to his Merits love him, and no further.

 Rober. I thus confirm it.

                    [*Gives his Hand to* Fulgentio.

 Camiola. And, as ere you hope,   [*To* Bertoldo.
Like me, to be made happy, I conjure you
To reassume your Order ; and in fighting
Bravely against the Enemies of our Faith,
Redeem your mortgag'd Honour.

 Gonza. I restore this :——   [*The white Cross.*
Once more Brothers in Arms.

 Bert. I'll live and die so.

 Camiola. To you my pious Wishes! And, to end
All Differences, Great Sir, I beseech you
To be an Arbitrator, and compound
The Quarrel, long continuing, between
The Duke and Dutchess,

Rober. I'll take it into
My special Care.

Camiola. I'm then at Rest.—Now, Father,
Conduct me where you please.

       [*Exeunt* Paulo *and* Camiola.

Rober. She well deserves
Her Name, *The Maid of Honour!* May she stand
To all Posterity a fair Example
For noble Maids to imitate! Since to live
In Wealth and Pleasure is common; but to part with
Such poison'd Baits is rare, there being nothing
Upon this Stage of Life to be commended,
Tho' well begun, till it be fully ended.   [*Exeunt.*

We are now come to the Conclusion of *the Maid of Honour:* A
Piece which in my Judgment does *Honour* to its Author, and well deserves to be presented upon the *English* Stage.

END OF THE SECOND VOLUME;

www.ingramcontent.com/pod-product-compliance
Lightning Source LLC
Chambersburg PA
CBHW022028110726
47901CB00006B/1687